UNDERSTANDING THE U.S.

IN IRAQ AND AFGHANISTA

Understanding the U.S. Wars in Iraq and Afghanistan

Edited by Beth Bailey and Richard H. Immerman

NEW YORK UNIVERSITY PRESS
New York and London

NEW YORK UNIVERSITY PRESS
New York and London
www.nyupress.org

References to Internet websites (URLs) were accurate at the time of writing. Neither the author nor New York University Press is responsible for URLs that may have expired or changed since the manuscript was prepared.

ISBN: 978-1-4798-7143-8 (hardback)
ISBN: 978-1-4798-2690-2 (paperback)

For Library of Congress Cataloging-in-Publication data, please contact the Library of Congress.

New York University Press books are printed on acid-free paper, and their binding materials are chosen for strength and durability. We strive to use environmentally responsible suppliers and materials to the greatest extent possible in publishing our books.

Manufactured in the United States of America

10 9 8 7 6 5 4 3 2 1

Also available as an ebook

To those who served

CONTENTS

ACKNOWLEDGMENTS

We must begin by thanking the contributors to this volume for their intellectual engagement, their professionalism, and their good humor. Their conversations at the workshop that initiated this project in October 2013 took us in some unanticipated directions and strengthened both the collection as a whole and the individual essays. We also thank Clara Platter for her early embrace of this work. Her encouragement, which included attending the initial workshop and the offer of an advance contract, made our job as editors much easier. Clara and Constance Grady made NYU Press a pleasure to work with. We also thank faculty at the Army War College, particularly Tami Davis Biddle and her colleagues in the Department of National Security and Strategy, for helping to jump-start the project. Ironically, many of those faculty members could not attend the October conference because of the sequester. Gregory Daddis, from the U.S. Military Academy at West Point, and Katherine Epstein, from Rutgers, Camden, did attend, chairing sessions and offering insightful commentary. Carly Goodman, the Thomas Davis Fellow at Temple University's Center for the Study of Force, proved vital to the organization of the conference. She also prepared the volume's chronology. Carly's successor as the Thomas Davis Fellow, Silke Zoller, painstakingly assembled the terms and list of terms.

We also want to express our appreciation to Managing Editor Dorothea Halliday, Angelo Repousis, who prepared the index, and our copy editor, Joseph Dahm. Finally, we greatly appreciate the financial support of the Hertog Foundation and the Center for the Study of Force and Diplomacy at Temple University.

As is always the case, our friends and families offer support in countless different ways. We thank them all.

Introduction

BETH BAILEY AND RICHARD H. IMMERMAN

Understanding the U.S. wars in Iraq and Afghanistan demands that we confront the complexity of their origins, their prosecution, and their legacies—and the ongoing uncertainty about their outcomes. It also depends, to an extent often underappreciated, on recapturing the sense of shock, of fear, and of powerful resolve that gripped the nation in the wake of the terrorist attacks of September 11, 2001. That's not to suggest that histories of these wars should begin with that date; this volume clearly argues otherwise. Nor is it to suggest that the events of 9/11 were the sole cause of these wars, or that the decisions to go to war in Afghanistan and then Iraq were the only, or even the most logical, possible reactions to those attacks. The authors of this volume, in the main, make other claims. Nonetheless, the profound shock of 9/11 shaped America's course to war; the emotions unleashed by those attacks made possible actions that might otherwise never have been taken—or that would, at least, have provoked longer and more difficult debate. The attack on the U.S. "homeland" changed the political dynamic of America's foreign relations.

***

The first plane slammed into the World Trade Center at 8:46 on a sunny Tuesday morning. It took scarcely more than three minutes before CNN was airing live footage of what anchor Carol Lin called "clearly something relatively devastating happening there this morning on the south end of the island of Manhattan."[1]

It's surprising, in retrospect, how willing people were to believe it an accident, how long it took for the word "terrorism" to be used. As reporters scrambled for information, more than one news anchor told listeners that this wasn't the first time a plane had crashed into a building in Manhattan: an army bomber, flying in dense fog, had collided with the Empire State Building in 1945. On Fox news, shortly before 9:03, when a second plane flew directly into the Trade Center's south tower, anchor John Scott asked a former investigator with the National Transportation Safety Board if he could "think of any reason for a pilot to slam into a building of this height on a day like today if it wasn't intentional." The investigator offered a long list of possibilities: the pilot might have had "difficulty"; he "might have had engine failure"; he "might have been with his head down in the cockpit instead of looking where he was going"; he might have been flying into the sun; he "could have been confused." Even *after* the second plane struck, CNN was airing speculation that something might have gone wrong with the U.S. flight navigation system. On MSNBC, soon after the second collision, anchor Glen Walker noted that the World Trade Center had been "the subject of terrorist attacks in the past." "I would hate to speculate," he said, repeatedly, but "that possibility leaps to mind."[2]

But confusion soon gave way to certainty that the United States was under attack. At 9:29 a.m., in comments lasting less than a minute, President George W. Bush spoke with resolve: "Terrorism against our nation will not stand."[3] Eight minutes later a third hijacked jetliner hit the Pentagon. By this time, people all over the world were watching the cascading horror. The south tower of the World Trade Center collapsed just before ten; the north fell half an hour later. There were reports of a commercial aircraft driven into the ground in rural Pennsylvania, and speculation about where it had been headed. Images from that day are burned into the memories of those who, at home, at their workplace, wherever they were, watched on television: the planes striking the towers, again and again, in constant replay; firefighters and police confronting a task beyond any capacity; human beings plummeting more than a thousand feet to earth; the towers collapsing in clouds of dust and debris; the faces of those fleeing the encroaching cloud; the survivors, blank-faced and shrouded white in dust.

Only the World Trade Center and the Pentagon bore the physical brunt of attack, but the nation as a whole felt its impact. No one knew, then, that al Qaeda's plans had run their course before noon fell that Tuesday; Americans remained braced for what might come next. Skyscrapers were evacuated in cities around the nation, as were Disney's theme parks and Minnesota's enormous Mall of America. Parents, in scenes of chaos, pulled children from school in Atlanta and in Austin and in Albuquerque; they kept them home in Anchorage, where most people had woken up to a world already changed.

On the day after, in its September 12 edition, the *New York Times* noted that "the sense of security and self-confidence that Americans take as their birthright suffered a grievous blow, from which recovery will be slow."[4] There was a powerful sense at the time that September 11 marked a bright line, a division between before and after, a day following which nothing would ever be the same. It is difficult, now, to summon the aching emptiness of America's airports in the months that followed, to imagine the deserted malls and sports stadiums and tourist sites, to recapture the anxiety that newly suffused daily life—or, sadly, the spontaneous outpouring of sympathy from people throughout the world.

In the days and months that followed the attacks, key senior members of the Bush administration struggled with the sense that they'd failed to protect the nation, that they had allowed (in Secretary of Defense Robert Gates's words) "a devastating attack on America" to "take place on their watch."[5] In fact, the president had received a series of briefings from the U.S. Intelligence Community about the imminence of a terrorist attack, beginning in the spring of 2001 and culminating with the August 6 Presidential Daily Brief bearing the heading "Bin Laden Determined to Strike in the U.S."[6] Shaken by the attacks—and not at all certain they were the last—the administration was willing to take virtually any action to protect the nation from further terrorist strikes. Those responsible for national security made 9/11 their touchstone and their ultimate justification, fully resolved to overcome (again in the words of Secretary Gates) "any obstacle—legal, bureaucratic, financial, or international" to the urgency of their mission.[7]

The catastrophic attacks on the World Trade Center and the Pentagon called forth compassion and generosity from the American people: long lines formed at local Red Cross blood donation centers throughout the nation, and in the days immediately following the attacks Americans donated $2.2 billion to assist victims and their families.[8] But Americans also responded with fear, much of it irrational and incapacitating. People across the nation—including those in outlying suburbs and in the small towns of rural America—worried not only about the security of the nation, but also about their own safety from terrorist attack. In this climate of fear, promises of safety and of security moved the electorate and fostered public support for extraordinary actions.

And, finally, there was a growing resolve to respond, as a nation, to the attacks on U.S. soil. On September 20, President Bush told the nation and the listening world, "Tonight, we are a country awakened to danger and called to defend freedom. Our grief has turned to anger and anger to resolution. Whether we bring our enemies to justice or bring justice to our enemies, justice will be done." Then he issued a list of nonnegotiable demands to the Taliban regime in Afghanistan, from where Osama bin Laden had coordinated the attacks. First and foremost was delivery to the United States of "all the leaders of al Qaeda that hide in your land." Two weeks later, on October 7, the United States (along with its ally, the United Kingdom) began combat operations in Afghanistan.[9] Bush's popularity surged to 92 percent, the highest presidential approval rating ever recorded. America, seared by the events of 9/11, was at war.

***

The U.S. response to the attacks of September 11, 2001, both immediately and over the subsequent years, revived fundamental questions about America and its global posture that stretch back to its emergence as a great power after World War I and intensified during the Cold War. America's response likewise generated new questions that already have caused historians and others among the informed public to reconsider and may force many of them to revise the prevailing narrative of the twentieth century. That history centers on rivalries between great powers, two world wars, and, most prominently, a Cold War that lasted almost fifty years. These new questions will almost certainly also frame domestic and international politics for most if not all of the twenty-first century. To no one's surprise, therefore, debates about the drivers, efficacy, and consequences of the response to 9/11 are heated, and achieving a consensus remains elusive.

These questions could not be more fundamental to understanding and assessing both U.S. international relations and American identity and self-image. They begin by raising conflicting explanations for America's behavior: Does or should the United States act because of its ideals, values, and perceived mission either to police the globe or to reform and even remake nations large and small to conform to U.S. ideals and values? Or does or should the United States seek to promote and protect its national interests, whether one defines those interests as security, prosperity, or, more generally, the American way of life? These broad questions do not lend themselves readily to either/or answers. Indeed, Woodrow Wilson suggested that the answer is "and" when he spoke about making the world safe for democracy as the justification of America's entry into World War I. Once the United States did become involved the war, Wilson went a step further by formulating a program for peace that synthesized American ideals and self-interest. These Fourteen Points highlighted self-determination, the liberal exchange of goods and ideas, and, most important, a league of nations based on shared interests and a universal respect for international law. If the global community followed his prescriptions, Wilson proclaimed, the product would be worldwide peace and prosperity, ensuring that World War I indeed ended all wars.

Americans debated the merits of this Wilsonian ideal for the remainder of the twentieth century. As that century gave way to the next, the wars in Iraq and Afghanistan provoked an equally fundamental question that likewise had defied resolution since America's founding—but especially in the years following World War II, as the United States accepted the roles and responsibilities of a world power. Historically the nation identified its vital interests, those interests for which it was prepared to fight, as located in the Western Hemisphere and in Europe. The Cold War erupted over a divided Europe, and the United States first signaled its rejection of George Washington's "Great Rule" prohibiting "entangling alliances" by agreeing to collective security agreements with the nations of Latin America (the Inter-American Treaty of Reciprocal Assistance, or Rio Pact) in 1947 and to the North Atlantic Treaty establishing the North Atlantic Treaty Organization (NATO) in 1949. Yet for reasons that ranged from geopolitical (preventing dominoes from falling) to psychological (protecting America's reputation and credibility) to ideological (combating the spread of communism on the one hand and promoting the spread of republicanism on the other), in the latter half of the twentieth century the United States fought wars not where its historic core interests lie but on the periphery—in Korea, in Vietnam, and, in the century's last decade, in Iraq (the First Gulf War in 1991). While many Americans supported these wars, others found them incomprehensible and often objectionable. These critics, who spanned the political spectrum, referred to them pejoratively as ill-advised crusades or, worse, imperialist adventures.

Because these debates about America's proper role in the world carried over to the twenty-first century, their legacies complicate our understandings of the Iraq and Afghanistan Wars. The consensus within and beyond the United States was that al Qaeda's attack on New York and Washington, D.C., egregiously violated international norms as well as international laws. People around the world overwhelmingly sympathized with the United States; 9/11 became synonymous with Pearl Harbor as a day of infamy. Yet the tragedy of 9/11 also raised new questions that collided with the many unanswered ones from the past. After all, unlike the situation in 1941, the enemy, the offending power (loosely defined), was not a state. Al Qaeda had no territory to invade, no military to confront, and no government against which to declare war and ultimately compel to surrender. The rules of engagement by which Americans conduct wars, and for that matter the international laws and treaties that govern how all nations are supposed to conduct wars (and treat prisoners of those wars), did not unambiguously apply.

Yet Americans demanded retaliation against the attack, and President George W. Bush was eager to accommodate them. But how, where, and to what end? President Franklin Roosevelt's decision after Japan's attack on Pearl Harbor in 1941 was a relatively simple one (as if these kinds of decisions are ever simple). He declared war on the aggressor and launched a military effort to force Tokyo's surrender. The fact that Japan's ally, Germany, declared war on the United States allowed Roosevelt to avoid a potential political and strategic nightmare. After September 11, 2001, President Bush faced a more complicated set of decisions. The aggressor lacked not only a government and a capital city, but also territory and infrastructure. It was more diffuse. Instead of allies it had affiliates.

President Bush finessed this issue by articulating the first Bush Doctrine. "We will make no distinction between the terrorists who committed these acts and those who harbor them," he proclaimed to the nation the evening of September 11, 2001, in his first public address following the attacks.[10] Al Qaeda was based in Afghanistan, so the United States deployed first paramilitary and then military forces to that country. But he declared war not on Afghanistan but on terror, a global war on terror. "Our war on terror begins with al Qaeda, but it does not end there," the president told a joint session of Congress on September 20. "It will not end until every terrorist group of global reach has been found, stopped and defeated."[11]

What it meant to wage war against a tactic and an emotion was obscure to citizens of the United States and of nations around the world. The Bush administration never sought to provide a precise definition, but the manifestations of such thinking rapidly became evident. Even as the ousted Taliban foot soldiers (many of whom, ironically, were former *mujahideen*, the Islamic warriors or jihadists who had, with clandestine support of the United States, for the decade between 1979 and 1989 fought the Soviets and their Afghan clients) who had initially sheltered al Qaeda faded into the Afghanistan hinterland, and even as Osama bin Laden, Taliban leader Mullah Omar, and their lieutenants escaped the mountains of Tora Bora and crossed the border into Pakistan, the administration made explicit that it considered Iraq the central front in the war against terror. The Bush administration's claim that there was a link between bin Laden and Iraq dictator Saddam Hussein never gained much traction, even in Washington. More convincing, though, was the charge that Saddam had concealed from the international community a quantity of weapons of mass destruction (WMDs), both chemical and biological, and that he was seeking to reconstitute the nuclear program that he had initiated in the run-up to the First Gulf War in 1991. That potential generated terror among Iraq's neighbors, the United States, and beyond. The existential threat posed by al Qaeda and other terrorist networks was almost incomprehensible to Americans; it obscured the boundary between the "homeland" and the foreign, and could take years if not generations to defeat. The threat the administration claimed that Saddam posed, however, was more familiar, more intelligible, more concrete, and—from the viewpoint of the administration— more manageable.

The United States launched Operation Iraqi Freedom, the invasion of Iraq, on March 19, 2003. In this fashion the global war on terror (GWOT) bred two distinct wars—one in Afghanistan and the other in Iraq. Once again, questions and challenges emerged that had bedeviled American policy makers and strategists long before 9/11. Defeating Saddam Hussein and his Republican Guard proved remarkably but not unexpectedly easy. But that ease caused as many problems as (some might argue more problems than) it solved. The destruction of Saddam's forces left no obstacle to uncovering Iraq's cache of WMDs or its nuclear facilities. None were found. The United States had long prided itself on relying on force only as a last resort and waging war only with the greatest reluctance. In Iraq, however, both the precipitant for taking military action and the nation's relationship to the war on terror evaporated. Furthermore, the president had justified the invasion on the grounds that any nation had the right to take preemptive measures when its security—and that of its allies—was in imminent danger. The results of Operation Iraqi Freedom exposed Iraq as far from an imminent danger. This outcome did more than make a mockery of American boasts about U.S. intelligence capabilities and cast doubt on U.S. military strategy and doctrine. It also discredited long-standing claims about U.S. exceptionalism and its status as the indispensable nation.

The conflict in Iraq, much like the past war in Vietnam, engaged the United States in the kind of war for which it was the least equipped to fight. Few of Saddam's forces surrendered; most melted away to their villages. Of these, many were Sunni Muslims, Saddam loyalists, or former Ba'athists (Saddam Hussein had been the leader of Iraq's Ba'ath Party). They became the pillars of resistance movements that assembled to fight the American forces they saw as occupiers and the government in Baghdad that the United States had established. Also fighting the Americans, while at the same time fighting the Sunnis, were Shi'ite Muslims, who constituted the primary support for the post-Saddam Baghdad government and received assistance from Iraq's regional rival and America's worst regional adversary, Iran. The consequence was escalating sectarian violence as government forces, competing private armies, and disorganized insurgents struggled for control. U.S. forces were not well trained or well supplied for such unconventional warfare.

The United States had confronted parallel conditions in Vietnam, with similarly poor results. In the wake of that war, American political and military leaders had first vowed and then planned never to repeat the experience. In future wars, they emphasized, America would deploy overwhelming force, fight on its terms, formulate and articulate unambiguous objectives, and develop a clear exit strategy. Furthermore, as President Bush had repeatedly emphasized in the 2000 election campaign, the "humble" global posture that the United States would pursue under his leadership precluded its undertaking nation building.[12] Yet the Bush administration violated virtually all these post-Vietnam principles. In an attempt to counter public opposition to the war (which had grown as it became clear that the administration had misled the nation about the reasons for going to war) and in order to have any chance of success in the difficult early years of struggle, the Bush administration turned to nation building. Accompanying the surge of some thirty thousand additional troops in 2007 was a new counterinsurgency doctrine that fundamentally committed the United States to placing American soldiers in harm's way for the purpose of building a new nation in Iraq.

Whether nation building will succeed in Iraq remains to be seen. But after some initial causes for optimism, the prospect of a unified nation in Iraq, one with a capacity for effective governance, seems distant—if at all achievable. The same holds true for Afghanistan, which had provided safe haven for al Qaeda and was thus the initial front in the GWOT. By opening a second front in Iraq the Bush administration had provided time and space for the Taliban to revive in Afghanistan and reignite violence. Afghanistan, moreover, proved even less hospitable to nation building than Iraq. American military efforts did succeed in rooting out—or more accurately decapitating—al Qaeda (Osama bin Laden was killed in neighboring Pakistan in 2011), but the Taliban soon reemerged with a vengeance. Afghanistan's capacity for governance was less than that of Iraq, its corruption was more pervasive and ran deeper, and whereas Saddam was surrounded by regional enemies, powerful elements in Pakistan nurtured the Taliban. For all these reasons the counterinsurgency doctrine developed for Iraq was inadequate if not inapplicable for Afghanistan. The war in Afghanistan has now eclipsed that in Vietnam as the longest in America's history.

The wars in Iraq and Afghanistan gave form to the GWOT, and thus that broader war can be traced to the forces unleashed by the Soviet invasion of Afghanistan in 1979 and the Islamic Revolution in Iran that same year. For that reason, 1979 may someday overshadow 1989 (when the collapse of the Berlin Wall served as a catalyst for the end of the Cold War) as a watershed in the evolution of global politics. Understanding the wars in Iraq and Afghanistan, accordingly, requires understanding both the historic processes and the contemporary dynamics that precipitated and sustained them. This collection of essays provides a basis for developing these understandings even as it provokes further questioning and inquiry.

***

This volume contains thirteen essays, organized into four sections. The first section offers overviews of the wars and arguments about their origins; the second evaluates the possibilities and limits of American military and diplo-matic strategy; the third examines those who fought and places the wars in broader political and cultural context; and, finally, the fourth speculates on the lessons and legacies of wars whose outcomes may not be clear for decades. The essays, read together, offer a multifaceted look at these wars. At the same time, each chapter can stand alone, serving as a freestanding essay on one or another aspect of these wars. In order to make that possible, some of the same key events appear in multiple chapters.

We begin with two overviews of the wars in Afghanistan and Iraq. In "The Wars' Entangled Roots: Regional Realities and Washington's Vision," Michael Reynolds starts with a straightforward explanation for America's invasion of Afghanistan: it was in response to attacks on American soil waged by a ter-rorist organization based in that nation. However, he notes, the "reasons why a non-state organization led by two Arab citizens of nominally pro-American states assaulted the United States and why that organization was based in Afghanistan are anything but straightforward." And the origins of the war in Iraq, he notes, are even less so. In this essay, Reynolds (an Associate Professor of Near Eastern Studies at Princeton) situates these wars in the local dynam-ics of the Middle East. In 1979, the Soviet invasion of Afghanistan and the Islamic Revolution in Iran "overturned the geopolitical order" of the region. Indigenous struggles over social and economic change, inflamed by religious claims, had sparked deep and divisive conflict. Because the countries of the Middle East possess vast quantities of the world's oil, it was virtually guar-anteed that powers outside the region would take interest and intervene. In the 1990s, Washington began to see the maintenance of global security as a moral duty and a prerequisite for America's own security. It identified the Middle East as a region of importance not only for its energy resources but also as a test case and proving ground for America's global mission. One can-not understand why the United States went to war in Afghanistan and Iraq, Reynolds argues, without comprehending how regional struggles intersected with Washington's pursuit of its vision of world order.

Terry Anderson, Professor of History at Texas A&M and author of *Bush's War* (2011), turns from the wars' origins in the Middle East to their origins in the United States. Anderson traces U.S. engagement from September 11, 2001, through the failing Iraqi state of 2015, situating "Bush's wars" in Iraq and Af-ghanistan in relation to the broader war on terror, the Patriot Act, the incar-cerations at Guantanamo Bay, the "rendition" of suspected terrorists to "black sites" beyond U.S. legal jurisdiction and consequent legitimization of torture, and the doctrine of preemptive war. Anderson portrays Operation Enduring Freedom in Afghanistan as necessary. This operation, which initially relied on CIA teams with extensive knowledge of Afghanistan's culture and politics and which ultimately drew the participation of twenty-five nations, proved a limited success. In contrast, he argues, Bush and his administration launched Operation Iraqi Freedom with no fundamental knowledge or understanding of Iraq, its people, or its history, "dragg[ing] the United States into the greatest foreign policy blunder in American history."

Following these overviews, scholars who have in significant ways contributed to policy making related to the wars assess the possibilities and limits of American military and diplomatic strategy. Richard Immerman, who served as assistant deputy director of national intelligence (2007–9) and directs Temple University's Center for the Study of Force and Diplomacy, analyzes the role intelligence played in the origins and conduct of these wars. The purpose of intelligence, he argues, is to reduce policy makers' uncertainty and to provide them with a "decision advantage." There is little evidence that in either the Iraq or Afghanistan Wars the U.S. Intelligence Community (IC) achieved these goals. There is likewise little evidence, however, that this failure affected the policy decisions of the George W. Bush or Barack Obama administrations. Both presidents placed a higher priority on the IC's paramilitary capabilities in their effort to terminate America's engagement in the wars than they did on its collection and analytic capabilities when deciding initially to engage in the wars.

Political scientists Stephen Biddle (who before accepting an appointment as Professor of Political Science and International Affairs at George Washington University served on General David Petraeus's Joint Strategic Assessment Team in Baghdad in 2007 and as a Senior Advisor to Petraeus's Central Command Assessment Team in 2008–9) and Duke University Professor of Political Science and Public Affairs Peter Feaver (who from 2005 to 2007 served as Special Advisor for Strategic Planning and Institutional Reform on the George W. Bush National Security Council) then evaluate the strategic choices made by the Bush administration. They argue that the GWOT consisted of a series of strategic decisions, each with its own consequences, intended and unintended. The conventional wisdom treats U.S. strategic choices as a series of "ninety–ten" decisions: some obviously right, others just as obviously wrong. But in fact the war was a series of "fifty-five–forty-five" decisions, close calls where the arguments for and against were in most cases fairly evenly balanced—even if outcomes make the choices appear obvious in retrospect. Using counterfactual scenarios to make their points, Biddle and Feaver argue that different choices at key junctures in the wars in Iraq and Afghanistan would not have produced dramatically different outcomes. Thus there may well be a greater degree of "equifinality" (different paths can lead to the same outcome) in the GWOT than is commonly assumed.

Next, Conrad Crane, lead author of the U.S. Army-Marine Corps counterinsurgency manual (2006) and Director of the Army Military History Institute at Carlisle Barracks, Pennsylvania, discusses "Military Strategy in Afghanistan and Iraq: Learning and Adapting Under Fire at Home and in the Field." Crane argues that the U.S. military efforts in Afghanistan and Iraq contrasted starkly. In Afghanistan, the military relied on an innovative combination of indigenous forces, Special Operations Forces, and airpower in its initial strategic movement to contact. Neither the U.S. military nor political leadership expected the "catastrophic success" that came as the Taliban fell, leaving "ownership" of the country to the invading forces. Before a coherent strategy to stabilize Afghanistan could be designed and implemented, the United States shifted critical assets to Iraq. Not until 2009 did the military apply counterinsurgency doctrine to Afghanistan, and by then any chance to create a legitimate Karzai government had passed. In Iraq, conversely, disjointed planning for stability operations followed a well-orchestrated initial assault. General George Casey launched a counterinsurgency program intended to build up Iraqi security forces, but sectarian violence intensified until General Petraeus implemented a redesigned counterinsurgency doctrine and successfully lobbied for the "surge." Petraeus benefited from good timing and good fortune, but what success he had was tenuous at best.

Finally, Jonathan Horowitz, a Legal Officer at the Open Society Justice Initiative, discusses the ethical and legal parameters of these wars. In "Human Rights as a Weapon of War," Horowitz argues that the United States "weaponized" human rights in both Iraq and Afghanistan. Leaders in the U.S. government used the human rights abuses of the Taliban, al Qaeda, and Saddam Hussein to create public support for going to war in Afghanistan and in Iraq. Once deployed, the military exploited aid and humanitarian assistance, along with emphasis on securing the rule of law, to help expand its reach and to "win the hearts and minds" of local populations. While many communities in Iraq and Afghanistan initially received the U.S. military with good faith and with confidence that its presence would improve their livelihoods and security, U.S. human rights abuses significantly undermined that positive initial reception. Nonetheless, Horowitz argues, the problems created by the weaponization of human rights would likely exist even without the abuses that undermined U.S. moral authority.

We then turn away from high-level policy and strategic decision making to the experiences of war, both foreign and domestic. In the section titled "Waging and the Wages of War," four scholars analyze the experience of combat and of antiwar protest, of war's portrayal in news media and in popular culture. Lisa Mundey, formerly a historian at the U.S. Army Center of Military

History and currently an Associate Professor of History at the University of St. Thomas, discusses combatants' experiences. Focusing on members of the U.S. military, she reminds us of the human scale and consequences of war. The wars in Iraq and Afghanistan were the first extended wars fought by the all-volunteer force, and Mundey shows us who served and compares those troops to those who fought the wars of America's recent past. In both Iraq and Afghanistan, she emphasizes, much of the experience depended on *when* and on *where*—when in the course of the war, and where one was located, not only geographically, but also from the austerity of the field to the striking comfort of well-defended bases.

David Farber, Roy A. Roberts Distinguished Professor in the University of Kansas Department of History, has written extensively on the antiwar movements of the 1960s, as well as on more recent conflicts in *Taken Hostage: America's First Encounter with Radical Islam.* He analyzes a different sort of combat in "Fighting (Against) the Wars in Iraq and Afghanistan." While the Afghan War produced relatively few opponents, the Iraq War from beginning to end was opposed by many well-informed and influential elite figures, as well as by masses of people inside and outside the United States. Nonetheless, the Bush administration was able to prosecute the war as it saw fit and without the kind of disruptive and radical protests that challenged the Vietnam War–era presidencies of Johnson and Nixon. The explanation, Farber argues, is that the political framing of the Iraq and Afghanistan Wars as key to a global war on terror, the changing nature of the mass media, the polarized nature of political debate in the United States during the Bush years, and Americans' views of the all-volunteer military played major roles both in disarming the antiwar movement and in allowing the Bush administration unusual latitude to fight the wars in Afghanistan and Iraq.

Sam Lebovic, an Assistant Professor of History at George Mason University who studies freedom of the press, analyzes "Limited War in the Age of Total Media." Despite the proliferation of media channels and the ease of access to the media, he argues, the American public never acquired adequate knowledge of these wars. Journalists themselves failed to portray the nature and complexity of the wars, relying heavily on official sources and official framing. Moreover, the state manipulated the media, censoring, for example, the portrayal of war casualties. More significantly, the American public showed little hunger for more accurate reporting. In an age of proliferating cable news channels and Internet media outlets, viewers were easily distracted and less interested in hard news. And in the years since the Vietnam War, as images of warfare and violence have become more common, the public has become increasingly desensitized to the horrors of war. As a result of the twin problems of inadequate media coverage of the wars and a public that was too often uninterested in and unaffected by them, the American people were ill equipped to offer consent to or critique of U.S. policy.

Andrew McKevitt, Assistant Professor of History at Louisiana Tech University, examines the popular culture of the wars. Wide-ranging misinformation from the Bush administration about the origins and process of these wars, he argues, filtered into popular culture, which tended to conflate all opponents and to implicitly connect all military action to the attacks of 9/11. The "metaphorical construct" of the GWOT underlay a wide array of television programs, films, literature, music, and video games that "both reflected and shaped the ways Americans made sense" of the wars and their origins. Situating the wars as part of a global (epic) war on terror (an existential battle) made it easy to transpose them to the realm of epic fantasy. Works that attempted to portray the wars realistically rarely gained traction; those that portrayed an epic struggle between good and evil, in contrast, captured the American imagination and helped shape perceptions of the all-too-real struggles on the other side of the world.

The book concludes with a section on the lessons and legacies of the wars. David Kieran, an Assistant Professor at Washington and Jefferson College who writes about war and society, investigates the wars' legacies for their veterans. While most service members returned to civilian life with relative ease, aided by programs such as the G.I. Bill, others struggled with profound physical or psychological wounds, the trauma of sexual assault, the difficulty of securing employment in the midst of economic recession, and—significantly—problems in securing care from the Veterans Administration. The shortcomings in assistance offered to veterans are most fundamental, Kieran argues, because those responsible did not anticipate the length and brutality of the wars, leaving the VA always responding to problems rather than anticipating needs.

Robert Brigham, Professor of History at Vassar College and author of works including *Is Iraq Another Vietnam?* (2006), draws cautionary lessons from the U.S. war in Iraq. The Bush administration went to war in Iraq, he argues, with the expectation that a distinctly American story would emerge. This did not happen. The greatest lessons of the Iraq War are, first, that there is often no political corollary to America's overwhelming military power and, second, that the United States does not possess transformative power—at least not at acceptable risk and costs. Despite enormous expenses in blood and treasure, the United States failed to alter the Iraqi political outlook and policies because it lacked leverage with a government in Baghdad that was uncommitted to promoting national reconciliation and concord by creating a more just and equitable society. Its inability to deliver on the revolutionary change it promised has cost America credibility and influence in the region.

The final essay, on the lessons and legacies of the war in Afghanistan, is by Aaron O'Connell, an Associate Professor of History at the U.S. Naval Academy and a Lieutenant Colonel in the U.S. Marine Corps Reserve; O'Connell served as a Special Advisor to General David Petraeus in Afghanistan and also as Special Assistant to the Chairman of the Joint Chiefs of Staff, General Martin Dempsey. O'Connell evaluates the goals, costs, and outcomes of what is now America's longest war, concluding that, in sum, "American efforts were at best a wildly inefficient partial success and at worst a failure." From this experience, he argues, American policy makers should identify lessons about how states cooperate and compete with each other, what constitutes an appropriate mission for the U.S. military, America's limited capacity for exporting its values and culture, and, perhaps the most important lesson of all, the vital importance of looking to the past as a guide for future action.

***

Reading these essays, it is clear that the authors are not speaking with one voice. Obviously, they are writing about different topics. But they also make arguments that conflict with one another—sometimes slightly, sometimes profoundly. They emphasize different points, stress different factors, place weight differently when explaining origins or evaluating outcomes. That's no accident. This volume wasn't meant to offer an encyclopedic account of the wars, nor one in which the questions about the wars' origins, prosecution, and legacies are transformed into a seamless narrative. Instead, the essays provide entry into a broad conversation about the meaning and significance of the U.S. wars in Iraq and Afghanistan, in hopes that the understandings offered will allow readers to make informed arguments of their own.

These understandings will also allow readers to formulate new questions. When this project began, at the head of the U.S. government was a president who took great pride in his having fulfilled his promise to bring the Iraq and Afghanistan Wars to an end. The withdrawal of U.S. forces began six months into President Obama's first administration and was completed in December 2011. The same year that the last U.S. soldier left Iraq, President Obama announced the start of the drawdown in Afghanistan. "We're starting this drawdown from a position of strength," he remarked. U.S. "troops will continue coming home at a steady pace as Afghan security forces move into the lead. . . . By 2014, this process of transition will be complete."[13]

The global environment has evolved dramatically since Obama uttered those remarks, and not for the better. Despite the turmoil over Ashraf Ghani's

2014 election as president of Afghanistan after Hamid Karzai's decade-long tenure, the withdrawal of American forces is on track, albeit it is almost certain to proceed more slowly than Obama projected. In 2014 a new government came to power Iraq, too, when Haider al-Abadi succeeded Nouri al-Maliki as prime minister. Yet President Obama is speaking no longer of America's position of strength but of "pervasive unease" and a "cycle of conflict."[14] The political complexion in Afghanistan and neighboring Pakistan all but ensures continued instability and violence in the region. In Iraq, the situation is worse. Not only have sectarian bombings, assassinations, and related mayhem reminiscent of the Bush years exploded again, but large swaths of territory have fallen to the Islamic State (also called the Islamic State of Iraq and Syria, ISIS, or the Islamic State in the Levant, ISIL). This offshoot of al Qaeda seeks to establish a caliphate (theocratic Muslim empire) that envelopes Iraq, Syria, and beyond. Indeed, the Islamic State exploited the insurgency against the Bashar al-Assad regime in Syria to acquire territory in that state as well, and has designs on Jordan, Lebanon, Israel, and Turkey.

The emergence of the Islamic State as an even more ruthless and ambitious network of terrorists than al Qaeda reveals the complex consequences of the wars in Afghanistan and Iraq and the uncertain future. The Islamic State is not the direct product of those wars. It is the product of the collision of forces—political forces, religious forces, military forces, international forces—unleashed by those wars. Assessing the Islamic State as a threat to both America's core values and vital interests, an extremely reluctant and deeply conflicted President Obama recommitted U.S. forces to Iraq and extended their use to Syria. Referring to the U.S. military action not as a war but a "counterterrorist campaign," he has vowed that with the support of regional allies the United States can "degrade and ultimately destroy" ISIS without deploying American boots on the ground. Whether that's possible remains an open question. Capturing the difficulties the administration faces, *New York Times* columnist Thomas Friedman writes that "our enemy is barbarous, our regional allies are duplicitous, our European allies are feckless, and the Iraqis and Syrians we're trying to help are fractious."[15]

As the essays in this volume chronicle, the Obama administration has sought a substitute for the Bush administration's brand of war. It has banked on a complex combination of actions: drone strikes and the training and supply (often covertly) of forces it assesses as sympathetic to American goals and interests, on the one hand, and the mitigation—if not elimination—of government corruption and the building of the capacity to govern as an antidote to radical Islamist terrorism, on the other. Critics on the right have lambasted the president for not doing enough, critics on the left for doing too much. In all likelihood his successor, whether Democrat or Republican, will confront the same and perhaps even more intractable forces and challenges as did Bush and has Obama. In 1945 and 1946 few Americans could imagine that the country would be locked in a Cold War with the Soviet Union for almost the next half century. Will historians fifty years from now have coined a name for the period, beginning in 2001 (or perhaps in 1979), when America became enmeshed in an unending succession of "low intensity" conflicts with a shifting set of elusive enemies whom it could not defeat but from whom it could not escape? This volume cannot provide the answer. But it can help to understand the problems and pose the proper questions.

NOTES

1 CNN Breaking News, September 11, 2001, https://www.youtube.com/watch?v=wbsLoyCfBKo. Quote begins at 27 seconds.

2 Ibid.; Fox News Alert, September 11, 2001, https://www.youtube.com/watch?v=oAynWrt1tY8&index=1&list=PL8157E4A31D54579E; MSNBC Breaking News, September 11, 2001, https://www.youtube.com/watch?v=dd5QL60Y8fQ; for army bomber, see Fox footage at 5:20 and MSNBC at 1:13; for Fox NTSB discussion, see Fox at 7:21; for CNN on navigation system, see CNN, September 11, 2001, 8:48 a.m.–9:29 a.m., https://archive.org/details/cnn200109110848-0929 at 18:38; for MSNBC "hate to speculate," see MSNBC at 11:25 through 13:00.

3 C-SPAN, http://www.c-span.org/video/?c3344379/bush-911, at 01:13.

4 R. W. Apple, Jr., "Nation Plunges into Fight with Enemy Hard to Identify," New York Times, September 12, 2001.

5 Robert M. Gates, Duty: Memoirs of a Secretary at War (New York: Knopf, 2014), 93.

6 Kurt Eichenwald, "The Deafness before the Storm," New York Times, September 10, 2012.

7 Gates, Duty, 93.

8 Douglas Starr, "Bad Blood: The 9/11 Blood-Donation Disaster," New Republic Online, July 29, 2002, http://douglasstarr.com/wp-content/uploads/2012/05/TNR-BAD-BLOOD-Starr.pdf; M. Ann Wolfe, Homeland Security: 9/11 Victim Relief Funds (Congressional Research Service, Library of Congress, updated March 27, 2003).

9 "President Bush Address to a Joint Session of Congress" (September 20, 2001), http://edition.cnn.com/2001/US/09/20/gen.bush.transcript/.

10 "President Bush Address to the Nation" (September 11, 2001), http://georgewbush-whitehouse.archives.gov/news/releases/2001/09/20010911-16.html.

11 "President Bush Address to a Joint Session of Congress" (September 20, 2001).

12 "Transcript of the Second Gore-Bush Presidential Debate" (October 11, 2000), http://www.debates.org/index.php?page=october-11-2000-debate-transcript.

13 "Remarks by the President on the Way Forward in Afghanistan" (June 22, 2011), http://www.whitehouse.gov/the-press-office/2011/06/22/remarks-president-way-forward-afghanistan.

14 "Remarks by President Obama in Address to the United Nations General Assembly" (September 24, 2014), http://www.whitehouse.gov/the-press-office/2014/09/24/remarks-president-obama-address-united-nations-general-assembly.

15 "Statement by the President on ISIL" (September 10, 2014), http://www.whitehouse.gov/the-press-office/2014/09/10/statement-president-isil-1; Thomas Friedman, "What's Their Plan? Obama's Strategy for Fighting ISIS Isn't All about Us," *New York Times*, September 14, 2014.

PART I

The Wars and Their Origins

1

The Wars' Entangled Roots

Regional Realities and Washington's Vision

MICHAEL A. REYNOLDS

Afghanistan has surpassed Vietnam as America's longest war. At the time of this writing, the U.S. armed forces are still fighting there, where they have been engaged in combat since 2001. This makes America's third longest war the one in Iraq, where Americans fought for nearly nine years (2003–12). Despite the exceptional lengths of these two conflicts, most Americans have only a vague understanding of them and of how and why at the beginning of the twenty-first century they found their soldiers fighting in two countries across the globe. The war in Afghanistan has a superficially straightforward explanation: on September 11, 2001, a terrorist organization based in Afghanistan carried out attacks on American soil that resulted in the deaths of over three thousand people. In order to avenge those deaths and protect the American and other populations from further attack, the U.S. invaded Afghanistan. Yet the reasons why a non-state organization led by two Arab citizens of nominally pro-American states assaulted the United States and why that organization was based in Afghanistan are anything but straightforward.

If, for most Americans, the origins of the war in Afghanistan are shrouded in some confusion, those of the war in Iraq are impenetrable. America's leaders had asserted to domestic and international audiences an urgent need for America to invade Iraq, overthrow its ruling government, and preemptively eliminate its weapons of mass destruction and programs to develop them. The failure to uncover any such weapons following the invasion tarnished the reputation and credibility of the United States, as observers were left to conclude that the United States was either colossally inept or brazenly duplicitous. Contrary to assurances, the Iraq War turned out to be costly in lives, treasure, and reputation. The invasion and subsequent occupation cost the United States a staggering estimated one trillion dollars. Nearly forty-five hundred American servicemen and -women lost their lives, while almost thirty-seven thousand were wounded (not to mention over fifteen thousand Iraqi civilians killed by Coalition forces).[1] William E. Odom, former U.S.

Army lieutenant general and director of the National Security Agency, a soldier and scholar not given to hyperbole, famously opined that the "invasion of Iraq may well turn out to be the greatest strategic disaster in American history."[2] Odom issued this assessment in 2005, six years before U.S. forces completed their withdrawal from Iraq. The passage of time has only buttressed his judgment.

The war did remove from power Saddam Hussein, who for more than a decade had menaced the U.S. position in the region and who in that period had deliberately caused the deaths of tens of thousands of his own people. Yet the greatest strategic beneficiary of the Iraq War was not the United States or the Iraqi people, whose liberation became a justification of the war, but an implacable enemy of the United States: Iran. America's overthrow of Saddam Hussein transformed Iraq from a nasty but effective bulwark blocking Iranian influence into a platform from which Iran projects power into Syria and beyond. Meanwhile, Sunni radicals aligned with another foe of the United States, al Qaeda, found Iraq a useful symbol with which to mobilize anti-American as well as anti-Iranian and anti-Shi'i sentiment in their recruiting and operations inside Iraq and beyond. By 2014, such radicals exploited the erosion of governmental institutions to seize large swaths of territory in both Iraq and Syria and declare the establishment of an Islamic state.

The emergence in the heart of the Middle East of a large, transnational violent challenger to the regional status quo and the global order represents a stark failure of American policy, as it was precisely such a scenario that Washington sought to avert by intervening in Iraq and Afghanistan. Compounding the confusion about the American invasion is its origin. It was not Iraq that forced war upon the United States but the opposite. This, for many, distinguished the war in Iraq from the war in Afghanistan. The masterminds of the September 11, 2001, terrorist attacks had been based in Afghanistan, and a military intervention to destroy them was seen as an exercise of the right, even obligation, to self-defense. The Iraq War, by contrast, was a "preemptive war" or "war of choice."[3] It was a war that Washington sought out and initiated largely on its own terms.

Even if one rejects the characterization of the invasion of Iraq as America's greatest strategic blunder, it is indisputable that the invasion exacted costs far higher than predicted and delivered benefits far less than its proponents promised. How could the United States have committed such a colossal error? How could it have decided to initiate a war that would squander America's resources and undermine its position in the Middle East and throughout the world while strengthening America's enemies? The American decision to go to war with Iraq in 2003 indeed is a puzzle. To explain it, many have pointed to the role of individuals: President George W. Bush, Vice President Dick Cheney, and/or furtive networks of lesser officials in the executive branch. Those explanations cannot be wholly satisfactory. The case for war was not made in the dark or behind the scenes. Iraq and its dictatorial strongman, Saddam Hussein, were not unfamiliar to Americans. They had been continuous subjects of the political conversation in America for well over a decade before 2003, and the decision to invade Iraq had the express backing of a broad spectrum of American elite opinion in both politics and the media.[4]

In order to begin to understand why America went to war in Afghanistan in 2001 and Iraq in 2003, it is necessary first to grasp how in the Middle East internal conflicts over fundamental social changes meshed with the geopolitics of great power and regional rivalries to generate anti-American currents in Iran, Afghanistan, and Iraq. During the latter two decades of the Cold War, the United States took on the role of guarantor of security in the Middle East. With the end of the Cold War, key American decision makers aspired for the United States to play a similar role globally. Toward this end they formulated an assertive national security doctrine that tied America's security to America's maintenance of order throughout the world. That doctrine had a logic, albeit an aggressive one. But it also had a flaw: the conceptualization of global politics as a realm populated almost exclusively by integral nation-states. It thereby left Washington baffled by the phenomena of al Qaeda and Ba'athist Iraq, and blind to the fragility of the Afghan and Iraqi states and the demands of warfare against non-state actors.

Regional Currents: 1979 as Watershed

Identifying the beginning of a chain of events that culminates in a given historical outcome is always an exercise in conjecture. With that in mind, 1979 does offer a compelling starting point for the exploration of the regional dynamics and global ambitions that led to the American military interventions in Afghanistan and Iraq. In that year, the Soviet Union invaded Afghanistan and the Islamic Revolution swept Iran. These two events overturned the geopolitical order of the Middle East. Although they occurred amid the Cold War, they were the products more of local processes and factors than of superpower ones, and they created challenges to U.S. foreign policy that have persisted into the twenty-first century. Indeed, the fundamental aim of the American interventions in Afghanistan and Iraq was to resolve these challenges in Washington's favor.

Afghanistan

Despite its remote location in the Eurasian landmass, the mountainous and comparatively poor land of Afghanistan in the late twentieth century was no virgin territory for Great Power conflict. It had been a pivotal site of the so-called Great Game in the nineteenth century, when agents of the British Empire sought to block their Russian competitors from advancing southward from Central Asian Turkestan toward India, the empire's "jewel in the crown." During the Cold War Afghanistan again found itself playing the role of buffer state. To the north, it bordered the Soviet Union, the successor to imperial Russia. Afghanistan shared with the peoples of Soviet Central Asia ethnic, linguistic, religious, and cultural ties, and Soviet authorities accordingly kept a wary eye on the country. Moscow could tolerate the existence inside Afghanistan of comparatively small and innocuous agencies like the American Peace Corps and the American Agency for International Development, but it was allergic to any large-scale American presence on its borders.

In the greater Middle East, the United States in the 1970s emerged as a successor of sorts to imperial Britain. Great Britain's announcement in 1968 that it was abandoning its role as guarantor of security in the Persian Gulf left the United States as the region's constabulary. The U.S. interest in Afghanistan was driven by concern for Iran and the oil-rich Persian Gulf. The Arab-led oil boycott of 1973 had caused world oil prices to quadruple in the space of just six months, and had thereby sent the industrialized economies of the West into a tailspin. The boycott made it painfully evident just how vital to the West the free and uninterrupted flow of oil from the Persian Gulf was. Keeping those oil fields free from Soviet hands or influence was essential.

Having just extricated itself from the Vietnam War, however, America in the 1970s had no appetite for new security commitments in Asia. U.S. President Richard Nixon's solution to this bind, dubbed the "Nixon Doctrine," was to rely on local allied powers to police their regions. Washington planners identified the Kingdom of Saudi Arabia and Iran as the two pillars of stability in the Gulf and sought to build them up. The coffers of these two oil-exporting countries were overflowing due to the recent vast increases in oil prices, allowing them to spend lavishly on expanding and equipping their militaries with American-made weapons systems.[5] The *shah* (king) of Iran, Mohammad Reza Pahlavi, was pressing upon his population a program of industrializing modernization and was therefore eager to receive U.S. economic, technological, and military aid.

Afghanistan in the 1950s and 1960s had functioned as a neutral buffer state where Soviets and Americans could operate alongside each other by maintaining low profiles and relatively small numbers. By the 1970s, however, developments inside Afghanistan were making the modus vivendi of the previous decades unsustainable. A rift was emerging among Afghan elites over the future of their country. In particular, a segment of the landlocked and rural country's educated urban elite had grown impatient with the slow pace of Afghanistan's economic and technological development. Literacy was low, infant mortality was high, and outside the major cities electricity was absent. Indeed, mud brick remained the dominant construction material in the countryside.[6] Thus in 1973, Mohammed Daoud Khan toppled Afghanistan's monarch. Daoud was a member of the Afghan royal family, but he demonstratively installed himself not as a new monarch but as the country's first president. The aspirations of Daoud and his followers paralleled those of the shah in neighboring Iran, namely the accelerated economic and technological development of their country. But whereas the shah looked to America, Daoud and his Marxist People's Democratic Party found inspiration in the Soviet model of modernity.

Still, a radical faction of the new ruling party grew dissatisfied with Daoud's relative moderation, and in spring 1978 this faction overthrew him. Disregarding the counsel of their Soviet advisers in the country not to push too much reform too quickly, Afghanistan's new rulers aggressively pursued their vision of socialist progress.[7] They imposed revolutionary reforms in the areas of land ownership, education, and family law simultaneously to vanquish "feudalism."

Socialists, however, were not the only political force inside Afghanistan. There were others who drew political inspiration from Islam, and they, too, had been mobilizing on university campuses and elsewhere. Their vision of Afghanistan's future departed sharply from that of the socialists, and Afghanistan's politics began to polarize between advocates of Soviet-style modernization and exponents of revivalist Islam. Already in 1973, tribal leaders under the influence of Islamists began to talk openly of jihad (struggle in the name of God) against the government. In neighboring Pakistan, authorities saw these Islamists as a useful counterweight against the pro-Soviet government in Kabul. The Pakistanis lent them support, boosting their reach and clout.[8] By 1978, multiple Afghan voices were calling for a jihad against Kabul. Tribal chiefs and local notables resented the central government's bid to expand its power at their expense, while the population at large found government-imposed reforms like the introduction of mixed-gender schooling culturally offensive and unacceptable. Soon enough, scattered local rural rebellions coalesced and an insurgency started to take shape.[9]

Already by the spring of 1979 Afghanistan's socialist government was losing control. Moscow grew alarmed. Afghanistan lay astride Soviet Central
Asia, and the Afghans' cultural and ethno-linguistic ties to the Central Asians
raised the possibility that rebellion might spill over the border. Moscow had
suspicions that Afghanistan's ruler was involved with the CIA, and feared
that the Americans' recent loss of bases in Iran would propel them to seek
facilities in Afghanistan.[10] Moreover, central to the Soviet Union's Marxist-
Leninist ideology was a rigidly linear concept of progress. According to that
concept, a country's advancement from feudalism or capitalism to socialism
was irreversible. The fall of a socialist government thus would raise the possibility that Marxism-Leninism might be flawed and shake confidence in the
inevitability of the world triumph of communism. Indeed, precisely for this
reason Moscow had intervened militarily in 1956 and again in 1968 in Eastern
Europe to prop up socialist regimes in Hungary and Czechoslovakia, respec-
tively. But in an ironic twist of sorts, this time Moscow identified an excess of
socialist zeal, not its absence, as the problem. Using their special forces, the
Soviets engineered a bloody coup against Afghanistan's sitting president in
December 1979 and installed a more moderate faction of the ruling party.[11]

To assist the new government Moscow deployed the officially titled "Limited Contingent of Soviet Forces in Afghanistan." Consisting of roughly eighty
thousand men, the contingent's mission was to help the new government stabilize the country. As its name implied, its size, operations, and duration of
stay in Afghanistan were to be circumscribed. The Soviets expected that after
using military force to restore government and order, the implementation of
reforms in public health, agriculture, and education would win the Afghan
people over to the new government's side.[12] They believed that the "force of
example" would prove more effective and cheaper than the "force of arms."[13]

Whereas Moscow's political elite calculated that the deployment of Soviet troops would quell the resistance, the General Staff had predicted the
presence of Soviet troops would galvanize it.[14] On this, the General Staff was
correct. The regime's opponents grew in numbers. Declaring their struggle
a sacred one, they began calling themselves *mujahideen*, that is, those who
wage jihad.

The Afghan mujahideen were poorly armed at the outset of the war, but
they soon found themselves the beneficiaries of a formidable international
support network that included the United States, Pakistan, China, Egypt, and
the Gulf Arab states. Motives for supporting the mujahideen varied. Some
backers, such as the United States and China, assisted them as a way to trap,
bleed, and exhaust the Soviets in a quagmire. For Muslims, Islamic solidarity served as an additional motive. Volunteers from throughout the Muslim

world came to Afghanistan to wage jihad. The Sunni Arabs of the Gulf, and the Saudis in particular, funneled billions of dollars to the fighters through official, semiofficial, and private channels. These Arabs saw the mujahideen not only as a bulwark against Soviet aggression but also as conduits for the spread of the more austere Salafi interpretation of Islam followed in Arabia. The political elites also saw support for jihad as a means to bolster their own legitimacy as Muslim rulers. Cash-poor Egypt contributed by playing a key role in training the mujahideen. Afghanistan thus became a nexus for militant Islamist circles around the globe, as the cause drew them together and thickened the ties between them.[15]

Pakistan, given its location on Afghanistan's border, saw the Soviet invasion as especially ominous. Pakistan's president from 1978 to 1988, Chief of the Army Staff General Staff Muhammad Zia ul-Haq, seized the chance to take charge of routing military, monetary, and other forms of aid from outside donors to the Afghan fighters. A devout Muslim who sought to also bring Muslim Afghanistan closer to help counter India, Zia ul-Haq used his leverage over the aid to further the Islamization of the Afghan resistance. He assigned to Pakistan's Inter-Service Intelligence monopoly control of the aid and ensured that only favored Afghan Islamists received support.[16]

With rear bases secure across the border in Pakistan and access to a steady flow of weapons, the Afghan mujahideen proved a tenacious foe to the PDPA (People's Democratic Party of Afghanistan) government and its Soviet backers. The Kremlin, however, was unwilling to expand its contingent in Afghanistan beyond 120,000 men. Therefore, as the Soviet army met stiffening resistance, it resorted to firepower-intensive but often indiscriminate tactics such as carpet bombing to drive villagers out of the countryside and into refugee camps. The Soviet conduct of the war devastated Afghanistan, destroying the rural economy, shattering Afghan society, killing an estimated one million Afghans, and forcing over five million refugees into Pakistan and Iran.[17] The inability of the Soviet army and its Afghan allies to prevail despite employing such measures for several years convinced Soviet Premier Mikhail Gorbachev that there was no prospect for victory. He commenced the withdrawal of Soviet forces from the country in 1988 and completed it in 1989.[18]

The exit of Soviet forces did not mean the end of Afghanistan's civil war. That war and the parties waging it had evolved. The war had started before the Soviet intervention as a conflict between a militantly socialist and centralizing government and a largely religious rural society. Stymied by the indomitable mujahideen, a chastened PDPA gradually shed its socialist trappings. In 1990 it even declared Afghanistan an "Islamic state" in a bid to win popular support and preserve itself. It was much too late. At the beginning of the war most Afghan fighters had no programmatic Islamist agenda, but Pakistan's manipulation of aid to support Islamism over the course of a decade of war led many to adopt precisely such an agenda. As war, pestilence, famine, and death ravaged and emptied the Afghan countryside, a new generation came of age in the refugee camps of Pakistan. Dependent on the largesse of Arab Gulf and Pakistani-sponsored Islamist charities for sustenance and education, these young Afghans grew up believing the application of a rigid and un-compromising interpretation of Islam to be a moral imperative and the only way to restore political order to their ravaged country. These would compose the ranks of the Taliban, a word whose meaning of "students" betrayed the origins of the movement in the *madrasas*, or Islamic schools, in Pakistan.[19]

To the surprise of many Western observers, the PDPA survived the with-drawal of Soviet forces. It did not, however, make it long past the collapse of the Soviet Union. Deprived of outside support in 1991, Kabul fell to the muja-hideen the following year. No longer facing a common enemy, the former reb-els fell out with each other. War-weary and disillusioned Afghans looked with modest hope upon a new force of young zealots who promised to bring order and justice to the country under the banner of Islam. These were the Taliban. They moved against the mujahideen warlords and by 1997 had brought under their control most of Afghanistan, with the exception of a pocket in the north. There, their opponents, the so-called Northern Alliance, composed mainly of ethnic Tajiks, Uzbeks, and Hazaras, would remain bottled up. Not inciden-tal to the Taliban's success was Pakistan's vigorous support. The Pakistanis saw backing the Pashtun-dominated religious movement in Afghanistan as a means to guarantee "strategic depth" against their archrival India, preclude the possibility of Pashtun separatism on Pakistan's side of the border, and project Pakistani influence on the flow of oil and gas from Central Asia.[20]

Fighting alongside the Taliban were Muslim militants from varied parts of the globe. Originally having arrived to wage jihad against the Soviets, some had stayed on, seeing in the Taliban ideological confederates. Among them was a young man from a wealthy Saudi family named Osama bin Laden. He had been one of the first Saudis to take an interest in the Afghan struggle, ar-riving there just two weeks after the Soviet invasion at the age of twenty-two. Two years later he formed a brigade of similarly minded Arab jihadists. As the Soviet army began its withdrawal in 1988, he and his associates, including an Egyptian doctor named Ayman al-Zawahiri, founded al Qaeda, an organiza-tion dedicated to global jihad. Although driven by a conviction in the need to wage jihad against infidel aggressors and to oppose Muslim regimes that were insufficiently or improperly Islamic, bin Laden had not yet entered into open opposition to the monarchy of his native land, Saudi Arabia. Bin Laden's decision to turn on Saudi Arabia would follow from a separate train of events triggered by another upheaval in 1979, the Islamic Revolution in Iran.

America, Iran, and Iraq: Geopolitics and Bedfellows

The Middle East during the Cold War was, like much of the world, a site of competition between the United States and Soviet Union. But, as the Arab oil embargo of 1973 demonstrated, unlike much of the world the Middle East possessed a resource essential to all: oil. With its concentration of roughly half of the world's oil reserves, the Persian Gulf in particular loomed large among the concerns of American defense planners. During the 1970s, a young civilian analyst at the Pentagon studying the Gulf presciently pointed to the state of Iraq as deserving special attention. His name was Paul Wolfowitz. Iraq, Wolfowitz noted, had the potential to become a regional hegemon. It was also a Soviet military client and an avowed foe of Israel, and as such a foe of U.S. interests in the region. Iraq therefore needed to be watched.[21]

Yet events in the following decade turned Iraq not into America's prime opponent in the region but instead into a de facto ally. Next door to Iraq, the shah of Iran shared ambitions broadly parallel to those of the government in neighboring Afghanistan. He, too, aspired to transform his country into a technologically advanced and powerful one. And, like Afghanistan's socialists, he believed Islam to be retrograde and pursued policies to diminish its influence. Toward that end, he promoted Western, "modern" styles of dress, consumption, and behavior while also celebrating Iran's pre-Islamic Sassanid past. Many Iranians found the shah's Kulturkampf against Islam objectionable. Moreover, although surging oil revenues brought rapid economic growth in the 1970s, that growth was imbalanced and fueled inflation that ate away the incomes of poor and middle-class Iranians. By 1978, large swaths of Iranians found the shah's contempt for their faith and his disregard for their economic plight intolerable. Mass protests broke out that year, leading to a protracted standoff that concluded with the shah's flight from Iran in 1979. The fall of the shah opened the way for one of his leading opponents, the religious authority Ayatollah Ruhollah Khomeini, to take control of the burgeoning rebellion against the Pahlavi dynasty and direct popular passions against the monarchy into support for theocratic rule and ultimately an Islamic revolution.

Iran's transformation from a U.S.-backed defender of the status quo into a revolutionary Islamic republic turned the region's geopolitics upside down. U.S. policy in the Persian Gulf had relied upon a strong, stable, and pro-American Iran to maintain regional order and block Soviet influence. Overnight Iran had become the most virulent foe of the United States in the region, and perhaps the world. Despite his own opposition to the United States, Iraq's leader Saddam Hussein found nothing to celebrate in his neighbor's Islamic Revolution. Revolutionary Islam directly challenged the Ba'athist ideology on which Saddam was trying to build the Iraqi state. Where Saddam's Iraq espoused socialist revolution and pan-Arab solidarity, Khomeini's Iran proclaimed Islamic Revolution and Muslim solidarity. Moreover, Saddam had to worry that Islamic Revolution in overwhelmingly Shi'i Iran would hold special appeal to Iraq's Shi'is, who made up 60 to 65 percent of Iraq's population. Although Ba'athism in the name of pan-Arab ethnic solidarity did not recognize sectarian divides, Saddam's regime did not so much abrogate a tradition of Sunni Arab dominance in Iraq as cloak it. Khomeini's message of revolution and Shi'i empowerment held the potential to tap into Iraqi Shi'i dissatisfaction. Khomeini made appeals directly to his coreligionists inside Iraq, and Iran began to host Shi'i Iraqi activists agitating against the Ba'athist regime. Fear that the Islamic revolutionary regime threatened the unity of the Iraqi state and his personal rule was a prime motive in Saddam's decision to invade his neighbor in September 1980.[22]

Saddam Goes to War with Iran

Saddam that fall had good reason to believe he could successfully use force to squelch the appeal of the Islamic Revolution, perhaps even topple Khomeini. The Iranian state was still engulfed in revolutionary chaos; its military in particular was in shambles. Much of the pro-shah officer corps was either in exile or facing political persecution, while its American-supplied weaponry and equipment were in disrepair due to an American embargo on spare parts. Iraq's armed forces advanced swiftly into Iran initially. In a matter of months, however, the Iraqis' offensive bogged down, as their operational and logistical limits revealed themselves and as Iranians rallied behind Khomeini.[23]

By the spring of 1982 Iran had reversed the momentum of the war and put Iraq on the defensive. Although backing Iraq's aggrandizement would not serve U.S. foreign policy, blocking Iran's certainly would. When Iran's armies began threatening to drive into Iraqi territory, the United States improved ties to Iraq and extended direct and indirect assistance. Washington authorized the export to Iraq of valuable military technology, welcomed the sale to Iraq of weapons by third parties such as France, and provided battlefield intelligence to the Iraqi army.[24] One of the most jarring photographs to reemerge in the wake of the 2003 U.S. invasion of Iraq was one from 1983. It showed Donald Rumsfeld in his capacity as the special envoy of the U.S. president greeting Saddam Hussein with outstretched arms and a genial handshake.

The United States was not alone in aiding Iraq against Iran. The Soviet Union, France, China, Italy, Germany, and Brazil were among those selling arms and/or military technology to Iraq. Saudi Arabia and the other Sunniruled Arab Gulf states saw revolutionary Shi'i Iran as a real geopolitical and ideological threat. Iran was menacingly large, and its Islamic Revolution unsettled the Gulf monarchies. Saudi Arabia's monarchy rested on an uneasy pact with religious authorities. A rebellion of Shi'is followed by the sudden seizure of Mecca's Grand Mosque by several hundred armed Sunni radicals in 1979—amid Iran's own revolution—graphically revealed the volatility of Saudi religion and politics.[25] The ruling family in Bahrain, a Sunni dynasty linked to the Saudis, sat perched nervously above a predominantly Shi'i population. These states had their own incentives to back Saddam, and they provided Baghdad with critical financing and facilitated the delivery of weapons and war materiel to Iraq. Among the weapons that Iraq employed against Iran was poison gas, first using it in the summer of 1983.[26] Saddam credited chemical weapons with staunching Iran's advance. His decision to target Tehran with ballistic missiles, he believed, drove Iran eventually to make peace.[27]

Washington's tilt in his favor did little to endear Saddam to America. In fact, as we know from his recorded conversations, Iraq's leader was convinced that the United States was extending assistance to Iran in the same subtle ways it was aiding Iraq.[28] As it turned out, he was not incorrect. Not wishing for either side to prevail, Washington in the course of the war secretly lent support to both.[29]

After eight grueling years of war, Iraq and Iran made peace in 1988. The war left Iraq bloodied and bankrupt. Although the casualty figures are in dispute, with the Iraqi government putting deaths at 250,000 and others suggesting as many as 600,000 died, there is no debate that Iraqi battlefield deaths were significant.[30] Iraq's debts to foreign creditors ran to eighty-five billion dollars, an amount roughly three times bigger than the country's GDP. At least half of these debts were to the Gulf countries. Saddam, however, believed he was the one due recompense. He presented the war not as a failed gamble on his part to exploit Iran's weakness but as a successful, if costly, defense of the Arabs from the Persian onslaught.[31] And because Iraq had incurred a gravely disproportionate toll in both blood and treasure fighting on behalf of all Arabs, it deserved repayment.[32]

One way the Arab Gulf states might have compensated Iraq would have been to limit their oil production for the sake of driving up the price of oil while simultaneously permitting Iraq to boost its exports in order to maximize its profits. Instead, Iraq's neighbor Kuwait persistently pumped oil in excess of its OPEC quota, thereby helping suppress global oil prices and drive down Iraq's revenues. Saddam interpreted Kuwait's overpumping as a hostile act. In addition, he accused Kuwait in 1990 of diverting oil underground from Iraq's side of the border, in effect stealing Iraqi oil.[33]

Saddam was not the first Iraqi to covet Kuwait's territory and resources. A traditional Iraqi skepticism about Kuwait's legitimacy, coupled with umbrage at Kuwait's impudence and lack of gratitude for Iraq's defense against Iran, undoubtedly made his decision to invade the country easier. More significant, however, was the conviction forming in Saddam's mind that the difficulties in which his country found itself were the result neither of poor policy decisions nor of the vicissitudes of the world oil market but of outside forces that aimed to weaken and destabilize his regime.[34] Speaking in March 1990, Saddam warned, "America is coordinating with Saudi Arabia and the UAE and Kuwait in a conspiracy against us. They are trying to reduce the price of oil to affect our military industries and our scientific research, to force us to reduce the size of our armed forces. . . . You must expect from another direction an Israeli military airstrike, or more than one, to destroy some of our important targets as part of this conspiracy."[35]

The waning of Soviet power and the fall of pro-Soviet communist regimes in Eastern Europe in 1989 also unnerved Saddam, and not simply because the Soviet Union had been his patron. He worried that the absence of a strong Soviet Union would embolden the United States to act without restraint around the globe. As Saddam informed his subordinates, the United States in the post–Cold War world was ascending to a position of unprecedented supremacy. There it would stay for some five years before other world powers would balance it. During this window Iraq would be vulnerable.[36] The United States and the Gulf Arabs were not the only ones plotting against him, Saddam believed. Israel, too, was working to undermine Iraq. In a speech delivered in April 1990, he lashed out at Israel, and in an infamous allusion to his possession of chemical weapons, threatened to "burn half" of that country. U.S. diplomats worried that Saddam's defiant rhetoric, as bad as it was on its own, would create more problems by stiffening Arab opposition to Israel and blocking the possibility of a settlement on Palestine.[37]

Saddam Seizes Kuwait and Bin Laden Breaks with Saudi Arabia

Saddam invaded Kuwait on August 2, 1990, occupying the country in two days. By seizing Kuwait, Saddam did more than take control of that country's considerable resources. He had placed his army in position to threaten the fragile Kingdom of Saudi Arabia and the other Gulf states. The armed forces of Saudi Arabia, let alone those of the still smaller Gulf states, were no match for Iraq's. If left unchecked, Saddam would be able to exert significant control over more than half of the world's oil reserves, with a concomitant influence over the global price of oil.[38]

Saddam's invasion alarmed the Saudi royal family. If they were to defy Saddam's bid at regional dominance, they recognized, they would need outside help. Among those who offered to defend the kingdom was the young Saudi exile, bin Laden. Although bin Laden was critical of the Saudi royal family for what he saw as its insufficiently Islamic rule, Ba'athism, with its elevation of Arab nationalism over Islam, was anathema to him. He loathed the idea of either Ba'athist or American soldiers marching in the holy land of Arabia. Reversing his opposition to the Saudi establishment, bin Laden approached several Saudi officials to offer his men in defense of the kingdom on condition that they permit no American forces in Arabia. Given the miniscule size of his brigade, the offer was comical, and indeed the head of the Saudi General Intelligence Directorate reportedly laughed out loud when he heard it.[39] The consequences of the Saudi king's rejection of the offer, however, would be far from funny.

The United States to the Rescue

The royal family was more receptive to an offer from American President George H. W. Bush to defend the kingdom. Bush, although preoccupied with the momentous unraveling of communism and the looming crack-up of the Soviet Union, concluded that Saddam's action demanded a swift and decisive response. His reasons were several. Iraq's invasion of Kuwait was a flagrant violation of territorial sovereignty, a bedrock principle of international order and law. This would have been a matter of concern at any time, but two factors magnified its significance for Bush. One was that the invasion coincided with the implosion of Soviet power. The retreat of the Soviet Union from its role as a pole of global politics portended an uncertain future for world order. To tolerate or overlook the conquest of one sovereign state by another would set a dangerous precedent in a time of flux. The other was that possession of Kuwait put Saddam in position to control vast Gulf oil reserves and manipulate world oil markets, as explained above.

Washington promptly began airlifting troops to Saudi Arabia and mobilizing international support in the form of a coalition to eject Saddam. Saddam found himself almost entirely isolated. The Americans rallied their traditional Cold War allies in Europe and Asia with ease. Indeed, many Arab states, Egypt, Kuwait, Morocco, Oman, Qatar, Saudi Arabia, Syria, and the United Arab Emirates, enthusiastically deployed troops to the Arabian Peninsula alongside America and its Western allies. A total of twenty-nine countries joined the coalition. It was an extraordinary diplomatic achievement on the part of Bush and his secretary of state, James Baker. On November 29, 1990, the United Nations authorized the American-led coalition to use force to eject Iraq from Kuwait if Saddam failed to withdraw from Kuwait by January 15, 1991.

Saddam believed that his Republican Guard units would halt the coalition's coming assault much as they had defied Iran's. He was confident that Americans, unlike Iraqis, could not sustain any conflict that would result in ten thousand or more casualties per week.[40] Thus, despite the coalition's obvious overwhelming superiority, Saddam refused to budge. On January 17, 1991, the United States and its allies commenced an extended air campaign against Iraqi forces. Iraq, in response, launched surface-to-surface Scud missiles against Saudi Arabia and Israel. These missile attacks could have only a symbolic effect. Scuds are inaccurate, and Iraq had limited numbers of them. But their use against Israel was not a vain gambit. As a state founded in the aftermath of the Nazi effort to annihilate the Jewish people, Israel saw the defense of its population as its very raison d'être. To deter attacks, it had adopted a severe policy of retaliation. By striking Israel, Saddam hoped to provoke Israel to hit back. An Israeli attack on Iraq, he calculated, would compel his Arab opponents to rally to his side and thereby cause the coalition against him to fall apart. Despite the loss of over seventy lives in the course of the Scud attacks, Israel refrained from responding to Saddam's provocation.[41] The coalition held.

On February 20, the coalition forces mounted a full-scale offensive into Kuwait. The Iraqi defenses collapsed almost instantly. After just one hundred hours of combat on the ground, Kuwait was liberated. Operation Desert Storm, as the military operation to liberate Kuwait was code-named, had been a stunning success. The coalition suffered only 190 casualties (113 of which were American) due to enemy fire, an almost negligible fraction of the ten thousand casualties U.S. planners had predicted.[42] Yet although Iraq's armed forces in and around Kuwait had been routed, Saddam and his regime in Baghdad remained intact. Nonetheless, Bush declared a cease-fire.

Bush's decision not to drive on to Baghdad to unseat Saddam was one of the war's most controversial. Some lambasted Bush for passing on a chance to dispose of a troublesome regional foe of U.S. power. Others regretted that Bush's decision allowed Saddam to remain in power and continue to abuse and inflict suffering upon the people of Iraq.[43]

Bush and his advisors, with little dissent, explained that they ruled out an invasion of Iraq in 1991 for two reasons. The first was that UN Resolution

678 authorized only the ejection of Iraqi forces from Kuwait. It made no allowance for invading Iraqi territory, let alone pursuing Saddam's forces to Baghdad. A decision by Washington to continue on to Baghdad would have precipitated the collapse of the allied coalition by compelling the Arab countries to withdraw from it in protest of what they would see as an illegitimate act of aggression against a fellow Arab state. Second, they feared that the removal of Saddam would have triggered the shattering of Iraq into Kurdish, Sunni Arab, and Shi'i Arab parts and opened a regional vacuum that would have drawn Iraq's neighbors into prolonged struggle.[44]

While unwilling to commit U.S. forces to overthrow Saddam, Bush was not averse to goading Iraqis to topple him. Speaking in a Voice of America broadcast on February 15, Bush said, "There is another way for the bloodshed to stop: and that is, for the Iraqi military and the Iraqi people to take matters into their own hands and force Saddam Hussein, the dictator, to step aside." He reiterated, the "Iraqi people should put him [Saddam] aside" on March 1.[45] Inspired in part by Bush's words, Iraq's Shi'i population in the south and Iraq's Kurds in the north rose in revolt. Although they constituted a majority of Iraq's total population, the Shi'is had from the Ottoman era forward been relegated to a second-class status of sorts. Their links to their coreligionists in Iran had aroused Saddam's suspicion and provoked repression.

As for Iraq's Kurds, they had periodically defied Iraq's central government since the state's founding and had suffered retaliation accordingly. Most infamously, Iraqi forces under Saddam employed poison gas in the Anfal campaign of 1988–89 to destroy over three thousand Kurdish villages, killing some two hundred thousand Kurds and displacing over a million more.[46] In early March 1991 the Shi'i and Kurdish rebels enjoyed initial successes, seizing cities and provinces throughout southern and northern Iraq. Baghdad and the center, however, remained under government control.

Although in battered condition, Iraq's armed forces retained enough strength to handle the lightly armed rebels. They suppressed first the Shi'is and then the Kurds, ruthlessly killing tens of thousands and rounding up thousands more for jail. In response to the crackdown, the United States, Britain, France, Australia, the Netherlands, Saudi Arabia, and Turkey established "no-fly zones" in the north of Iraq over the thirty-eighth parallel and in the south below the thirty-third parallel. They forbade Iraqi aircraft from flying over these territories. To enforce this ban, coalition air forces—primarily American, British, and French—began flying regular patrols in those airspaces. In the north, this was sufficient to enable the Kurds to establish de facto autonomy. The no-fly zones, however, marked the extent of coalition's intervention. As reprehensible as Saddam may have been, the United States and its allies saw the preservation of Iraq's unity under him as preferable to Iraq's dissolution without him.[47]

The defeat in Kuwait and the uprisings rattled Saddam and tarnished his regime. Whereas during the war with Iran the regime had celebrated the Iraqi soldier as the embodiment of Iraq, the army's poor performance in Kuwait and the examples both of soldiers who rebelled and of those who suppressed the rebels made this henceforth impossible.[48] Still, Saddam concluded that he, not his enemies and certainly not the United States, had emerged triumphant from what he dubbed "the mother of all battles." In his mind, Bush had used Kuwait as a pretext to go to war against Iraq to achieve dominance over the region and its oil. But Bush had failed. Because Iraq's forces were unbowed, he had been compelled to declare a ceasefire.[49] Saddam's success in quashing the rebellions steeled his resolve to maintain power and to prevail over all enemies, foreign and domestic.[50]

Dilemmas of Containing Iraq

America greeted its servicemen returning from Operation Desert Storm with a heroes' welcome complete with a ticker tape parade. The victory in Kuwait, nevertheless, failed to resolve America's fundamental problem in the Gulf of containing Iran; arguably, it made that problem worse. A weakened Iraq was of lesser use in balancing Iran, and it was now incontrovertibly hostile to the United States and U.S. interests in the region. Washington's solution was to pursue a policy of "dual containment," that is, seek to box in the influence and ambitions of both the Ba'athist and Islamic republics simultaneously. The policy's appeal was that it purported to resolve this basic dilemma, but its flaw was that in reality it could not.[51]

Containing Iraq required the United States to deploy military forces sufficient to achieve two goals. One was to maintain the no-fly zones over northern and southern Iraq. The other was to base sufficient numbers of troops, equipment, and supplies to deter Saddam from invading his neighbors. This was no small burden, for the United States had military obligations around the globe. The possibility that Iraq might acquire an arsenal of weapons of mass destruction (WMDs)—chemical, biological and especially nuclear—complicated the containment policy. The acquisition of WMDs would allow Iraq to neutralize America's conventional deterrent by making the potential costs of taking military action against Iraq prohibitively high. Such a dynamic would not depend on an ability to strike the continental United States. The threat of a WMD strike against U.S. or allied forces in the region or the societies hosting those forces could be enough. And whereas to counter Iraq's conventional forces one could afford to wait to respond until they had crossed Iraq's borders in clear violation of a neighbor's sovereignty, one would have no comparable territorial or chronological buffer zone in which to respond to Iraq's brandishing of WMDs. Saddam could wield the threat of WMDs from inside Iraq's territory.[52]

The Question of Iraq's Weapons of Mass Destruction: A Haunting Phantom

During the 1990–91 Gulf War, coalition intelligence bodies made the disquieting discovery that Iraq's chemical weapons stores were substantial and that its nuclear weapons program was more advanced than anyone had suspected.[53] The UN came to the same conclusion. Thus as part of the war's settlement, the UN insisted that Iraq submit to weapons inspections. Toward that end the UN created UNSCOM, the United Nations Special Commission on Disarmament, and assigned it the mission to discover and destroy any nuclear, biological, or chemical weapons stores or facilities inside Iraq. To encourage Iraq to comply, the UN subjected Iraq to a sanctions regime that prevented it from selling oil to earn foreign currency and sharply limited what it could import. The appeal of economic sanctions was that they offered a way to coerce Iraq without violence. The calculation was that by limiting Iraq's access to outside goods and to the means to pay for them, popular dissatisfaction with Saddam would build and eventually compel him to either change course or be overthrown.

Washington hoped for a coup that would dislodge Saddam but preserve Iraq's territorial integrity. The hope rested on the belief that among the Iraqi officer corps there must be disgruntled patriots who would see that Saddam was leading their country to ruin and then decide to take him out. Yet even America's clandestine efforts to foment such a coup came to naught.[54]

The fact was that Saddam was skilled in the prevention, preemption, and neutralization of coups and other internal threats. He had, after all, gotten his start in politics in his early twenties as an assassin and understood all too well what conspirators were capable of. He was an assiduous student of Joseph Stalin, and not for reasons of mere historical curiosity.[55] Saddam, like Stalin, was expert at the manipulation of cadres to protect against treachery. He placed personal loyalty above any other characteristic for appointments and appointed and promoted military officers and regime officials accordingly.[56] He ensured that those around him had a direct, personal stake in the perpetuation of his regime, and that all feared incurring even the slightest suspicion of dissent or disloyalty.[57] He created overlapping and competing government bodies and inhibited lateral flows of information between his subordinates to breed rivalry and sow distrust and thereby block conspiracies from forming. Saddam intensified these measures after the uprisings of 1991, when he made "coup proofing" his regime his utmost priority.[58]

The economic sanctions that the United States and United Nations imposed on Iraq with the goal of stoking popular discontent and bringing about Saddam's fall perversely had the opposite effect. They bolstered the relative strength of Saddam's regime in two ways. First, by targeting the more sophisticated parts of Iraq's economy, the sanctions devastated Iraq's formerly large middle and professional classes—precisely the constituency that specialists had once predicted would one day transform Iraq into an industrial, urbanizing, and technologically advanced power akin to Taiwan or South Korea. Moreover, Saddam revitalized tribal ties by cutting deals with tribal chiefs, offering them greater freedom in return for their fealty, thereby undermining the state to amplify his personal influence. Second, the shortages caused by sanctions made Iraqis more, not less, dependent on the regime for access to now scarce goods. Loyalty to Saddam and his regime and personal connections became all the more important. Regime insiders and Saddam loyalists managed also to profit disproportionately from the black markets that emerged.

The Noose Loosens

Saddam's repression and gross violations of human rights were known to the world. But the imposition of sanctions caused observers to shift attention to suffering under the sanctions regime, and deflected criticism away from Baghdad toward Washington. Critics began to blame not Saddam but the United States for the deaths of hundreds of thousands of Iraqi children from malnutrition and inadequate medicine.[59] U.S. diplomats were, at a minimum, astoundingly tone-deaf in responding to these charges.[60] The sanctions against Iraq began to appear as ineffective and cruel. As one U.S. analyst put it in the mainstream American journal *Foreign Affairs*, "American policymakers need to recognize that the only 'box' into which sanctions put Iraqis is coffins."[61]

In an attempt to alleviate the impact of sanctions on innocent Iraqis, the UN proposed in 1996 an "oil for food" arrangement that allowed Saddam now to sell two billion dollars worth of oil every six months and exchange the proceeds for food and other humanitarian supplies under UN supervision. Saddam begrudgingly agreed to it, seeing the arrangement as a way to boost his revenues in the short term and as a step in the longer term toward weakening and ending the sanctions altogether. Iraq's lenders, particularly France and

Russia, were anxious for Iraq to resume exporting oil so that it might pay its debts.[62] Saddam quietly began to reach out to former regional foes like Oman, Qatar, and the United Arab Emirates, as well as potential counterweights to the United States like China, playing in particular on the latter's discomfort with sanctions for human rights abuses.[63]

Containing Saddam Hussein's Iraq constituted a top priority of American foreign policy during the 1990s. The exercise was costly, however. It acted as a drain on military personnel, equipment, and budgets. By spending roughly one billion dollars a year on operations in the Gulf alone to hem in Iraq in addition to the myriad costs of maintaining forces in the region, the effort exacted a toll on the preparedness and morale of U.S. forces. This is not to say that the policy failed. To the contrary, as Daniel Byman noted at the time, judged by its initial goals of keeping Iraq militarily weak and its neighbors safe, the containment policy was an "impressive success."[64] But Saddam's doggedness in waiting out the sanctions wore down American resolve. Among UN Security Council members, the United States could rely only on Britain. China, Russia, and even France were often critical of U.S. policy toward Iraq. The ongoing U.S. military effort generated friction in the region even with long-standing partners like Turkey, Egypt, and Saudi Arabia. The need to maintain the no-fly zones and deter the Iraqi army required the deployment of air, ground, and naval forces to Turkey and the Persian Gulf. For different reasons, the presence of U.S. forces supporting the containment of Iraq in Turkey and Saudi Arabia complicated America's relations with these two countries.

Stressed Ties: The United States, Turkey, and Saudi Arabia

The Turkish Republic has from its beginnings been constitutionally allergic to outside military interventions on its borders as a matter of identity and principle. Although a NATO ally and recipient of U.S. military aid, Turkey understands itself as a product of a resistance movement led by its founder Mustafa Kemal Atatürk, who after the end of World War I established the republic in defiance of the European imperial powers' plans to partition Anatolia. Atatürk's success had come after more than a century of relentless European encroachment upon a steadily shrinking Ottoman Empire. The memory of imperial intervention and partition was strong among the Turks, who saw the weakening of their Iraqi neighbor as a threat to the unity of their own state.

The flight in 1991 of hundreds thousands of Iraqi Kurds from Saddam's repression across the border into Turkey, nevertheless, prompted Ankara to push for intervention to protect the Kurds inside Iraq and thereby halt the influx. The result was Operation Provide Comfort, in which the United States, Britain, France, the Netherlands, Australia, and Turkey cooperated to distribute humanitarian aid to Kurds inside Iraq and enforce a no-fly zone for Iraqi aircraft above the thirty-sixth parallel. In 1997, the United States, Britain, and Turkey decided to maintain the no-fly zone, now under the name Operation Northern Watch. Essential to the success of both operations was the airbase located in Incirlik, Turkey.

The Turkish armed forces' participation in the northern no-fly zone notwithstanding, Ankara remained profoundly uneasy about collaborating in an effort that, by keeping Saddam's forces at bay, was enabling Iraq's Kurds to build a government of sorts. The Iraqi Kurds' de facto autonomy could one day become de jure independence. That independence in turn might lead to Turkey's partition, since perhaps 15 percent of Turkey's own population was Kurdish and much of that concentrated in Turkey's southeast near Iraq. Belief that the United States in Iraq was deliberately pursuing a multistage project to create an independent Kurdish state and use it to weaken or even divide Turkey was widespread.[65] The Turkish General Staff had in 1990 blocked the suggestion of Turkey's president to join the UN coalition against Saddam precisely because it feared fracturing the Iraqi state and loosing the Kurds.[66] Turkey in the 1990s found itself entering the second decade of a war with the separatist Kurdistan Workers' Party (Partiya Karkeren Kurdistan or PKK). The war against the PKK, which would claim some thirty thousand lives by the end of the decade, was the biggest and most divisive issue in Turkish politics, and it was directly tied to Iraq, where the PKK maintained bases beyond Turkey's reach. Deep suspicion of U.S. motives in Iraq and resentment at having to support the Americans even as they facilitated Kurdish separatism thus introduced a chronic irritant into Turkish-American relations.

Although Turkey continued to participate in Operation Northern Watch until its end in 2003, disagreements over Iraqi Kurdistan remained an impediment to closer ties between Turkey and the United States through the buildup to the invasion of Iraq and then thereafter. Indeed, when in 2002 U.S. commanders requested permission from Ankara to use Turkish territory to mount an offensive into Iraq, the Turkish General Staff uncharacteristically refrained from expressing an opinion. Such reticence from an institution widely seen as close to and even dependent upon the United States was widely interpreted inside Turkey as a signal of distrust. Taking the cue from the General Staff, the Turkish parliament rejected the request, forcing the U.S. military to abandon a key part of its invasion plan.[67]

Like Turkey, Saudi Arabia also faced a violent internal threat that was tied to Iraq, or more precisely to the presence inside the kingdom of U.S. forces based there to contain Saddam. The arrival of those forces had caused bin Laden openly to oppose the Saudi royal family. Bin Laden was not alone. The presence of non-Muslims on the sacred soil of the Arabian Peninsula was a contentious issue for many Muslims inside and outside the kingdom.[68] That discontent had been anticipated. From the beginning of the confrontation over Kuwait, Americans and Saudis had agreed that it would be undesirable to maintain a U.S. troop presence inside Arabia for long. In August 1990 U.S. Secretary of Defense Dick Cheney had assured Saudi King Fahd that America would withdraw its forces from the kingdom as soon as victory over Iraq had been achieved. It was not an idle pledge. By 1993, the United States had reduced the number of its military personnel in Saudi Arabia from half a million to fewer than one thousand. Saddam's deployment of three Republican Guard divisions along Kuwait's border in 1994, however, forced the United States to scramble to dispatch thirty thousand men to the Gulf in response. Thereafter the United States gradually increased its presence inside the kingdom, boosting the number of personnel to over seven thousand in 2000.[69]

Saddam understood the Saudi vulnerability. Already in 1990 he had begun cultivating religious opposition to the American presence in Arabia. Drawing parallels between that presence and the Israeli occupation of Jerusalem and sounding the themes of the self-serving wealthy Arabs, the honor of the Arab man, the dignity of the Arab woman, the sanctity of the holy cities of Mecca and Medina, and the "perfidy of Zionism," he "masterfully fused" the languages of Arabism and Islam. As the coalition forces swelled, the audience for his rhetoric increased.[70] Defeat did not diminish the audience. Whereas, the Egyptian Mohamed Heikal observed, the Americans believed that by defeating Saddam they had rendered a service for which the Arabs should be grateful, Arabs were sorrowful, not relieved, about Iraq's destruction. When polled after the Gulf War, three-fourths of Arab elites expressed the belief that the war had been a conspiracy engineered by outsiders to split and subjugate the Arab world.[71] Saddam continued in the 1990s to make good use of Islamist agents and networks to agitate on the issue.[72]

In 1995 a group calling itself the Islamic Movement for Change warned that if American forces were not withdrawn from Arabia, it would carry out attacks. It followed through that November when it detonated a car bomb at a U.S. military building in Riyadh, killing six. The following year, militants used a massive truck bomb to blast a complex called Khobar Towers that housed U.S. servicemen. Nineteen Americans lost their lives.[73] Two months later, the London-based Arabic newspaper *Al-Quds Al-Arabi* published a "Declaration of War against the Americans Occupying the Land of the Two

Holy Places." Signed by bin Laden, it labeled the American presence around Mecca and Medina the "latest and greatest" of aggressions against Muslims.[74] Then in 1998, bin Laden, al-Zawahiri, and three others joined under the name World Front for Jihad against Jews and Crusaders to declare it the personal duty of all Muslims to attack Americans, civilian and military, wherever they could find them in order to compel the "Crusader-Jewish" alliance to withdraw from the Al-Aqsa Mosque in Jerusalem, the Arabian Peninsula, and indeed all the Muslim lands. That summer, on the day marking the eighth anniversary of the arrival of U.S. forces in Arabia, suicide bombers drove truck bombs into the U.S. embassy compounds in Kenya and Tanzania, killing over two hundred, the vast majority of whom were local Africans. Two years later, al Qaeda struck the U.S. Navy destroyer USS *Cole* with a suicide boat bomb in the port of Aden, killing seventeen American sailors. These attacks indicated the depth of opposition to the presence of U.S. forces in Arabia and testified to the growing resourcefulness of anti-American Islamists.

The Saudis and other regimes in the region were sensitive to this resentment of the American presence. Popular anger over the toll U.S.-led sanctions were inflicting on Iraq's population reinforced it. The first Arab satellite television news channel, Al Jazeera, debuted in 1996, and its footage of suffering Iraqis galvanized hostility toward America. Thus when in 1998 the United States proposed to respond to Iraqi violations of the northern no-fly zone and incursions into the Kurdish north with cruise missile and air strikes, Turkey and Saudi Arabia both refused to cooperate. The Turks worried they were facilitating Kurdish separatism that would be directed eventually against them, while the Saudis feared being tagged as collaborators with America in the bullying and abuse of a fellow Arab country. The desire to put distance between themselves and the United States over Iraq strengthened with time. Whereas Washington and Riyadh had bonded almost instantly in 1990 in response to Iraq's invasion of Kuwait, less than a decade had passed before the issue of Iraq was dividing them.[75] Washington was well aware of the tensions that its forward military presence and policy of containment were generating; the desire to resolve those tensions became another incentive to finish Saddam once and for all.

Saddam could see that the international coalition against him was fraying and the will to maintain sanctions was weakening. Countries from France to China were eager to do business and turn profits with Iraq, and opinion around the world was blaming not Baghdad but Washington for the toll that sanctions were exacting on the Iraqi population. In 1997 and 1998 Saddam instigated crises that threatened to disrupt UNSCOM investigations, and his armed forces expressed defiance of U.S. and British air patrols by turning on antiaircraft targeting radars and taking similar provocative acts.

Saddam stood unchastened and unrepentant. He continued to rebuild support home and abroad. Despite the Ba'athist emphasis on secularism, Saddam during the 1990s cultivated religious believers and Islamists. He sent Iraqi religious authorities abroad who by virtue of their nominal clerical status could serve as his diplomats and emissaries. He also sponsored the establishment of institutions of religious learning inside Iraq, recruiting foreign students who could later serve as goodwill ambassadors and help overcome Iraq's isolation.[76] Bolstering legitimacy among domestic audiences was another motive for Saddam's public embrace of faith, which included such demonstrative projects as the construction of the "Mother of All Battles Mosque" in honor of the 1991 Gulf War and the production of a Koran written in ink allegedly made from his own blood.[77] Saddam retained his megalomaniacal belief in himself as a world-historical figure on par with the Babylonian king Nebuchadnezzar II and Saladin, two liberators of Jerusalem from the land of Iraq. Saddam's links to Hamas and offers of monetary support to the families of Palestinian suicide bombers demonstrated his determination to play a larger role in the region.[78]

American officials, too, sensed all too well that the sanctions were collapsing. Prominent Republicans in 1997 had begun calling for "regime change" in Iraq, and in October 1998 President Bill Clinton made this an official goal of U.S. policy by signing into law the Iraq Liberation Act. Passed with broad bipartisan support, the act called for supporting "a transition to democracy in Iraq." That December, frustrated by Saddam's recalcitrance and the repeated Iraqi violations of the northern no-fly zone and incursions into the Kurdish north, the United States and Britain decided to act without UN authorization. They mounted a four-day air campaign against Iraq dubbed Desert Fox. Although it damaged Iraq's infrastructure, the campaign did nothing to shake Saddam's rule and instead reinforced the image of the United States and Britain as bullies. Indeed, the operation prompted the other three members of the UN Security Council—France, Russia, and China—to call openly for an end to the oil embargo. It was the sanctions regime, not the Ba'athist one, that was falling apart.[79] Dual containment was failing badly, Saddam was as intractable as ever, and in the United States Clinton's Republican critics assailed him for his fecklessness on Iraq. Iraq had morphed from regional distraction into a persistent and major headache for the Clinton administration.

U.S. Grand Strategy: Empire of the World and for the World

George W. Bush inherited that headache when he assumed the presidency in 2001. Bush appointed to key positions in his administration some of the most vociferous advocates for toppling Saddam, including his vice president, Dick Cheney, secretary of defense, Donald Rumsfeld, and deputy secretary of defense, Paul Wolfowitz. All three believed in the need for American global primacy. Wolfowitz believed also in the righteousness of American primacy. The experiences of World War II and the Cold War powerfully informed his worldview. The failure of the liberal democracies to confront dictatorships in the 1930s permitted the horrors of Hitler and the Axis powers, whereas the willingness of the United States to resist tyranny in the Cold War led not only to the downfall of Soviet communism but to the strengthening and spread of democracy in Latin America and Asia. American leadership thus was good not only for America but also for the world, as it secured international peace through the deterrence of potential aggressors and facilitated the spread and consolidation of democratic governance around the globe.[80] Saddam, with his tyranny, repression of his own people, contempt for international law, and ambition for greater power, manifested precisely the sort of threat America was obliged to neutralize for its own sake and the world's.

Rumsfeld, by contrast, was engaged in a crusade in which Iraq was to be only one skirmish. As secretary of defense, Rumsfeld saw his mission to be a total overhaul of the U.S. armed forces, the transformation of the American military from a large but ponderous bureaucracy suited to fight the bygone wars of the twentieth century into a nimbler yet harder-hitting organization built for the twenty-first century. The U.S. armed forces at the end of the twentieth century may have appeared unassailable, but history was replete with examples of complacent and stagnant armies outsmarted, surprised, and outfought by opponents who embraced doctrinal, organizational, and technological innovation. In the more diffuse threat environment of the twenty-first century, the accelerating rate of technological advancement suggested that challengers would emerge, mutate, and grow more rapidly than ever. Saddam and his apparent quest for WMDs seemingly illustrated precisely this dynamic. The United States therefore needed a military machine that, by leveraging its advantages in information, stealth, and precision, could react more quickly and overwhelm and defeat its opponents with less manpower and less firepower. After setting out on this project of reform, Rumsfeld concluded that the biggest obstacle to change was the U.S. military bureaucracy. The enemy was the Pentagon.[81] The preoccupation with transformation would subtly inform the U.S. decision for war against Saddam Hussein.

9/11, the United States, and Iraq

The attacks of 9/11 riveted Washington's attention on the organizational perpetrator of those attacks, al Qaeda. The head of al Qaeda was in Afghanistan. When the Taliban refused Washington's demand to hand over bin Laden, the United States, joined by the United Kingdom, initiated Operation Enduring Freedom in October to destroy terrorist training camps and infrastructure in Afghanistan. Coordinating with the Northern Alliance, they drove the Taliban from power in a matter of weeks. Although the United States and its allies failed to catch or kill bin Laden, the swift rout of the Taliban suggested that America's foes were perhaps paper tigers and would crumble when confronted. American planners, not entirely unlike their Soviet predecessors, expected that the establishment of good centralized governance and effective state institutions would "drain the swamp," that is, transform Afghanistan from a war-torn and lawless "failed state" where terrorists could operate with impunity into an orderly and prosperous society inhospitable to terrorist movements or insurgencies.

The deceptively smooth initial success in Afghanistan made it easier for Washington to turn America's eyes to Iraq. But the fact is that those eyes had never strayed too far. Already in the immediate wake of the attacks of 9/11, key members of the Bush team had expressed a desire to direct the inevitable American response to those attacks toward the overthrow of Saddam. Rumsfeld and Wolfowitz in Washington and Undersecretary of Defense Douglas Feith in Europe were making the case for regime change in Iraq mere hours after the hijacked planes hit their target.[82] The Bush administration subsequently asserted that Saddam was tied to al Qaeda and in possession of a robust WMD program. Since it became well established after the invasion that Saddam had no active WMD program and that his links to al Qaeda were real but tenuous,[83] such behavior might seem a clever albeit cynical application of the maxim to "never let a serious crisis go to waste."[84] Coupled with National Security Advisor Condoleezza Rice's impatient dismissal of skepticism toward the White House's assertions about the advanced state of Saddam's nuclear program—"We don't want the smoking gun to be a mushroom cloud," a not-so-subtle hint at the possibility that the United States might receive confirmation of the existence of Saddam's nuclear program only after his agents have detonated a smuggled nuclear device on American territory[85]—this approach suggests a brazen disregard for evidence and a calculated effort to manipulate public opinion.

The fact, however, is that virtually all outside intelligence bodies, including those of countries that opposed the war, earnestly believed that Iraq had active WMD programs.[86] Moreover, the shock effect of 9/11 cannot be underestimated. The scale and ingenuity of those attacks stunned Americans, who had not been able to even conceive of an operation carried out by men with no more than box cutters wreaking such havoc, let alone on the American continent. Imagining that terrorists might smuggle a nuclear device into the United States was, by contrast, all too easy. As Frank Harvey has argued, in the context of aftermath of 9/11, "downplaying the threat from Saddam's WMD would have been viewed by almost everyone as reckless and irresponsible." Moreover, a string of prior intelligence failures of underestimation primed outside, and especially American, intelligence analysts to overestimate dangers. The surprise discovery in 1991 that Saddam had far more advanced WMD capabilities than anyone had predicted, the CIA's inability to foresee Iran's and North Korea's development of ballistic missiles, and the CIA's failure to anticipate India's test of nuclear weapons in 1998 reinforced the emerging bias to err toward the overestimation of capabilities.[87]

This is not to excuse the Bush administration's rush to judgment and poor use of intelligence. It is, rather, to illustrate that the administration was not alone in its errors and that the errors were not entirely willful. Indeed, the Americans and others were all too correctly reading the signals that Saddam was sending. Saddam, after all, had been striving to project the impression that Iraq had WMDs. The intended audience for this impression, however, was not the United States or its allies, but rather Iraq's neighbor and primary threat, Iran. The war with Iran had battered Iraq, and the subsequent defeat in Kuwait, the uprisings, and sanctions further weakened Iraq. Saddam thus came to conclude, not illogically, that WMDs might be his best deterrent against future Iranian aggression.

Although after 1991 Iraq could no longer produce WMDs, Saddam decided he could at least create the appearance that he might possess them. Saddam made the creation of that impression a foreign relations priority. As part of a strategy of "deterrence by doubt," Saddam established a special unit dedicated to concealing Iraq's WMD programs.[88] Iran remained foremost in his mind. In June 2000 Saddam gave a speech in which he said that the world could not expect Iraq to surrender the rifle and rely only on the sword for self-defense, a thinly veiled reference to WMDs. Only after they had interrogated Saddam did the puzzled Americans understand that at the time he had been sending a warning to Iran.[89] Writing with hindsight, CIA Director George Tenet summarized the paradox in the American view of Saddam and Saddam's view of the United States: "Before the war, we didn't understand he was bluffing, and he didn't understand that *we were not*."[90]

Conclusion

The early twentieth century subjected the societies of the greater Middle East to a scale and intensity of socioeconomic change that was unprecedented for them. As revolutionary developments in manufacturing, medicine, military technology, agriculture, communications, and other spheres simultaneously made themselves felt, they upended existing patterns of economic, cultural, and political behavior. The projection of European power over those societies, sometimes in the form of colonialism, accompanied those changes, endowing them with a political valence that problematized their local adoption and assimilation. Disagreement over the degree and manner of adaptation to those developments often defined political struggles. The vitality of the region's predominant religious faith, Islam, and its claim to cultural hegemony complicated matters further by injecting into the conflict a metaphysical dimension, thus raising the stakes and making compromise more difficult to attain. The result often was polarized strife between radical self-styled "modernizers" who advocated breaking symbolically with the past and assimilating aspects of European and global culture and proponents of reviving a "purer" and more "authentic" Islam.

Struggles of this nature helped precipitate the Soviet Invasion of Afghanistan and the Islamic Revolution in Iran in 1979. The geography of the greater Middle East and in particular its possession of oil, the lifeblood of the modern world, ensured that global geopolitical rivalries and concerns would intertwine with these regional clashes and conflicts to generate the chain of events narrated above.

Yet even as long-term conflicts in Afghanistan and Iraq continued to grind onward and grind up the Afghani and Iraqi states, Washington was distilling an ambitious vision of national security that took it for granted that in global politics the primary actors were and would remain states. All too sensitive to the long-term vulnerability of American power in a rapidly changing world, Washington was woefully ignorant of the course of history in the greater Middle East, where, far from fostering the next great challenge to world order, the region's societies were consuming themselves, trapped in overlapping and interlocking conflicts. It was into those layered conflicts that the United States injected itself so forcefully and decisively in 2001 and 2003.

Now, well over a decade later, it has become all too clear that the interventions in Afghanistan and Iraq have failed to meet their objectives to bring stability, democratic rule, and prosperity, but they have succeeded in exacerbating local conflicts. In Afghanistan, a fragile central government exists more as a dependent of foreign aid than as the sovereign representative of the Afghan people. Among the people, ethnic and sectarian rifts are deeper now than three decades ago. All the while the Taliban abides, waiting for the final American withdrawal to reassume its prior dominance. In Iraq, the state is a husk, a polite fiction maintained not by the population of Iraq but by the international community that rightly fears that recognizing Iraq's de facto partition will only trigger a round of further conflicts that draw in Iraq's neighbors. The emergence of the self-styled Islamic State of Iraq and Syria in 2013, however, is forcing the issue of the reality of the Iraqi state.

The intervention in Iraq, justified in large measure by the argument that the installation of democratic governance under U.S. tutelage was necessary to preclude the further incubation and spread of "terror and extremism" in the Muslim world, has led to precisely the opposite. Exponents of terror no longer operate in the shadows and in the crevices of failed states; they now openly control large swathes of territory in the heart of the Middle East.

Some saw in the Arab Spring of 2011 the redemption of the U.S. effort in Iraq. Those uprisings, however, have not brought democracy and open societies, but instead have contributed to the spread of violent Islamism to Libya, the consolidation of martial law in Egypt, and the explosion of civil war in Syria. The paroxysm of violence that grips the greater Middle East will at some point subside, and it may sometime in the future leave in its wake more open, just, and prosperous societies. But this is hardly certain, and perhaps not even likely. The failures of the two U.S. interventions and of the Soviet in Afghanistan, despite their vast differences, may have a common lesson to teach. All three interventions sought to resolve localized conflicts expressed in the idiom of Islam, and all predicated their strategies on the belief that the use of superior military force to quell resistance would open the way to socioeconomic and political progress that in turn would gradually remove the causes of conflict. Yet in each case, their reform efforts achieved disappointing results, while the military campaigns more often than not spread conflict. Just as adding water to an oil-based fire does not douse but rather spreads flames, so, too, have outside military interventions fanned conflicts rather than contain and overcome them.

NOTES

1 The total number of violent civilian deaths was 114,212. Figures on Iraqi losses are from the Iraq Body Count project, https://www.iraqbodycount.org/analysis/numbers/2011/. For a critique of the project's methodology, see John Tirman, *The Deaths of Others: The Fate of Civilians in America's Wars* (New York: Oxford University Press, 2011), 328–32.

2 Quoted in Albert L. Weeks, *The Choice of War: The Iraq War and the Just War Tradition* (Santa Barbara, CA: Praeger, 2009), 6.

3 Jeffrey Record, "The Bush Doctrine and War with Iraq," *Parameters*, 33 (Spring 2003): 4–21.

4 For a patient and thorough refutation of the argument for conspiracy, see Frank P. Harvey, *Explaining the Iraq War: Counterfactual Theory, Logic, and Evidence* (Cambridge: Cambridge University Press, 2012).

5 Tore T. Petersen, *Richard Nixon, Great Britain, and the Anglo-American Alignment in the Persian Gulf and Arabian Peninsula* (Portland, OR: Sussex Academic Press, 2009).

6 Thomas Barfield, *Afghanistan: A Cultural and Political History* (Princeton: Princeton University Press, 2010), 217–18.

7 Vladimir Snegirev and Valerii Samunin, *Virus "A": Kak my zaboleli vtorzheniem v Afganistan* (Moscow: Rossiiskaia gazeta, 2011), 201–2.

8 Vahid Brown and Don Rassler, *Fountainhead of Jihad: The Haqqani Nexus, 1973–2012* (London: Hurst, 2013), 45; Aleksandr Liakhovskii, *Tragediia i doblest' Afgana* (Moscow: GPI Ispolkoma, 1995), 23–24.

9 Barfield, *Afghanistan*, 225–33; Odd Arne Westad, *The Global Cold War: Third World Interventions and the Making of Our Times* (Cambridge: Cambridge University Press, 2006), 307.

10 Liakhovskii, *Tragediia i doblest' Afgana*, 119–20; Snegirev and Samunin, *Virus "A,"* 543.

11 Roderic Braithwaite, *Afgantsy: The Russians in Afghanistan, 1979–89* (Oxford: Oxford University Press, 2011), 58–102; Vladislav M. Zubok, *A Failed Empire: The Soviet Union in the Cold War from Stalin to Gorbachev* (Chapel Hill: University of North Carolina Press, 2007), 259–64.

12 Braithwaite, *Afgantsy*, 123

13 Mark Galeotti, *Afghanistan: The Soviet Union's Last War* (London: Frank Cass, 1994), 16.

14 Liakhovskii, *Tragediia i doblest' Afgana*, 117.

15 Brown and Rassler, *Fountainhead of Jihad*, 7–8. On the Saudi role, see Thomas Hegghammer, *Jihad in Saudi Arabia: Violence and Pan-Islamism since 1979* (Cambridge: Cambridge University Press, 2010), 24–30.

16 Neamotallah Nojumi, "The Rise and Fall of the Taliban," in *The Taliban and the Crisis of Afghanistan*, ed. Robert D. Crews and Amin Tarzi (Cambridge, MA: Harvard University Press, 2008), 91–92.

17 Galeotti, *Afghanistan*, 17, 142; Larry P. Goodson, *Afghanistan's Endless War: State Failure, Regional Politics, and the Rise of the Taliban* (Seattle: University of Washington Press, 2001), 60–69.

18 Artemy Kalinovsky, *A Long Goodbye: The Soviet Withdrawal from Afghanistan* (Cambridge, MA: Harvard University Press, 2011).

19 Nojumi, "Rise and Fall of the Taliban," 93–100; Barfield, *Afghanistan*, 281.

20 Amin Saikal, *Modern Afghanistan: A History of Struggle and Survival* (New York: I.B. Tauris, 2006), 352; Nojumi, "Rise and Fall of the Taliban," 101–3.

21 Richard H. Immerman, *Empire of Liberty: A History of American Imperialism from Benjamin Franklin to Paul Wolfowitz* (Princeton: Princeton University Press, 2010), 205.

22 F. Gregory Gause, III, "The International Politics of the Gulf," in *International Relations of the Middle East*, ed. Louise Fawcett (Oxford: Oxford University Press, 2009), 274.

23 Charles Tripp, *A History of Iraq* (Cambridge: Cambridge University Press, 2000), 224.

24 Ibid., 231.

25 Toby Jones, "Rebellion on the Saudi Periphery: Modernity, Marginalization and the Shi'a Uprising of 1979," *International Journal of Middle East Studies* 38 (May 2006): 213–33; Thomas Hegghammer and Stephane Lacroix, "Rejectionist Islam in Saudi Arabia: The Story of Juhayman al-Utaybi Revisited," *International Journal of Middle East Studies* 39 (February 2007): 103–22.

26 Javed Ali, "The Iran-Iraq War: A Case Study in Non-Compliance," *Non-Proliferation Review* 8 (Spring 2001): 47–48.

27 Charles Duelfer, "Comprehensive Report of the Special Advisor to the DCI on Iraq's WMD with Addendums" (Washington, DC: Central Intelligence Agency, 2004), 1:24, 26; 3:9.

28 Kevin M. Woods, David D. Palkki, and Mark E. Stout, *The Saddam Tapes: The Inner Workings of a Tyrant's Regime, 1978–2001* (New York: Cambridge University Press, 2011), 19.

29 Robert M. Gates, *Duty: Memoirs of a Secretary at War* (New York: Knopf, 2014), 178–79. This support included the Iran-Contra scandal when Reagan administration officials in 1985–86 sold antitank and antiaircraft missiles to Iran in violation of an official U.S. arms embargo on Iran.

30 See Charles Kurzman, "Death Tolls of the Iran-Iraq War," October 31, 2013, https://kurzman.unc.edu/death-tolls-of-the-iran-iraq-war/.

31 See, for example, the report for a Ba'ath regional conference: *al-Taqrīr al-markazī lil- mu'tamar al-quṭrī al-tāsi'* (Baghdad: Ḥizb al-Ba'th al-'Arabī al-Ishtirākī, 1983). Western analysts sometimes echoed this theme: Christine Moss Helms, *Iraq: Eastern Flank of the Arab World* (Washington, DC: Brookings Institution, 1984). My thanks to Sam Helfont for these sources.

32 Rachel Bronson, *Thicker Than Oil: America's Uneasy Partnership with Saudi Arabia* (New York: Oxford University Press, 2006), 164.

33 Ibid., 192.

34 Gause, "International Politics of the Gulf," 277; F. Gregory Gause, III, "Iraq's Decisions to Go to War, 1980 and 1990," *Middle East Journal* 56 (Winter 2002): 53.

35 Gause, "International Politics of the Gulf," 278.

36 Ibid., 53, 56, 61.

37 Ibid., 278; Joseph Wilson, *The Politics of Truth* (New York: Carroll and Graf, 2004), 95.

38 Daniel Yergin, *The Prize: The Epic Quest for Oil, Money, and Power* (1991; repr., New York: Free Press, 2008), 751, 754–55.

39 Bronson, *Thicker Than Oil*, 196.

40 Sanford Lakoff, "Desert Snowstorm: Revisionism and the Gulf War," *Journal of Policy History* 6 (April 1994): 218, 221–22.

41 Laura Zittrain Eisenberg, "Passive Belligerency: Israel and the 1991 Gulf War," *Journal of Strategic Studies* 35 (September 1992): 304–29.

42 Michael Gordon and Bernard E. Trainor, *The Generals' War: The Inside Story of the Conflict in the Gulf* (Boston: Little, Brown, 1995), 132–33.

43 William L. Dowdy and Barry R. Schneider, "On to Baghdad? Or Stop at Kuwait? A Gulf War Question Revisited," *Defense Analysis* 13 (December 1997): 319–27.

44 John Ehrenberg, J. Patrice McSherry, Jose Ramon Sanchez, and Caroleen Marji Savej, eds., *The Iraq Papers* (New York: Oxford University Press, 2010), 27.

45 "Statement by Bush on Iraq's Proposal for Ending Conflict," February 15, 1991, *New York Times*, February 16, 1991, http://www.nytimes.com/1991/02/16/world/war-gulf-bush-statement-excerpts-2-statements-bush-iraq-s-proposal-for-ending.html; "The President's News Conference on the Persian Gulf Conflict," March 1, 1991, American Presidency Project, http://www.presidency.ucsb.edu/ws/?pid=19352.

46 David McDowall, *A Modern History of the Kurds*, 3rd ed. (New York: I.B. Tauris, 2005), 357–63.

47 Tripp, *History of Iraq*, 246–48; As President George H. W. Bush put it, "We seek Iraq's compliance, not its partition." "Warning to Baghdad; Excerpts from Bush's Talk," *New York Times*, August 27, 1992.

48 Dina Rizk Khoury, *Iraq in Wartime: Soldiering, Martyrdom, and Remembrance* (Cambridge: Cambridge University Press, 2013), 216–17.

49 Woods, Palkki, and Stout, *Saddam Tapes*, 211–15.

50 Kevin M. Woods et al., *Iraqi Perspectives Project: A View of Operation Iraqi Freedom from Saddam's Senior Leadership* (Washington, DC: Joint Center for Operations Analysis, 2006), 52.

51 F. Gregory Gause, III, "The Illogic of Dual Containment," *Foreign Affairs* 73 (March 1994): 56–66.

52 On the difficulties involved, see Barry R. Posen, "U.S. Security Policy in a Nuclear-Armed World, or: What If Iraq Had Nuclear Weapons?," *Security Studies* 6 (Spring 1997): 1–31.

53 Daniel Byman, "After the Storm: U.S. Policy toward Iraq since 1991," *Political Science Quarterly* 115 (Winter 2000–2001): 496.

54 Robert Baer, *See No Evil: The True Story of a Ground Soldier in the CIA's War on Terrorism* (New York: Crown, 2002).

55 Said K. Aburish, *Saddam Hussein: The Politics of Revenge* (London: Bloomsbury, 2000), 178; Joseph Sassoon, *Saddam Hussein's Ba'th Party: Inside an Authoritarian Regime* (Cambridge: Cambridge University Press, 2012), 193–94.

56 Sassoon, *Saddam Hussein's Ba'th Party*, 103–7. This fact goes a long way toward explaining the dysfunction of the Iraqi military. See also Woods et al., *Iraqi Perspectives Project: A View of Operation Iraqi Freedom*.

57 Sassoon, *Saddam Hussein's Ba'th Party*, 138, 143–44, 193–201; Tripp, *History of Iraq*, 250.

58 Sassoon, *Saddam Hussein's Ba'th Party*, 130. On "coup proofing," see James T. Quinlivan, "Coup-proofing: Its Practice and Consequences in the Middle East," *International Security* 24 (Fall 1999): 131–65.

59 David Rieff, "Were Sanctions Right?," *New York Times*, July 27, 2003.

60 For example, when asked in 1996 by an American television correspondent whether the sanctions were worth the deaths of half a million Iraqi children, then-ambassador to the UN Madeleine Albright replied, "I think this is a very hard choice, but the price—we think the price is worth it." Madeleine Albright, *Madam Secretary* (New York: Harper Perennial, 2013), 276–77.

61 F. Gregory Gause, III, "Getting It Backward on Iraq," *Foreign Affairs* 78 (May–June 1999): 56.

62 Sarah Graham Brown, *Sanctioning Saddam: The Politics of Intervention in Iraq* (New York: I.B. Tauris), 56–104.

63 Tripp, *History of Iraq*, 253.

64 Byman, "After the Storm," 493, 516.

65 Baskın Oran, *Kalkık Horoz: Çekiç Güç ve Kürt Devleti* (Ankara: Bilgi Yayınevi, 1996); Necip Torumtay, *Değişen Stratejilerin Odağında Türkiye* (Ad Yayıncılık, 1996), 245–46; Arda Sualp, "Çekiç Güç Kürt Devleti Kuruyor," *Aksiyon*, October 10, 1995, http://www.aksiyon.com.tr/aksiyon/haber-1103-26-cekic-guc-kurt-devleti-kuruyor.html.

66 Baskın Oran, ed., *Türk Dış Politikası: Kurtuluş Savaşından Bugüne Olgular, Belgeler, Yorumlar, vol. 2: 1980–2001* (Istanbul: İletişim, 2001), 255; Cüneyt Arcayürek, *Kriz Doğuran Savaş* (Ankara: Bilgi Yayınevi, 2000), 131–34; William Hale, *Turkish Foreign Policy since 1774* (New York: Routledge, 2013), 160.

67 Fikret Bila, *Sivil darbe girişimi ve Ankara'da Irak savaşları* (Ankara: Ümit, 2003).

68 Hegghammer, *Jihad in Saudi Arabia*, 30–31; Mamoun Fandy, *Saudi Arabia and the Politics of Dissent* (New York: St. Martin's, 1999), 71–72, 145–46, 189–90.

69 Bronson, *Thicker Than Oil*, 218–19.

70 Jerry Long, *Saddam's War of Words: Politics, Religion, and the Iraqi Invasion of Kuwait* (Austin: University of Texas Press, 2004), 31, 161–66.

71 Ibid., 182.

72 Samuel Helfont, "Saddam and the Islamists," *Middle East Journal* 68 (Summer 2014): 359–61.

73 Bronson, *Thicker Than Oil*, 214–16.

74 Usama bin Laden, "Declaration of War against the Americans Occupying the Land of the Two Holy Places," in *Princeton Readings in Islamist Thought*, ed. Roxanne L. Euben and Muhammad Qasim Zaman (Princeton: Princeton University Press, 2009), 437.

75 Bronson, *Thicker Than Oil*, 220–21.

76 Helfont, "Saddam and the Islamists," 361–64.

77 Sassoon, *Saddam Hussein's Ba'th Party*, 265–67.

78 Assaf Moghadam, "Palestinian Suicide Terrorism in the Second Intifada: Motivations and Organizational Aspects," *Studies in Conflict and Terrorism* 26 (March 2003):

72; Kevin M. Woods and James Lacey, *Iraqi Perspectives Project: Saddam and Terrorism* vol. 1 (Alexandria, VA: Institute for Defense Analyses, 2007), 13–16, 20, 24–245. On Saddam's earlier invocations of Nebuchadnezzar and Saladin, see Long, *Saddam's War of Words*, 30, 76, 79, 108–9, 115.

79 Tripp, *History of Iraq*, 254, 259; Michael Dunne, "The United States, the United Nations and Iraq: 'Multilateralism of a Kind,'" *International Affairs* 79 (March 2003): 266–67.

80 James Mann, *Rise of the Vulcans: The History of Bush's War Cabinet* (New York: Penguin, 2004).

81 Keith L. Shimko, *The Iraq Wars and America's Military Revolution* (Cambridge: Cambridge University Press, 2010), 133–34.

82 Richard A. Clarke, *Against All Enemies: Inside America's War on Terror* (New York: Free Press, 2004), 30–31; George Tenet, *At the Center of the Storm: My Years at the CIA* (New York: HarperCollins, 2007), 306; Bob Woodward, *Plan of Attack: The Definitive Account of the Decision to Invade Iraq* (New York: Simon & Schuster, 2004), 24–25.

83 From 1994 to 1996 Saddam's representatives discussed with bin Laden the possibility of joint operations against Saudi Arabia and the foreign troops based there. Helfont, "Saddam and the Islamists," 362.

84 This maxim is sometimes known as "Rahm's Rule," in honor of Clinton's chief of staff, Rahm Emanuel, who uttered a similar formulation.

85 Aiden Warren, *Prevention, Pre-emption, and the Nuclear Option: From Bush to Obama* (New York: Routledge, 2011), 40.

86 Robert Jervis, *Why Intelligence Fails: Lessons from the Iranian Revolution and the Iraq War* (Ithaca, NY: Cornell University Press, 2010), 133–34, 138–39, 155; Harvey, *Explaining the Iraq War*, 241.

87 Harvey, *Explaining the Iraq War*, 241–42.

88 Ibid., 244–49; R. Gordon and Bernard E. Trainor, *Cobra II: The Inside Story of the Invasion and Occupation of Iraq* (New York: Pantheon, 2006), 118–19; Tenet, *At the Center of the Storm*, 311.

89 Charles Deulfer, *Hide and Seek: The Search for Truth in Iraq* (New York: Public Affairs, 2009), 406; Tenet, *At the Center of the Storm*, 332.

90 Emphasis in the original. Tenet, *At the Center of the Storm*, 333.

2

9/11

Bush's Response

TERRY H. ANDERSON

On September 11, 2001, nineteen terrorists commandeered three passenger airplanes, flew them into the World Trade Center and Pentagon, killing over twenty-seven hundred, and changed the future of the United States. Shortly after those attacks, President George W. Bush turned to political adviser Karl Rove and said, "I am here for a reason, and this is how we're going to be judged."[1]

This essay examines George W. Bush and his administration's responses to that tragedy. The president declared his war on terror, ordered the attack on Afghanistan, and invaded Iraq—all within nineteen months after 9/11.

War on Terror

Nine days after the attack, on September 20, the president gave one of the most significant speeches of his first term. "Who attacked our country?" he asked rhetorically. A "loosely affiliated terrorist organizations known as al Qaeda," he responded. The president then introduced Americans to their leader, "a person named Osama bin Laden," promising that America will "pursue nations that provide aid or safe haven to terrorism."

In that same speech the president used the phrase "war on terror": "Our war on terror begins with al Qaeda, but it does not end there. It will not end until every terrorist group of global reach has been found, stopped and defeated."[2] This was not the first time a president had employed that term; but the Bush administration made it a part of the American lexicon. Linguistically the term made no sense. Terror is a tactic, like Germany's World War II blitzkrieg or Japan's preemptive strike on Pearl Harbor. In December 1941 the United States went to war not against the blitzkrieg or sneak attack but against nations: Germany and Japan. Bin Laden accepted responsibility for the attack. America's "greatest buildings have been destroyed, thank God for that," he said on a videotape. "There is America, full of fear. . . . Thank god for that."[3] In response, Bush demanded that the Taliban regime in Afghanistan hand over the terrorist. By refusing and thereby providing bin Laden with safe haven, the regime became a legitimate target.

Thus, the president could have asked Congress for a declaration of war against Afghanistan because it was harboring bin Laden and his network of terrorists. Almost certainly, Congress would have supported a declaration of war. But given the growth of executive power since World War II, and that no president has requested a declaration of war since 1941, Bush and his advisers never considered asking Congress. Instead, the president declared a "war on terror," a vague term against a vague enemy. The administration argued that it had the right to deploy any type of U.S. force to pursue "every terrorist group" until they were "found, stopped and defeated."[4] That was an enormous chore. During the previous generation the State Department had listed over forty groups involved in terrorism throughout the world, almost all of which never had attacked the United States or its interests. That raised a question: who would define the terrorist enemy? The Bush administration claimed that it would, void of oversight from Congress and any national or international agencies. That remained the situation until January 2007, when the Republicans lost control of Congress.

The administration's use of "war on terror" also had domestic implications. Former national security adviser Zbigniew Brzezinski wrote that the term contributed to a "siege mentality," and "a culture of fear in America," one that continued for years.[5]

That fear was exacerbated just one week after the 9/11 tragedy. Someone mailed letters to news organizations, including NBC and the New York Post, which contained traces of the bacterial disease anthrax. The letters killed one man, sickened others, and sent a wave of anxiety throughout the nation. Three weeks later the postal service delivered anthrax to two Democratic senators, including Senate Majority Leader Tom Daschle of South Dakota. Both mailings contained messages. The letter to Daschle read, "YOU CANNOT STOP US. WE HAVE THIS ANTHRAX. YOU DIE NOW. ARE YOU AFRAID? DEATH TO AMERICA. DEATH TO ISRAEL. ALLAH IS GREAT."[6] The anthrax attacks killed five and made seventeen others ill in the weeks after September 11.

The fear also appeared in October, when the Bush administration supported and Congress passed the USA Patriot Act. Both legislative chambers passed the law with little debate only forty-five days after 9/11. The act enhanced powers of immigration agents to detain and deport immigrants suspected of terrorism, and it expanded the definition of terrorism to include domestic events. It also increased the authority of law enforcement agencies to search telephone and email communications, and financial, medical, and other personal records. But it did not allow the administration to wiretap people without a court order or to arrest citizens and detain them without charging them with a crime, rights protected by habeas corpus and the Fourth Amendment. That being the case, Bush signed a secret executive order authorizing the government to eavesdrop on Americans' international calls and emails without a court warrant, an act of dubious legality since 1978 when, after the Watergate scandal, Congress had passed the Foreign Intelligence Surveillance Act.[7]

While the immediate fear subsided, its results were woven into daily life. The public was reminded of 9/11 every time they went to the airport. While few objected to the new Transportation Security Administration and its screening of passengers, other citizens tired of the warning signs in airports of the "level of danger" from a terrorist attack. While there were five levels, green to red, the Department of Homeland Security usually kept the warning on orange, "High Risk of Terrorist Attacks," a practice ended by the Barack Obama administration in 2011.

Bush also responded to 9/11 by adopting secret policies. Vice President Dick Cheney made this clear just four days after the tragedy when he appeared on *Meet the Press*. To defeat the terrorists, he said, America will "have to work . . . the dark side, if you will. We've got to spend time in the shadows in the intelligence world. A lot of what needs to be done here will have to be done quietly, without any discussion. . . . If you're going to deal only with sort of officially approved, certified good guys, you're not going to find out what the bad guys are doing. You need to be able to penetrate these organizations."[8]

Cheney's words signaled the beginning of extralegal behavior that reached far beyond problematic eavesdropping. Detention and torture during interrogations—behavior that previous U.S. administrations had condemned and that the triumphant allies made illegal by the Geneva Accords after World War II—became standard practice. In the weeks after 9/11, the government arrested at least 1,200 persons because of "possible links to terrorism." The FBI apprehended 762 Muslim aliens, mostly on immigration violations; 184 were "high interest" suspects and held under maximum security within the United States. Many were not charged or told why they were being held. Moreover, there was little effort made to distinguish between legitimate terrorism suspects and people arrested primarily because of their Middle Eastern names or appearance.[9]

Afghanistan

At the same time, Bush was preparing for combat in Afghanistan. Just three days after 9/11, the Senate voted 98 to 0 and the House 420 to 1 to give the president "all necessary and appropriate force" to respond to the terrorist attacks. The administration rapidly took a number of public measures. Bush first demanded that Afghanistan's Taliban government close all terrorist camps and hand over al Qaeda leaders—or face an attack. He then pressured Pakistan's President Pervez Musharraf to cooperate with the United States in the war against al Qaeda, and issued an executive order freezing the assets of groups and individuals suspected of aiding terrorists.

Because the Taliban regime refused to comply with Bush's demands, and with virtually all the world supporting military action against al Qaeda, the president prepared for a military campaign in Afghanistan. Bush met with his security team on September 17 and signed a secret order that outlined the plan for war. The order also gave the CIA authorization to conduct a range of covert actions "to disrupt terrorist activity," including renditions, disinformation campaigns, cyber-attacks, and "permission to kill, capture and detain members of al Qaeda anywhere in the world." After the meeting CIA director George Tenet declared, "All the rules have changed"; his counterterrorism chief, Cofer Black, declared, "The gloves came off."[10]

The administration labeled the war in Afghanistan Operation Enduring Freedom. The Taliban told their people that they would humiliate the Americans like the indigenous Muslim resistance, the mujahedeen, had humiliated the Soviets in the 1980s. They did not. Allies and friends lined up to help the United States. Britain, Canada, Germany, Australia, and other U.S. allies contributed infantry forces, deployed aircraft, or offered logistical support. France and Italy provided aircraft carrier battle groups, engineering teams, and transport aircraft. Japan sent fleet refueling ships and other aircraft. Eventually, more than twenty-five nations contributed personnel, equipment, or services to the fight against al Qaeda and the Taliban.

Operation Enduring Freedom began just eight days after 9/11, on September 27, when the CIA inserted the first covert team, code named Jawbreaker, inside Afghanistan. On October 7 Bush announced that U.S. forces had begun air strikes "on terrorist camps of al Qaeda, and the military installations of the Taliban regime in Afghanistan." The first attacks targeted the Taliban's air defense installations, defense ministry, electrical grids, and command centers, and hit the important cities of Kabul, Kandahar, and Mazar-i-Sharif. At the same time the CIA moved Special Operations troops and U.S. Special Forces teams into Afghanistan. CIA operatives were communicating and negotiating with the various warlords and their troops who made up the indigenous resistance to the Taliban, the Northern Alliance, who resided in the northern part of that nation.

The U.S. plan was to deploy massive aid and air power to support the Northern Alliance. The alliance would conduct the ground operations against the Taliban militia and their al Qaeda allies, which included foreign Arabs, Chechens, Pakistanis, and Uighurs. CIA teams met with tribal leaders and promised these impoverished people immediate aid for those who joined with the Northern Alliance. As fall began turning into winter, the teams called in the U.S. Air Force. Guided to exact locations by Global Positioning System satellites, the planes conducted over a hundred airdrops of almost 1.7 million pounds of tents, clothes, food, medicine, horse feed and saddles, guns and munitions, even Korans. "Each drop was tailored to the specific requests of teams on the ground," wrote Henry "Hank" Crumpton, the CIA officer who directed the campaign from his headquarters in Langley, Virginia. "Imagine the power conferred upon the Afghan tribal leader who sided with the United States, whose clan's needs fell from the sky within seventy-two hours of his request. Their desperation was addressed, and their leader won honor and prestige among his people."[11]

The plan worked because the CIA was prepared. In a few weeks seven teams were in Afghanistan, and all members understood the language and culture of their hosts. One was Gary Berntsen, a twenty-year veteran of the CIA's Clandestine Service, and another was Gary Schroen, age fifty-nine, fluent in Farsi and Dari. The average age of team members was forty-five, with more than twenty years on the job. The CIA gave these professionals maximum flexibility to conduct operations, collect intelligence, and pinpoint bombing targets.

American aid and airdrops fed and armed the Afghans, saving American lives, but the strategy also meant that U.S. forces would have to rely on tribal warlords. Mohammed Fahim Khan operated in the northeast corner of Afghanistan and led a confederation of Tajiks. Rashid Dostum, an ethnic Uzbek, was based in the mountains south of Mazar-i-Sharif. Ismail Khan, a Tajik, operated in the Herat region, close to the Iranian border, as did Mohammed Mohaqqeq of the Hazara ethnic group. And Atta Mohammed, a Tajik, was sometimes a confederate and at other times a rival of Dostum. Eventually, the Northern Alliance was composed of Tajiks, Uzbeks, and Hazaras, all with various loyalties; some had even fought with the mostly Pashtun Taliban in the 1990s only to switch sides later. It seemed that the northern warlords were united only in their hatred of the Taliban.

The warlords also were unreliable and usually more motivated by money and self-interest than by a desire to fight the Taliban. When Jawbreaker, the first CIA team, arrived in the Panjshir Valley of northeastern Afghanistan, it carried three million dollars in hundred-dollar bills, which the team was authorized to use to prompt the warlords to begin the offensive against the Taliban. Within a month Jawbreaker had received from CIA headquarters another ten million. In order to get the warlord Mohammed Fahim Khan to attack and capture important northern towns, the CIA paid him five million.[12]

What at the time appeared like victory in Afghanistan took only seventy-eight days because the Taliban was not equipped to fight a modern war. Riding to battle in pickup trucks, their troops were easily spotted by U.S. planes and Predator drones, which launched precision air strikes. After just two weeks Taliban lines had been decimated and the Northern Alliance was sweeping through Afghanistan. On November 9 they captured the northern city of Mazar-i-Sharif. That triggered the collapse of Taliban forces; many began to change sides while others made strategic withdrawals, either back to their villages or to the tribal regions of northwestern Pakistan, often Waziristan, which was also inhabited by ethnic Pashtuns. Four days later the Northern Alliance seized control of Kabul. What remained of the Taliban militia surrendered on December 6 in the southern city of Kandahar, the spiritual capital of the Taliban movement. Two weeks later the allies celebrated the inauguration of the Afghan interim government led by a Pashtun from Kandahar, Hamid Karzai.

Operation Enduring Freedom seemed like a quick victory with few allied casualties. Yet the original aim of the invasion—to kill Osama bin Laden and destroy al Qaeda—was unsuccessful. The world's most notorious terrorist fled to Tora Bora, a cave and tunnel complex in the rugged Afghanistan mountains only twenty miles from Pakistan. The theater commander, General Tommy Franks, ordered about forty Special Operations troops and a dozen Special Forces soldiers to the area to call in air strikes. Instead of ordering U.S. troops to secure the border with Pakistan and attack Tora Bora, however, he decided to allow Afghan forces to take the lead. That turned out to be a mistake.

Bush declared, "We'll smoke him out of his cave," and in December he again pledged that bin Laden would be taken "dead or alive": "I don't know whether we're going to get him tomorrow or a month from now or a year from now. . . . But we're going to get him." Two weeks later, while vacationing at his Texas ranch, the president declared, "He is not escaping us."[13]

But bin Laden already had escaped. During the night of December 15, the terrorist got on his shortwave radio, praised his "most loyal fighters," asked them to "forgive me" should they die, and announced that the battle against the "crusaders" would continue "on new fronts." After leading them in a prayer, he slipped away. Bin Laden and his lieutenants arrived safely in the rugged Pashtun tribal lands of Pakistan. "Had bin Laden been surrounded at Tora Bora," wrote one expert at the time, "he would have been confined to an area of several dozen square miles; now he could well be in an area that snakes across some 40,000 square miles," a region, for comparison, about the size of Kentucky. Also escaping from Afghanistan was the Taliban leader Mullah Omar, his militia, and al Qaeda's number-two man, Ayman al-Zawahiri.[14]

Bush never got his man "dead or alive." The next president, Barack Obama, pulled the trigger on Osama bin Laden. On May 1, 2011, SEAL Team Six invaded bin Laden's compound in the Pakistani city of Abbottabad and killed al Qaeda's leader. After carefully documenting his identity, they took bin Laden's body and buried it at sea to ensure that there never would be pilgrimages to a shrine in his honor. Ayman al-Zawahri became al Qaeda's new leader, and as of 2014 he is believed to be hiding in Pakistan. The U.S. government has offered a twenty-five-million-dollar reward for information leading to al-Zawahiri's apprehension, and ten million for Mullah Omar, also believed to be in Pakistan.

Operation Enduring Freedom had another consequence related to the war on terror. In Afghanistan U.S. troops captured some six hundred suspected al Qaeda and Taliban soldiers, and CIA agents in other parts of the world rounded up suspected terrorists and placed them in "black sites," secret jails overseas. On November 13, 2001, the president signed an executive order proclaiming an "extraordinary emergency," thereby allowing the military to detain and try anyone whom the administration deemed an "enemy combatant," not in American courts but by military tribunals. The accused would have no access to the usual standards applied by federal courts and no review procedures. Detainees could receive the death penalty and would have no right to remain silent; hearsay evidence and statements made during torture would be admissible. Bush claimed that the military tribunals would treat the detainees fairly, but that claim missed the point. Congress had not declared war, so the Bush administration did not have the powers of a wartime president to void the balance of powers and the Bill of Rights.

By January 2002 the first detainees were arriving at Camp X-Ray, at Guantanamo Bay, Cuba. During that month, Justice Department and White House memos informed the president that international law, particularly the Geneva Conventions, did not apply to the Taliban or al Qaeda. That claim would be contested for years, but it was what the president wanted to hear. The administration stripped enemy combatants of all the usual American legal rights, even habeas corpus—a court order to determine if a prisoner has been lawfully detained and a right guaranteed by the U.S. Constitution. Later that year

Secretary Rumsfeld approved "special interrogation techniques"—a euphemism for torture—for the detainees.

In just months after the September 11 emergency, the administration had set aside national laws that prohibited warrantless surveillance of American citizens. It also bypassed international laws that protected foreigners from torture, secret detention, and extraordinary rendition (capturing suspects and taking them to other countries for secret interrogation and torture).

There were problems with the administration's policies toward the 770 "terrorist suspects" from over forty countries eventually imprisoned at Guantanamo that went beyond constitutional issues. Some of those captured after battle obviously were enemy warriors. Camp X-Ray did house confirmed terrorists, including the admitted mastermind of the September 11 attacks, Khalid Sheikh Mohammed. But some were citizens of allies—Britain and Australia—and one, Jose Padilla, was a U.S. citizen. Moreover, later investigations revealed that most of the jailed were not terrorists. As the United States bombed Afghanistan, the Taliban leadership had quickly evacuated, leaving the battlefield filled with uneducated volunteers and conscripts, many of whom knew nothing about global terrorism and had been impressed into military service; some were teens, one fourteen and another thirteen, and two were children, ten and twelve. U.S. planes had dropped leaflets advertising bounties for the enemy, littering the country with promises of five thousand dollars, ten thousand, even "wealth and power beyond your dreams." Afghan warlords usually were paid cash based on the number of men they could hand over to the Americans. This financial incentive in an impoverished nation resulted in many locals making false reports to settle old grudges or lying about people to whom they or their family owed money.[15]

An investigation found that dozens and perhaps hundreds of detainees were wrongfully imprisoned on the "basis of flimsy or fabricated evidence, old personal scores or bounty payments." Another investigation determined that a majority of the prisoners were not caught on the battlefield, but came into U.S. custody from third parties, mostly from Pakistan, after that government targeted Arabs living in their nation after 9/11. In fact, no one really knew how many of the men imprisoned at Camp X-Ray actually were terrorists or affiliated with either al Qaeda or the Taliban. In 2002, the U.S. secretary of the army noted that at least a third of the prisoners did not belong at Guantanamo; later the base commander stated that half the prisoners were there by mistake. By the end of the second Bush administration in January 2009, only 6 of the remaining 240 detainees had been charged with involvement with the 9/11 attacks.[16]

Such issues did not trouble the Bush administration. Vice President Cheney labeled the Guantanamo prisoners "the worst of a very bad lot," while Defense Secretary Rumsfeld called them "the most dangerous, best-trained, vicious killers on the face of the earth," and basically threw away the key as they sat in legal limbo for years. Although the Guantanamo Bay detention camp was U.S. property, the administration claimed that it was outside the protection granted by the U.S. Constitution: "a legal black hole," as one attorney called Camp X-Ray.[17] It would take two and a half years before the Supreme Court would begin ruling against the administration, beginning in 2004 with *Rasul v. Bush* and *Hamdi v. Rumsfeld*. Over the years many detainees deemed not a threat to the United States were slowly sent home or to another nation that would accept them. By August 2014 there remained about 149.

Iraq

Meanwhile, the administration conducted its third and final response to 9/11—the invasion of Iraq.

Why Iraq? There are two basic interpretations of the origins of Bush's War in Iraq. In numerous comments, books, and memoirs, the former president and his team have been consistent with their reasons for the war. According to Bush's memoir, *Decision Points*, Saddam was a ruthless dictator who had attacked and killed his neighbors and own people, continually violated international demands, sponsored terror, and aimed to develop weapons of mass destruction (WMDs). He was not only an enemy of the United States—he was a threat to it. "The lesson of 9/11," wrote the president, "was that if we waited for a danger to fully materialize, we would have waited too long. I reached a decision: We would confront the threat from Iraq."[18]

To the president and his team, a preemptive strike on Iraq was actually an act of defense. As Douglas Feith, former undersecretary of defense, explained, "President Bush ultimately decided that the risks of getting drawn into a renewed war on Saddam's terms were unacceptable. Weighing America's vulnerabilities against Saddam's record of aggression, he decided that it would be too dangerous to allow Saddam to choose the time and place of his next war with us."[19]

Most historians and other commentators disagree with the administration's interpretation. In general, they think that Bush misled the nation into an unnecessary war in Iraq. They argue that the tragedy of September 11 opened the door for the president to claim that Saddam was involved in the attack and was manufacturing WMDs for himself and terrorists to use against the United States and the West.[20]

The Bush administration had long been interested in Saddam Hussein and Iraq. More than eight months before the attacks of 9/11, during the first meeting of the National Security Council on January 30, 2001, National Security Advisor Condoleezza Rice brought up how Saddam was "destabilizing" the Middle East. CIA Director Tenet then rolled out a grainy photograph of a factory that "produces either chemical or biological materials for weapons manufacture." But one NSC member, Treasury Secretary Paul O'Neill, commented, "I've seen a lot of factories around the world that look a lot like this one. What makes us suspect that this one is producing chemical or biological agents for weapons?" It was a good question; Tenet admitted that his agency did not know what was being produced at the factory.

"From the very beginning," said O'Neill, "there was a conviction, that Saddam Hussein was a bad person and that he needed to go." Going after Saddam was "topic A. . . . It was all about finding a way to do it," O'Neill continued, noting that he was surprised that no one in that meeting had asked "Why Saddam?" and "Why Now?"[1]

A State Department memo that mentioned "possible regime change" in Iraq was introduced at the NSC's meeting two days later. But in public, over the next eight months, the administration stated that Saddam was "contained" and posed no threat to his neighbors or to the United States. During that same time, CIA Director Tenet and "Terrorism Czar" Richard Clarke warned the administration of another threat—from Osama bin Laden's al Qaeda. Between the inaugural in January and September 11, Tenet later wrote, "Bush received 44 morning intelligence reports from the CIA mentioning the al Qaeda threat, and not once did he say . . . 'let's begin a process to stop the attack.'"[22]

Yet to be fair, there was significant information missing. "Throughout the summer of 2001," said National Security Agency Director Michael Hayden, "we had more than thirty warnings that something was imminent." They usually were intercepted messages, "Something spectacular is coming," but the warnings contained no specific details—no what, where, or when. Consequently, no one knows if 9/11 could have been prevented.[23]

Then, the terrorist attack on September 11, 2001, changed everything. Over the weekend of September 15–16 the president held a war council at Camp David. During the first session Defense Secretary Rumsfeld asked what the administration should do about Iraq. His deputy, Paul Wolfowitz, made the case for striking that nation during "this round" of the war on terrorism. The resulting briefing paper specified "three priority targets for initial action: al Qaeda, the Taliban, and Iraq." The president, however, returned the focus to al Qaeda, and the rest of the sessions concerned how to fight a war in Afghanistan.

While the United States was conducting Operation Enduring Freedom in Afghanistan, during the long Thanksgiving weekend, Bush asked his secretary of defense if the Pentagon had a war plan for Iraq. Rumsfeld said he was reviewing it with General Tommy Franks. "Let's get started on this," ordered Bush, "and get Tommy Franks looking at what it would take to protect America by removing Saddam Hussein."[24]

Publicly, Bush revealed his thoughts on Iraq just four months after 9/11 in his 2002 State of the Union address: "North Korea is a regime arming with missiles and weapons of mass destruction. . . . Iran aggressively pursues these weapons and exports terror. . . . Iraq continues to flaunt its hostility toward America and to support terror. The Iraqi regime has plotted to develop anthrax, and nerve gas, and nuclear weapons for over a decade. . . . States like these, and their terrorist allies, constitute an axis of evil, aiming to threaten the peace of the world." Those regimes sought WMDs, Bush continued, which they could provide to terrorists and then "attack our allies or attempt to blackmail the United States." We have to act, he declared, for "the price of indifference would be catastrophic."

Bush's "Axis of Evil" speech should have sounded alarm bells. He mentioned the Taliban enemy fleeing Afghanistan and then turned to three nations that had nothing to do with the attack on September 11: North Korea, Iran, and Iraq. "If there was a serious internal debate within the administration over what to do about Iraq," wrote conservative columnist Charles Krauthammer, "that debate is over." Democratic Representative Ike Skelton of Missouri agreed; both felt that the speech was basically a "declaration of war."[25]

Later, at West Point on June 1, 2002, Bush proclaimed what became known as the Bush Doctrine. America's previous reliance on containment, he stated, was obsolete against "unbalanced dictators with weapons of mass destruction" and their "terrorist allies." "If we wait for threats to fully materialize, we will have waited too long," he warned. The "war on terror will not be won on the defensive. We must take the battle to the enemy, disrupt his plans, and confront the worst threats before they emerge." That meant that Americans had "to be ready for preemptive action when necessary to defend our liberty and to defend our lives."

The press interpreted the address as the administration intended. A *New York Times* reporter called it a "toughly worded speech that seemed aimed at preparing Americans for a potential war with Iraq."[26]

In order to prepare, the administration needed allies. When his father attacked Saddam's army and liberated Kuwait in 1991, George H. W. Bush had forged a coalition of twenty-eight nations, including seven Arab ones.

These allies had a force of almost five hundred thousand in the Persian Gulf area, along with the approval of the UN Security Council. Thus, the younger Bush began attempts to form a "coalition of the willing" to invade Iraq in July 2002—the same time that the administration privately decided to go to war.

Although the president and his subordinates later maintained that they had not reached the decision to go to war before Secretary of State Powell presented the American case for war to the United Nations in February 2003, ample evidence suggests that they had decided the previous summer. Richard Haass, director of policy planning at the State Department, reported that he expressed concern about foreign policy toward Iraq to Condi Rice the previous summer. "You can save your breath, Richard," she said. "The President has already made up his mind on Iraq."[27] Unless Iraq conceded to the administration's demands, war was a forgone conclusion. Books by journalist Bob Woodward and by at least three former insiders—terrorism adviser Richard Clarke, NSC participant Paul O'Neill, and White House Press Secretary Scott McClellan suggest that timing.

But the most significant evidence came from a later British leak to the press on May 1, 2005—the Downing Street Memorandum. "Secret and Strictly Personal—UK Eyes Only" was the heading on the minutes of Tony Blair's meeting with his top advisers on July 23, 2002. It detailed a recent meeting between Sir Richard Dearlove, chief of Britain's secret intelligence service, and Bush and his senior advisers. Dearlove's impression of the meeting was that the president had decided to attack Saddam's regime. The minutes record, "There was a perceptible shift in attitude. Military action was now seen as inevitable. Bush wanted to remove Saddam, through military action, justified by the conjunction of terrorism and WMD. But the intelligence and facts were being fixed around the policy. . . . There was little discussion in Washington of the aftermath after military action." The administration wanted Britain to deploy "up to 40,000" troops in the invasion, "perhaps with a discrete role in Northern Iraq entering from Turkey, tying down two Iraqi divisions."

The Downing Street Memo quoted other British officials who attended the July 23 meeting. "Bush had made up his mind to take military action, even if the timing was not yet decided," said Foreign Secretary Jack Straw, calling the case "thin" because "Saddam was not threatening his neighbors and his WMD capability was less than that of Libya, North Korea or Iran." Straw argued that the Anglo-Americans should present Saddam with an ultimatum "to allow back in the UN weapons inspectors" which would "help with legal justification for the use of force." The British attorney general agreed, stating that "regime change was not a legal basis for military action" and that an attack could be legal only if it was done in self-defense, for humanitarian reasons, or with authorization from the United Nations. That troubled Prime Minister Blair, who hoped that Saddam would "refuse to allow in the UN inspectors. . . . If the political context were right," he continued, "people would support regime change."[28]

Having made up its collective mind to go to war in July, the Bush administration now had to sell the war to the American public. But there was a problem: the vast majority of citizens were not interested in waging war in the Middle East against a nation that posed little threat to America and had easily been beaten in the 1991 Gulf War. In early September 2002 a CBS News opinion poll found that there was "no consensus on adopting a pre-emptive strike in general—except where a nuclear attack against the United States is contemplated."[29]

Thus, the administration established the White House Iraq Group, WHIG. Composed of Rice, presidential adviser Karl Rove, vice presidential adviser I. Lewis "Scooter" Libby, and White House Chief of Staff Andrew Card, Jr., it devised "talking points," according to Press Secretary Scott McClellan, "to coordinate the marketing of the war to the public." When a reporter asked Card in September why the administration waited until after Labor Day to begin selling the people on military action against Iraq, Card replied, "From a marketing point of view, you don't introduce new products in August." WHIG invented most of the talking points, including one the speakers constantly reiterated: Saddam's smoking gun could be a mushroom cloud—a nuclear attack.

The administration's concentrated barrage began in September 2002. The president began by inviting eighteen senior members of the House and Senate to the White House on September 4. Aides handed them a letter from Bush. "America and the civilized world face a critical decision in the months ahead," it began. "The decision is how to disarm an outlaw regime that continues to possess and develop weapons of mass destruction." Bush told congressional leaders that he would work with them, but that he needed a resolution that would grant him the authority to confront Saddam, including the use of military force. He wanted a vote on the resolution within six weeks—before members left town to campaign for reelection. Senate Majority Leader Tom Daschle (D-SD) asked if it would be better to wait until after the election in order to take politics out of such an important vote concerning war. What was the rush? What was new about Saddam, and what was the immediate threat? If there was a new threat, where was the evidence? Rather than answer directly, Bush simply proclaimed, "We just have to do it now."[30]

On September 7, while on the campaign trail for the upcoming congressional elections, Bush declared in Cincinnati that the Iraqis were "six months away from developing a weapon. I don't know what more evidence we need." The next day Bush's subordinates blitzed the Sunday morning talk shows, *Meet the Press, Face the Nation,* and *Late Edition.* "We don't want the smoking gun to be a mushroom cloud," said Condoleezza Rice. "We do know, with absolute certainty, that he is using his procurement system to acquire the equipment he needs in order to enrich uranium to build a nuclear weapon," remarked Cheney. The vice president also added a new potential fear: "One of the real concerns about Saddam Hussein . . . is his biological weapons ability, the fact that he may at some point try to use smallpox, anthrax, plague, some other kind of biological agent against other nations, possibly including even the United States." Rumsfeld tied it all together: "Imagine a September 11 with weapons of mass destruction," which would kill "tens of thousands of innocent men, women, and children." Later that month he told Congress, "No terrorist state poses a greater or more immediate threat to the security of our people, and the stability of the world, than the regime of Saddam Hussein."[31]

On the first anniversary of the terrorist attacks, Bush appeared in a prime time address from Ellis Island. "We will not allow any terrorist or tyrant to threaten civilization with weapons of mass murder. Now and in the future, Americans will live as free people, not in fear, and never at the mercy of any foreign plot or power." The next day the president took his message to the United Nations. After recounting the numerous resolutions that the UN had passed against Iraq but Saddam continued to violate, Bush claimed that "Iraq employs capable nuclear scientists and technicians. It retains physical infrastructure needed to build a nuclear weapon. Iraq has made several attempts to buy high-strength aluminum tubes used to enrich uranium for a nuclear weapon. Should Iraq acquire fissile material, it would be able to build a nuclear weapon within a year." Bush continued, "Iraq possesses a force of Scud-type missiles" and is working on long-range missiles that could "inflict mass death throughout the region." It also "possesses biological and chemical weapons." Bush concluded by drawing a line in the sand: the "purposes of the United States should not be doubted. The Security Council resolutions will be enforced . . . or action will be unavoidable. And a regime that has lost its legitimacy will also lose its power."

Bush's speech did not have much impact on most members of the United Nations, but it did on Saddam. On September 16, Iraq announced that UN weapons inspectors—whom he had expelled in 1998—would now be readmitted into his country without conditions. That was a diplomatic coup for Bush, and UN inspectors began preparing for their trip to Iraq. Yet the administration appeared uninterested in allowing them to determine if Saddam had WMDs. Instead, it continued to build a case for attacking Iraq. On September 20 Bush hosted a private meeting with Republican governors at the White House, telling his political allies, "It is important to know that Iraq is an extension of the war on terror." "There is a case to be made," he stressed, "and I have to make it."[32]

The administration built its case throughout the month by attempting to establish a link between Saddam and bin Laden. Cheney told *Meet the Press* that "new information . . . has come to light" linking one of the 9/11 hijackers with "a senior Iraqi intelligence official a few months before the attack on the World Trade Center." On September 25 Rice added, "There clearly are contacts between al Qaeda and Iraq that can be documented . . . there's a relationship here. . . . And there are some al Qaeda personnel who found refuge in Baghdad." Bush continued the charge, "You can't distinguish between al Qaeda and Saddam when you talk about the war on terror," and Rumsfeld commented, "We have what we consider to be credible evidence that al Qaeda leaders have sought contacts with Iraq who could help them acquire . . . weapons of mass destruction capabilities." Later Rumsfeld described the evidence of Saddam–al Qaeda ties as "bulletproof."[33]

The president rejoined the chorus with a major address on October 7, just days before Congress was slated to vote on the Iraq resolution. Bush introduced the speech by warning of the "grave threat" from Iraq: "The danger is already significant, and it only grows worse with time. . . . We know that the regime has produced thousands of tons of chemical agents, including mustard gas, sarin nerve gas, VX nerve gas" and that "Iraq possesses ballistic missiles with a likely range of hundreds of miles." The president maintained that Saddam was trying to acquire "manned and unmanned aerial vehicles that could be used to disperse chemical or biological weapons," including "missions targeting the United States." In addition, he claimed, "evidence indicates that Iraq is reconstituting its nuclear weapons program" making it possible for Saddam to build a bomb "in less than a year." Then, Saddam would be able to dominate the Middle East, threaten America, and pass nuclear technology to terrorists. He concluded, "Facing clear evidence of peril, we cannot wait for the final proof, the smoking gun that could come in the form of a mushroom cloud."

The administration also took its message to Congress. Rumsfeld appeared before the House Armed Services Committee and declared that Saddam "has amassed large clandestine stocks of biological weapons, including anthrax and botulism toxin and possibly smallpox. His regime has amassed large clandestine stockpiles of chemical weapons, including VX and sarin and mustard gas."[34] Moreover, Iraq now could attack the United States. Cheney told members of Congress that Iraq's threat consisted of a fleet of UAVs—unmanned aerial vehicles. "I was looked at straight in the face," recalled Florida Democratic Senator Bill Nelson, "and told that Saddam Hussein had the means of delivering those biological and chemical weapons of mass destruction by unmanned drones. . . . Further, I was . . . told that UAVs could be launched from ships off the Atlantic coast to attack eastern seaboard cities of the United States."[35]

Under pressure, Congress voted in favor of the Joint Resolution to Authorize the Use of United States Armed Force Against Iraq in October. But the title was misleading. The resolution authorized the president to use armed forces only under two conditions: to "defend the national security of the United States against the continuing threat posed by Iraq" and to "enforce all relevant United Nations Security Council Resolutions regarding Iraq." Although the administration would claim that it had congressional approval for a war against Iraq, nothing in the resolution gave the president power to launch a preemptive strike on Iraq.

Meanwhile, UN weapon inspectors moved into Iraq early in December and began "no knock" inspections. While the world awaited news about WMDs, Rumsfeld preempted the findings. If the inspectors did not find WMDs, he declared, it would prove that the inspections process had been successfully defeated by the Iraqis. We "don't want to see a smoking gun from a weapon of mass destruction," Rumsfeld added. "With a weapon of mass destruction you're not talking about 300 people or 3,000 people being killed, but 30,000, or a hundred thousand."

By the end of January 2003 two organizations had been scouring Iraq for sixty days, the International Atomic Energy Agency (IAEA) and the United Nations Monitoring, Verification and Inspection Commission (UNMOVIC). On January 27 their directors presented their findings to the UN. IAEA Director Mohamed ElBaradei reminded the audience that in 1998 his organization had verified that Iraq had no nuclear capabilities. During the last two months it had conducted 139 inspections at 106 locations to determine if Saddam had rebuilt those capabilities. UNMOVIC head Hans Blix had a team of about 250 inspectors inside Iraq and had conducted some 300 visits to 230 different sites. Blix reported that UNMOVIC did not know if all biological weapons had been destroyed and that his inspectors had found a few missiles that had a range of slightly over ninety miles and some gas warheads for artillery rockets; those missiles and warheads were destroyed. He informed the world that the inspections continued and that his report did not "contend that weapons of mass destruction remain in Iraq, but nor do they exclude that possibility." Simply stated, there was "lack of evidence" of WMDs. ElBaradei was more direct: "No prohibited nuclear activities have been identified during these inspections," or "evidence of efforts . . . to revive the country's nuclear weapons program."[36]

In his State of the Union address the next day, Bush spoke as if the inspections had never taken place:

> Our intelligence officials estimate that Saddam Hussein had the materials to produce as much as 500 tons of sarin, mustard and VX nerve agent. In such quantities, these chemicals agents could kill untold thousands. . . . The British Government has learned that Saddam Hussein recently sought significant quantities of uranium from Africa. Our intelligence sources tell us that he has attempted to purchase high-strength aluminum tubes suitable for nuclear weapons production. . . . The dictator of Iraq is not disarming. To the contrary; he is deceiving. . . . Saddam Hussein has gone to elaborate lengths, spent enormous sums, taken great risks to build and keep weapons of mass destruction. . . . Evidence from intelligence sources, secret communications, and statements by people now in custody reveal that Saddam Hussein aids and protects terrorists, including members of al Qaeda. Secretly, and without fingerprints, he could provide one of his hidden weapons to terrorists, or help them develop their own. . . . Imagine those 19 hijackers with other weapons and other plans this time armed by Saddam Hussein.

Bush promised he would send Secretary Powell to the UN in a week with "information and intelligence" on Iraq. He pledged to consult with other nations. "But let there be no misunderstanding: If Saddam Hussein does not fully disarm, for the safety of our people and for the peace of the world, we will lead a coalition to disarm him."

That coalition meant for the most part the British, and on January 31 Prime Minister Blair arrived at the White House. Bush told him that the United States would invade whether or not there was a second UN resolution supporting an invasion and even if weapons inspectors found no evidence that Saddam was producing WMDs. Bush already had ordered two hundred thousand troops to take positions in the Middle East. Blair responded that he was "solidly with the president" and would do whatever it took to disarm Saddam. Bush replied, "The diplomatic strategy had to be arranged around the military planning," and the two men agreed to start the military campaign on or around March 10. Neither thought it likely "there would be internecine warfare between the different religious and ethnic groups."[37]

On February 5, 2003, Secretary of State Powell took the administration's case to the United Nations. Armed with numerous satellite photos, Powell claimed the "existence of mobile production facilities used to make biological agents," adding, "Our conservative estimate is that Iraq today has a stockpile of between 100 and 500 tons of chemical weapons agent." He continued, "We know that Iraq has at least seven of these mobile biological agent factories," and in a month they could produce enough agents to "kill thousands upon thousands of people." Powell restated the link between Iraq and al Qaeda and declared that Baghdad had provided the terrorists "help in acquiring poisons and gases." He then surprised the diplomats by refuting ElBaradei: "we have more than a decade of proof" that Saddam "remains determined to acquire nuclear weapons."[38]

Americans like to believe their leaders, and the barrage of such claims over more than six months had an impact on popular opinion. A CBS News/*New York Times* poll released two weeks after the September 11, 2001, attacks found that only 6 percent thought bin Laden had collaborated with Saddam in the strikes against America. But by the time of the Iraq invasion in mid-March 2003, CBS News found that 53 percent believed that Saddam had been involved in September 11. Other polls showed that a similar percentage were even convinced that the attackers were Iraqis—when not one was from that country.

Since leaving office Bush and his team have given identical talking points on the Iraq War. They continually write or state that "everyone thought Saddam had WMDs," the proclaimed reason for the war. There are two problems with this excuse—it is neither true nor relevant. Some in the CIA, like Paul Pillar, were not sure that the dictator had those weapons, and the Germans warned the administration that one featured American source, "Curveball," had fabricated stories about mobile production facilities. Some Britons were likewise dubious. On March 22, 2002, the political director of the British Foreign Office, Peter Ricketts, wrote to his boss, Foreign Secretary Straw, that "even the best survey of Iraq's WMD programmes will not show much advance in recent years" of nuclear, chemical, or biological weapons. He cautioned that the "programmes are extremely worrying but have not, as far as we know, been stepped up." How could the Bush administration, without one weapon inspector inside Iraq, know more about Saddam's alleged WMDs than hundreds of UN weapon inspectors conducting "no knock" inspections at all possible facilities inside that nation?[39]

Moreover, the WMD cause was irrelevant. Numerous nations in the world possess WMDs, and the United States has not attacked or even threatened them. Bush went to war for four key reasons: because he hated Saddam, because he and his advisers wanted to bring about a democratic Middle East, because he thought the war would be quick and cheap, and for oil. As early as January 29, 2001, the president established his National Energy Policy Development Group, chaired by Cheney. The group included executives from Exxon Mobil, Enron,

British Petroleum, Duke Energy, the American Petroleum Institute, and a leader in the anti-Saddam Iraqi National Congress, Ahmed Chalabi. By March, Cheney and his energy task force were examining maps of Iraq's oil fields and pipelines and had a list of companies interested in doing business in a post-Saddam Iraq. A couple months after the 2003 invasion a reporter asked Paul Wolfowitz why we attacked Iraq and not a nation developing an atomic bomb, North Korea, and he bluntly declared one of the administration's real reasons for the war: "Look, the primarily difference—to put it a little too simply—between North Korea and Iraq," said the deputy defense secretary, "is that we had virtually no economic options with Iraq because the country floats on a sea of oil."[40]

Bush and his top advisers, who had no knowledge about Saddam or Iraq and its people, dragged the United States into the greatest foreign policy blunder in American history. Their characterization of the war in Iraq as defensive is specious. If Saddam was building WMDs, and he was not, the target would be his hated enemy—Iran—whom he fought for eight years in the 1980s. As former Republican Senator and Secretary of Defense Chuck Hagel wrote, "The administration cherry-picked intelligence to fit its policy, used fear and the threat of terrorism to intensify its war sloganeering . . . and dampened the possibility of dissent by denying that it had decided to go to war even though it had already made that decision before the debate even began. It is shocking how little Congress or the media challenged the Bush administration."[41]

Bush's response to 9/11 remains with the nation today. We still are fighting the war on terror, still have detainees at Guantanamo, and still are confronting a Taliban insurgency in Afghanistan. Moreover, after more than seven years at war, and after a heavy price in treasury and blood, the Bush administration succeeded in creating a failed state in Iraq. In many ways it remains a threat to peace in the Middle East.

NOTES

1 Bob Woodward, *Bush at War* (New York: Simon & Schuster, 2002), 205.

2 All of Bush's speeches and many statements are at http://www.johnstonarchive.net/policy/bush-speeches.html.

3 "Text: Bin Laden's Statement," *Guardian*, October 7, 2001, http://www.theguardian.com/world/2001/oct/07/afghanistan.terrorism15.

4 President Bush's speech, September 20, 2001.

5 Zbigniew Brzezinski, "Terrorized by 'War on Terror': How a Three-Word Mantra Has Undermined America," *Washington Post*, March 25, 2007.

6 CNN transcript, October 24, 2001, http://transcripts.cnn.com/TRANSCRIPTS/0110/24/se.13.html.

7 James Risen, *State of War: The Secret History of the CIA and the Bush Administration* (New York: Free Press, 2006), 47–59; and see Cary Stacy Smith and Li-ching

Hung, *The Patriot Act: Issues and Controversies* (Springfield, IL: Charles C Thomas, 2010).

8 "The Vice President appears on Meet the Press," September 16, 2001, http://georgewbush-whitehouse.archives.gov/vicepresident/news-speeches/speeches/vp20010916.html. And see Jane Mayer, *The Dark Side: The Inside Story of How the War on Terror Turned into a War on American Ideals* (New York: Doubleday, 2009).

9 Human Rights Watch, "'We Are Not the Enemy': Hate Crimes Against Arabs, Muslims, and Those Perceived to Be Arab or Muslim after September 11" (November 2002 and February 14, 2006), http: //hrw.org/reports/2002/usahate/.

10 George Tenet, *At the Center of the Storm: My Years at the CIA* (New York: HarperCollins, 2007), 208.

11 Henry A. Crumpton, "Intelligence and War: Afghanistan, 2001–2002," in *Transforming U.S. Intelligence*, ed. Jennifer E. Sims and Burton Gerber (Washington, DC: Georgetown University Press, 2005), 162–79.

12 Gary C. Schroen, *First In: An Insider's Account of How the CIA Spearheaded the War on Terror in Afghanistan* (New York: Presidio Press, 2005), 36–37; Bob Woodward, *Plan of Attack: The Definitive Account of the Decision to Invade Iraq* (New York: Simon & Schuster, 2004), 139–43.

13 Presidential statements, September 17 and December 28, 2001.

14 Mary Anne Weaver, "Lost at Tora Bora," *New York Times*, September 11, 2005; Terry H. Anderson, *Bush's Wars* (New York: Oxford University Press, 2011), 85–88.

15 Tom Lasseter's five part series, "Guantanamo: Beyond the Law," *McClatchy-Tribune*, June 2008; Corine Hegland, "Guantanamo's Grip," *National Journal*, February 3, 2006; and on treatment and children, Joseph Margulies, *Guantanamo and the Abuse of Presidential Power* (New York: Simon & Schuster, 2006), introduction.

16 Margulies, *Guantanamo and the Abuse of Presidential Power*, chap. 4, and Sherry Jones's documentary, *Torturing Democracy*.

17 "Rumsfeld: Afghan Detainees at Gitmo Bay Will Not Be Granted POW Status," FoxNews.com, January 28, 2002; Johan Steyn, "Guantanamo Bay: The Legal Black Hole," *International and Comparative Law Quarterly* 53 (January 2004): 1–15.

18 George W. Bush, *Decision Points* (New York: Crown, 2010), 229.

19 Douglas J. Feith, *War and Decision: Inside the Pentagon at the Dawn of the War on Terrorism* (New York: Harper, 2008), 223–24.

20 Anderson, *Bush's Wars*, 228–33.

21 Ron Suskind, *The Price of Loyalty: George W. Bush, the White House, and the Education of Paul O'Neill* (New York: Simon & Schuster, 2004), 72–75, 84–86.

22 Tenet, *At the Center of the Storm*, 104–5; Richard Clarke, interview, *Fresh Air*, National Public Radio, September 22, 2004, http://www.npr.org/templates/story/story.php?storyId=3931123.

23 Thomas H. Kean and Lee H. Hamilton, *The 9/11 Report* (New York: St. Martin's, 2004), chap. 8.

24 Woodward, *Plan of Attack*, 1–3.

"

25 Thomas, E. Ricks, *Fiasco: The American Military Adventure in Iraq* (New York: Penguin, 2006), 35.

26 Elisabeth Bumiller, "U.S. Must Act First to Battle Terror, Bush Tells Cadets," *New York Times*, June 2, 2002.

27 Richard N. Haass, "The Dilemma of Dissent," *Newsweek*, May 18, 2009.

28 *Times* (London), May 1, 2005, http://www.thesundaytimes.co.uk/sto/news/uk_news/article91033.ece.

29 CBS News poll, September 7, 2002.

30 Michael Isikoff and David Corn, *Hubris: The Inside Story of Spin, Scandal, and the Selling of the Iraq War* (New York: Crown, 2006), 21–25; Scott McClellan, *What Happened: Inside the Bush White House and Washington's Culture of Deception* (New York: Public Affairs, 2008), chap. 8.

31 Frank Rich, *The Greatest Story Ever Sold: The Decline and Fall of Truth from 9/11 to Katrina* (New York: Penguin, 2006), chap. 4.

32 McClellan, *What Happened*, 139–41.

33 Eric Schmitt, "Rumsfeld Says U.S. Has 'Bulletproof' Evidence of Iraq's Links to Al Qaeda," *New York Times*, September 28, 2002.

34 Testimony before the House Armed Services Committee, September 18, 2002. Rumsfeld made this statement at least two other times, on September 27, 2002, and January 20, 2003.

35 James Bamford, *A Pretext for War: 9/11, Iraq, and the Abuse of America's Intelligence Agencies* (New York: Doubleday, 2004), 330–31.

36 ElBaradei's statement to the UN, "The Status of Nuclear Inspections in Iraq," January 27, 2003, and his *The Age of Deception: Nuclear Diplomacy in Treacherous Times* (New York: Henry Holt, 2011), chap. 3; Hans Blix, *Disarming Iraq: The Search for Weapons of Mass Destruction* (New York: Pantheon, 2004), 135–41.

37 Bush-Blair meeting from Richard Norton-Taylor, "Blair-Bush Deal before Iraq War Revealed in Secret Memo," *Guardian*, February 3, 2006, http://www.theguardian.com/world/2006/feb/03/iraq.usa; and Don Van Natta Jr., "The Reach of War: Leaders; Bush Was Set on Path to War, Memo by British Adviser Says," *New York Times*, March 27, 2006.

38 http://www.washingtonpost.com/wp-srv/nation/transcripts/powelltext_020503.html.

39 Isikoff and Corn, *Hubris*, 27; and see "The Secret Downing Street Memo," *Times* (London), May 1, 2005.

40 Michael Abramowitz and Steven Mufson, "Papers Detail Industry's Role in Cheney's Energy Report," *Washington Post*, July 18, 2007; Neil Mackay, "Official: US Oil at the Heart of Iraq Crisis," *Sunday Herald* (Scotland), October 2, 2002, http://www.myiwc.com/forums/showthread.php?t=2816; "Deputy Secretary Wolfowitz Q&A Following IISA Asia Security Conference," March 31, 2003, http://www.defense.gov/transcripts/transcript.aspx?transcriptid=2704.

41 Chuck Hagel with Peter Kaminsky, *America: Our Next Chapter* (New York: HarperCollins, 2008), 38.

PART II

The Possibilities and Limits of American Military and Diplomatic Strategy

3

Intelligence and the Wars in Iraq and Afghanistan

RICHARD H. IMMERMAN

Commenting in 1950 on the accuracy of intelligence reports that the U.S. public expected the fledgling Central Intelligence Agency to produce, newly appointed CIA Director Walter Bedell Smith purportedly remarked that Americans "expect you to be on a communing level with God and Joe Stalin, and I'm not sure they are so much interested in God."[1] Smith exaggerated, but not by much. Americans' expectations (both within and beyond the Beltway) about the value of intelligence for conducting foreign policy and promoting national security are uniformly unrealistic. Collecting intelligence is hard, and analyzing it is even harder. The most one can expect from intelligence, in the words of a veteran official, is to "reduce uncertainty, identify risks and opportunities, and by doing so, deepen understanding so that those with policymaking responsibilities will make 'better' decisions." These are limited but nonetheless valuable goals. Done right, intelligence can provide policy makers with a "decision advantage."[2]

Intelligence, particularly strategic intelligence, was not done right during the lead-up to and conduct of either the Iraq War or the Afghanistan War. It thus did little to reduce policy makers' uncertainty or to provide them with a decision advantage. This judgment, however, begs questions about who was responsible for this failure and therefore for its consequences. This essay argues that, although the Intelligence Community (IC) did not perform well, its customers—America's policy makers—are primarily culpable for the grief that befell the United States in both Iraq and Afghanistan.[3] First in the aftermath of the September 11, 2001, attacks on the World Trade Center in New York and the Pentagon Building in Washington, D.C., and then when waging two wars, the architects of America's national security relied far too little on intelligence in reaching their decisions, forfeiting any advantage it could have provided them.

Policy makers did not depend on intelligence to guide their decisions because they did not feel the need to; too many high-ranking officials' minds were closed. Furthermore, they too often saw intelligence reports, and those who wrote them, as obstacles to actions they were predisposed to take. By the second term of the George W. Bush presidency, moreover, and throughout that of Barack Obama, administration officials used the IC largely to assist in taking those actions—primarily by managing the drone campaign and undertaking other covert, paramilitary operations. For this reason intelligence played a larger role in efforts to prosecute and terminate the wars than it did in decisions to engage in the wars.

This is not to say that in the lead-up to the wars in Iraq and Afghanistan the IC served policy makers well. Intelligence reporting on Afghanistan, Saddam Hussein's Iraq, and stateless terrorist networks such as al Qaeda severely challenged American capabilities. The CIA's inability to predict the Soviet invasion of Afghanistan in 1979 heads almost all lists of the agency's greatest Cold War failures. By covertly providing billions of dollars in arms and materiel (funneled through Pakistan's intelligence service, the Inter-Services Intelligence Directorate or ISI) to Muslim guerrilla warriors, the mujahedeen, in their battle against the Soviets and their Afghan clients, the CIA did contribute to the Kremlin's decision to withdraw from Afghanistan in 1989. "WE WON" cabled the agency's chief of station in Islamabad, Pakistan, after Moscow called it quits in what another CIA veteran described as an "intelligence war between the United States and its allies and the Soviets and their ally, the Afghan communist party" and "the most successful covert intelligence operation in U.S. history."[4]

In the sense that a Soviet defeat meant a U.S. victory, the CIA station chief was right. Still, throughout that conflict intelligence analysts displayed little understanding of the complexity of the country's internal dynamics or appreciation of the emergence of the Taliban as a political force. The withdrawal of CIA operatives from Afghanistan quickly followed that of the Soviet troops. By the time the Taliban captured Kabul, established an Islamist government headed by Mullah Muhammed Omar, and turned Afghanistan into a base for global jihadism in the latter half of the 1990s, U.S. intelligence capabilities there were virtually nonexistent.[5]

Since the Iran Hostage Crisis of 1979 and the protracted Iran-Iraq War that raged over much of the next decade, the intelligence role in Iraq, in contrast to Afghanistan, focused more on analysis than operations. And initially it performed well in this capacity. Although the CIA lacked the assets necessary to collect human intelligence (HUMINT), the IC drew on photographs taken from satellites (IMINT) to monitor the build-up of Iraqi forces along the Kuwait border in 1990 and provide advance warning that it was "highly likely" that Saddam intended to invade Kuwait.[6] Once the invasion occurred in August of that year, CIA assessed it unlikely that economic sanctions would compel Saddam to withdraw his forces, a judgment that was probably accurate. The agency also estimated that the international community was likely to support a U.S. military response not only by cheering from the sidelines but also by contributing troops, money, or both. This judgment was accurate. Moreover, CIA analysts outperformed General Norman Schwarzkopf's Central Command intelligence staff by correctly evaluating the damage to Iraq's military capabilities inflicted by the America-led coalition as dramatically less than that claimed by Schwarzkopf.

Overshadowing these successes, nevertheless, was the CIA's inability accurately to evaluate Saddam Hussein's weapons of mass destruction (WMD) programs in the early 1990s; their underestimation would influence intelligence assessments a decade later. Because the CIA had few assets on the ground in Iraq to provide HUMINT, the United States had little appreciation of his WMD capabilities. A postwar study of the "successes" and "failures" of U.S. intelligence during Operations Desert Shield and Desert Storm conducted by a subcommittee of the House Armed Services Committee judged that because of insufficient information, the IC's estimates of Saddam's cache of biological weapons were too ambiguous to be useful. Intelligence on Iraq's chemical capabilities was better. But the committee also found fault with the community's assessments of Iraq's nuclear program.[7]

At the start of 1990, according to U.S. estimates, Iraq was five, perhaps ten years away from acquiring a nuclear weapon. But intelligence received from Israel that summer suggested that Iraq was further along in its efforts to produce the requisite enriched uranium, which shortened the time that the IC estimated Iraq required to achieve a nuclear capability.[8] But it was information collected by United Nations inspectors in 1991 and 1992, after the First Gulf War, which revealed more accurately the state of Saddam's nuclear program. These inspectors learned that by the time that Iraq invaded Kuwait, it possessed the capacity to produce enough enriched uranium for several nuclear bombs, that Saddam had funded the program with virtually no limits, and that the United States was "totally unaware of more than 50 percent of all the major weapons installations in Iraq." Furthermore, because Saddam could readily conceal facilities to build and store unconventional weapons and because the equipment was mobile, it was less vulnerable to attack than the United States had anticipated.[9]

Concluding that Saddam could never be trusted, the IC resolved never again to underestimate Iraq's capacity to conceal nuclear or other weapons of massive destruction. This resolve grew stronger as the CIA's covert efforts to topple Saddam in the mid-1990s failed even as his regime crushed a Kurdish insurrection that the CIA encouraged, funded Palestinian terrorists, and provoked anxiety among U.S. regional allies from those states that shared the Persian Gulf with Iraq extending to Turkey. Yet even though Iraq, unlike Afghanistan, remained a priority for U.S. intelligence throughout the decade of the 1990s, the IC's ability to monitor—let alone influence—developments there eroded further.

U.S. intelligence had suffered prior to the First Gulf War because, devoid of "boots on the ground" in Iraq, it was unable to collect HUMINT. Nothing improved this situation in the years following Saddam's defeat. John Deutch, whom President Bill Clinton appointed director of central intelligence (DCI) in 1995, believed that intelligence acquired from intercepting communication signals and satellite photography (SIGINT and IMINT) should take precedence over HUMINT. He also so vigorously opposed using foreign assets with records of criminal behavior or human rights abuses that he issued a directive prohibiting their recruitment. This prohibition probably had little effect in Iraq. Saddam did not allow anyone into his inner circle who was not family or with whom he did not have a long history. CIA officials nevertheless complained that Deutch's edict made a bad situation worse.[10] Moreover, the agency's budget was a casualty of the post–Cold War quest for a "peace dividend." U.S. intelligence, consequently, depended on UN inspectors to detect efforts on the part of the Saddam regime to reconstitute its WMD, including its nuclear, program. Saddam kept these inspectors at arm's length until 1998. That year he expelled them.

At the same time, the evolving threat of stateless terrorist networks diverted attention from both Afghanistan and Iraq. Yet the IC performed no better in that realm. In 1986 DCI William Casey had established a Counterterrorism Center. But its mandate was almost exclusively to conduct covert operations against terrorists as opposed to identifying who they were and assessing their motivations and intentions. Further constraining the CIA's capacity for analyzing issues related to terrorism was the makeup of its analytic workforce. The agency dedicated a high proportion of its analysts to the Soviet Union, which was poor preparation for understanding stateless terrorism.

Yet even as the agency struggled to reassign and retrain its analysts after the 1991 collapse of the Soviet Union, the uptick in terrorist attacks was unmistakable. In June 1995 President Clinton signed Presidential Decision Directive-39, "U.S. Policy on Counterterrorism." It made the DCI responsible for pursuing an "aggressive program of foreign intelligence collection, analysis, counterintelligence and covert action" aimed at reducing U.S. vulnerabilities to international terrorism.[11] Almost precisely one year after Clinton signed the directive, nineteen U.S. servicemen died when Islamic militants associated with Hezbollah, an Islamic organization based in Lebanon, bombed the U.S. military barracks at Khobar Towers in Saudi Arabia.

Deutch resigned as DCI at the end of Clinton's first term; the Senate confirmed George Tenet as his successor in July 1997. For reasons having to do with both the national interest and the institutional interest of the CIA, Tenet quickly moved to position the agency at the center of a ramped-up counterterrorism campaign by reviving its capacity for covert operations. He did not move quickly enough. On August 7, 1998, only a year after Tenet's confirmation, terrorists bombed the U.S. embassies in Nairobi, Kenya, and Dar es Salaam, Tanzania. The IC identified Osama bin Laden as the mastermind. In the late 1980s bin Laden, the scion of a wealthy Saudi family who had joined the mujahedeen resistance to the Soviets in Afghanistan, had put together a loosely organized network called al Qaeda (the Base). Its purpose was to wage holy war against foreign influence in Islamist territories. The United States, with its forces stationed in bin Laden's native Saudi Arabia, was from al Qaeda's perspective the chief offender and thus its primary target.

By the mid-1990s al Qaeda had shifted its headquarters from the Sudan to Afghanistan, where it received protection from the Taliban. Two weeks after the August 1998 bombing of the U.S. embassies, Clinton ordered a missile strike on al Qaeda's training camp at Zawhar Kili in eastern Afghanistan. According to CIA intelligence, bin Laden was attending a meeting there. Scores were killed or wounded, but bin Laden was not among them. The Pakistani ISI may have tipped off the Taliban, which warned bin Laden.[12] Pakistan supported the Taliban as an ally in its conflict with India over Kashmir and as a buffer should it experience unrest among its own Pashtun population.

For the Clinton administration and the CIA, bin Laden and al Qaeda overtook Iraq and Afghanistan as priorities. In 1999 Tenet appointed J. Cofer Black to head up the CIA's Counterterrorism Center. Black had been following bin Laden's trail since serving as the CIA station chief in Khartoum, Sudan, in 1993, and he kept close tabs on the progress of the "Bin Laden [code-named 'Alec'] Station." This was the special unit led by Michael F. Scheuer and housed in a building separate from but close to the CIA's Langley headquarters. The agency had established the station in 1996 to track the wealthy Saudi.[13] Clinton signed a memorandum in December 1999 authorizing the CIA to use lethal force if necessary to cripple the terrorist organization. The agency's operatives, however, even the most highly trained personnel in the Office of External Development's "non-official cover" program, were unable to penetrate al Qaeda. Furthermore, neither the Counterterrorist Center nor the Alec Station acquired "actionable intelligence." Bin Laden remained out of harm's way.[14]

On October 12, 2000, al Qaeda–directed terrorists blew up the USS *Cole* in the harbor of Aden, Yemen. Seventeen Americans died. The next month

Americans elected George W. Bush president (the final outcome had to await the Supreme Court ruling in December). The new president and his national security team dismissed Clinton's hunt for bin Laden and al Qaeda as an overwrought obsession. In their view Saddam Hussein's Iraq, owing to its present capabilities, its potential capabilities, and its alleged sponsorship of other terrorists' capabilities, represented a far more severe threat than did, in the words of Deputy Secretary of Defense Paul Wolfowitz, the "little terrorist in Afghanistan."[15] Their overriding concern was with states, especially those states that it believed were willing to violate international law and that could potentially acquire nuclear weapons. The new administration intended defense against nuclear missiles, not terrorism, to be the cornerstone of its national security strategy.

Bush retained George Tenet as DCI. And throughout the administration's first eight months, no one sought more strenuously than he to convince the president that Clinton's emphasis on counterterrorism was legitimate. During this period, in fact beginning with the transition, Tenet personally briefed Bush dozens of times on the IC's judgment that bin Laden intended to attack the United States. But it was Michael Morrell, a senior CIA analyst who later served as the head of the agency's Directorate of Intelligence and its acting director, who briefed the president on August 6, 2001, while Bush was vacationing at his ranch in Crawford, Texas. The lead item in that day's President's Daily Brief was a report titled "Bin Laden Determined to Strike in U.S." Although available intelligence did not point toward a specific date, the purpose of the report, according to one of its authors, was to warn the president that the risk was so high, and the danger so imminent, that he should take extraordinary precautions.[16]

The administration, surely influenced by its predisposition to perceive the threat of al Qaeda as less severe than that of nuclear-armed outlaw states, was unimpressed by the CIA's alert. Bush interpreted the brief as an effort to provide historical context to the contemporary situation, not to signal any change in the assessment. But the CIA's intent was to signal a change, and that estimate proved sound. Shortly before nine o'clock Eastern time on the morning of September 11, 2001, a hijacked airliner slammed into the north tower of New York City's World Trade Center. Before the morning was over, a second airliner struck the other Twin Tower, a third crashed into the Pentagon, and a fourth, en route to the Capitol Building in Washington, D.C., was brought down in rural Pennsylvania by courageous passengers. The CIA rapidly identified al Qaeda as responsible for the calamity, which claimed more lives than the Japanese attack on Pearl Harbor.

Almost as rapidly, the agency began to make amends for what it conceded was a failure to detect the preparations for the attack and its implementation strategy. Cofer Black, the head of the CIA's Counterterrorism Center, briefed the National Security Council on a plan to take revenge on al Qaeda on September 13. In but a few weeks, he boasted, the terrorists responsible for the outrage would have "flies walking across their eyeballs." At Camp David two days later, Tenet provided a more detailed briefing to Bush on what came to be called Operation Enduring Freedom. On September 17 President Bush instructed the CIA to execute it.[17]

By early October agency operatives had returned to Afghanistan, having left with the Soviets in 1989. Preceding and then collaborating closely with Special Operations Forces from the U.S. and British militaries, the agency's paramilitary operatives (the seven-member Northern Afghanistan Liaison Team, code-named Jawbreaker and led by Gary Schroen) quickly reestablished contacts with the Northern Alliance's anti-Taliban warlords. Schroen's team provided them with intelligence and, according to Bob Woodward, some seventy million dollars in money and supplies.[18] Jawbreaker (later succeeded by Team Juliet, led by Gary Bernstein) also coordinated its efforts with the CIA's station in Islamabad, Pakistan, and other operatives previously stationed in Uzbekistan to direct Predator drones (unmanned aerial vehicles) on surveillance missions over Afghanistan. After the arrival of U.S. military forces and the official launch of Operation Enduring Freedom on October 7, relations between CIA operatives in Afghanistan and General Tommy Franks's Central Command, and even between those operatives and offices at the agency's Langley headquarters, most notably the Counterterrorism Center, were at times strained. Nevertheless, over the subsequent months CIA agents in the field (ultimately a total of about 110) provided vital support by collecting real-time, "actionable" intelligence, identifying and helping to guide American bombs to designated targets, and interrogating prisoners. CIA officer Johnny "Mike" Spann became the operation's first fatality when he was killed on November 25. By that day the allied Taliban and al Qaeda forces had lost the battles for Mazar-e-Sharif and Kabul in the north, and with CIA assistance were being pummeled, presumably along with Osama bin Laden himself, in the Tora Bora cave complex near Afghanistan's eastern border.[19]

In early December the Taliban's southern stronghold of Kandahar fell. Its leader, Mullah Omar, fled to the Tora Bora mountains to join bin Laden and his al Qaeda colleagues in hiding. In March 2002, following the defeat of the remnants of al Qaeda and the Taliban, major combat operations ended. By then, American bombers had steadily clobbered Tora Bora. An estimated

seven hundred thousand pounds of ordinance landed on the mountains between December 4 and 7 alone.[20]

Victory eluded the Americans, nevertheless. Bin Laden, his chief lieutenant Ayman al-Zawahiri, Mullah Omar, and others were able to find shelter
in the tunnels and bunkers built with CIA money in the 1980s by the Afghans who fought the Soviets. Moreover, consistent with Secretary of Defense Donald Rumsfeld's insistence that the U.S. military maintain a "light
footprint," General Franks refused to deploy the reinforcements that Henry
Crumpton, who commanded the CIA's "forces" in Afghanistan, requested
for the purpose of preventing the enemy from fleeing. Whether additional
troops could have blocked all avenues of escape from Tora Bora is an open
question. What is not is that the al Qaeda and Taliban survivors fled over
the border to Pakistan. The Bush administration was unconcerned. Already
it had redirected the crusade against terrorism to target Saddam Hussein's
regime in Iraq. Presuming, without reliable intelligence, that Saddam Hussein had assisted bin Laden in executing the 9/11 attacks, the managers of
America's national security had begun to develop war plans against Iraq in
early November. The U.S. Intelligence Community was spiraling toward
irrelevancy.[21]

James Woolsey, Deutch's predecessor as DCI, was a leading champion of
the theory that tied Saddam Hussein to bin Laden. But the agency's sources
did not support the claim. In Tenet's words, the "intelligence did not show any
Iraqi authority, direction, or control over any of the many specific terrorists
acts carried out by al-Qa'ida."[22] Rumsfeld, nevertheless, described evidence of
the link as "bulletproof," and to marshal support he established a two-person
Policy Counter Terrorism Evaluation Group (PCTEG) to comb through the
files of the CIA and the Defense Intelligence Agency (DIA). The PCTEG
claimed that the files showed "consultation, training, financing, and collaboration" between Saddam and al Qaeda. Rejecting this claim as "Feith-based
analysis," a play on the name of Paul Wolfowitz's deputy, Douglas Feith, the
CIA held to its position.[23]

The CIA's evaluation of the administration's accusation that Saddam Hussein possessed chemical and biological weapons and sought actively to develop nuclear weapons was less resolute and more complicated. Bush and his
closest advisors alleged that Saddam not only possessed (and was determined
to acquire more) WMDs, but he also was prepared to supply them to bin
Laden and other terrorists. The CIA continued to resist connecting Saddam
to bin Laden. But the agency, including Director Tenet, did share the assessment of Bush, Cheney, Rumsfeld, Wolfowitz, Feith, National Security Advisor
Condoleezza Rice, and Secretary of State Colin Powell that Saddam intended

to augment a cache of WMDs that he had successfully concealed since expelling the UN inspectors in 1998 with a nuclear capability.[24]

Still bereft of human assets in Iraq, the CIA relied on U-2 spy planes, drones, and other technological means to collect intelligence on the danger Saddam posed. It remained unable to uncover evidence of WMDs, however, let alone of Saddam's intentions. This inability did not shake the belief of Bush and his chief advisors in Saddam's guilt. In his January 2002 State of the Union speech, the president devoted more attention to Iraq than to any of the other states that comprised what he labeled the "axis of evil." Among his many allegations, Bush indicted the regime's effort "to develop anthrax, and nerve gas, and nuclear weapons for over a decade." The challenge for the IC was to confirm that this effort continued. Moreover, the IC sought intelligence that would reveal that Saddam Hussein already had WMDs available to use and to share.[25]

Having observed Saddam's reprehensible behavior for decades, CIA analysts had little reason to doubt that Saddam had hidden in Iraq a stockpile of WMDs. The IC collected no evidence disconfirming this assumption. But neither did it collect confirming evidence. So it hedged on its judgments. The effect on an administration that had already rushed to judgment was inconsequential. But a conflicted Congress sought a more conclusive estimate, if only to support whichever direction its members were leaning toward or to justify, even if reluctantly, going along with an invasion. In September 2002 members, Congress requested a new National Intelligence Estimate (NIE).

By October 3 the National Foreign Intelligence Board (now the National Intelligence Board), composed of senior leaders from across the IC, had approved a ninety-two-page NIE on "Iraq's Continuing Programs for Weapons of Mass Destruction." It was new only in the most technical definition. Because of time constraints and the absence of current intelligence, the NIE was a synthesis of previous reports and estimates. In addition, violating the most basic tenets of analytic tradecraft, the authors conflated "fact" with assumptions and failed to identify the gaping holes in their data. Kept too much in the dark by collectors, moreover, they insufficiently expressed their confidence, or lack thereof, in the reliability of their sources. They likewise did not warn their readers that the IC had serious doubts about the credibility of some of those sources. The most notorious of these problematic sources was "Curveball," an Iraqi defector to Germany who concocted evidence that Saddam had hidden from inspectors mobile laboratories that produced biological weapons. German intelligence, British intelligence, and many in both the CIA and DIA doubted Curveball's claims, but the NIE omitted mention of these doubts.[26]

The IC's failure to detect Saddam's secret WMD programs prior to the First Gulf War made it easier for intelligence analysts to accept as logical the premise that if Saddam had pursued such programs before, he must be doing so again. This logic also led analysts to inflate the probability of worst-case scenarios, thus making themselves more vulnerable (to quote the CIA's own self-study) to "Iraq's intransigence and deceptive practices." The NIE's first key judgment read, "We judge that Iraq has continued its weapons of mass destruction (WMD) programs in defiance of UN resolutions and restrictions. Baghdad has chemical and biological weapons as well as missiles with ranges in excess of UN restrictions; if left unchecked, it probably will have a nuclear weapon during this decade." The claim was as inaccurate as it was categorical. Comparisons are difficult, but the *New York Times* could not have been far off when it described the NIE as "one of the most flawed documents in the history of American intelligence."[27]

Those in favor of and opposed to the invasion of Iraq, at the time and subsequently, have held the NIE responsible for their positions. That charge is exaggerated if not baseless. The most a policy maker can expect of intelligence is for it to provide a decision advantage. The policy maker should never hold it responsible for that decision. Furthermore, very few in Congress, the White House, the State and Defense Departments, or elsewhere in Washington actually read the estimate. And its critics outside of (and perhaps some inside) government read a different document, most likely the NIE's "Key Judgments," which under pressure the administration released out of context. Some may also have read a white paper that Congress insisted that the National Intelligence Council, the interagency body that generates reports reflecting the IC's collective judgment, produce at the unclassified level. But unlike an NIE, the white paper was not coordinated among the IC's different agencies. Neither it nor the released Key Judgments included the caveats and acknowledgments of dissents (primarily by the State Department's Bureau of Intelligence and Research) that appeared in the NIE itself, even if only in footnotes.[28]

This is not to absolve the IC. The CIA titled its after-the-fact examination of its estimates about Saddam Hussein "Misreading Intentions." The postmortem insightfully explains how Saddam, appreciating how precarious was his position, had in the run-up to the invasion genuinely sought to provide the international community with the information it sought. But he could not work out a way to do so without admitting that he had for years concealed and lied about this very information. At the same time, he did not want to sacrifice his deterrent against enemies by acknowledging publicly that he had destroyed his chemical and biological weapons capacity and ceased efforts to obtain a nuclear one. The CIA, guided by Saddam's history of "cheat and retreat," was deceived as much as Israel and Iran, the key targets of his deception. The agency fell victim to what it euphemistically labeled "analyst liabilities."[29]

For this reason administration efforts to politicize the intelligence on Iraq, while inappropriate, were immaterial. There is no reason to conclude that the October 2002 NIE or any other analytic product would have reached different judgments had the administration signaled its preference to invade Iraq less blatantly, let alone had Vice President Cheney refrained from visiting CIA headquarters to look over analysts' shoulders as they sifted through data.[30] But there is also no reason to suspect that the administration would have behaved any differently had the IC correctly read Saddam's intentions and assessed his capabilities.

The fact that Secretary of State Colin Powell was skeptical of claims made by the president and most of his core advisors and yet pushed no less strenuously to invade Iraq supports this argument. In his infamous State of the Union address on January 28, 2003, Bush referred explicitly to Saddam's supposed effort to purchase from Niger "yellow cake" uranium, which with further processing can be used to make nuclear weapons. The basis for that allegation, which the administration's critics cite frequently to illustrate its politicization of intelligence, was a British report, the so-called September Dossier, that relied on forged documents. Harboring reservations about the report's credibility, the CIA advised against Bush citing it. He nevertheless did.[31]

Powell did not in his equally infamous address to the UN General Assembly a week later. The secretary of state was more cautious about the evidence he used to charge Saddam Hussein. That his indictment was no less vigorous or categorical illustrates how prevalent was the presumption of Saddam Hussein's guilt. More systematically than Bush, Powell drew on the available intelligence to close the administration's case. With Tenet seated at his shoulder as a stamp of approval, the widely respected secretary of state proclaimed that "every statement I make today is backed up by sources, solid sources." He then highlighted the extraordinary means that he alleged that Saddam had taken and was still taking to conceal a range of WMDs and his continuing efforts to develop and acquire others. In what became the most notorious example, Powell cited four different sources to condemn Iraq for maintaining mobile production facilities capable of producing "a quantity of biological poison equal to the entire amount that Iraq claimed to have produced in the years prior to the Gulf War." Chief among these sources was Curveball, whom, despite IC doubts about his credibility, Powell described as a defector "currently hiding in another country with the certain knowledge that Saddam Hussein will kill him if he finds him." The subtext of the address was that because of its unique capabilities, the United States, in contrast to the United Nations and all its member nations, had access to the most sensitive intelligence.[32]

Powell later publicly apologized for his pitch. But, he explained, his duty was to mobilize support for the administration's policy—which was to invade Iraq. Powell "wanted to sell a rotten fish," a former intelligence officer commented. "His job was to go to war with as much legitimacy as he could scrape up."[33] He performed this assignment so well that his allegations were invulnerable to criticism. Although the intelligence Powell cited for his authority was unreliable, no official of any government or nongovernmental organization, or any scholar or journalist, had the evidence to challenge him. As a consequence, it was U.S. intelligence that became the scapegoat for the ensuing grief that befell both the United States and Iraq.

On March 19, 2003, however, when President Bush announced the initiation of Operation Iraqi Freedom, the preemptive invasion aimed at ridding the world of Saddam and the threat he posed, he had successfully mobilized domestic and even international support. In less than two months Baghdad fell, Saddam and his sons fled into hiding, and Bush proclaimed an end to military operations. Behind the president when he made this proclamation aboard the USS *Lincoln* was a banner with the words "Mission Accomplished" blazoned on it. But the fundamental mission—to find and destroy Saddam's cache of WMDs—had not yet begun. That mission turned out to be impossible. Notwithstanding the administration's claims that U.S. intelligence was solid, Iraq was devoid of hidden WMDs.

Even as the American people and the globe's population became progressively aware that the U.S. Intelligence Community had gotten the threat posed by Iraq very wrong, the Bush administration, the Iraqis, and America's military became progressively more aware of a different threat that U.S. intelligence had gotten right. In August 2002 the National Intelligence Council, in a report titled "The Perfect Storm: Planning for Negative Consequences of Invading Iraq," had warned of the danger of the invasion turning into a boon for al Qaeda by destabilizing the region and providing safe havens from which terrorists could operate. Six months later, still before Bush green-lighted Operation Iraqi Freedom, the NIC produced two additional reports: "Principal Challenges in Post-Saddam Iraq" and "Regional Consequences of Regime Change in Iraq." Together they estimated that a U.S. invasion would generate profound ethnic and religious factions within Iraq that would likely collide violently. A "surge of political Islam and increased funding for terrorist groups" throughout the Muslim world would probably result, was the quote that appeared in the *Washington Post*.[34]

By the time the *Post* and other sources disclosed these intelligence reports to the public in 2007, the failure to locate WMDs in Iraq had already gravely damaged the CIA's reputation. That the agency had forecast the eruption of the sectarian violence that was producing so many casualties among both the Iraqis and Americans was at this point of little importance—on the home front or the battlefield. The agency's image, and some argue its capability to assist the war fighters as well, was further undermined by revelations about the CIA's use of extraordinary renditions (kidnapping suspected terrorists and spiriting them off to countries known for sanctioning torture) and enhanced interrogation techniques, which agency personnel employed. These techniques included waterboarding, which involved tying the prisoner down at a slight incline, covering his nose and mouth with a cloth, and pouring water over his face to simulate drowning. The press and human rights groups publicized waterboarding as the CIA's preferred means of torture. But waterboarding was but one of a list of interrogation methods sanctioned by a team of psychologists under contract to the agency.[35]

Whether these techniques constitute "torture" remains fiercely debated. What impact the ban had on U.S. intelligence gathering is debated no less. By 2005, the year Congress prohibited the "cruel, inhuman, and degrading treatment" of any prisoner held by the United States, growing numbers of Americans in and out of Washington were reaching the point where for them the IC's failure in collection and reporting prior to the invasion was almost beside the point.[36] The Iraq War was claiming more and more victims with no end in sight, terrorist networks, many of which were claiming to be affiliated with al Qaeda, were increasing, and bin Laden himself appeared to be all but mocking U.S. efforts to find him. Rather than benefiting the conduct of the war, CIA behavior was contributing to the dramatic shift in U.S. public opinion against the war. Polls showed that by 2006 a majority of Americans thought it a mistake and wanted it over, regardless of the outcome.[37]

But the combination of the U.S. military surge in 2007, the shift to a revised counterinsurgency doctrine that accompanied General David Petraeus's assuming command of U.S. (and multinational) forces that year, war weariness on the part of the Iraqis, and the emergence of an indigenous opposition to al Qaeda in Iraq signaled a change in America's fortunes. The next year Barack Obama, who had been an early opponent of what he judged a "war of choice" and a vocal advocate of a U.S. withdrawal, announced his candidacy for president. In November 2008 Americans elected him.

The U.S. Intelligence Community underwent its most radical transformation since the CIA's establishment in 1947 even before Obama's election. At the end of 2004 President Bush signed into law the Intelligence Reform and Terrorism Prevention Act (IRTPA). Chief among IRTPA's provisions was the establishment of a new official, the director of national intelligence, who would oversee the CIA as well as the fifteen other official elements of the IC. For the CIA especially, this "demotion" added insult to the injury it had suffered from the debacle over the NIE on Iraq's WMD program (and to a lesser extent the charge that by not "connecting the dots" it had failed to prevent the 9/11 tragedy). Indeed, in large part the intelligence reform legislation resulted directly from the Senate investigation of the prewar intelligence on Iraq, which placed paramount responsibility on the CIA, not the administration, for the ill-advised invasion of Iraq. Put another way, there is a direct connection between the CIA's indictment for all but causing the Iraq War and the legislation that cost the director of the CIA the title of chief of American intelligence.[38]

The resurgence of the war in Afghanistan transformed the CIA in ways that may prove as dramatic as that of the IC as a whole. Only a month into his first year as president, President Obama, to the surprise of no one, announced that he intended to wind down the War in Iraq by withdrawing U.S. combat troops by August 2010 and America's remaining forces by the end of the next year. In December 2009, however, to the surprise of many, Obama announced he would deploy an additional thirty thousand troops to Afghanistan, a surge comparable to Bush's in Iraq in 2007. From his perspective, Bush's decision to divert U.S. attention and resources to Iraq had allowed the Taliban to regain the initiative in Afghanistan. Thus he was risking thirty thousand more American lives to wage "a war of necessity." "I am convinced that our security is at stake in Afghanistan and Pakistan," Obama spoke to the nation from the U.S. Military Academy at West Point on December 1. "This is the epicenter of violent extremism practiced by al Qaeda."[39]

For more than six years the U.S. Intelligence Community had been producing assessments that warned the White House about deteriorating conditions in Afghanistan, which U.S. forces there came to call the "Lumpy Suck" because its mountainous terrain was so conducive to never-ending guerrilla warfare. The warnings began prior to the decision to invade Iraq and continued unabated. Not that the IC's intelligence had gotten dramatically better since the 1970s. Reporting on the escalation of insurgent attacks, the Afghan government's loss of control over large swaths of territory, and the increase in crime and narcotics trafficking was easy. So, too, was assessing the feebleness of the corruption-plagued army, police force, and even more important, regime of Hamid Karzai. But neither the CIA nor DIA, which are responsible for collecting HUMINT, and certainly not the National Security Agency or National Geo-Spatial Agency, which collect and process SIGINT and IMINT, could provide quality information about the nature of the enemy. The key questions—who were Taliban, who were al Qaeda, and to what extent were they allied—were left unanswered. Notwithstanding the 2004 intelligence reform legislation, the "disjointed and dysfunctional" relationships among the more than twenty intelligence organizations that competed for both authority and collection systems in Afghanistan produced more paralysis than insight.[40]

Exacerbating this situation was the relationship between Afghanistan and Pakistan. U.S. intelligence long suspected Pakistan, including its ISI, of sympathizing with and possibly abetting Afghanistan's Taliban. The reason was that Pakistan's priorities differed from America's. It was primarily concerned with India, which it identified as its greatest enemy, and the allegiance of its own Pashtun population. In addition, Pakistan had its own "Taliban." While independent of the Taliban in Afghanistan and much more focused on its opposition to the government in Islamabad, it shared a strict interpretation of Islam. Finally, many Pakistanis were convinced that sooner or later, the Americans would leave and the Afghan Taliban would win.[41]

Until its last days in office, the Bush administration paid insufficient heed to warnings about Afghanistan. It did not challenge the reporting. Rather, preoccupied with Iraq, where American forces were committed in numbers that precluded their deployment to Afghanistan, its options in Afghanistan were too limited to take aggressive countermeasures. At least it could not do so publicly and in a way that required substantial military forces. Yet incrementally and covertly, the administration did begin to employ a tactic that it estimated could slow the momentum of if not defeat the Taliban in Afghanistan, continue to cripple al Qaeda, and not seriously risk further eroding U.S. military capabilities or provoke a domestic reaction. By the end of the Bush presidency the United States was using unmanned aerial vehicles, drones, to provide much better support to military operations by meeting field commanders' intelligence, surveillance, and reconnaissance requirements.[42] Beginning in the administration's last year it began to use these same instruments to decapitate the leadership of al Qaeda and both Talibans. For this purpose it would rely on the CIA.[43]

So even as the CIA remained a scapegoat for the ill-fated war in Iraq, and its prominent place in the IC fell with the enactment of the IRTPA, it became the linchpin in the war in Afghanistan—and its concomitant in Pakistan. The drones' purpose when U.S. forces first arrived in Afghanistan in 2001 was to provide aerial reconnaissance to support combat operations. They were soon reconfigured to carry missiles and other munitions, however, and their first use for "targeted killing" came in early 2002 in Paktia province in Afghanistan. But the presumed target, Osama bin Laden, was a case of mistaken identity.[44]

Initially the armed drone campaign was limited to Iraq and Afghanistan and basically represented an extension of the conventional warfare in those theaters. In 2008, however, with al Qaeda and its surrogates entrenched in the lawless mountain area that overlaps the porous border between Afghanistan and Pakistan, CIA director Michael Hayden, as reported by New York Times veteran reporters Eric Schmitt and Thom Shanker, requested authorization from the lame duck Bush administration to escalate the drone campaign with or without Pakistan's concurrence. It agreed, and the successor Obama administration expanded the campaign still. Since 2008 the United States has launched more than a thousand drone strikes on Afghanistan and hundreds more against Pakistan. Moreover, the "disposition matrix," popularly known as the "kill list," has expanded to include targets in Yemen, Somalia, and elsewhere. Because these are countries with which the United States was not at war, America could not officially acknowledge its use of lethal force. Under American statute, such covert killings must come under the authority of the CIA. As a consequence, to quote Schmitt and Shanker, the drone campaign resulted in the director of the Central Intelligence Agency becoming "America's combatant commander in the hottest covert war in the global campaign against terror."[45]

That covert war escalated rapidly. In Pakistan the Bush administration authorized 45 strikes between 2004 and 2008. Obama authorized his first two strikes the third day he was in office, and from 2009 through 2012 he authorized 255 more. To use another example, Bush authorized a single strike in Yemen. Obama approved 38 in his first term. These strikes, managed by CIA personnel out of harm's way, have occurred against the backdrop of the end of combat operations in Iraq and the impending end of combat operations in Afghanistan. They have provoked intense controversy, especially because among those killed by drones have been American citizens. Nevertheless, the "body count," even if the identities are only occasionally disclosed and have unquestionably included civilians, has allowed President Obama to claim progress in the global war on terror even as he takes credit for bringing America's forces home and reducing the number of American casualties. The CIA's contribution to degrading the capabilities of al Qaeda and to a lesser extent the Taliban, especially when coupled with its role in the successful 2011 raid on bin Laden's compound that finally killed al Qaeda's leader, has resurrected its stature. But its achievements in drone warfare and other paramilitary operations have come at the cost of its core mission: the collection and analysis of intelligence.[46]

Obama's selection in 2011 of David Petraeus as CIA director epitomizes the agency's increasing militarization. By 2011 Petraeus was arguably the most celebrated U.S. military commander since the Vietnam War. He had orchestrated the redesigned counterinsurgency doctrine, and consequently was identified with turning the tide in the Iraq War. Subsequently, Obama turned to Petraeus to take command of the U.S. and international forces fighting in Afghanistan from the cashiered General Stanley McChrystal. That he was unable to turn the tide in that war as well did not tarnish his reputation for leadership and brilliance.

While Petraeus directed the CIA, producing intelligence estimates was a secondary concern in the IC. It came no closer to answering questions about how many—if any—al Qaeda remained in Afghanistan or across the border in Pakistan, about the ties between al Qaeda and the Taliban, or about the relationship between the Taliban and Pakistani government. But the drone campaign continued to expand dramatically, and the press coverage of it expanded commensurately. The *Washington Post* quoted a former intelligence official remarking that at the time of Petraeus's appointment the CIA was "chugging along." His leadership "turned it into one hell of a killing machine."[47]

In the waning days of the 2012 presidential election the press reported that Petraeus asked to expand the CIA's drone force. But before the administration could reach a decision, Petraeus, caught up in a scandal over an extramarital affair, abruptly resigned. Obama selected John Brennan to succeed him. Brennan was a longtime veteran CIA official whom the newly elected president brought with him to the West Wing in 2009 to manage the drone campaign as his special advisor on homeland security and counterterrorism. Under his management the campaign was successful—if the number of killed Taliban and terrorist leaders is the barometer. Still, Brennan agreed with many senior CIA officials and retired veterans that the militarization of the CIA was corroding the analytic capabilities of the agency to the extent that it was impairing its contribution to both the war in Afghanistan and America's global posture. Brennan advised the administration to leave "lethal action to its more traditional home in the military, where the law requires greater transparency." The CIA and IC could then focus on collection and analysis.[48]

Although he may slow down the pace of the drawdown of American troops in Afghanistan to increase the likelihood that the progress he credits to his administration "sticks," President Obama remains committed to reducing the size of U.S. forces there dramatically by the end of 2015, with the goal of all but eliminating their presence by the end of 2016.[49] While in concert with U.S. Special Operations Forces the CIA, writes the *New York Times'* Michael Schmidt, has escalated the number of commando raids that often yield valuable intelligence, the agency is drawing down its personnel in Afghanistan as well. According to press reports, the Kabul station will nevertheless remain the largest anywhere, and having trained and funded the Afghan intelligence service, the CIA will continue to "keep tabs" on it.[50]

The drone campaign will march on, but to what extent and under what authority remain in question. The *New York Times* headline story on May 23, 2013, reported that Obama intended gradually to transfer control of the drone attacks to the Pentagon. A bit more than two months later another *Times* story quoted Secretary of State John Kerry claiming that the administration had a timeline to end the drone campaign in Pakistan "very, very soon." Yet Kerry's State Department quickly issued a statement clarifying that although ending the drone strikes was an aspiration, there was no set timetable.[51]

The dustup reflects the tension within the administration between building a better relationship with Afghan President Ashraf Ghani than it had with his predecessor, Hamid Karzai, seeking to improve relations with Prime Minister Nawaz Sharif's Pakistani government, and not surrendering what it still considers its most valuable weapon in the Afghanistan War. The conflict in Afghanistan is sure to persist after the last U.S. troop has been withdrawn, whatever that date. The danger of battle-hardened insurgents—and the Islamist State is only the current exemplar—gaining access to Pakistan's nuclear arsenal will be no less severe. Consequently, even as violence in Iraq is once again escalating, the United States is certain to remain engaged in Afghanistan. But its effort will be even more dependent on intelligence. The history of intelligence's contributions to both the Iraq and Afghanistan Wars suggests that for that effort to be effective, the IC's priorities will need to be reversed: collection and analysis must take priority over operations. Given the CIA's militarization, however, that reversal will require a cultural revolution.[52]

NOTES

1 Quoted in Paul R. Pillar, *Intelligence and U.S. Foreign Policy: Iraq, 9/11, and Misguided Reform* (New York: Columbia University Press, 2011), 9.

2 Thomas Fingar, *Reducing Uncertainty: Intelligence Analysis and National Security* (Stanford, CA: Stanford University Press, 2011), 25; Jennifer E. Sims, "Decision Advantage and the Nature of Intelligence Analysis," in *The Oxford Handbook of National Security Intelligence*, ed. Loch Johnson (New York: Oxford University Press, 2010), 389–403.

3 Currently some sixteen elements, such as the CIA, Defense Intelligence Agency, National Security Agency, Federal Bureau of Investigation, and Bureau of Intelligence and Research, compose America's Intelligence Community.

4 Bruce Riedel, *What We Won: America's Secret War in Afghanistan, 1979–89* (Washington, DC: Brookings Institution, 2014), x.

5 Steve Coll, *Ghost Wars: The Secret History of the CIA, Afghanistan, and Bin Laden, from the Soviet Invasion to September 10, 2001* (New York: Penguin, 2004).

6 Richard L. Russell, "CIA's Strategic Intelligence in Iraq," *Political Science Quarterly* 117 (Summer 2002): 194–204.

7 U.S. House of Representatives Committee on Armed Services, Report of the Oversight and Investigations Subcommittee, "Intelligence Successes and Failures during Operations Desert Shield/Storm," 103rd Cong., 1st Sess. (Washington, DC: Government Printing Office, 1993), 23–24.

8 Russell, "CIA's Strategic Intelligence in Iraq," 201.

9 House Report, "Intelligence Successes and Failures," 23–24.

10 Ronald Kessler, *The CIA at War: Inside the Secret Campaign Against Terror* (New York: St. Martin's, 2003), 21–28.

11 "U.S. Policy on Counterterrorism" (PDD-39, June 21, 1995), http://www.fas.org/irp/offdocs/pdd/pdd-39.pdf.

12 Coll, *Ghost Wars*, 405–11.

13 Anonymous [Michael Scheuer], *Imperial Hubris: Why the West Is Losing the War on Terrorism* (Washington, DC: Brassey's, 2004).

14 James Bamford, *A Pretext for War: 9/11, Iraq, and the Abuse of America's Intelligence Agencies* (New York: Doubleday, 2004), 188–221.

15 Quoted in Richard A. Clarke, *Against All Enemies: Inside America's War on Terror* (New York: Free Press, 2004), 231–32.

16 Peter Bergen, *The Longest War: The Enduring Conflict between America and al-Qaeda* (New York: Free Press, 2011), 48; Terry McDermott, *The Hunt for KSM: Inside the Pursuit and Takedown of the Real 9/11 Mastermind, Khalid Sheikh Mohammed* (New York: Little, Brown, 2012), 152.

17 Bergen, *Longest War*, 53–67.

18 Bob Woodward, *Bush at War* (New York: Simon & Schuster, 2002), 50–62, 317.

19 John A. Bonin, *U.S. Army Forces Central Command in Afghanistan and the Arabia Gulf during Operation Enduring Freedom: 11 September 2001–March 2003* (Carlisle, PA: Army Heritage Center Foundation, 2003); Robert L. Grenier, *88 Days to Kandahar: A CIA Diary* (New York: Simon & Schuster, 2015).

20 Bob Woodward, *Plan of Attack: The Definitive Account of the Decision to Invade Iraq* (New York: Simon & Schuster, 2004), 4–6, 12.

21 Henry A. Crumpton, *The Art of Intelligence: Lessons from a Life in the CIA's Clandestine Service* (New York: Penguin, 2012), 257–61.

22 George Tenet, *At the Center of the Storm: My Years at the CIA* (New York: HarperCollins, 2007), 341–58.

23 Bergen, *Longest War*, 138–40.

24 John B. Judis and Spencer Ackerman, "The Selling of the Iraq War, The First Casualty," *New York Review of Books* 50 (June 30, 2003), http://www.tnr.com/article/the-first-casualty; Thomas Powers, "The Vanishing Case for War," *New York Review of Books* 50 (December 4, 2003), http://www.nybooks.com/articles/archives/2003/dec/04/the-vanishing-case-for-war/?pagination=false.

25 Woodward, *Plan of Attack*, 107–9; text of President George W. Bush's State of the Union Address, January 29, 2002, http://www.washingtonpost.com/wp-srv/onpolitics/transcripts/sou012902.htm.

26 Fingar, *Reducing Uncertainty*, 89–108; Robert Jervis, *Why Intelligence Fails: Lessons from the Iranian Revolution and the Iraq War* (Ithaca, NY: Cornell University Press, 2010), 123–55; Bob Drogan: *Curveball: Spies, Lies, and the Con Man Who Caused a War* (New York: Random House, 2007).

27 Intelligence Assessment, "Misreading Intentions: Iraq's Reaction to Inspections Created Picture of Deception" (January 5, 2006), http://www.gwu.edu/~nsarchiv/news/20120905/CIA-Iraq.pdf; "Iraq's Continuing Programs for Weapons of Mass Destruction" (Key Judgments from NIE, 2012), http://www.fas.org/irp/cia/product/iraq-wmd.html; David Barstow, William J. Broad, and Jeff Gerth, "How the White House Embraced Disputed Arms Intelligence," *New York Times*, October 3, 2004.

28 Pillar, *Intelligence and U.S. Foreign Policy*, 13–42; "Iraq's Continuing Programs"; "Iraq's Weapons of Mass Destruction Programs" (White paper, October 2002), https://www.cia.gov/library/reports/general-reports-1/iraq_wmd/Iraq_Oct_2002; National Intelligence Estimate, "Iraq's Continuing Programs for Weapons of Mass Destruction" (sanitized; October 30, 2002), http://www.fas.org/irp/cia/product/iraq-wmd-nie.pdf.

29 Intelligence Assessment, "Misreading Intentions."

30 Tyler Drumheller, *On the Brink: An Insider's Account of How the White House Compromised American Intelligence* (New York: Carroll & Graf, 2006), 43–44. For the contrasting argument, see Joshua Rovner, *Fixing the Facts: National Security and the Politics of Intelligence* (Ithaca, NY: Cornell University Press, 2011), 137–84.

31 President George W. Bush, State of the Union Address, January 28, 2003, http://georgewbush-whitehouse.archives.gov/news/releases/2003/01/20030128-19.html; Joseph C. Wilson, IV, "What I Didn't Find in Africa," *New York Times*, July 6, 2003; "Iraq's Weapons of Mass Destruction: The Assessment of the British Government" (September 2002), http://www.gwu.edu/~nsarchiv/NSAEBB/NSAEBB254/doc05.pdf.

32 Secretary Colin L. Powell, remarks to the United Nations Security Council, February 5, 2003, http://www.washingtonpost.com/wp-srv/nation/transcripts/powell-text_020503.html.

33 Quoted in Walter LaFeber, "The Rise and Fall of Colin Powell and the Powell Doctrine," *Political Science Quarterly* 124 (Spring 2009): 89.

34 Walter Pincus, "Before War, CIA Warned of Negative Outcomes," *Washington Post*, June 3, 2007; Walter Pincus and Karen DeYoung, "Analysts' Warnings of Iraq Chaos Detailed," *Washington Post*, May 26, 2007.

35 Jane Mayer, *The Dark Side: The Inside Story of How the War on Terror Turned into a War on American Ideals* (New York: Doubleday, 2009), 139–81; Mark Dan-

ner, "US Torture: Voices from the Black Sites," *New York Review of Books* 56 (April 9, 2009), http://www.markdanner.com/articles/show/151; U.S. Senate, Select Committee on Intelligence, "Committee Study of the Central Intelligence Agency's Detention and Interrogation Program" (Declassification Revisions, Executive Summary, December 3, 2014), http://www.intelligence.senate.gov/study2014/executive-summary.pdf.

36 Mark Mazzetti, *The Way of the Knife: The CIA, A Secret Army, and a War at the Ends of the Earth* (New York: Penguin, 2013), 126.

37 Carl Hulse and Majorie Connelly, "Poll Shows a Shift in Opinion on Iraq War," *New York Times*, August 24, 2006.

38 U.S. Senate, Select Committee on Intelligence, 108th Congress, "Report on the U.S. Intelligence Community's Prewar Intelligence Assessments on Iraq" (ordered reported July 7, 2004), http://web.mit.edu/simsong/www/iraqreport2-textunder.pdf; *The 9/11 Commission Report: The Final Report of the National Commission on Terrorist Attacks upon the United States* (New York: Norton, 2004).

39 "Obama's Address on the War in Afghanistan, December 1, 2009," *New York Times*, December 2, 2009, http://www.nytimes.com/2009/12/02/world/asia/02prexy.text.html?ref=asia.

40 Matthew M. Aid, *Intel Wars: The Secret History of the Fight Against Terror* (New York: Bloomsbury Press, 2012), 10–38, 65–67.

41 Carlotta Gall, *The Wrong Enemy: America in Afghanistan, 2001–2014* (Boston: Houghton Mifflin Harcourt, 2014).

42 Robert M. Gates, *Duty: Memoirs of a Secretary at War* (New York: Knopf, 2014), 126–28.

43 Mark Mazzetti, "C.I.A. Takes on Bigger and Riskier Role on Front Lines," *New York Times*, January 1, 2010.

44 John Sifton, "A Brief History of Drones," *Nation*, February 27, 2012, http://www.thenation.com/article/166124/brief-history-drones#.

45 Eric Schmitt and Thom Shanker, *Counterstrike: The Untold Story of America's Secret Campaign Against Al Qaeda* (New York: Times Books, 2011), 99–103; Sarah Krebs and Michael Zenko, "The Next Drone Wars: Preparing for Proliferation," *Foreign Affairs* 93 (March–April 2014): 71.

46 Jane Mayer, "The Predator War: What Are the Risks of the CIA's Covert Drone Program?," *New Yorker*, October 26, 2009, http://www.newyorker.com/reporting/2009/10/26/091026fa_fact_mayer; Lloyd C. Gardner, *Killing Machine: The American Presidency in the Age of Drone Warfare* (New York: New Press, 2013); David Ignatius, "Leon Panetta Gets the CIA Back on Its Feet," *Washington Post*, April 25, 2010.

47 Greg Miller and Julie Tate, "CIA Shifts Focus to Killing Targets," *Washington Post*, September 1, 2011.

48 Karen DeYoung, "A CIA Veteran Transforms U.S. Counterterrorism Policy," *Washington Post*, October 24, 2012.

49 Michael S. Schmidt, "U.S. Open to Slowing Troop Pullout from Afghanistan," *New York Times*, February 22, 2015.

50 Matthew Rosenberg and Eric Schmitt, "U.S. Is Escalating a Secretive War in Afghanistan," *New York Times*, February 13, 2015; Greg Miller, "CIA Closing Bases in Afghanistan as It Shifts Focus amid Military Drawdown," *Washington Post*, July 23, 2013.

51 Charlie Savage and Peter Baker, "Obama Plans Shift on Drone Strikes and Guantánamo," *New York Times*, May 23, 2013; Mark Mazzetti and Mark Landler, "Despite Administration Promises, Few Signs of Change in Drone War," *New York Times*, August 3, 2013.

52 Richard H. Immerman, *The Hidden Hand: A Brief History of the CIA* (Malden, MA: Wiley-Blackwell, 2014), 225–28.

4

Assessing Strategic Choices in the War on Terror

STEPHEN BIDDLE AND PETER D. FEAVER

At the end of the day, this was still a 55–45 situation.
—President Barack Obama, 2011

Two successive U.S. administrations have waged the so-called war on terror. The "war" has consisted of a series of key strategic decisions, each with its own set of intended and unintended consequences. While the ultimate outcome of many decisions remains uncertain even as the United States draws down its forces, enough is known to allow for provisional judgments.

The conventional wisdom treats U.S. strategic choices in the war on terror as a series of ninety–ten decisions: decisions obviously right, or obviously wrong, where the judgment of wisdom or folly is vindicated by ensuing events. In contrast, we argue that the war was a series of fifty-five–forty-five decisions—some calls perhaps even closer than that—where the arguments for and against most choices were more evenly balanced than a superficial estimate of the outcome might suggest.

We base this conclusion on a series of counterfactuals that consider the likely consequences of the options rejected by decision makers at the time. To see the war as a series of ninety–ten calls is to imply that different choices would have led to radically better (or worse) outcomes. Logically, any such judgment rests on implicit counterfactuals. Yet these counterfactuals are rarely assessed in any depth. Instead, the debate typically examines the actual consequences of the choices made in great detail, with critics emphasizing costs actually incurred and supporters highlighting benefits actually realized. Neither approach is logically sufficient. We thus consider the counterfactuals directly. Our purpose is to judge whether we like the world of today better or worse than the world that probably would have obtained by 2015 had decision makers chosen differently in the early stages of the war on terror.

Perhaps unexpectedly, the outcomes we trace from most counterfactual scenarios look surprisingly close to today's world. We argue that for the most part different choices would have produced neither a radically better nor a radically worse 2015 outcome. Simply put, a large variety of potential choices would lead to similar long-term results, even if they got there via different routes.[1] Hence we see these choices as close calls: all involved options that posed risks and dangers and all were likely to incur major costs; none offered low-cost, low-risk means to a safe future.

We intend to neither defend nor criticize decision makers, in either the Bush or Obama administrations. We make no effort to assess officials' motives or intentions or veracity. We have our own views on the relative wisdom or folly of certain players, and the two of us disagree on certain key questions. But what distinguishes our approach from other assessments is that we exploit knowledge available to us now but not to officials then to carefully examine the likely consequences of alternatives not taken.

Of course we recognize the inherent uncertainty in counterfactual analysis. We know what did happen, but cannot prove what might have happened if other choices had been made. War is subject to chance and happenstance; complex chains of events pose multiple opportunities for error or unanticipated outcomes. The reality we have today is partly shaped by the lingering impact of decisions made a decade ago and partly by more recent decisions. In this chapter, we focus on several of the earliest decisions after the 9/11 attacks and conclude that they cannot be blamed or credited with as much blame or credit as partisans would like. But it is also the case that our assessment of the conditions today depend on further counterfactual judgments about more recent policy decisions—analysis that is beyond the scope of this chapter. Our confidence in our findings is therefore inherently limited. But these limits affect all analyses that assess choices by their results. All studies of cause and effect rest implicitly on counterfactual claims. The chief difference between our analysis and most others in today's debate is that we make explicit a logic chain that is no less critical to others' findings, even if unstated, than it is to ours. By making that logic explicit, we hope to illuminate the problem in ways that make the limitations and uncertainties in any such findings clearer.

We also recognize the impossibility of analyzing every alternative policy in the logical universe. For each major choice, we identify and analyze two primary counterfactual alternatives, which we argue are representative of the best options that were available to policy makers. We can think of countless others, but we believe none had a significantly greater likelihood of changing our fundamental conclusion.

We begin by describing in general terms the consensus grand strategy driving American foreign policy since the end of the Cold War that the 9/11 attacks seemed to challenge. We next evaluate two early grand-strategic choices made shortly after 9/11 as an initial means to demonstrate the utility of our approach: the decision to elevate the terrorism threat to first rank, and the decision to invade Afghanistan. We conclude with a discussion of the implications of this approach for the menu of strategic choice confronting U.S. strategists today and in the future.

Post–Cold War Grand Strategy

The 9/11 attacks were the most consequential global event since the collapse of the Soviet Union and called into question the grand strategy that had guided U.S. policy since the end of the Cold War. Grand strategy is "an academic term referring to the plans and policies undertaken in order to balance national ends and means at the broadest national level."[2] There is a lively debate among experts as to whether grand strategy really exists, or whether leaders normally make policy through a series of ad hoc decisions and then subsequently craft a strategic logic when writing their memoirs.[3]

Even scholars who would credit the United States with having followed a (largely successful) grand strategy called containment during the Cold War argue that no similarly coherent grand strategy emerged to take its place in the post–Cold War era.[4] President Clinton would appear to agree; he famously said, "strategic coherence . . . was largely imposed after the fact by scholars, memoirists and the 'chattering classes.'"[5] We argue, however, that while post–Cold War U.S. national security policy may not have had a popular label as widely known as "containment," for the past twenty years the United States has followed at least as coherent and bipartisan a grand strategy as it did during the Cold War.

The prime aim of American grand strategy over the past twenty years has been to avoid another Cold War, that is, to avert the rise of a hostile rival that could match the United States on key power dimensions and thus pose challenges to U.S. security interests across the globe. The grand strategy that policy makers pursued to meet this goal consisted of four main pillars. Pillar I involved dissuading the rise of a hostile rival by use of a "velvet-covered iron fist." The iron fist meant maintaining defense spending in excess of what was needed to meet near-term threat, thus staying far ahead of would-be rivals. The velvet glove meant giving would-be rivals stakes in global order in excess of their real power. Thus, U.S. policy makers sought to resolve the core areas of dispute with the European Union and Japan and give Russia an equity stake through concessions and enticements such as a seat at the G8, the forum composed of the world's leading economic powers. The velvet glove is most readily seen in the "responsible stakeholder" approach to China. While both candidate Bill Clinton and candidate George W. Bush campaigned on promises of getting tough with China, each, once elected, quickly adopted a more conciliatory posture.[6]

Pillar II of the grand strategy involved making the world more like America politically by promoting the spread of democracy. Of course, promoting U.S. values has been a hallmark of its strategy (at the very least, of rhetorical strategy) from the earliest days of the Republic. But with the end of the Cold War, abetting a new wave of democratization became a more explicit and higher-priority foreign policy goal.[7] Policy makers believed that the spread of democracies would further improve global security because, according to democratic peace theory, mature democracies resolve disputes peacefully rather than go to war.

Pillar III of the grand strategy was the economic counterpart to pillar II. Its goal was to make the world more like America economically by promoting globalization, market capitalism, and free trade.[8] Policy makers believed pillars II and III were mutually reinforcing. Market democracies—states that embraced both a liberal political order and a liberal economic order—would be the most stable; political progress would lead to greater economic prosperity; and economic prosperity would lock in democratization. Together, these two pillars would secure a global status quo that left the United States as the sole superpower.

The fourth pillar of the post–Cold War grand strategy involved identifying and confronting the gravest near-term threat: the spread of weapons of mass destruction (WMDs) to rogue states. Strategists recognized that rogue states with WMDs did not pose as great a threat as the Soviet Union once did, but they were the most lethal threat to the existing global order. Clinton's CIA Director James Woolsey explained, "It's as if we were fighting with a dragon for some 45 years and slew the dragon and then found ourselves in a jungle full of a number of poisonous snakes."[9]

The Clinton administration did show some inclination to add a fifth pillar, elevating the problem of "failed states" and the solution of "assertive multilateralism" to the top rank of grand-strategy emphasis, but the ambiguous U.S. experiences in Somalia, Haiti, Rwanda, Bosnia, Sudan, and Kosovo meant that this pillar had less bipartisan support.[10]

While we know of no single document that lays out the post–Cold War grand strategy explicitly in these terms, we would argue that this outline is readily discernible in the primary strategy documents that successive administrations did develop.[11] President Clinton made pillar II (democratic goals) and pillar III (economic goals) explicit in his National Security Strategy, released in July 1994; indeed, the Clinton administration labeled it "A Strategy of Enlargement and Engagement," seeking a deliberate echo of Cold War containment policy. Candidate Bush campaigned against the Clinton emphasis on failed states and promised other shifts in tone (including a more "humble" foreign policy), but the essence of what he advocated essentially involved a reorientation back to the four main pillars.[12] There was, then, remarkable bipartisan continuity and support at the level of post–Cold War grand strategy.

The Decision to Elevate the Terrorism Threat to the First Rank

The events of 9/11 generated major change in U.S. grand strategy almost immediately. The most basic of these changes was to define terrorism as a priority coequal, to if not more urgent than, the existing four pillars. Before 9/11, terrorism was a minor consideration in U.S. grand strategy. There were dissenters who believed that terrorism was underemphasized and merited greater attention. But at no point had the terrorist threat competed with the four pillars of existing U.S. grand strategy for effort or resources. After 9/11, however, terrorism rose almost immediately to the first rank of national security threats.

But while policy makers elevated terrorism, they did not downgrade the other four pillars. Terrorism became a fifth pillar. As such, it was grafted onto the existing strategy rather than replacing it.

This was hardly the only possibility. One alternative option would have been to leave terrorism in its prior status as a lesser challenge—retaining the four existing pillars, and continuing to treat counterterrorism as a subordinate threat. Another option not taken would have been to elevate terrorism but downgrade the others, replacing a four-pillar grand strategy with a one-pillar alternative of defeating terrorism.

Either alternative had precedents. Great Britain, for example, had faced a major terrorism threat stemming from Northern Ireland. Yet it never raised this to a priority equal to its NATO commitment against the Soviet Union.[13] Conversely, the United States in the Civil War, World War I, and World War II made the immediate war itself the nearly exclusive focus of American strategy, setting other concerns aside for the duration. Even in the long Cold War, the primary U.S. competition with the Soviet Union took precedence over other security challenges, which got short shrift in budgets, military force design, and diplomacy.[14] After 9/11, by contrast, the terrorism threat received massive effort, but without significantly diverting resources from the existing four pillars. The more than one trillion dollars spent, according to Congressional Research Service estimates, on the war on terror was accompanied by more than another one trillion on other defense spending.[15] The Navy and Air Force, for example, although playing only secondary roles in Afghanistan,

Iraq, and counterterror special operations, nevertheless retained almost the entire force structure they had in 2000.

Counterfactual: A Terrorism-Subordinate Policy

Making terrorism a subordinate priority would have involved a radically lower counterterror expenditure after 9/11; avoidance of major military action in Afghanistan, Iraq, or elsewhere; and avoidance of demands to comply to U.S. wishes such as those that the Bush administration made to Afghanistan and Pakistan. Such a policy would have continued existing policies for a "velvet fist" relationship with China (pillar I), incrementalist promotion of democracy abroad (pillar II), support for economic globalization (pillar III), and multilateral nonproliferation efforts (pillar IV). This alternative would permit low-profile, low-cost, and low-risk counterterror action (such as small-scale cruise missile or drone strikes, or occasional Special Operations raids, as the Clinton administration and its predecessors approved). But these actions had to be consistent with leaving counterterrorism in a subordinate status in terms of U.S. grand strategy.

What would the world of 2014 look like if this alternative had been adopted? First, al Qaeda would probably have been much more active after 2001, and probably stronger today. This is partly because bin Laden or others might have seen a U.S. failure to retaliate for 9/11 as a sign of weakness and therefore undertook further aggression and expanded recruitment. We disagree on the importance of this effect (Feaver sees it as central, Biddle as secondary). We agree, however, that al Qaeda would have had strategic incentives to escalate if the United States had downplayed 9/11 in this fashion. Terrorists seek to goad states into reacting in order either to exhaust state opponents through their own exertions or to win converts by provoking increased state oppression. When states react to terror attacks with massive force, they advance either goal. If bin Laden had failed to provoke this response with 9/11, his logical reaction would have been to escalate until he did. A U.S. policy of "rope-a-dope" could thus be expected to encourage harder punches.

Al Qaeda would also have been better positioned to deliver harder punches than it can do today. Without the invasion of Afghanistan, bin Laden would still enjoy sanctuary under an openly supportive Taliban regime. In 2001 the Taliban refused to renounce al Qaeda or turn over bin Laden even under a credible threat of invasion.[16] If U.S. grand strategy had refrained from such a war-risking ultimatum, the Taliban would surely have continued to offer bin Laden at least the same level of support. Such open support by Afghanistan, a committed state sponsor, would have made al Qaeda's planning and operational control of its far-flung global terror network much easier than it was after bin Laden was driven into hiding in Pakistan. Some would counter that without the Afghan and Iraq Wars as recruiting tools, al Qaeda would today be smaller. However, by 2011 when U.S. combat troops left Iraq, most experts recognized that al Qaeda, despite such recruits, was much weaker than it had been in 2001; that was the judgment even before bin Laden was killed.[17] Terrorists typically use violence as a recruiting and motivational tool; an unopposed surge of violence against distant America could well have offered a recruiting tool useful enough to offset the absence of the effect of the wars in Iraq and Afghanistan.[18]

While al Qaeda would probably have been more aggressive had the United States allowed it sanctuary in Afghanistan, the magnitude of the increase would have been subject to constraints. The lack of nuclear or biological weapons limits the lethality of purely conventional terrorism. More Americans died of peptic ulcers than terrorism even in 2001, the worst year on record for terrorist lethality in the United States.[19] Al Qaeda's pattern has historically been to plan big attacks carefully over long periods; this has produced large death tolls but with long intervals between strikes. It has never shown an ability to repeat spectacular attacks frequently over a long period. Even if al Qaeda could mount a 9/11-scale attack every year, it would still kill far fewer Americans than automobile accidents do. And al Qaeda's ability to escalate its violence would be subject to counterpressure from ongoing U.S. intelligence and counterterror efforts. Such pressure could never destroy al Qaeda, but it would complicate its planning and tend to suppress its lethality to some degree.

On balance, then, al Qaeda would probably have been more lethal than it was from 2001 to 2014 had the United States pursued a grand strategy after 9/11 that subordinated counterterrorism. But the net result would probably have been a pattern of chronic attacks whose costs would still be smaller than many other dangers in modern life. The increased death toll would be real, but probably not cataclysmic, unless al Qaeda gained access to WMDs. Without the invasions of Afghanistan and Iraq, the lives of more than six thousand American service members would not have been lost in those wars, forty-three thousand Americans would not have been seriously wounded, and much larger numbers of Iraqis and Afghans would not have been killed or wounded.

This alternative would likely yield other key differences. The U.S. economy, for example, would have suffered the cost of further terrorist attacks. While nontrivial, these would probably not have been catastrophic. Analyses of the 9/11 attacks themselves now generally conclude that their effects "were too small and too geographically concentrated to make a significant dent in the nation's economic output," as the Congressional Research Service put it.[20] On the other side of the ledger, the economy would have been spared perhaps one trillion dollars in defense spending relating to the war on terror since 2001. The net economic effect would depend on the nation's psychological response to chronic terrorism. Still, unless this effect was mammoth, it would be largely offset by the benefits of reduced defense expenditure.

In international politics, China would perhaps be less empowered today. Many criticize the war on terror as a distraction from a more important task of restraining China. Absent this U.S. distraction after 2001, perhaps China would be less assertive in 2014. Yet most analysts judge Chinese assertiveness as based primarily on long-term trends in relative economic growth. These trends would still favor China even without the war on terror. Perhaps the Chinese would today be more restrained at the margin, but the difference would probably be small.

As for the other main emphases of pre-2001 grand strategy, global trade would probably be no more affected than U.S. domestic economic growth by a counterfactual scenario of chronic but conventional terrorism. For better or worse, the central issue for democratization today is the Arab Spring, a phenomenon with little causal link to the original war on terror; it would probably be largely unaffected by its absence.[21] World opinion of the United States was sharply, and negatively, affected by the invasion of Iraq (and to some extent by U.S. war making against Muslims in Afghanistan). While the concrete consequences of anti-Americanism are hard to trace, these would presumably have been lesser if the United States had made a lower-key response to 9/11.

In this counterfactual, conversely, the preexisting Iraq problem would still be festering. World intelligence services would probably continue to believe that Iraq had WMDs; there would be no inspectors to show otherwise; the further erosion of the UN sanctions regime would have allowed Saddam Hussein to restart his WMD program, as we now know he likely intended to do, and so a possible alliance between Iraq and al Qaeda would continue to concern officials, as it had concerned both Clinton and Bush administration officials for years.[22]

Of course there are many uncertainties. If a continued safe haven in Afghanistan had enabled bin Laden to acquire a nuclear weapon or to master biological warfare on a large scale, then the toll under a terrorism-subordinate policy would have been immensely higher.[23] If public malaise had led to a lack of economic confidence, then the economic cost could have been substantial. Conversely, if more vigorous U.S. diplomacy in the Pacific had changed China's perceptions of its self-interest and spurred a more benign Chinese foreign policy, then the political benefits could have been significant, and world opinion of the United States would presumably be more favorable today. On balance, nevertheless, the likeliest outcome appears to be one of chronic but conventional terrorism against American civilians of a kind that the war on terror has largely averted, offset by the savings in defense expenditures and in lives, both of service members and civilians, in Afghanistan and Iraq.

Counterfactual: Terrorism-Dominant Grand Strategy

Our second alternative retains the historical strategy's emphasis on terrorism, and indeed elevates it, downgrading the other pillars of the existing strategy to subordinate status. For the nonproliferation pillar (IV), this would have had little practical effect; much of the focus of the historical war on terror was denying al Qaeda access to WMDs, as would any grand strategy that focused on the terror. This "terrorism-dominant" counterfactual would have some slight effect on the democratization and economic globalization pillars (II and III), which were not the most expensive pillars, in terms of resource allocation. Furthermore, as the Bush administration argued in the 2006 National Security Strategy that democratization and economic globalization were partly antiterror measures, those policies might have continued at roughly the same level. Thus the main effect of this counterfactual would be on pillar I: the velvet fist strategy to dissuade potential great-power rivals from competing with the United States. In particular, substantial resources would have been diverted from U.S. conventional military capability in order to underwrite the one-trillion expenditure and high ground-force operational tempo needed to sustain the war on terror and especially its campaigns in Afghanistan and Iraq.

The world this counterfactual would create would differ from current conditions in two main respects. First, the United States would have spent much less on defense after 2001. Assuming that the war on terror per se was unchanged, we might expect the same post-2001 defense supplemental budgets but a smaller base budget. For example, if we assume that post-2001 base budgets were held constant at 2001 levels—no actual cuts, but no increases in the nonsupplemental base—then the United States would have spent almost $1.2 trillion less than it actually spent between 2001 and 2011.[24] This probably overestimates the savings: the "base budget" includes, for example, the cost of expanding the Army and Marine Corps to wage the wars in Afghanistan and Iraq, and the military pay increases deemed necessary for wartime recruitment. These expenditures would be needed for the historical war on terror even if pillar I, the "velvet fist," were downgraded, so some increase in the "base" budget would probably have been necessary even without pillar I.

But much of the base budget's growth is because the United States chose to maintain a preeminent conventional military even while creating a counterinsurgency force for Afghanistan and Iraq.[25] At a minimum, this counterfactual would imply a decrease of hundreds of billions of dollars of defense expenditure between 2001 and 2014, with substantial future additional savings through the transition of the Afghan War to Afghan government control.

Savings on this scale might have improved national economic performance and cushioned the severity of the post-2008 financial crisis. They would also have reduced the scale of austerity measures needed to address the federal deficit in the aftermath of the crisis. In 2001, the Congressional Budget Office projected a cumulative federal budget surplus of $2.3 trillion by 2011, whereas the United States that year actually faced a cumulative debt of $10.4 trillion. The Pew Center estimates that perhaps 15 percent of the difference is attributable to post-2001 defense spending increases, of which they allocate one-third to purposes other than Afghanistan and Iraq.[26] While the defense budget is thus only part of the problem, it is a notable part. The Bush administration decision to add the war on terror to a preexisting strategy rather than to replace that strategy played an important role in raising the national debt.

Offsetting these economic advantages would be several disadvantages. Strategists designed the "velvet fist" to encourage a more benign Chinese foreign policy; deliberate disinvestment in the pillar's military underpinning could be expected to promote the opposite. Moreover, a shift away from concerns with great-power balancing would make sense only during wartime. The war on terror is already a very long war, but presumably it will eventually end. When it does, the challenge of great-power competition will reemerge. If the United States were to take a decade-long conventional-procurement holiday and restructure its military systematically for counterinsurgency in the interim, the result could be a serious loss of relative standing by the time the nation tried to pivot from counterinsurgency back to concerns with balancing China. The cost of rebuilding the American military at that point would be much larger, somewhat mitigating the economic savings of this counterfactual from 2001 to 2011.

On balance, this counterfactual implies a trade-off between economic benefits in the near term and excess costs in defense transformation thereafter, plus an expectation of more assertive Chinese behavior in the interim.

The Decision to Invade Afghanistan

After deciding to wage a war on terror, the Bush administration faced a number of critical decisions on strategy. Among the earliest of these involved Afghanistan. The Bush administration's choice was to act quickly against the

Taliban regime. Airstrikes began on October 7, 2001, and soon thereafter several Special Operations Forces (SOF) teams were inserted on the ground to act as spotters for the air attacks and to cooperate with allied Afghan forces of, first, the Northern Alliance and, later, the Southern Alliance in their civil war against the Taliban. The result was a surprisingly rapid overthrow of the Taliban with very few U.S. casualties and al Qaeda's loss of state sanctuary and its subsequent flight into Pakistan. Later, however, a stubborn Taliban insurgency revived, killing over fifteen hundred American troops and many thousands of Afghans, and might yet topple the Afghan government.

While Afghanistan is sometimes treated as a "war of necessity," in fact invading Afghanistan the way the United States did was a choice—and not the only possible choice open to the Bush administration in 2001. The two basic alternatives were to do less, especially by opting for limited counterterrorism airstrikes or SOF raids rather than invasion, or to do more, especially with larger conventional forces. The United States could, for example, have declined to invade, leaving the Taliban in power, and instead targeted al Qaeda from the air to suppress its ability to plan terror attacks and weaken its leadership. (Limited versions of this approach would be consistent with the terrorism-subordinate grand strategy described above, but a more aggressive air-only program would fit a war-on-terror strategy, albeit one waged differently than that actually commenced in 2001.) This might have resembled the counterterrorism proposals attributed to Vice President Joseph Biden for Afghanistan after 2008: Biden reportedly advised downgrading the importance of nation building and other counterinsurgency activities aimed at winning the battle for hearts and minds and focusing on strikes aimed at the terrorist leadership and conducted primarily by drones and Special Forces.[27]

Alternatively, in 2001 the Bush administration could have deployed a much larger conventional ground force in lieu of the small-footprint SOF approach actually chosen. Other possibilities include variants on the master alternatives of less and more than actually employed: the United States could have sought regime change with the same combination of SOF, allies, and airstrikes actually used, but might have withdrawn all U.S. forces immediately after the Taliban fled (a regime-change-only option). Or it could have acted immediately as it did in 2001, but followed up with a large force of conventional soldiers as these became available to provide security and to stabilize the new regime of Hamid Karzai.

Here, too, the alternatives would not necessarily have been realistic given the political context of September 2001 and the personalities and views of the key actors. But they were open possibilities all the same, so we ask whether either might have produced a significantly better result by 2014.

Counterfactual: Counterterrorism Alone in Afghanistan in 2001

The consequences of a "counterterrorism alone" policy would be similar to those of the terrorism-subordinate counterfactual described above, as the U.S. government would have attempted to suppress al Qaeda rather than invading Afghanistan in an attempt to annihilate the organization. One could thus expect a stronger al Qaeda in 2015 pursuing chronic but probably noncatastrophic terrorism against Americans, along with reductions in costs, including those of a long counterinsurgency campaign in Afghanistan. The main difference from the terrorism-subordinate counterfactual is that a much more aggressive counterterrorism activity is implied by a war against terrorism. The costs of such a campaign would thus be marginally higher than in the first counterfactual, and the scale of terrorism against Americans marginally lower.

A more important difference is that "counterterrorism alone" would present problems of conflict termination and escalation management. Air strikes are better at suppressing than defeating an enemy; against a resolute opponent, campaigns limited to the air can drag on if the target digs in and refuses to concede. This is tolerable if the effort is small, cheap, quiet, and modest in its ambitions, as were the U.S. intelligence efforts against terrorism before 2001. Few called for an end to actions against terrorists after interventions like that against the terrorists who attacked the Italian cruise ship *Achille Lauro* in 1985, even though this action had no prospect of destroying the enemy or ending the conflict.[28]

In contrast, framing the conflict as a war treats the enemy as a threat of the very first rank and reorients American grand strategy accordingly. Thus the stakes are raised, making it that much more painful if success is elusive. An aerial counterterrorism campaign alone would have been unlikely to topple the Taliban or cause them to hand over bin Laden. Before the ground force spotters arrived, the air campaign had already started to run out of targets by the end of October 2001, with no sign of concession from the Taliban. An air-only effort would have been likely to drag on. Calls for escalation or disengagement would have been heard, given the inherent prominence of the air campaign and its visibility as a proclaimed act of war. The Taliban were battle-hardened from decades of war and would likely have outlasted U.S. domestic public or political will for such a hobbled air campaign.

Disengagement—in the terrorism-subordinate policy described above—could have produced a worse outcome than actual circumstances. Escalation, by contrast (in this terrorism-priority counterfactual), looks much like the actual choice made in 2001, but with the appearance of early failure as a drag on its efficacy. If the counterterrorism-only option had been all the United States was prepared to do in Afghanistan, then the terrorism-subordinate option would probably have yielded better results.

Counterfactual: Large-Force Conventional Invasion of Afghanistan in 2001

In principle, sending a large conventional force in 2001 instead of small commando teams might have had two important advantages. Had this alternative enabled the United States to catch bin Laden in 2002, rather than letting him escape to Pakistan as he did, it might have shortened the war on terror. And if it had secured Afghanistan against guerrilla penetration after 2002, it might have dampened or averted today's insurgency. Neither outcome can be excluded. Nevertheless, we believe the outcome would most likely be similar to the way things now look.

A larger conventional ground force would have improved the chances of intercepting bin Laden at Tora Bora in 2001. Many have argued that had the United States abandoned its reliance on ill-motivated Afghan forces and used just the American troops that were already available in a more aggressive effort to seal the battlefield, then bin Laden could have been captured.[29] Others disagree.[30] But few believe that interception would have been a sure thing, and most see it as a high-risk gamble, albeit a worthwhile one. As Peter Krause puts it, "Significant challenges at each step of the operation made success far from assured, and the operation presented here is admittedly extremely ambitious and risky."[31]

A greater conventional-force effort would have required airlifting thousands of U.S. soldiers into some of the most forbidding terrain on the planet, supplying them from the air for weeks or months of battle, and hoping they could prevent a single individual from evading them through any of the dozens of interconnected caves and mountain foot trails used for centuries as smuggling routes. Changeable mountain weather that grounded aircraft could have left the blocking forces without supply or medical evacuation for extended periods. Deployment delays could have alerted bin Laden, giving him time to escape. Observation of incoming aircraft by al Qaeda fighters or sympathetic civilians could have tipped him off. A crashed or shot-down helicopter could have changed the mission from man-hunting to rescue, thereby diverting limited airmobile capabilities.

Some challenges, such as heavy-lift helicopter availability, would have been eased if the administration had chosen to delay the whole operation until a large conventional force could arrive. But it was the faster-than-expected U.S.

response that pinned bin Laden in Tora Bora in the first place. It is far less likely that bin Laden would have stayed holed up in Tora Bora while watching a slow and ponderous accumulation of heavy U.S. forces; seasonal weather might have stretched the deployment and subsequent campaign well into late summer 2002.

Other problems could have been made worse. Most advocates of a U.S. cordon at Tora Bora begin from the premise that bin Laden had been sighted there and chose to linger for multiple weeks (as he did). Without this lucky sighting, or without his willingness to delay there, even a large force would have faced a virtually impossible challenge in trying to close one of the most porous borders in the world and prevent the passage of a single individual traveling incognito with a small security team. The large-force counterfactual would have exacerbated this challenge. It would imply a very different campaign, with different timing, dynamics, and conduct, on both sides. Perhaps this new war would have produced a bin Laden sighting of its own, perhaps in Tora Bora or some other location no harder to reach. Perhaps he would have cooperated by sitting still long enough to be captured. But if we change the conditions this much, we introduce so many other differences that it becomes very hard to know whether we could still expect a lucky sighting of a famously elusive target who then did not immediately flee. Thus while a larger force would probably have improved the odds of eliminating bin Laden in 2001, we cannot know by how much, and the prospects would have been highly imperfect even so.

The conventional-force counterfactual suggests some hope for better prospects of averting today's insurgency. In the historical case, the weakness of available security forces gave the Taliban, having rebuilt their strength in Pakistan, easy access to Afghan territory and population. A larger U.S. force would have presented a much tougher target, and it could have provided the trainers, mentors, and partners needed for a much faster expansion and reform of Afghan security forces. A large, sustained conventional force deployment could also have helped quell Karzai's growing fears of U.S. abandonment after 2003, when the Bush administration handed the Afghanistan mission off to NATO in order to focus U.S. attention on Iraq.[32] This fear of abandonment has given rise to a range of hedging behaviors by the Afghan government— from political alliances with warlords and malign power brokers to incentives for corruption—that have hindered the legitimacy normally seen as essential for success and that have facilitated Taliban access to victimized populations.

A clear U.S. commitment to stabilizing Afghanistan militarily could also have reduced Pakistani incentives for harboring Afghan Taliban expatriates. Most now believe that Pakistan, too, fears that the United States will abandon the region prematurely, resulting in Karzai's collapse and a Pakistan confronted with dangerous instability on its western border. Islamabad thus offers sanctuary to Afghan Taliban factions that it believes will take over when this happens and provide a tolerable alternative to chaos; in the process they undermine the prospects for Karzai's success. A stable Karzai's government with clear and sustained U.S. support would diminish Pakistani incentives to hedge. Perhaps Islamabad would be willing to act against Taliban safe havens on their soil.[33]

Yet experience since 2001 also suggests a strong possibility of a major insurgency a decade later regardless, albeit one waged on different grounds. First, Mullah Omar, Jalaluddin and Sirajuddin Haqqani, Gulbuddin Hekmatyar, and the other leaders of the primary Taliban factions have proven to be highly determined foes. The insurgency continues, even though the United States more than tripled its troop strength in Afghanistan between 2008 and 2011, from around 30,000 to 100,000. Together with major growth in indigenous Afghan forces and a reinforced non U.S. NATO contingent, by 2011 this produced an allied security force of over 425,000. Yet the insurgency continued. It may yet be possible to negotiate a settlement in which these or other Taliban leaders agree to stand down in exchange for political concessions of some kind, and it is possible that they would have chosen not to attempt a return after 2001 if faced with a hard enough target. But these insurgents are willing to accept considerable cost and hardship in pursuit of restoration of their power in Afghanistan. From what we now know, it seems likelier that they would have attempted an insurgency even if they had faced a much larger security force in 2001.

A much larger foreign military presence would also have posed political and legitimacy challenges for the Karzai government. Occupation by foreign troops is rarely welcome. They may be tolerated if unequivocally needed for security against an unpopular enemy, but foreign soldiers who do not seem necessary quickly wear out their welcome. Where a common threat unifies the occupying force and the occupying population—such as the Soviet enemy in U.S.-occupied post–World War II Germany—very long-term foreign military presences are accepted. Where a common threat is lacking, as in Israel's occupation of Lebanon from 1982–2000, or Vietnam's presence in Cambodia from 1979–89, nationalism soon turns the population against the occupiers.[34] In Afghanistan today, the Taliban insurgency is a clear threat, and the overwhelming majority of Afghans fear and reject the Taliban as a prospective ruler. One reason they continue to tolerate an intrusive foreign military presence is because they believe that foreign troops are all that stand between them and a future of chaos or Taliban restoration.

In the conventional-force alternative counterfactual, however, a large foreign presence would remain after 2001 in a presumably quieter Afghanistan. The very purpose of the deployment would be to prevent Pakistan-based Taliban, which for a prolonged period had invisibly rebuilt its strength, from reentering Afghanistan or threatening Afghan civilians. If this plan worked as intended, it would dampen the common threat perception that would justify the foreign presence to the population. It is unlikely that such a force would actually dissuade the likes of Omar, the Haqqanis, or Hekmatyar from plotting a return; their behavior since 2001 indicates remarkable patience and commitment to building an insurgency from Pakistan. But it is likely that a large foreign deployment would have slowed or deferred the onset of military action by them; it could have lengthened significantly the time they would need for quiet rebuilding in Pakistan in order to mount a credible threat.[35] In the meantime, Afghans would be asked to tolerate a large, intrusive foreign military presence with no immediate, visible enemy to justify it.

This scenario suggests an important danger: that the public could turn against such an occupation before a unifying threat materialized. Such public sentiment would in turn strengthen the insurgency and (once it had rebuilt and engaged in active operations inside Afghanistan) undermine the foreign troops' effectiveness against it. The Taliban have long promoted resistance to foreign occupation as a major plank in their political platform, and while this had limited persuasive power against a foreign troop presence clearly designed to protect against an unpopular insurgency, it would be more effective against a presence that had already worn out its welcome and become a cause of resentment.

Evidence suggests that Afghan patience with the foreign presence was fraying a bit even in the historical case, notwithstanding its limited and nearly invisible pre-2008 configuration. Through the end of 2008, fewer than thirty thousand American and fewer than thirty thousand other foreign troops were present in a country of a quarter million square miles and almost thirty million people.[36] In a rural society with a widely distributed, low-density population and limited media penetration, most Afghans never saw a foreign soldier during this period. It took the Taliban only three to five years to rebuild to a strength where they could threaten this light security presence. Yet this was long enough for at least some of the foreign troops to wear out their welcome. In May 2006, for example, the brakes failed on a U.S. Army cargo truck as it descended a hill north of Kabul, and the truck hit twelve cars in rush-hour traffic, killing five Afghan civilians. This traffic accident spurred a riot in which at least fourteen people were killed and over ninety injured.[37] The traffic accident, a relatively minor incident in itself, intensified a simmering resentment of what Afghans saw as an arrogant and self-interested foreign presence. U.S. tactics tended to aggravate this problem: in the era before the Army published its official doctrine on best practices in the revised field manual, FM 3-24, "Counterinsurgency" (which emphasized winning hearts and minds by protecting civilians from harm), practices designed to protect military forces often encouraged U.S. aggressiveness and so spurred local resentment. As late as 2010, four years after the manual went into effect, logistics convoys were still bulling their way through Kabul traffic jams, angering local residents and provoking hostility to the foreign presence.[38]

During 2001–06, before the manual had yet exercised influence, such behavior was more widespread. In the historical case, the relatively light foreign military footprint and the relatively early return of the Taliban both promoted public acceptance of the foreign presence as a necessary evil to defeat the Taliban. But in a counterfactual where a much larger presence stayed on for a longer period with no apparent Taliban threat, much lower levels of public tolerance would be expected, along with a much more effective antiforeign propaganda campaign by the Taliban once its insurgency appeared.

A variation on this conventional force counterfactual would be to support a much larger indigenous Afghan security force, thus helping to overcome the problem of nationalism. In the historical case, Afghan forces remained very small: in 2003, the Afghan National Army had only six thousand troops. By comparison, in March 2013 it numbered nearly two hundred six thousand.[39] Such an expansion could have been implemented much sooner, beginning immediately after the overthrow of the Taliban. A large Afghan force might have prevented the Taliban from gaining a foothold, and without the legitimacy challenges associated with a sustained presence of a hundred thousand American troops.

Two problems would confront such an alternative. First, large foreign forces are normally thought necessary to train and supplement novice indigenous militaries. A primary function for the hundred thousand U.S. troops now in Afghanistan is precisely that: to train, mentor, and partner with the new Afghan Army and Police in the field. Nationalist resistance to foreign troops might be reduced if the latter operated together with indigenous forces, but large foreign forces would still be needed to make a large new Afghan military effective. And in the absence of an evident threat, it is unclear whether this large foreign presence would be accepted even if it were partnered with Afghans.

More important, large Afghan forces would require massive external funding. Since 2002 the United States has allocated over forty-three billion dollars to train, equip, and sustain the Afghan National Security Forces.[40] With an actual war in process, and with Afghan forces seen as substitutes for Americans in waging it, these expenditures have been tolerated by the U.S. Congress, but only barely. It is very unlikely that Americans would have been willing to pay anything like this sum to support an Afghan military of this size, or anything close, with no apparent threat to require it. It is thus equally unlikely that a large indigenous Afghan force could have been funded during the quiet period before the Taliban insurgency grew strong enough to pose a serious threat.

On balance, a large early conventional presence would have offered some advantages, but it would also have posed severe political problems. At the extreme, it might have led to a broader nationalist insurgency in place of the Taliban's Islamist revanchism. At a minimum, nationalist resistance would have diminished the effectiveness of a large U.S. force as a counterweight to the Taliban insurgency when that insurgency eventually appeared. Any of these possibilities would tend to offset the counterinsurgency benefits of a larger U.S. presence after 2001.

Conclusions and Implications

The war on terror involved a host of major decisions, any of which could have been made differently. As an initial probe, we have considered two such choices—the decision to elevate terrorism to become the fifth pillar of U.S. grand strategy in 2001, and the decision to topple the Taliban regime in Afghanistan and leave a small international force on the ground to secure the successor Karzai government—and four counterfactual alternatives: the option to leave terrorism in a subordinate position in 2001, the option to elevate terrorism as a priority while downgrading the other four pillars of grand strategy, the option to restrict the Afghan intervention to aerial counterterrorism without a ground component, and the option to invade Afghanistan with a large conventional ground force.

Each of these options implies a different world more than a decade later if it had been adopted in 2001–2. Some of these differences would be improvements. The terrorism-subordinate counterfactual, for example, would probably have reduced defense expenditures and the loss of life in Afghanistan and Iraq. The terrorism-dominant and counterterrorism-alone policies would probably have saved money. The large conventional invasion alternative would have improved the odds of capturing bin Laden in 2001.

Because each has drawbacks that offset their advantages, however, none seems likely to have produced a radically better world than today's. The terrorism-subordinate alternative, for example, would probably have led to years of chronic conventional terrorism against the United States. The terrorism-dominant alternative would probably have allowed increased Chinese assertiveness in the Pacific and incurred a larger bill for reshaping the U.S. military after Afghanistan. The counterterrorism-alone option in Afghanistan would probably have elevated the terror threat to the United States, as well as creating a dilemma as to how to end the war. The large conventional invasion option would have increased U.S. defense expenditure while risking a nationalist reaction in Afghanistan that could have provoked an insurgency apart from, and possibly worse than, that currently posed by the Taliban.

Some options may seem in retrospect like better choices, but we are struck by the absence of radically superior *or* decisively inferior alternatives. The strategic challenges that 9/11 created for the United States simply do not look wholly avoidable by any of the options open to decision makers at the time. A determined terrorist opponent in today's world can credibly threaten chronic, ongoing attacks despite intercontinental distances. The measures required to end such threats—especially regime change to eliminate the terrorists' state sponsors and havens—create dynamics that make long, grinding counterinsurgency commitments difficult to avoid. This leaves Americans with a choice among unattractive alternatives: tolerate some terrorist violence against innocent American civilians, or invest enormous sums in blood and treasure to avert this.

Moreover, the only options that offer a higher-probability way out of this costly counterinsurgency—terrorism-subordinate and counterterrorism-alone strategies—pose enormous domestic political challenges. Terrorism is extremely hard for democratic governments to ignore. The attacks may kill few people in objective terms, but they frighten much larger groups. The September 11 attacks shocked Americans of all parties, ages, and creeds. Dramatic acts of violence against innocent civilians prompt powerful calls for governments to act, even where action will be more costly in lives and treasure than the attacks it is meant to prevent. There was an overwhelming public outcry for revenge and protection in the United States after 9/11. Even if one concluded in hindsight that the most effective response to the 9/11 attacks would have been to respond with a low-key effort focused chiefly on intelligence, espionage, and limited counterterrorism airstrikes, without promises to destroy al Qaeda or to end the threat of global terror, it is hard to imagine any American president choosing such a path.[41]

Even if George W. Bush had been inclined to take a minimal response, criticism from both parties would have made such a policy unsustainable. If al Qaeda had actually managed to mount a second attack on the United States without a vigorous U.S. military response in the interim, the domestic outcry would have been immediate and politically fatal to the incumbent. And the successor president would likely have reversed the policy to pursue a more aggressive strategy.

Given the character of democracies faced with sudden terrorist attack, all realistic options impose a major risk of suffering and sacrifice.

This dynamic suggests that these strategic post-9/11 decisions were neither ninety–ten nor ten–ninety calls. For each of the decisions considered above, the balance of cost and benefit appears closer, even when their counterfactual implications are explicitly assessed, with outcomes less different from the historical case than other analyses that have considered only one side of the cost-benefit ledger have claimed. To us, this suggests that these decisions were, instead, a series of fifty-five–forty-five close calls.

Of course this conclusion is specific to the two decisions considered here. Analyzing other decisions since 2001—such as the decisions that got the United States into the 2003 Iraq War, the decisions that got the United States out of the Iraq War, the responses to the Arab Spring, and others—might generate a very different assessment. We have not yet done the analysis needed to reach a firm conclusion on those other decisions, but our analysis of the early decisions leaves us with a provisional hypothesis: the choices after 2001, even ones that look obviously wise or foolish in light of current events, were probably closer calls than the conventional wisdom believes just as the initial decisions were.

Moreover, any counterfactual analysis is subject to the inherent uncertainties of the enterprise. Yet tentative initial implications can be drawn. Perhaps the most important of these is the utility of expanding the spectrum of options for the future. Faced with a set of fifty-five–forty-five alternatives, it is certainly better to pick fifty-five than forty-five, but far better would be to get a sixty-five–thirty-five or seventy-five–twenty-five option onto the menu.

New technology or some radical new military operational concept might theoretically provide better alternatives, but it seems improbable. Counterterrorism strikes, for example, will certainly become more precise, but a lack of precision or an inability to destroy a really critical target was not the problem limiting counterterrorism options in 2001. The real problem was that limited violence delivered from afar cannot overcome combatants on the ground with virtually unlimited commitment. If terrorists or insurgents see their wars as vital interests, then limited airstrikes (including by drones) or intermittent raids by Special Operations Forces can rarely do more than temporarily suppress or contain the threat they might pose. Conversely, major invasions can control populations and deny terrorists haven or state support, but only at a cost that will often exceed the real stakes for a distant United States. Better counterinsurgency training or equipment or organization can help reduce those costs, but only at the margin, and efforts to engage in counterinsurgency on the cheap can easily result in very expensive campaigns. To control territory by force is irreducibly expensive and will remain so for the foreseeable future.

This raises the question of whether the primary means of widening the option space might be by reshaping the politics of terrorism and Americans' expectations of security in the longer run. If the long, grinding wars of the last dozen years look in hindsight to be undesirable, would it be better to lower U.S. expectations of security and to condition Americans to view terrorism as unpreventable, as something they simply must learn to live with? The linked assumptions that terrorism is preventable and that defeating the threat is the way to prevent it creates escalatory pressures that make wars hard to avoid. In 2001, the closest thing to a sixty-five–thirty-five option may have been the one that was the least realistic politically: a limited response to 9/11 and tolerance of some degree of terrorism. This choice might or might not have been the best: it has major downsides of its own, and its acceptability turns on views about risk that will vary from person to person. If that had been the choice made, one can well imagine analytical exercises conducted after more than a decade of war that ask what we are doing wrong that we have had to suffer so many follow-on terrorist strikes at the hands of an al Qaeda that looks not much weaker than it did in the immediate aftermath of 9/11.

For something like the minimal response even to be a viable *option* in the future would require a different domestic political environment than the one that faced George W. Bush in 2001. That cannot happen overnight, or in the immediate aftermath of a spectacular attack, but would require sustained political debate. We are not optimistic it could happen in a democratic political environment where partisan rivals have so much incentive and opportunity to highlight the costs of choices taken by the party in power, and to downplay the costs of alternatives. We cannot even be sure that the American public would have opted decisively for the minimal response if all of the alternatives had been thoroughly aired and weighed. The public might even have opted for the current result: long, hard wars that cost far more than expected but that yielded the death of bin Laden and a substantially degraded al Qaeda that was never able to launch a follow-on strike on U.S. soil. This might have been preferred to a world in which al Qaeda launched repeated intermittent strikes with seeming impunity, while the WMD ambitions of the terrorists came ever closer to realization.

We are sure, however, that a real choice would require careful consideration of complex counterfactual analyses such as the ones we have attempted here. Reasonable people can disagree even when the analysis is carefully done, but without the analysis, the debate is likely to be far less reasonable.

NOTES

With the permission of Stanford University Press, "Assessing Strategic Choices in the War on Terror" was adopted from *How 9/11 Changed Our Ways of War*, edited by James Burk (2013).

1 Contingency also played a role in the outcomes of post-9/11 U.S. grand strategy. It may be that decisions that seem obviously wrong because of generally negative consequences were just unlucky, while obviously right ones were lucky. We disagree between ourselves as to the relative weight to assign between equifinality, the principle that different paths often lead to the same outcome, and contingency, the principle that outcome depends on the path followed. Feaver gives contingency more scope than does Biddle. But we agree that prevailing analyses have ignored the equifinality feature, and so we focus our argument here.

2 Peter D. Feaver, "Debating American Grand Strategy after Major War," *Orbis* 53, no. 4 (2009): 548.

3 See, for example, Richard K. Betts, "Is Strategy an Illusion?," *International Security* 25, no. 2 (2000): 5–50; Christopher Layne, *The Peace of Illusions: American Grand Strategy from 1940 to the Present* (Ithaca, NY: Cornell University Press, 2007); John J. Mearsheimer, "Imperial by Design," *National Interest*, no. 111 (January–February 2011): 16–34.

4 For example, this is the basic conclusion of Hal Brands, *From Berlin to Baghdad: America's Search for Purpose in the Post–Cold War World* (Lexington: University Press of Kentucky, 2008); John Lewis Gaddis, "What Is Grand Strategy?" (lecture, Duke University, February 26, 2009), www.duke.edu/web/agsp/grandstrategypaper.pdf; Jeremi Suri, "American Grand Strategy from the Cold War's End to 9/11," *Orbis* 53, no. 4 (2009): 611–27.

5 Strobe Talbot, *The Russia Hand: A Memoir of Diplomacy* (New York: Random House, 2002), 133.

6 Both the Clinton and George W. Bush administrations pursued a secondary hedge in the form of improved relations with India, China's most serious regional rival, even though those improved relations came at the cost of further accommodation of Indian geostrategic demands regarding nuclear weapons. For more on the "responsible stakeholder" strategy, see Robert B. Zoellick, "Whither China: From Membership to Responsibility?" (remarks, National Committee on the United States and China Relations, New York, September 21, 2005), www.disam.dsca.mil/pubs/INDEXES/Vol%20 28_2/Zoellick.pdf. For more on the outreach to India, see Ashley J. Tellis, "The Merits of Dehyphenation: Explaining U.S. Success in Engaging India and Pakistan," *Washington Quarterly* 31, no. 4 (2008): 21–42.

7 On U.S. efforts to promote democracy in the post–Cold War era, see Thomas Carothers, *U.S. Democracy Promotion During and After Bush* (Washington, DC: Carnegie Endowment for Peace, 2007).

8 On U.S. efforts to promote a liberal economic order, see John Williamson, "What Washington Means by Policy Reform," in *Latin American Readjustment: How Much Has Happened*, ed. John Williamson (Washington, DC: Institute for International Economics, 1989).

9 James Woolsey, "Former CIA Directory Woolsey Deliver Remarks at Foreign Press Center" (March 7, 2000), cryptome.org/echelon-cia.htm.

10 For more on Clinton's ineffective efforts at "assertive multilateralism," see Richard N. Haass, "Paradigm Lost," *Foreign Affairs* 74, no. 1 (January–February 1995): 43–58.

11 Indeed, to a remarkable degree, the outline of this approach is evident in the draft Defense Planning Guidance (DPG) that the Department of Defense developed in 1992. The draft DPG is available at www.gwu.edu/~nsarchiv/nukevault/ebb245/doc03_extract_nytedit.pdf.

12 The Bush campaign view of grand strategy can be found in Condoleezza Rice, "Promoting the National Interest," *Foreign Affairs* 79, no. 1 (January–February 2000): 32.45–62.

13 See Paul Dixon, "British Policy towards Northern Ireland 1969–2000: Continuity, Tactical Adjustment and Consistent 'Inconsistencies,'" *British Journal of Politics & International Relations* 3 (2001): 340–68.

14 See John Lewis Gaddis, *Strategies of Containment: A Critical Appraisal of Postwar American National Security Policy* (Oxford: Oxford University Press, 1982).

15 Amy Belasco, "The Cost of Iraq, Afghanistan, and Other Global War on Terror Operations since 9/11" (Congressional Research Service Report for Congress, March 2011). For a critical analysis, see Carl Conetta, "An Undisciplined Defense: Explaining the $2 Trillion Surge in U.S. Defense Spending" (Project on Defense Alternatives, Commonwealth Institute, January 18, 2010), www.comw.org/pda/fulltext/1001PDABR20.pdf.

16 The Taliban did offer to turn Bin Laden over to an Islamic court, first in Afghanistan and later to an unspecified third country, if the United States first provided the Taliban with convincing evidence of Bin Laden's guilt, but this offer was widely seen as a delaying ploy and was quickly rejected. See Kathy Gannon, "Bush Rejects Taliban Bin Laden Offer," *Washington Post*, October 14, 2001.

17 Peter Bergen, "Ten Years On: The Evolution of the Terrorist Threat since 9/11" (testimony before House Armed Services Subcommittee on Emerging Threats, June 22, 2011), newamerica.net/publications/resources/2011/ten_years_on_the_evolution_of_the_terrorist_threat_since_911; Peter Bergen and Bruce Hoffman, *Assessing the Terrorist Threat: A Report of the Bipartisan Policy Center's National Security Preparedness Group* (Washington, DC: Bipartisan Policy Center, 2010), 2.

18 In 2015, the core of al Qaeda remains weak, but the larger threat posed by other militant Islamist networks is stronger than that posed by the core, with al Qaeda eclipsed by the Islamic State of Iraq and the Levant (ISIL). ISIL grew out of al Qaeda in Iraq, another organization that was greatly weakened by 2011; its resurgence today has little to do with the 2001 choices that we analyze here. We have not done the analysis to determine whether other choices in the intervening years—for instance, the decision to invade Iraq in 2003 or the decision not to intervene earlier in Syria, or others—were crucial for effecting the rise of ISIL.

19 Elizabeth Arias and Betty L. Smith, "Deaths: Preliminary Data for 2001," *National Vital Statistics Reports* 51, no. 5 (2003): 4, 16, www.cdc.gov/nchs/data/nvsr/nvsr51/nvsr51_05.pdf.

20 Gail Makinen, coordinator, *The Economic Effects of 9/11: A Retrospective Assessment* (Washington, DC: Congressional Research Service, September 27, 2002), 58. See also former Undersecretary of Commerce Robert Shapiro in Robert Shapiro, "Al Qaeda and the GDP," *Slate*, February 28, 2003, www.slate.com/id/2079298; Robert Looney, "Economic Costs to the United States Stemming from the 9/11 Attacks," *Strategic Insights* 1, no. 6 (August 2002). These economic costs might have been greater absent the steps taken by the Bush administration and Congress to overcome the psychological and economic shocks of 9/11. In the counterfactual, where al Qaeda is able to mount sustained (albeit intermittent) attacks, the economic costs could have been substantially higher, if only because of a devastating impact on consumer confidence.

21 President Bush did raise the profile of democracy in the Middle East with his "Freedom Agenda," and Iraq became the first major Arab country in modern times to draft a constitution, ratify it in a free referendum, and then conduct mostly free and fair democratic elections under the auspices of that democratically approved constitution. However, few participants in the Arab Spring uprisings have invoked the Iraqi transition to democracy as a favorable inspiration, which is why we likewise consider any linkage of the Arab Spring to the war on terror grand strategy as secondary.

22 The most authoritative account of Iraqi ambitions remains the 2004 "Comprehensive Report of the Special Advisor to the Director of Central Intelligence on Iraq's WMD," known as the Duelfer Report, available from https://www.cia.gov/library/reports/general-reports-1/iraq_wmd_2004/index.html.

23 It was probably concerns about al Qaeda's quest for WMD that drove the Bush administration's actual grand strategy choices.

24 Department of the Treasury, "General Explanations of the Administration's Fiscal Year 2012 Revenue Proposals" (February 2011), 29–34, www.treasury.gov/resource-center/tax-policy/Documents/Final%20Greenbook%20Feb%202012.pdf.

25 Conetta, "Undisciplined Defense."

26 Pew Charitable Trusts, "The Great Debt Shift: Drivers of Federal Debt since 2001" (April 5, 2011), www.pewtrusts.org/uploadedFiles/wwwpewtrustsorg/Fact_Sheets/Economic_Policy/drivers_federal_debt_since_2001.pdf.

27 On Biden's proposals, see Bob Woodward, *Obama's Wars* (New York: Simon & Schuster, 2010), 159–201.

28 On the *Achille Lauro* incident, see Brian Michael Jenkins, *The Aftermath of the Achille Lauro* (Santa Monica, CA: RAND, 1985).

29 See, e.g., Peter J. P. Krause, "The Last Good Chance: A Reassessment of U.S. Operations at Tora Bora," *Security Studies* 17 (October 2008): 644–84; Senate Foreign Relations Committee, "Tora Bora Revisited: How We Failed to Get Bin Laden and Why It Matters Today" (November 2009), foreign.senate.gov/imo/media/doc/Tora_Bora_Report.pdf; Philip Smucker, *Al Qaeda's Great Escape* (Washington, DC: Brassey's, 2004), 97–98, 132–39.

30 Michael DeLong, *Inside CENTCOM* (Washington, DC: Regnery, 2004), 55–56; Tommy Franks, "War of Words," *New York Times*, October 19, 2004.

31 Krause, "Last Good Chance," 648.

32 Under this counterfactual, the United States might also have matched the larger military effort with larger state- and nation-building efforts, perhaps yielding more progress. This is the core thesis of Dov Zakheim, the senior Department of Defense official with responsibility for Afghanistan policy during this critical period. See Dov Zakheim, *A Vulcan's Tale: How the Bush Administration Mismanaged the Reconstruction of Afghanistan* (Washington, DC: Brookings Institution, 2011).

33 Stephen Biddle, "Long Term Goals for Afghanistan and Their Near Term Implications" (testimony for Steps Needed for a Successful 2014 Transition in Afghanistan: Hearing before the Senate Foreign Relations Committee, 112th Cong., 1st sess., May 10, 2011), foreign.senate.gov/imo/media/doc/Biddle%20Testimony.pdf; Alissa Rubin, "As U.S. Pulls Back, Fears Abound over Toll on Afghan Economy," *New York Times*, June 22, 2011; Rubin, "Afghans Fear West May See Death as the End," *New York Times*, May 3, 2011; Rubin, "Pakistan Pushed Afghans for Closer Ties, Officials Say," *New York Times*, April 28, 2011.

34 David M. Edelstein, "Occupational Hazards: Why Military Occupations Succeed or Fail," *International Security* 29, no. 1 (Summer 2004): 49–91.

35 Another complication to the counterfactual analysis is the effect of Pakistani government pressure on Taliban elements inside Pakistan territory. While this pressure was never as great as the United States wanted it to be, it was substantially greater before Prime Minister Pervez Musharraf made an ill-fated deal with the tribal elements in 2006 that substantially eased the burden on the Pakistan-based Taliban, and permitted their revival in the last half of the decade.

36 Ian S. Livingston and Michael O'Hanlon, "Afghanistan Index: Also Including Selected Data on Pakistan" (Washington, DC: Brookings Institution, January 10, 2014), 4–5, http://www.brookings.edu/~/media/Programs/foreign%20policy/afghanistan%20index/index20140110.pdf; CIA World Factbook, "Afghanistan," https://www.cia.gov/library/publications/the-world-factbook/geos/af.html.

37 Carlotta Gall, "Afghans Riot after Deadly Crash by U.S. Military Truck," *New York Times*, May 29, 2006.

38 Biddle, personal observation, Kabul, January 2010.

39 Livingston and O'Hanlon, "Afghanistan Index," 6.

40 U.S. Government Accountability Office, February 23, 2012, http://www.gao.gov/assets/590/588816.pdf. The funding level as of 2015 is estimated as sixty-five billion dollars. See Matthew Rosenberg, "U.S. Suddenly Goes Quiet on Effort to Bolster Afghan Forces," *New York Times*, January 29, 2015.

41 The two authors of this chapter do not even agree on whether this is the best option in hindsight, given uncertainties about al Qaeda's quest for WMD in a counterfactual world where al Qaeda, having successfully bloodied the United States, still enjoyed Taliban sanctuary, while Saddam Hussein (and others) were slipping out of the loosening nonproliferation noose.

5

Military Strategy in Afghanistan and Iraq

Learning and Adapting under Fire at Home and in the Field

CONRAD C. CRANE

Writing about contemporary military operations is perilous. Authors like Tom Ricks and Bob Woodward base their "instant histories" primarily on interviews.[1] Content depends upon who is willing to talk and their agendas. Uniformed leaders are usually reluctant to discuss ongoing missions, and documentary evidence, even if not classified, often takes years to appear. Furthermore, initial impressions and storylines usually undergo many revisions over time. The best military histories appear decades after events.

One must therefore be cautious when writing any account of U.S. military strategy in the recent conflicts in Afghanistan and Iraq. Likewise, one must not separate those histories from the legacies of the preceding decade. The apparent rapid and decisive success of Operation Desert Storm in 1991 launched a deluge of claims that warfare had changed. Debates raged about whether the new technologies displayed portended a full-blown Revolution in Military Affairs. Airpower advocates trumpeted the results of the air campaign against Iraq and later operations in the Balkans to advocate expanding USAF missions.[2] The bombing campaign to force the Serbs out of Kosovo inspired historian John Keegan to declare that conflict the first ever successfully won by the air arm alone. The perceived success helped reinforce the concept of "Shock and Awe" that gained many adherents before war was launched on Iraq in 2003.[3]

Even ground forces succumbed to this technological euphoria. The 1993 Army operations manual, Field Manual 100-5, was based on the premises that the United States would always be able to use "overwhelming force as a way to achieve decisive victory with minimum cost to friendly forces," and to exploit "near perfect, near-real-time intelligence systems."[4] Central Command systems analysts envisioned a battlefield where friendly forces were almost invulnerable, enemy forces were easily detected and destroyed, and improved weapon accuracy would significantly reduce ammunition expenditures.[5] There seemed no enemy that could stand up to American conventional military power. While President George H. W. Bush declared in 1991 that Operation Desert Storm had "kicked the Vietnam Syndrome," which had made the United States reluctant to risk its military might to achieve anything but the most vital national objectives, in reality that victory had reinforced the propensity of leaders in uniform to favor only the use of vastly superior mass for clear and vital aims.[6]

This sense of American omnipotence also affected political leaders, but in different ways. With the end of the Cold War, key leaders saw the possibility of achieving a "new world order" and, like Secretary of State Madeleine Albright, believed that the United States was "the indispensable nation" to create it.[7] Building upon the policies of his predecessor, President Bill Clinton's National Security Strategy of "Engagement and Enlargement" replaced the paradigm of containment with one based on the theory that supporting and spreading democracy would make the world more peaceful—a concept that still influences the nation's actions today.[8]

Chairman of the Joint Chiefs of Staff General Colin Powell, however, who served under both George H. W. Bush and Bill Clinton, strongly resisted the humanitarian interventions and nation building that this paradigm suggests. He wrote in his memoir that he almost had an "aneurysm" in 1993 when, during the debate over Bosnian intervention, then-ambassador to the UN Albright complained, "What's the point of having this superb military that you're always talking about if we can't use it?"[9] But after Powell retired later that year, the number of American military deployments, often on peacekeeping or nation-building missions, soon reached a level five times that of 1990.[10] At the same time, the military was undergoing significant reductions. A military force that stood at about 2.1 million uniformed personnel in the late 1980s had shrunk to 1.4 million a decade later.[11] The Army, for instance, went from an active strength of 770,000 in 1989 to 495,000.[12] But still the overseas deployments expanded, and strain on the force grew. When George W. Bush ran for president in 2000, one of his campaign promises was to relieve the stress on the armed forces by reducing their involvement in stability operations like peacekeeping and nation building, irregular missions with complex cultural, political, economic, and diplomatic requirements in addition to conventional combat skills .[13]

Some of the lessons of the 1990s had influenced military doctrine at least by the summer of 2001, though conventional preferences remained apparent. The most complex irregular mission is counterinsurgency, the comprehensive civilian and military effort to defeat the organized use of subversion and violence to seize, nullify, or challenge political control of a region, usually by attacking established governing authority. America's unsuccessful campaign in

Vietnam had motivated the military to try to avoid such missions, rather than learn to conduct them better. The treatment of counterinsurgency in Field Manual 3-0, "Operations," which replaced 100-5, took only one page, and its emphasis was primarily on having hosts solve their own problems. Desert Storm provided the most historical examples, although there were some from Balkan peace operations. Vietnam was mentioned only twice. The United States was criticized for providing so much military support to the South Vietnamese that it undermined the authority and credibility of their government and army.[14] This unique perspective on the American involvement in the war provides another sign of service reluctance to engage in counterinsurgency in 2001.

There were many reasons for the continuing neglect of unconventional or irregular missions like stability operations and counterinsurgency. The creation of Special Operations Command (SOCOM) in 1986 created an unhealthy intellectual bifurcation that gave Special Operations Forces no incentive to focus beyond the small-scale, irregular warfare they had waged in Central America and encouraged conventional forces to ignore such operations altogether. Stability operations did not figure into Department of Defense force structure calculations, nor did they attract budget dollars, while the general success and few casualties of such missions in the 1990s encouraged the assumption that they were really just a lesser included set of capabilities within the conventional war-fighting tasks of general purpose forces. And after the inconclusive results in Somalia and Haiti, and the lack of political progress in the Balkans, many senior military leaders still saw such long and frustrating missions, in General Powell's words, as "halfhearted warfare for half-baked reasons."[15]

When President George W. Bush took office in 2001, his secretary of defense, Donald Rumsfeld, launched an effort to transform the American military. Impressed with concepts like "Shock and Awe," Rumsfeld wanted to exploit new technologies and further reduce the size of ground forces.[16] The 9/11 attacks did not change his goals, but they did affect the worldview of his president. Bush now perceived a security threat from fanatic extremists who could not be deterred and who would resort to any means to harm Americans, including weapons of mass destruction if they could be procured. Such enemies had to be killed or captured in the short term. But the only long-term solution, according to this understanding, was to drain the swamp that was producing the alligators. That required bringing stability and democracy to Middle Eastern hotbeds that spawned the threat.

The first swamp to be eliminated was Afghanistan. The September 2001 attacks on the World Trade Center and the Pentagon created immense political and public pressure for an American response against the perpetrators. After the Taliban government refused to turn over Osama bin Laden to the United States, President Bush asked Congress to authorize stronger action. In response, Congress issued a Joint Resolution authorizing the president "to use all necessary and appropriate force against those nations, organizations, or persons he determines planned, authorized, committed, or aided the terrorist attacks that occurred on September 11, 2001, or harbored such organizations or persons, in order to prevent any future acts of international terrorism against the United States by such nations, organizations or persons."[17] It is doubtful al Qaeda's leaders anticipated the ensuing military action. Far from any American bases, Afghanistan is a landlocked and mountainous country the size of Texas. In response to al Qaeda–linked attacks on embassies in 1998, President Clinton had just launched cruise missiles against terrorist training camps in Afghanistan. His successor would do far more.

Before September was over, U.S. intelligence and military personnel had been inserted into Afghanistan to join with forces of the Northern Alliance, mostly composed of ethnic minorities from the north and west of the country opposed to the majority Pushtun tribes who supported the Taliban. Logistic difficulties were immense. Afghanistan's internal transportation networks were primitive, and external access was available only through Central Asia or Pakistan. The latter had helped create the Taliban, but considerable American diplomatic pressure persuaded reluctant Pakistani leaders to allow basing through their nation.

For the U.S. Central Command, Special Operations Forces in Afghanistan were executing a "strategic movement to contact" as a foundation for launching Operation Enduring Freedom. There was no completed campaign plan or thought about the future of Afghanistan. Under great pressure for quick action, the staff planned as it executed. Expectations were that before harsh winter set in the Northern Alliance, helped by American advice and airpower, could secure a foothold with an airfield in the north, which conventional forces then gathering in Uzbekistan could use to mount an offensive in the spring.[18]

Air strikes to destroy Taliban defenses and communications began on October 7. Two months later, Taliban rule ended and their leaders went into hiding. No one foresaw such a quick and total collapse. There was much serendipity involved in American success. Because the leader of the Special Operations Forces (SOF) team deployed to assist General Abdul Rashid Dostum was a former high school rodeo rider in Kansas, he was able to train his men to ride the Afghan ponies necessary to travel through the difficult mountainous terrain. At the key engagement at Bai Beche on November 5, he called in air strikes on entrenched Taliban positions after Dostum's cavalry had been repulsed. Due to a misunderstanding, Dostum mounted another assault at the same time. The worried SOF commander watched as the bombs threw up a blast of dirt and smoke just as the cavalry arrived, allowing them to get behind the position. After the defenders fled, Atta Mohammed's Northern Alliance forces captured Ac'capruk. The whole Taliban position in the north collapsed, and the capital of Kabul fell without a fight on November 13. The focus of operations then turned to the southern stronghold of Kandahar. Allied forces under the command of Pushtuns Hamid Karzai and Gul Agha Shirzai, with their supporting SOF teams and American airpower, attacked the city from both sides. On the night of December 6, Mullah Omar and other Taliban leaders abandoned the city and scattered to the mountains, leaving control of Afghanistan to their enemies.[19]

The performance of American airpower in Afghanistan appeared to justify Secretary Rumsfeld's decision to impose limits on the number of ground troops that could deploy there. Results seemed to reinforce his transformation agenda and to avoid getting conventional forces bogged down there like the Soviets had in the 1980s. The policy backfired at the end of November, however, when local Afghan militia—recruited and advised by SOF and the CIA and backed up by massive American airpower—could not contain al Qaeda elements at Tora Bora. Senior leaders, including Osama bin Laden, escaped into Pakistan. The final operation of this phase of the Afghan War, called Anaconda, in early March 2002 against another al Qaeda stronghold, repeated many of the same mistakes of Tora Bora. Again hundreds of enemy fighters got away. Anaconda also revealed many problems with command and control among American ground and air forces, most of which were corrected later.[20]

Sensing the opportunity to create a new Afghanistan, the United States scrambled to take advantage of its unexpected "catastrophic success." A conference convened in Bonn, Germany, in December 2001, and without any consultations with CENTCOM, set up an interim Afghan government under the leadership of Hamid Karzai. At this time the Americans felt lucky to have found Karzai, a Pushtun with no "blood on his hands" from fighting against them. But the United States remained reluctant to get involved in nation building, and the UN was likewise wary of getting too heavily committed. The challenges were enormous. Socioeconomically, Afghanistan ranked in the bottom ten countries in the world, and it was almost bereft of human capital after decades of strife. Unable to create a comprehensive development plan, a donor conference in Tokyo adopted a "lead nation" approach for aid in January 2002, allocating separate responsibilities to the United States (Afghan

Army), United Kingdom (counternarcotics), Japan (disarmament, demobilization, and reintegration), Italy (judicial system), and Germany (police). The disjointed system was distrusted by Afghans, grossly underfunded, and incomplete. Although eventually scrapped, it set the precedent for future assistance to the country—never adequate to achieve real reform, but more than enough to fuel rampant corruption.[21]

Even as Karzai was elected president of a highly centralized government (a questionable form for Afghan conditions) established by a new constitution, U.S. interest and resources became focused on the next major target of the global war on terror: Iraq. The Bush administration viewed Saddam Hussein as a supporter of terrorists and a potential source of weapons of mass destruction for them. The Iraqi leader was playing a dangerous game, trying to appease UN weapons inspectors charged with verifying the destruction of his WMDs while maintaining enough ambiguity to achieve "deterrence by doubt" to keep enemies in Iran and opponents in Iraq in check. Saddam believed that revealing the total absence of WMDs would be riskier than alarming the United States.[22] He was wrong.

Central Command started planning for Operation Vigilant Guardian, a limited objective attack to secure oil fields and create battle space, soon after the 9/11 attacks. Early in 2002 planners began considering a larger assault to isolate Baghdad. Despite warnings from some analysts that it was reckless to draw too many conclusions from the unique Afghan scenario or to expect so much from technology, Secretary Rumsfeld sent military reform advocate Douglas Macgregor to CENTCOM headquarters in early 2002 to argue that a 15,000-soldier armor-heavy ground force would be enough to conquer Baghdad, with an additional 15,000 infantry added later to stabilize the country after the regime fell. Though Macgregor was rebuffed, Rumsfeld continued to pressure CENTCOM to reduce the size of its assault force, which February plans set at 275,000 troops.[23]

During the next year, the objectives for what would become Operation Cobra II expanded to include regime change in Iraq. The primary planning focus for CENTCOM and the Pentagon remained phase III of the campaign, combat operations to remove Saddam Hussein. Stabilization and reconstruction to replace him, phase IV, received far less attention. At the same time Rumsfeld was successfully cajoling CENTCOM to reduce the size of the force executing the increasingly complex plan. He desired a decisive campaign with a minimal ground force that would vindicate his vision for the new American military.

Senior Army leaders were particularly concerned about a lack of sufficient forces for the complex requirements of phase IV. Unfortunately, that service was disdained by the secretary of defense, who saw it as wedded to large and heavy formations that were antithetical to his own views. When shortly before the invasion was launched Army Chief of Staff General Eric Shinseki (who had considerable experience with stability operations in the Balkans) suggested during congressional hearings in February that "several hundred thousand" troops would be needed to restore Iraq, Secretary Rumsfeld and his deputy, Paul Wolfowitz, immediately claimed Shinseki's estimates were "wildly off the mark." Unable to envision that it might take more troops to secure the peace than to win the war, they were still pressing CENTCOM to limit attacking forces to a hundred thousand, often by challenging mobilization orders and trimming deployment lists. While within the purview of the secretary, this behavior undercut CENTCOM planners who assumed their routine troop requests would be honored.[24]

Army concerns about the inadequacy of phase IV planning for Iraq intensified as the invasion grew closer. In October 2002 Deputy Chief of Staff for Operations Lieutenant General Richard Cody and Army War College Commandant Major General Robert Ivany realized that the Army general who would be "mayor of Baghdad" after Saddam fell needed a clear plan for how to proceed. They assigned the mission to the college's Strategic Studies Institute. The project, completed in January 2003 and published shortly thereafter, highlighted insights from past occupations, examined the unique conditions in Iraq, and provided a detailed list of 135 tasks necessary to rebuild a state and guidance on who should accomplish them. The study acknowledged that the "possibility of the United States winning the war and losing the peace in Iraq is real and serious." It also stressed the importance of preserving the Iraqi Army and the dangers of withdrawing American troops before the job was completed. It concluded,

> To be successful, an occupation such as that contemplated after any hostilities in Iraq requires much detailed interagency planning, many forces, multi-year military commitment, and a national commitment to nation building.
>
> Recent American experiences with post-conflict operations have generally featured poor planning, problems with relevant military force structure, and difficulties with a handover from military to civilian responsibility.
>
> To conduct their share of the essential tasks that must be accomplished to reconstruct an Iraqi state, military forces will be severely taxed in military police, civil affairs, engineer, and transportation units, in addition to possible severe security difficulties.

The administration of an Iraqi occupation will be complicated by deep religious, ethnic, and tribal differences which dominate Iraqi society.

U.S. forces may have to manage and adjudicate conflicts among Iraqis that they can barely comprehend.

An exit strategy will require the establishment of political stability, which will be difficult to achieve given Iraq's fragmented population, weak political institutions, and propensity for rule by violence.[25]

The study was first distributed on the same day that Secretary Rumsfeld established the Office of Reconstruction and Humanitarian Affairs (ORHA) under Lieutenant General (ret.) Jay Garner to handle the transition to a new Iraqi regime. With the apparent reassignment of postwar responsibilities, the Army staff lost interest in the War College study. It was ignored in the secretary's office, and its pessimistic tone was not shared by other influential intelligence sources. Except for single instances of testimony to Congress by Shinseki and Secretary of the Army Thomas White, moreover, little if any dissent was expressed in the Pentagon about the inadequacy of postwar planning. The operation to establish a democratic, prosperous, and nonthreatening Iraqi state would reflect Rumsfeld's desires for a small ground force.

President Bush decided to launch Operation Iraqi Freedom on March 16, 2003. The next day he gave Saddam and his sons forty-eight hours to leave the country. On the 19th, military operations began with a stealth bomber attack on Saddam's suspected bunker and the destruction of Iraqi border observation posts. The Army's V Corps, the First Marine Division, and the British First Armored Division began the main assault from Kuwait on the 21st and 22nd. After unsuccessful negotiations for an invasion route through Turkey, the 173rd Airborne Brigade was dropped into Kurdish territory in northern Iraq to establish another front, while the 4th Infantry Division was deployed as a follow-on element in the south. Rumsfeld had managed to whittle total ground forces down to about 145,000.

Unlike Operation Desert Storm, where an extended period of bombing preceded the ground campaign, this time both were executed simultaneously, which surprised enemy generals. Results were impressive, and the joint campaign seemed to vindicate Rumsfeld's vision. The British quickly secured the major city of Basra in the south, while the 173rd Airborne Brigade liberated Kirkuk in the north. Elements of the 82nd and 101st Airborne Divisions cleared An Najaf and As Samawah, and secured the V Corps flanks so the 3rd Infantry Division could burst through the Karbala Gap to reach Baghdad. Airpower and ground assaults destroyed enemy forces that tried to resist. American psychological operations advised Iraqi soldiers to go home to avoid being bombed into oblivion; many did. By April 7, Baghdad was isolated. By the 10th, resistance in the city had collapsed completely. Victory seemed total.[26]

Yet the campaign was not as flawless as it appeared. Saddam and his sons, among many others, escaped Baghdad. While his sons were killed in July, Saddam eluded capture until December. "The enemy we're fighting is different from the one we war-gamed against," commented V Corps commander Lieutenant General Scott Wallace about the paramilitary Fedayeen commandoes who continued to offer resistance in the cities and threaten lines of communication.[27] Signs of sectarian strife appeared quickly in the north, and there was no plan to address the looting that erupted in Baghdad. The impact on an already decrepit Iraqi infrastructure, weakened by a decade of sanctions, was catastrophic. Poorly coordinated attempts to establish Jay Garner's ORHA team were floundering, foreshadowing the innumerable problems with phase IV to come.[28]

Many share the blame for the dysfunctional postwar situation that spawned insurgency in Iraq. The British quickly reduced their strength in Basra and allowed Shi'a militias to take control of much of the city. Consistent with his commitment to a rapid withdrawal, Rumsfeld reduced the number of follow-on forces and accelerated redeployments. Instead of having twenty brigades to execute occupation plans, only fourteen were available. General Tommy Franks's hasty retirement soon after the completion of major combat operations bequeathed the turmoil to his successor, General John Abizaid. CENTCOM planners, who had seen the War College study, had considered only the early part of phase IV, expecting that a new command, Combined Joint Task Force 7 (CJTF-7), would be created to handle the bulk of it. When that transition occurred, the unit designated to assume that role turned out to be the V Corps, under the command of the newly promoted Lieutenant General Ricardo Sanchez, with only a fraction of the intelligence and personnel assets available to higher headquarters like CENTCOM. In the first of many poor transitions between units in Iraq, the most capable and experienced staff sections redeployed, leaving behind an undermanned and underresourced CJTF-7 headquarters.[29]

Jay Garner planned to reconstruct Iraq with his makeshift team by quickly establishing an indigenous government. But he had been in Iraq only seventeen days when he received notification of his replacement by Ambassador L. Paul Bremer and the Coalition Provisional Authority, with a change in mission from liberation to a more difficult occupation. When Bremer arrived in May he unilaterally took two drastic actions that undercut ongoing plans to involve more Iraqis in shaping and securing their own future. First, he barred anyone in the top four levels of the ruling Ba'ath Party from holding a government job. That disenfranchised about thirty thousand people, many of them important technocrats who had been running the bureaucracy and infrastructure, including even teachers and police.

Bremer's second order was even more calamitous. He completely disbanded the Iraqi Army and sent them home without pay. Bremer's decrees not only required rebuilding the Army from scratch, upending CENTCOM plans to quickly supplement security forces, but also alienated more than three hundred thousand armed Iraqis. Although Bremer eventually paid them, they remained an unsupervised and embittered element.[30]

As the situation worsened, Americans argued over who was to blame. In a scathing editorial, noted military analyst Michael O'Hanlon faulted the military for allowing an invasion of Iraq with inadequate phase IV plans. He argued that officers should have publically resigned their commissions rather than execute such a flawed operation.[31] Other commentators emphasized the American tradition of military deference to civilian authority. Military officers must give their best advice, but then they are obligated to carry out the decisions of their civilian superiors whatever their personal opinion, just as General Shinseki did. And political leaders have the right to be wrong.

No matter who was most culpable for the mess in Iraq when O'Hanlon's editorial appeared in late 2004, well before then a violent and multilayered insurgency had erupted: deposed Ba'athists, Shi'a militias, Sunni tribes, and foreign militants supporting al Qaeda fought against foreign occupiers and each other. Eventually more than ninety named insurgent organizations fought the U.S.-led coalition and the new Iraqi government.[32] Despite denials in Washington, vehicle bombings in August 2003 of the Jordanian Embassy and UN compound in Baghdad showed the security situation was deteriorating. The latter attack killed twenty-two people, including the chief UN envoy to Iraq, and influenced that organization to leave the country. Sectarian violence spread quickly, and the poor relationship between Bremer and Sanchez hindered coordination of civilian and military actions. Parallel command chains, in which Bremer reported directly to the secretary of defense while Sanchez worked for Central Command, exacerbated the dysfunction. Further inflaming the situation was the April 2004 release of photographs depicting prisoner abuse by American soldiers at Abu Ghraib prison.[33]

By mid-2004 the inadequacy of the current command and control structure to deal with the complex insurgency was evident. A new Multi-National Force Iraq (MNF-I) was established to control two major subordinate commands, the combat forces of Multi-National Corps Iraq (MNC-I) and the trainers of Multi-National Security Transition Command Iraq (MNSTC-I).

General George Casey took command of MNF-I on July 1, 2004. The return of sovereignty to an interim Iraqi government a few days earlier in preparation for elections in January 2005 further complicated the command and control situation. The new American ambassador to Iraq, John Negroponte, now also had to work with a nascent and stubborn Iraqi government.[34]

General Casey divined his mission by interpreting President Bush's speeches and reading the UN Security Council resolutions setting the timeline for Iraq's political transition. General Abizaid reinforced that focus with instructions to concentrate on facilitating elections and building up Iraqi security forces. Nevertheless, one of the MNF-I commander's first missions was to eliminate insurgent safe havens that had emerged. First, Shi'a militia forces of Muqtada al-Sadr were defeated in An Najaf and the Sadr City area of Baghdad. Then, Army forces stabilized the Sunni stronghold in Samarra during October 2004, after which all attention turned to the assault on Falluja. Complaints from Iraqi leaders about excessive damage to the city had halted the first attempt to free it in April. Insurgents hailed that as a great victory. They would receive no such respite during Operation Al Fajr (New Dawn) in November. Marine forces with Army reinforcements cleared the city, destroying much of it in the process. Eighty-two Americans lost their lives in the operation, and another six hundred were wounded. Of an estimated forty-five hundred defenders, two thousand were killed and another twelve hundred captured. Still, some escaped to Samarra, reigniting resistance there.[35]

Those successes helped establish a secure environment for the first elections, held on January 30, 2005. Despite three hundred insurgent attacks on Election Day, eight million Iraqis voted, about 58 percent of those eligible. Just because elections occurred, however, does not mean that democracy was taking root. Sunnis largely boycotted the voting, ensuring the majority Shi'a would have an even more dominant role in governing and also shaping the new constitution, along with the more cooperative Kurds. A national referendum endorsed the constitution in October 2005. Ten million Iraqis voted, 80 percent for ratification, but Sunnis almost unanimously opposed it. December elections further solidified Shi'a dominance.[36]

In the meantime, there was significant military progress reducing violence throughout 2005, most notably by Colonel H. R. McMaster's Third Armored Cavalry Regiment in subduing Tal Afar and by Marines in parts of Anbar province. The insurgency seemed contained. A special task force was set up to counter the rise in attacks on American forces with improvised explosive devices (IEDs), which continued to cause the most casualties among coalition forces. The new MNSTC-I under Lieutenant General David Petraeus was starting to produce capable Iraqi Army units. Overall, General Casey's approach appeared to be working.[37]

Instead of bringing the country closer together, however, the elections hardened sectarian divides. As 2006 opened, Shi'a and Kurdish political factions struggled to form a government. Efforts to build up Iraqi security forces intensified, and Generals Casey and Abizaid still considered their campaign on track to transfer greater responsibility to them, reducing American forces accordingly. On February 22, however, an al Qaeda–detonated bomb destroyed the al-Askari Mosque, a sacred Shi'a holy site in troublesome Samarra. Shi'a militias retaliated by attacking Sunni neighborhoods and mosques in Baghdad and surrounding areas. Iraq spiraled into civil war and security deteriorated. Even the death of Abu Musab al-Zarqawi, al Qaeda's leader in Iraq, in an airstrike in June 2006, did not lessen the violence. A new Iraqi government under Nouri al-Maliki was installed in May, but the inexperienced leader's attempts to secure Baghdad failed miserably.[38]

A new generation of U.S. military leaders that had been forged in Somalia, Haiti, and the Balkans had come to realize that, to achieve national objectives, military forces had to be able to accomplish more than just killing people and breaking things. Their insights gained acceptance as events in Iraq began to spin out of control. The first significant sign of institutional change was the issuing of Defense Department Directive 3000.05 in November 2005, which declared that stability operations "shall be given priority comparable to combat operations."[39] But the most important institutional adjustment was the development of new Army and Marine Corps counterinsurgency doctrine, which appeared in December 2006.

As the situation in Iraq deteriorated, the Army produced an interim version of a counterinsurgency manual in 2004 that was tactical in focus. When Lieutenant General Petraeus returned to command the Combined Arms Center at Fort Leavenworth in late 2005, with responsibility for rewriting the interim doctrine, he realized a major revision was in order. Petraeus approached Lieutenant General James Mattis, a fellow division commander during Cobra II and now his Marine Corps counterpart at their Combat Developments Command. They agreed to combine efforts as part of a broader program to turn their respective services into better learning organizations for modern war. The creation of the new Army/Marine Corps counterinsurgency (COIN) manual resulted from the fortuitous linkage of two soldier-scholars with similar backgrounds and interests who received simultaneous assignments to change their respective services. Petraeus also drew on expertise from academia, think tanks, other government agencies, nongovernmental organizations, and allied nations.

The result was Field Manual 3-24/Marine Corps Warfighting Publication 3-33.5.[40] In many ways a revolutionary document, it incorporated new ideas about campaign design for complex problem sets and social-cultural intelligence to better understand the operational environment, and stressed the importance of contributions from civilian agencies. It also provided guidance for synchronizing information operations, training host nation security forces, restoring essential services, building good governance, and developing the economy. The first principle of counterinsurgency emphasized that unless the United States could leave behind a legitimate indigenous authority, COIN would fail. According to this doctrine, protecting the population was usually more important than killing and capturing insurgents. Counterinsurgents had to be adept at disaggregating enemy coalitions, determining which insurgents they could negotiate with, and identifying which ones required killing or capturing. The manual stressed the importance of continually learning and adapting to the changing conditions of a mosaic war that differed from region to region, and village to village.[41]

FM 3-24 was an instant sensation. Millions of copies were downloaded from the Internet, it was reviewed in the New York Times, and it was adopted as a textbook at major universities. Most important, it convinced America's military and its political leaders, as well as its enemies, that the nation had figured out how to win such a complex conflict. When General Petraeus took command in Baghdad in 2007, the new doctrine, and the confidence it engendered, were vital elements in his success.[42]

Nevertheless, the manual resulted from a flawed process that would have later repercussions. Ideally, policy drives doctrine. A national security strategy should have described how counterinsurgency would contribute to meeting national objectives. And a national military strategy should have described how the armed forces would apply counterinsurgency. But the process worked backward. Sarah Sewall, the director of Harvard's Carr Center of Human Rights and a driving force behind the manual, described it as "a moon without a planet to orbit" which "came out of the wrong end of the COIN equation."[43] Counterinsurgency is an operational approach, not a national strategy. Yet with a strategic vacuum, the manual came to fill that role. Just because a nation can execute counterinsurgency does not mean it should.

Furthermore, just because a nation proclaims it is executing counterinsurgency does not confirm that is true. Words without adequate resources and commitment are meaningless. For George Bush 2006 was a rough year. He had accepted the resignation of Secretary Rumsfeld; Iraq was a mess. Democrats had won control of both the House and Senate, and, congruent with public opinion, their presidential candidates were advocating withdrawal from Iraq. Despite these setbacks, the president decided that his best, if not last, chance to achieve his objectives in Iraq was to adopt a plan advocated by retired General Jack Keane, former Army vice chief of staff, and certain defense intellectuals, to deploy additional troops. General Casey, like many others, opposed bringing in more American forces before Iraqi reconciliation occurred. The president responded by selecting General Petraeus to take over MNF-I in February 2007. On January 10, in a broadcast from the White House Library, the president announced the new strategy. Rather than withdraw, he would add five Army brigades and four thousand Marines to the fifteen Army and Marine brigade teams already engaged in Iraq, as well as additional aid for economic assistance. The "Surge," combined with General Petraeus's new doctrinal approach, was intended to create breathing space for Iraqis to begin resolving the crucial issues confronting their nation.[44]

The new approach transformed the war. General Petraeus really needed four different surges to make it work. The first surge, an increase in military forces, eventually totaling about forty thousand troops, allowed him and the new commander of MNC-I, Lieutenant General Raymond Odierno, to secure Baghdad and its environs and keep insurgent forces on the run. The announcement of the reinforcements and the president's confirmation of American commitment to stay created an accompanying surge in Iraqi will to resist that was most evident in Anbar province. The "Awakening" of Sunni tribes turning against al Qaeda had already begun there, fostered by astute Army and Marine commanders along with oppressive al Qaeda policies. With a new sense of American commitment, more Sunnis now felt confident they could risk turning on the "foreign fighters" and trust Americans to intercede with the Shi'a dominated government. In this second surge, "COIN behind the wire"—innovative programs in the main detention camp at Bucca that taught prisoners to read, emphasized a moderate form of Islam, gave them job skills, adjudicated their cases more quickly, and returned the reformed inmates back to their community leaders—also reaped benefits with public support.

There was also a surge in American political will. On July 30 Michael O'Hanlon and Kenneth Pollack of the Brookings Institution published an op-ed in the New York Times titled "The War We Must Win." Fresh from a trip to Iraq, the two experts wrote that while they had been harsh critics of the Bush administration's policies, they now saw the possibility of achieving sustainable stability. Their piece forced even Democratic presidential candidates to acknowledge progress, and political debates began to focus on how to exploit success. The final and toughest surge to obtain proved to be an increase in U.S. government interagency support of the effort. When the State Department was unable to augment its personnel in Iraq, General Petraeus assigned the Provincial Reconstruction Teams to brigade commanders, making those colonels responsible for both military and civilian activities. That eliminated problems with security, coordination, and synchronization. He was also assisted greatly by the very close relationship he had with Ambassador Ryan Crocker.[45]

As with all successful military operations, luck was involved as well. Muqtada al-Sadr announced a unilateral truce, taking his Shi'a militias out of the picture and reducing accompanying Iranian meddling at a key time. There was plenty of money to pay off Sunni tribesmen to resist al Qaeda. Even the Iraqi government took some halting measures to reintegrate Ba'athists and Sunnis and treat them more fairly. Maliki actually mounted a military operation with the Iraqi Army, Charge of the Knights, to subdue Shi'a militias in Basra. Worn down by years of chaos, many Iraqis were eager to support any opportunity for peace. After multiple tours in Iraq, American soldiers and Marines had learned from harsh experience how to conduct counterinsurgency. No less important, the president remained personally engaged, insuring the operation received his guidance and a steady level of support.

When President Bush left office in 2009, he did so with an Iraq that seemed on its way to a stable future. But his successor, President Barack Obama, an early and consistent critic of that campaign, did not have the same personal interest or commitment. While there is plenty of blame to go around among Iraqis and Americans for the failure to finalize a Status of Forces Agreement to protect the rights of any U.S. military remaining in Iraq, the subsequent total withdrawal of American forces in December 2011 resulted in a significant increase in violence and Sunni-Shi'a friction. The U.S. embassy staff also diminished rapidly. The Iraqi government remained reluctant to trust the Sunnis, creating a self-fulfilling prophecy where insurgent elements again established strong footholds in Anbar. Resolving a mosaic war requires a mosaic peace, consisting of many local agreements and arrangements. And they quickly began to unravel without the presence of the Americans who had brokered them. The future of Iraq remains unclear as of this writing.

For President Obama, the "good war" was in Afghanistan. And in 2009 that was also the war that was going badly. After its rout in 2001, the Taliban had replenished itself in Pakistan. By late 2005 there were increasing insurgent attacks throughout Afghanistan, and signs of a true Taliban resurgence in the south. The Afghan National Army, which had grown by only thirty-six thousand since 2002, was far too small to handle the problem. Police training had progressed even less. With American forces concentrating on Iraq, more NATO troops were moved into the Pushtun heartland, Canadians to Kandahar, British to Helmand, and Dutch and Australians in Uruzgan. But they and Afghan forces were insufficient to handle the Taliban push when it came; by mid-2006, areas like Garmser in Helmand province were under full Taliban control. A few more advisers, the training of more Afghan soldiers and police, adequate aid money, and some land reform might have made a big difference between 2002 and 2006. But that opportunity was lost.[46]

Even with the reemergence of the Taliban threat, there was still no integrated counterinsurgency campaign in Afghanistan as late as 2009. Resources were inadequate for development programs, Afghan security forces remained small, and NATO countries could not even agree what counterinsurgency was let alone whether to conduct it. Air strikes or Special Operations Forces raids in remote areas often substituted for too few ground forces. Because who controls the ground controls the impression of results, the Taliban were often able to fabricate reports to reinforce perceptions these actions caused excessive civilian casualties.

Conditions in Afghanistan intensified the debate over counterinsurgency. Critics of the new COIN doctrine had emerged quickly, and the number expanded over time. In October 2006, columnist Ralph Peters penned a blistering critique of an early draft, claiming it was too soft and thus inadequate to deal with religious fanatics. He wanted a more enemy-centric approach.[47] Another criticism came from the scholar Edward Luttwak in the pages of *Harper's*. Terming the new doctrine "military malpractice," he agreed on its population centric-approach, but with a different focus. Luttwak believed it was necessary to intimidate the population by "out-terroriz[ing] the insurgents." For Luttwak, the proper role models were the Romans and the Nazis.[48]

At a 2007 conference American, British, German, and French doctrine writers unanimously rejected Luttwak's approach, based on international law, the realities of the current media environment, and a shared conviction that such an approach is counterproductive.[49] But those who agree with Luttwak respond that Western COIN efforts are doomed to failure. A uniquely American critique along this line was offered by analyst Jeffrey Record at about the same time. He posited that U.S. COIN will almost certainly fail because the military is not properly structured or motivated to conduct it, and the American people are easily frustrated by limited wars and conflicts where national interests are not obvious. Accordingly, the United States should avoid COIN unless it is unambiguously essential for national security.[50]

Some critics of the new doctrine were in uniform. The most prolific was Colonel Gian Gentile from the History Department at West Point. He commanded a battalion in combat in Iraq during 2006, and was a leading spokesman of a "conservative school" within the Army.[51] Gentile argued that the new doctrine was getting too much credit for success in Iraq. He asserted that the Army was moving too far and fast in the direction of reorienting to irregular warfare or French models of revolutionary warfare. In the process, it risked losing important fighting skills essential to deal with both conventional threats and tough insurgents. Gentile also feared that the Army and civilian policy makers might develop an overconfidence in COIN, leading to imprudent foreign policy decisions.[52]

Air Force writers added their input to the cacophony of critiques by positing that the United States could avoid protracted ground conflicts by adeptly applying airpower instead of taking a flawed "ground-centric" approach to COIN.[53] This latter argument is the most easily refuted, as events in Afghanistan especially have reinforced the fact that bombs from the air cannot substitute for boots on the ground in COIN when such deployments are necessary. The way to avoid large ground deployments instead is to rely on the other elements of national power to conduct the "population-centric" activities necessary for success, in lieu of the military. However, such civilian capacities are very limited, and not capable of operating on their own in dangerous security environments. There are still more musicians in the Department of Defense than foreign service officers in the Department of State.

Field Manual 3-24, moreover, had flaws. Though the writing team tried to create doctrine broadly applicable to any insurgency, the review process within the services drew the effort toward Iraq in particular. The writers also had to work quickly, producing the complex document in about nine months. They spent most of that time developing the Clear-Hold-Build approach to counterinsurgency demonstrated so successfully at Tal Afar. That approach requires both time and resources, and while it could work in Iraq, a nation with oil resources, large security forces, a history of central government, and significant and consistent American commitment, those same conditions did not exist in Afghanistan. And the manual paid little attention to cheaper or less direct methods.

* * *

Among President Obama's first duties after taking office in January 2009 was to consider a request for thirty thousand more troops from General David McKiernan, commander of the International Security Assistance Force (ISAF) and all troops in Afghanistan. Obama approved seventeen thousand combat troops and four thousand trainers, so they would be on the ground to help provide security for August elections. But Secretary of Defense Robert Gates and Chairman of the Joint Chiefs of Staff Admiral Mike Mullen considered McKiernan's request far too low if ISAF was intending to do doctrinal counterinsurgency. Further questioning and a visit to Afghanistan convinced Gates that General McKiernan was the wrong man to conduct such a campaign, and General Stanley McChrystal took command of ISAF in June 2009.

Having made his mark managing Special Operations Forces counterterrorism operations in Iraq for General Petraeus, McChrystal immediately arranged a formal assessment of the situation in Afghanistan similar to one conducted by Petraeus when he arrived in Iraq. As a result, the ISAF commander brought three options to the president: a low-end deployment of eleven thousand trainers of Afghan security forces, a high-end surge of eighty-five thousand troops (which is really what McChrystal needed), or a forty-thousand-troop addition (which is what he thought he could get). Most of the president's civilian advisers, most notably Vice President Joe Biden, favored a low-end counterterrorism approach rather than COIN with a smaller augmentation of twenty thousand troops, while those in uniform such as Mullin and Petraeus, now CENTCOM commander, supported McChrystal. The president compromised, authorizing a reinforcement of thirty thousand, but with a serious caveat. When Obama announced the surge on December 1, he promised that U.S. forces would start coming home in July 2011. This combination was the worst of both worlds—a troop increase that was inadequate for requirements but would increase American casualties, and a deadline that would hearten enemies and cause apprehension among allies.[54]

There were many other reasons the surge in Afghanistan did not have the same impact as in Iraq. Though billions of dollars were pumped into aid programs along with the military buildup, they mainly made rampant corruption worse. That problem was exacerbated by the persistent opium trade, and attempts to eradicate it or replace it with another cash crop failed miserably. Hamid Karzai knew that Americans did not really trust him and had hoped for his defeat in the 2009 elections. He thus was loath to pursue reforms that Americans thought were necessary. Key civilian advisors to the president continued to oppose the surge. So did the ambassador to Afghanistan, Karl Eikenberry, whose relations with both McChrystal and Karzai were frosty. Moreover, much of the impact of the surge was dissipated by the existence of a deadline, and by the fact that the Marines shunted too much of the increased numbers into the less important province of Helmand. The Clear-Hold-Build COIN campaign plan itself, which put considerable restrictions on air strikes and replicated much from Iraq, was probably not as appropriate in the poorer conditions of Afghanistan, and NATO forces and the Afghan Army never did much holding or building. Even though the administration considerably increased the number of drone strikes in Pakistan, that nation remained an important sanctuary for the resilient and adaptive Taliban, and the strikes further inflamed American relations with that key country as they complicated its own COIN efforts.

McChrystal soon resigned after a June 2010 *Rolling Stone* article revealed how freely his staff disparaged the president's close advisors. He was replaced by General Petraeus, who stepped down from his command of CENTCOM. Petraeus removed some of the combat restrictions and stepped up counterterror raids. He also established a separate task force to attack corruption, and again demonstrated his skill in all aspects of COIN, including seeking Taliban elements to negotiate with. He even improved relations with the ambassador. By the spring of 2011 there was military progress in stabilizing targeted violent areas, but the deadline for withdrawal was approaching. The war was costing a hundred billion dollars a year, and Obama had publicly promised he would begin the drawdown on time and bring home all surge troops in a year. His position had been reinforced by the death of Osama bin Laden, which made al Qaeda appear weakened. Petraeus argued that losing the troops would invalidate his campaign plan, but the president was insistent. Secretary Gates brokered a compromise that brought home the surge reinforcements by September 2012, the plan that the president announced in June 2011. The president argued that the surge had achieved its goals, increasing security, stabilizing more of the country, building Afghan security forces numbering a hundred thousand, opening new markets, and increasing opportunities for women. He had not been that positive in his discussions with Petraeus earlier, and revelations from others have questioned whether he ever had much confidence in the Afghan mission in the first place.[55]

Petraeus is quick to point out that although he really had the true surge forces for only about seven months, he did halt the momentum of the Taliban and even reverse it in some areas, create time and space for the training of the ANSF and creation of critical Afghan institutions, and conduct the transition of some security and governing tasks to the ANSF and those institutions, all while ensuring continued accomplishment of the overarching objective—that al Qaeda not establish a sanctuary in Afghanistan such as the one it had when it planned the 9/11 attacks and conducted the initial training of the attackers there as well.[56]

It is worth pondering what a more substantial commitment of manpower and/or time might have accomplished. At the same time as Obama's triumphant announcement of the surge's termination, a CIA report concluded that the country was heading toward stalemate: increased instability in the east and north offset gains in the south. But the drawdown has continued, at a faster pace than was even projected in 2011. The future of Afghanistan remains uncertain, just as does Iraq's. The parallels, nevertheless, are inexact. While the counterinsurgency campaign in Iraq should be seen as creating an opportunity for a political consolidation that never occurred, it can be questioned whether counterinsurgency was ever really tried in Afghanistan. This distinction notwithstanding, both cases reinforce the importance of the first principle of American COIN: the success of any such campaign hinges upon the possibility of establishing a legitimate indigenous governing authority to leave behind.

Perhaps the real legacy of Iraq and Afghanistan for American military strategy, besides reinforcing the lesson that even the most brilliant military operations cannot salvage a bad strategy produced by flawed assessments and short-sighted policies, is the 2012 Defense Planning Guidance. Reflecting resultant "COIN fatigue," it asserts that military forces "will no longer be sized to conduct large-scale, prolonged stability operations."[57] Whether the future will allow that remains to be seen.

NOTES

The views expressed in this chapter are those of the author and do not necessarily reflect the official policy or position of the Department of the Army, the Department of Defense, or the U.S. government.

1 Ricks wrote *Fiasco: The American Military Adventure in Iraq* (New York: Palgrave, 2006) and *The Gamble: General David Petraeus and the American Military Adventure in Iraq* (New York: Penguin, 2009). Woodward has written a series of books examining presidential decision making in Iraq and Afghanistan; his latest is *Obama's Wars* (New York: Simon & Schuster, 2010).

2 For example, see IRIS Independent Research, *Airpower and the Iraqi Offensive at Khafji* (CD-ROM; Arlington, VA, 1997).

3 John Keegan, "West Claimed Moral High Ground With Air Power," *London Daily Telegraph*, January 16, 2001; Harlan Ullman et al., *Shock & Awe: Achieving Rapid Dominance* (Washington, DC: National Defense University, 1996).

4 Deputy Chief of Staff for Doctrine, *Reader's Guide: FM 100-5, 1986–1993 Comparison* (Fort Monroe, VA: TRADOC, 1993), 1.

5 Earl Rubright, "Modern Warfare System Flow" (chart, CENTCOM headquarters, September 1, 1993).

6 Quoted in Ann McDaniel and Evan Thomas, "The Rewards of Leadership," *Newsweek*, March 11, 1991, 30.

7 Stated on NBC's *Today*, February 19, 1998, http://fas.org/news/iraq/1998/02/19/98021907_tpo.html.

8 William J. Clinton, *A National Security Strategy of Engagement and Enlargement* (Washington, DC; White House, 1994)

9 Collin Powell and Joseph Persico, *My American Journey: An Autobiography* (New York: Random House, 1995), 576.

10 Conrad C. Crane, *Landpower and Crises: Army Roles and Missions in Smaller-Scale Contingencies during the 1990s* (Carlisle, PA: U.S. Army War College, 2001), 2.

11 Allan R. Millett and Peter Maslowski, *For the Common Defense: A Military History of the United States of America* (New York: Free Press, 1994), 649–50.

12 John Sloan Brown, *Kevlar Legions* (Washington, DC: Center of Military History, 2011), 124.

13 Karen DeYoung, *Soldier* (New York: Knopf, 2006), 295.

14 Department of the Army, "FM 3-0, Operations" (Washington, DC: HQDA, June 2001), 9–16.

15 Powell and Persico, *My American Journey*, 149.

16 Dale R. Herspring, *Rumsfeld's Wars: The Arrogance of Power* (Lawrence: University Press of Kansas, 2008), 18–115.

17 Public Law 107-40, 107th Congress, September 18, 2001, http://www.gpo.gov/fdsys/pkg/PLAW-107publ40/html/PLAW-107publ40.htm.

18 Colonel (retired) John Agoglia, telephone conversation, January 30, 2014; Sean Naylor, *Not a Good Day to Die* (New York: Berkley Books, 2005), 11.

19 Stephen Biddle, *Afghanistan and the Future of Warfare: Implications for Army and Defense Policy* (Carlisle, PA: Strategic Studies Institute, 2002); Naylor, *Not a Good Day to Die*, 16.

20 Naylor's book presents the most thorough coverage of Tora Bora and Operation Anaconda.

21 David Isby, *Afghanistan* (New York: Pegasus, 2010), 334–39; Joseph J. Collins, *Understanding War in Afghanistan* (Washington, DC: NDU Press, 2011), 49–64. For military operations after the initial phase, see Center for Military History Publication 70-122-1, "The United States Army in Afghanistan: Operation Enduring Freedom: March 2002–April 2005," http://www.history.army.mil/html/books/070/70-122-1/CMH_Pub_70-122-1.pdf .

22 Michael R. Gordon and General Bernard E. Trainor, *Cobra II: The Inside Story of the Invasion and Occupation of Iraq* (New York: Pantheon, 2006), 64–65.

23 Ibid., 19–37.

24 Herspring, *Rumsfeld's Wars*, 115–25.

25 Conrad C. Crane and W. Andrew Terrill, *Reconstructing Iraq: Insights, Challenges, and Missions for Military Forces in a Post-conflict Scenario* (Carlisle, PA: U.S. Army War College, February 2003), http://www.strategicstudiesinstitute.army.mil/pubs/display.cfm?pubID=182.

26 For coverage of the actual conduct of the campaign to take Baghdad, see Gordon and Trainor, *Cobra II*, and Gregory Fontenot et al., *On Point: The United States Army in Operation Iraqi Freedom* (Fort Leavenworth, KS: Combat Studies Institute Press, 2004).

27 Lieutenant General William S. Wallace, quoted in Rick Atkinson, "General: A Longer War Likely: Ground Commander Describes Obstacles," *Washington Post*, March 28, 2003, A1.

28 Gordon and Trainor, *Cobra II*, 434–67.

29 Ibid., 463–85; Donald P. Wright et al., *The United States Army in Operation Iraqi Freedom, May 2003–January 2005: On Point II: Transition to the New Campaign* (Fort Leavenworth, KS: Combat Studies Institute Press, 2008), 25–80. On British difficulties with COIN in both Iraq and Afghanistan, see David H. Ucko and Robert Egnell, *Counterinsurgency in Crisis* (New York: Columbia University Press, 2013).

30 On early efforts at reconstruction, see Gordon W. Rudd, *Reconstructing Iraq: Regime Change, Jay Garner, and the ORHA Story* (Lawrence: University Press of Kansas, 2011). See also Charles H. Ferguson, *No End in Sight: Iraq's Descent into Chaos* (New York: Public Affairs, 2008)

31 Michael O'Hanlon, "Iraq Without a Plan," *Policy Review*, December 1, 2004, http://www.hoover.org/publications/policy-review/article/7655.

32 Chad Serena, *It Takes More Than a Network* (Stanford, CA: Stanford University Press, 2014), 1.

33 Wright et al., *United States Army*, 32–41.

34 Ibid., 171–76.

35 Ibid., 336–58; George W. Casey, Jr., *Strategic Reflections: Operation Iraqi Freedom, July 2004–February 2007* (Washington, DC: NDU Press, 2012), 8–10, 19–32, 41–42.

36 Casey, *Strategic Reflections*, 49–80.

37 Ibid., 88–89; Peter R. Mansoor, *Surge: My Journey with General David Petraeus and the Remaking of the Iraq War* (New Haven: Yale University Press, 2013), 22–25.

38 Mansoor, *Surge*, 26–33.

39 Department of Defense, "Directive 3000.05: Military Support for Stability, Security, Reconstruction, and Transition Operations" (November 28, 2005), http://www.fas.org/irp/doddir/dod/d3000_05.pdf. That emphasis on stability operations was reduced when the memorandum was rewritten in 2009, a sign of the "COIN fatigue" resulting from the long wars in Iraq and Afghanistan.

40 Headquarters, Department of the Army, "FM 3-24/MCWP 3-33.5 Counterinsurgency" (Washington, DC: GPO, December 2006), http://www.fas.org/irp/doddir/army/fm3-24.pdf.

41 While the U.S. Army and Marine Corps had tackled insurgencies many times in their history, they had never had a counterinsurgency doctrine this sophisticated, nor faced networked insurgencies so multilayered and complicated.

42 For a firsthand account of the writing, content, and impact of the manual, see Conrad Crane, "Doctrine: United States," in *Understanding Counterinsurgency: Doctrine, Operations, and Challenges*, ed. Thomas Rid and Thomas Keaney (New York: Routledge, 2010), 59–72.

43 Sarah Sewall, "Introduction to the University of Chicago Press Edition," in *The U.S. Army—Marine Corps Counterinsurgency Field Manual* (Chicago: University of Chicago Press, 2007), xl.

44 Mansoor, *Surge*, 51–56.

45 Mansoor provides the best coverage of the surge and its impacts.

46 Carter Malkasian, *War Comes to Garmser* (New York: Oxford, 2013), 91–102.

47 Ralph Peters, "Politically Correct War," *New York Post*, October 18, 2006.

48 Edward Luttwak, "Dead End: Counterinsurgency Warfare as Military Malpractice," *Harper's*, February 2007, 33–42.

49 Workshop on Counterinsurgency and Stability Operations: U.S., French, British, and German Approaches (Institut Français des Relations Internationals, Paris, June 4, 2007).

50 Jeffrey Record, "The American Way of War: Cultural Barriers to Successful Insurgency" (Cato Institute Policy Analysis 577, September 1, 2006).

51 Andrew Bacevich, "The Petraeus Doctrine," *Atlantic Monthly*, October 2008, found at http://www.theatlantic.com/doc/200810/petraeus-doctrine.

52 For examples of Gian Gentile's critiques, see "The Dogmas of War," *Armed Forces Journal International*, November 2007, http://www.afji.com/2007/11/3155836, and "A (Slightly) Better War: A Narrative and Its Defects," *World Affairs*, Summer 2008, http://www.worldaffairsjournal.org/2008%20-%20Summer/full-Gentile.html .

53 Charles Dunlap, "Making Revolutionary Change: Airpower in COIN Today," *Parameters* 38 (Summer 2008): 52–66.

54 The discussion of Afghanistan is based upon Rajiv Chandrasekaran, *Little America: The War Within the War for Afghanistan* (New York: Vintage, 2012).

55 Particularly revealing about the president's doubts and the infighting in Washington is Robert M. Gates, *Duty: Memoirs of a Secretary at War* (New York: Knopf, 2014).

56 Email to the author from General (ret) David Petraeus, March 25, 2015.

57 President Barack Obama, "Sustaining Global Leadership: Priorities for 21st Century Defense" (January 3, 2012), http://www.defense.gov/news/defense_strategic_guidance.pdf .

6

Human Rights as a Weapon of War

JONATHAN HOROWITZ

Human rights—the basic set of rights and freedoms to which all individuals are entitled simply by virtue of being human—are often framed as protections from state power and state violence. Such protection from the state is fundamental to definitions of human rights in the major international agreements that stemmed from World War II, and such protections have remained critical to definitions of human rights ever since. It is ironic, then, that states also use human rights as weapons in waging wars.

This chapter examines different ways the U.S. government—and its military, in particular—employed human rights in its twenty-first century wars as a means to defeat its enemies. We begin by tracing the ways that the first administration of George W. Bush (2001–4) used the human rights abuses of the Taliban, al Qaeda, and Saddam Hussein to garner public support for going to war in Afghanistan and in Iraq. Next, we look at how the U.S. military, largely through its counterinsurgency (COIN) approach, attempted to use aid and humanitarian assistance to diminish local support for the insurgencies in both nations, and then at how the U.S. military used "rule of law" as a counterinsurgency tool. Last, to offer a deeper understanding, this chapter explores the impact that the United States' own human rights abuses and violations of the laws of war had on its ability to effectively use human rights as a "weapon of war."

In so doing, this chapter raises questions about what one might call the weaponization of human rights: Should human rights ever be used as a weapon of war? Should the military be involved in humanitarian assistance and efforts to enforce the rule of law? If so, how, and with what limits or cautions? What consequences can—and should—a government's human rights record have on its war efforts? And, finally, what consequences can military-led humanitarian assistance and rule of law operations have on other parties in the conflict, such as nongovernmental humanitarian aid workers?

Overview of the U.S. Relationship with Human Rights

Today, the international system for human rights includes nine core human rights treaties,[1] each with a human rights body that monitor those treaties' obligations;[2] fifty-three "special procedures" that comprise thirty-nine thematic mandates and fourteen country-specific mandates as of November 1, 2014;[3] and an uncountable number of resolutions from various United Nations bodies declaring support for human rights, instituting sanctions for breaches of human rights, and setting out specialized human rights standards, guidelines, and principles. There are also regional human rights treaties, courts, and other human rights adjudication mechanisms in Europe, Africa, and the Americas.

In the years following World War II, the United States insisted that human rights were central to global reconstruction. It pushed to include human rights in the "purposes and principles" of the United Nations Charter (1945) and supported the creation of the Commission on Human Rights. That commission took the lead in drafting the seminal Universal Declaration of Human Rights (UDHR) that was subsequently adopted by the UN General Assembly in 1948; Eleanor Roosevelt, the commission's first chair, deserves much credit for the first steps in creating what is today the international human rights system.[4]

The U.S. advancement of an internationalized human rights system was in keeping with a preexisting American tradition of statements of rights marked by, for example, the U.S. Constitution's Bill of Rights, President Woodrow Wilson's concerns for global democracy and national self-determination during World War I, and President Franklin Roosevelt's 1941 "Four Freedoms" speech. Responding to Nazi Germany's expansion through Europe with claims of universal rights, Roosevelt asserted that every person in the world should have freedom of speech and expression, freedom to worship, freedom from want, and freedom from fear.[5]

By no means, however, has the United States provided unconditional support for the international human rights system. In 1953, President Dwight D. Eisenhower withdrew the United States from negotiations that yielded various human rights covenants.[6] The United States has also resisted key efforts to advance international economic, social, and cultural rights—in part because such rights were often associated with the Soviet Bloc and in part because some saw them as a tool for the redistribution of wealth. From the beginning, in fact, some U.S. politicians regarded the UDHR as a "socialist" document.[7]

In recent times, the United States has stood with South Sudan as the only other nation (at the time of publication) that has not ratified the Convention on the Rights of the Child and, in late 2012, the U.S. Senate failed to approve the ratification of the Convention on the Rights of Persons with Disabilities.[8] The United States has also refused to concede that the International Covenant on Civil and Political Rights applies extraterritorially—beyond its own borders—and has argued for its limited application in times of armed conflict, both of which are at odds with the findings of major human rights courts and institutions.[9]

American political leaders who oppose strengthening the international human rights system do so primarily for three reasons. Some object to the substance of specific international rules. Voicing broader concerns, other officials worry that international human rights law would infringe upon U.S. sovereignty and permit non-American institutions to hold the United States accountable to their rules. Finally, more broadly yet, some opponents have ideological objections. Whereas the United States has been relatively comfortable supporting international civil and political rights, the same cannot be said for economic, social, and cultural rights—which many U.S. opponents claim are incongruent with the values of a capitalist society that prides itself on meritocracy. None of these objections have prevented the U.S. government from embracing human rights principles—at least when it comes to civil and political human rights. At the same time, however, the U.S. government has routinely resisted the international human rights system because of fears that it could influence how the United States manages its domestic laws and national interests.

The U.S. relationship to human rights is also defined by the role human rights plays in U.S. foreign policy. There, its relationship with human rights institutions and application of human rights principles have been consistently inconsistent. U.S. presidents have stated, repeatedly, that it is in the interest of the United States for other nations to respect human rights. The U.S. 2010 National Security Strategy clearly stated that the United States "see[s] it as fundamental to our own interests to support a just peace around the world— one in which individuals, and not just nations, are granted the fundamental rights that they deserve." The strategy statement continued, "Nations that respect human rights and democratic values are more successful and stronger partners, and individuals who enjoy such respect are more able to achieve their full potential."[10]

What happens, however, when an administration concludes that its dedication to human rights conflicts with other interests, such as national security or economic growth? The Carter administration—notwithstanding its explicit promotion of human rights—at times put national self-interest above international human rights. As human rights scholar David Forsythe argued, the administration did "what it could for human rights, where it could."[11] Writing about President Bill Clinton's record, Forsythe concluded that "as long as a high national price, in blood or treasure, is not demanded to advance human rights, the United States is certainly for them—at least for the civil and political rights congruent with the American self-image."[12] In the post–September 11, 2001, world, that sentence holds largely true, but with one important change: "As long as a high national price, in blood, treasure, *or a softened stance against terrorism*, is not demanded to advance human rights, the United States is certainly for them." This complex history has shaped America's approach to human rights in the post-9/11 world, including when it went to war in Afghanistan and Iraq.

Weaponizing Human Rights

As the Bush administration moved toward war, first in Afghanistan and then in Iraq, it used the human rights abuses of its enemies to help justify military action. This tactic was not unusual; governments have regularly put forward human rights abuses as legal or moral justifications for going to war. Such was the case when President Clinton carried out military operations in the Federal Republic of Yugoslavia. This brand of warfare, now referred to as "humanitarian intervention" and based on understandings of an international "Responsibility to Protect," gained wide public attention after the international community failed to prevent atrocities in such places as Rwanda and Bosnia.[13] In other cases, including both Afghanistan and Iraq, human rights abuses by foreign governments were a peripheral justification, used primarily to increase public support for the war effort both at home and abroad.

In the case of Afghanistan, the immediate justification for American military action was al Qaeda's September 11 attack on the United States. With al Qaeda based in Afghanistan and the Taliban refusing U.S. demands to hand over those who planned and directed the attack, the United States launched its first airstrikes slightly less than a month after the World Trade Center towers fell. While the attacks of September 11 provided the legal justification for war, the Bush administration also used the language of human rights to portray al Qaeda and the Taliban as worthy of destruction. Describing al Qaeda as "people who hate freedom" (and thus as a worldwide threat), the Bush administration also emphasized the Taliban's abuses of other Afghans: "The Afghan people are victims of oppression and misrule of the Taliban regime. There are few places on earth that face greater misery," the president said on October 12, 2001.[14] First Lady Laura Bush focused on the plight of women under the Taliban, making her case in a radio address the next month: "Only the terrorists and the Taliban forbid education to women. Only the terrorists and the Taliban threaten to pull out women's fingernails for wearing nail polish. The plight of women and children in Afghanistan is a matter of deliberate human cruelty, carried out by those who seek to intimidate and control."[15] The language of human rights was fundamental to justifications for the U.S. war in Afghanistan.

In the case of Iraq, which America invaded less than a year and a half later, the Bush administration again relied on human rights violations to build public support for going to war. The principal justification for this "preemptive" war was the claim—later discredited—that President Saddam Hussein had access to and a willingness to use weapons of mass destruction (WMDs).[16] The Bush administration also asserted—incorrectly—that there were significant links between Saddam Hussein and al Qaeda that justified invading Iraq.[17] On top of these allegations the administration layered the incontestable facts of Saddam Hussein's human rights abuses to depict the president as a tyrant with no regard for humanity, one whose removal from power would benefit not only the Iraqi people but also the world at large.

Thus, in his March 15, 2003, radio address, four days before the war with Iraq began,[18] Bush recalled in vivid detail Saddam Hussein's willingness to use chemical weapons on the Iraq village of Halabja fifteen years earlier. This attack, he charged, illustrated the threat that Saddam posed to the world. In the same address he made a human rights argument. "We know from human rights groups," Bush said, "that dissidents in Iraq are tortured, imprisoned, and sometimes just disappear; their hands, feet, and tongues are cut off; their eyes are gouged out; and female relatives are raped in their presence."[19] Two days later the U.S. president promised Iraqis that the war would bring about a "free Iraq," one in which "there will be no more wars of aggression against your neighbors, no more poison factories, no more executions of dissidents, no more torture chambers and rape rooms."[20]

Just as it emphasized the human rights violations of Saddam Hussein, the Taliban, and al Qaeda, the Bush administration presented the United States as a guarantor of freedom and of human rights. During the invasion into Afghanistan, the president reassured Americans and the rest of the world that the nation was at war with terrorists, not with Arabs, Islam, or the people of Afghanistan: "The United States respects the people of Afghanistan . . . but we condemn the Taliban regime," he said on September 20, 2001.[21] He portrayed Americans as a "freedom-loving people" and the U.S. military as protectors of the Afghan people from those who "hate freedom."[22] Soon after the U.S. military campaign began, Laura Bush applauded the human rights achievements of the United States over national radio: "Because of our recent military gains in much of Afghanistan, women are no longer imprisoned in their homes. They can listen to music and teach their daughters without fear of punishment. . . . The fight against terrorism is also a fight for the rights and dignity of women."[23] And President Bush, in his speech to the UN General Assembly in September 2004, called America's interventions in Afghanistan and Iraq part of a "broad agenda to advance human dignity, and enhance the security of all of us." He continued, "The defeat of terror, the protection of human rights, the spread of prosperity, the advance of democracy—these causes, these ideals, call us to great work in the world."[24]

This rhetorical strategy—detailing the opponent's human rights abuses, emphasizing U.S. human rights support—played a critical role in America's case for war. But by its offer of carrying out relief operations, the administration made human rights integral to its war strategy as well. In the run-up to the Afghanistan War, for example, President Bush explained, "As we strike military targets, we'll also drop food, medicine and supplies to the starving and suffering men and women and children of Afghanistan."[25]

The need for humanitarian assistance in Afghanistan and Iraq was due, in part, to the status quo ante (the circumstances that existed before the war), and to natural disasters, including droughts, floods, and earthquakes. But it was also due to the wars, which displaced people from their homes; overwhelmed basic services, such as hospitals; restricted commerce; destroyed homes; infested farmland with mines; and wounded and killed civilians. Even before the United States invaded Afghanistan, the country had suffered from a roughly decade-long war with the Soviet Union, which was followed by a brutal civil war. Iraq, too, was a nation in distress well before the 2003 U.S. invasion; a 2003 UN report noted that "the Iran-Iraq war, the Gulf War and sanctions took a heavy toll on the health and education sectors, which had previously been among the best developed in the region."[26]

Humanitarian assistance is meant to alleviate human suffering, but in the Afghanistan (2001) and Iraq (2003) Wars it had another purpose: the U.S. military saw relief operations as an important counterinsurgency tool. The 2006 Army Field Manual on Counterinsurgency focused on the need to establish "a legitimate government supported by the people and able to address the fundamental causes that insurgents use to gain support." In order to achieve these goals, the manual stated, the host nation must "defeat insurgents or render them irrelevant, uphold the rule of law, and provide a *basic level of essential services* and security for the populace."[27]

The military was able to use relief operations as a counterinsurgency tool in Afghanistan and Iraq in large part through specific congressionally funded programs, including the Commander's Emergency Response Program, which provided "tactical commanders a ready source of cash for small-scale projects," including repairing public buildings, clearing roadways, and providing needed supplies to hospitals and schools. Other such congressionally authorized programs included the Iraq Relief and Reconstruction Fund, Iraq Freedom Fund, and the Commander's Humanitarian Relief and Reconstruction Program funds.[28]

Within the COIN paradigm of Clear-Hold-Build, relief operations fell most often within the "build" stage, after the insurgents were eliminated from an area ("clear") and security was maintained and insurgents were denied access and freedom of movement ("hold").[29] The military's provision of relief was based on the belief that, as Jamie Williamson, a legal advisor to the International Committee of the Red Cross, put it, "'Winning hearts and minds' is seen as a race for people's trust and confidence and convincing people that a better life lies ahead."[30] That trust and confidence, according to counterinsurgency theory, would lead the local population to reject the insurgents and side with the international forces and with the national government. Such allegiance could offer important benefits: local populations might provide intelligence to the United States and its allies and refrain from providing shelter and aid to the insurgents; the number of men who join the insurgents voluntarily might decline, and those subject to involuntary or forced recruitment efforts might be more likely to resist.

The military carried out COIN relief operations itself and facilitated and coordinated humanitarian assistance to local populations through the work of others. "Ideally, the military is simply providing the security for the humanitarian assistance by supporting other government, intergovernmental, and Host Nation agencies," reads the 2009 Army Field Manual on Tactics in Counterinsurgency. "When the Host Nation or other agency cannot perform its role, Army forces may provide the basics directly."[31] In Afghanistan, many of the international coalition's relief efforts were run through Provincial Reconstruction Teams (PRTs), which were at times led by the military and combined the skills of civilian, diplomatic, military, and development agencies. Iraq also saw multiactor relief strategies. In Tal Afar, for example, the U.S. military secured the area and then worked with the Department of State and the U.S. Agency for International Development's Office of Transition Initiatives to reestablish the economic system and provide key municipal services, including not only water and electricity, but also education, parks, and policing.[32]

The U.S. military also believed that strengthening the rule of law could, by increasing security, lead local populations to reject insurgents in favor of the United States and the host nation's government. In fact, it was the lack of rule of law—through a dysfunctional government—that made many Afghans initially favor Taliban rule in Afghanistan. According to Afghanistan country experts who studied the links between justice and security, "Justice is central to the self-image of the Taliban, and to their efforts to win the battle for popular support and gather legitimacy."[33] These experts described the Taliban's founding narrative as "the story of a group of *ulema* who confronted warring, debauched and predatory commanders, imposing order and eliminating crime through the implementation of *Sharia* law, with a grateful populace voluntarily coming over to their side as a result."[34]

"Nostalgic memories" of the Taliban's "harsh, but just" rule contrasted with the weak rule of law and prevalent sense of injustice under President Karzai's post–September 11 administration, in which "abuses ranging from land seizure to political marginalization [were] immediate causes of grievance that [had] alienated ordinary Afghans from the government, and pushed many to join or support the insurgency."[35] Going a step further, a Feinstein International Center study suggested that injustice in Afghanistan may have been a greater contributor to insecurity than the poverty, unemployment, illiteracy, social services, and infrastructure that aid and humanitarian assistance targeted.[36]

Civilian components of the U.S. government had long been working to bolster the rule of law in Iraq and Afghanistan, although they were criticized both for doing too little and for doing too much in an uncoordinated manner. In contrast, the U.S. military had placed relatively little importance on the rule of law. The 2004 predecessor to the 2006 Army Field Manual on Counterinsurgency mentioned "rule of law" only once, noting, "Most areas around the world are not governed by the rule of law, but instead rely upon tradition."[37] In Afghanistan, however—on which the remainder of this section now focuses—2009 marked the beginning of a more comprehensive military-led rule of law strategy that was aimed directly at fighting insurgents and creating stability.

The beginning of a troop surge in Afghanistan and the robust implementation of the COIN approach that General Petraeus employed in Iraq a few years earlier marked 2009.[38] This brought with it a new focus on the rule of law, which grew largely out of General Stanley McChrystal's recommendation, as the commander of ISAF, that a new Combined Joint Interagency Task Force on detention operations oversee U.S. detention and interrogation operations and provide support to Afghanistan's own corrections system.[39] General McChrystal perceived U.S. detention operations as a strategic liability if not handled carefully. He also judged Afghanistan's weak corrections system, which gave detained insurgents extensive opportunities to radicalize other prisoners, to be a breeding ground for new insurgents. To counter this situation, the United States built a new and improved detention facility, called the Detention Facility in Parwan (DFIP), to replace its notorious Bagram Theater Internment Facility. The task force (named CJIATF-435) also ran new Detainee Review Boards that instituted new and somewhat improved procedures, partly in response to charges of due process failures in the old system. At the same time, CJIATF-435 turned its attention to improving the Afghan corrections system.

What started as a detention-focused program expanded into the military's far more expansive Rule of Law Field Force--Afghanistan (ROLFF-A), headed first by Brigadier General Mark Martins. ROLFF-A then expanded further into the NATO Rule of Law Field Support Mission.[40] As part of these expansive rule of law efforts, the U.S. military was heavily involved in creating a new Afghan-led criminal justice facility, called the Justice Center in Parwan (JCIP), where the DFIP-held detainees stood trial before Afghan judges. The United States needed this DFIP/JCIP-based effort to succeed so that it could end the majority of its detention operations in time for its planned withdrawal (at the time scheduled for 2014) and still feel comfortable that the detainees it handed over to the Afghan government would not be set free and would be treated humanely.

Because of several significant problems, however, the JCIP did not prove sufficiently effective for the Americans, who were hoping that the JCIP would process more cases than it did and produce higher conviction rates and longer sentencing terms. As a result, while the JCIP remained open, the United States managed in 2011–12 to convince members of the Karzai administration to enact an internment regime that contained fewer rules and procedures for holding detainees compared to the Afghan criminal justice system. This effectively gave Afghans a means for detaining individuals who could not have been convicted under ordinary Afghan law. After the United States handed over around three thousand detainees, however, it became clear that the Afghan government preferred either to release these detainees or to funnel them through the JCIP's criminal justice system.[41] Ultimately, the U.S. plans for an Afghan internment regime failed and the Afghan authorities instead detained individuals under preexisting Afghan domestic law.

In explaining the thrust of the military's other rule of law efforts, former George W. Bush administration lawyer Jack Goldsmith noted, "The basic idea of ROLFF is to revive governance and rule of law functions in the Pashtun south where the insurgency is strongest during the 'hold' phase of COIN operations (i.e., just after an area has been cleared of insurgents)." He goes on to say, "General [Mark] Martins, his soldiers, and their Afghan partners are literally fighting to bring ordinary Afghans criminal justice capacity, dispute resolution services, and anti-corruption institutions, all with the aim of promoting the legitimacy of the Afghan government and defeating the insurgency. If that's not 'using law as a weapon of war' I don't know what is."[42]

General Martins himself did not embrace the notion of law as a weapon of war. He responded to Goldsmith, "If it merely becomes subordinated as a 'tool' or 'weapon' in the service of warfare, its authority and effectiveness will be undermined." But General Martins did call law a "powerful potential force in COIN," explaining, "When fighting an insurgency, a government that protects the population and upholds the rule of law can earn legitimacy—that is, authority in the eyes of the people."[43]

What to Consider When Using Human Rights in War

As we have now seen, the U.S. military used human rights as a weapon of war in a variety of ways, namely by capitalizing on its opponent's poor human rights record, conducting relief operations, and seeking to strengthen the rule of law. We will now assess the wisdom and consequences of it doing so.

In the opening months of the U.S. offensive into Afghanistan, many Afghans who believed strongly in notions of justice and democracy welcomed U.S. troops. As the months and years wore on, however, Afghans saw U.S. promises of stability and political change hampered significantly by U.S. strategic errors, such as empowering abusive warlords, taking overly militaristic approaches to governance, committing human rights abuses, and shrugging off accidental civilian casualties caused by airstrikes, night raids, and overaggressive convoy movements. Such contradictions between U.S. words and actions ultimately called into question for many Afghans the motivations, legitimacy, and credibility of U.S. military operations.

Both advertising the human rights abuses of your enemy to garner support for a war and using humanitarian aid and the rule of law as tools to defeat the enemy may appear, at first glance, to be appropriate and even effective. A key lesson from America's experience in Afghanistan, as well as in Iraq, nevertheless, is that human rights should not be used blindly as weapons of war, if at all. This is not to say that the military should not respect or promote human rights, for which there are legal, moral, ethical, strategic, and political reasons to do so. Rather, soldiers, commanders, and their civilian leaders must think seriously about the broad, strategic, and operational implications of using human rights as a central, or even secondary, tool for advancing military objectives. In Afghanistan, for example, the U.S. use of human rights as a weapon of war was on shaky ground from the start. The United States had long known of Taliban abuses in Afghanistan but never took serious action to mitigate those abuses prior to the war, something that human rights groups astutely pointed out. The human rights community had long been arguing that if the Taliban's abusive rule was not reined in, Afghanistan would become unresponsive to the rule of law and allow outlaw groups, such as al Qaeda, to find a base in that country.

Thus, when the United States used the Taliban's abuses to garner support for its 2001 invasion, it appeared to many that the United States was capitalizing on the suffering of the Taliban regime's victims. It was also problematic for the United States to recite Afghanistan's human rights problems when many Afghans saw the United States as having abandoned them to a bloody civil war that began after Afghans had, with American assistance, pushed out Soviet forces in the late 1980s. Also particularly problematic was the U.S. decision to arm the Northern Alliance directly after September 11, 2001, which included alleged war criminals with well-reported track records of atrocities.[44] In Iraq, too, the United States had supported the Saddam Hussein regime in its confrontations against Iran and then tried to downplay Saddam Hussein's gassing of his own people in 1998. An expert on Iraq wrote in 2003, "It is a good thing that Bush has highlighted these atrocities by a regime that is more brutal than most. Yet it is cynical to use them as a justification for American plans to terminate the regime. By any measure, the American record on Halabja is shameful."[45]

The U.S. government was equally on shaky ground when it used the language of human rights to garner support for the wars in Afghanistan and Iraq once it itself engaged in human rights violations. On October 8, 2003, with Iraq's president Saddam Hussein having been removed from power by the United States, President George W. Bush announced, "Iraq is free of a brutal dictator. Iraq is free of the man who caused there to be mass graves. Iraq is free of rape rooms and torture chambers. Iraq is free of a brutal thug. America did the right thing."[46] In May 2004, a different picture of U.S. actions in Iraq emerged—actions that were far from "the right thing" by any standard. Leaked to the media was an internal Department of Defense investigation report, along with shocking photographs that showed U.S. soldiers physically and mentally abusing detainees at the Forward Operating Base (FOB) Abu Ghraib, located twenty miles west of Iraq's capital of Baghdad. The report found that "between October and December 2003, at the Abu Ghraib Confinement Facility (BCCF), numerous incidents of sadistic, blatant, and wanton criminal abuses were inflicted on several detainees." The report described the abuses as systemic, illegal, and intentional.[47]

The report on Abu Ghraib—known commonly as the "Taguba Report" for its author Major General Antonio M. Taguba—provided a thirteen-point list of the types of abuses that military police personnel intentionally inflicted on detainees. These included, among others, punching, slapping, and kicking detainees; videotaping and photographing naked male and female detainees; forcibly arranging detainees in various sexually explicit positions for photographing; forcing detainees to remove their clothing and keeping them naked for several days at a time; positioning a naked detainee on a box, with a sandbag on his head, and attaching wires to his fingers, toes, and penis to simulate electric torture; and forcing groups of male detainees to masturbate themselves while being photographed and videotaped.[48]

The impact that the Abu Ghraib abuses had on the U.S. reputation around the world cannot be overstated. The abuses undercut the U.S. ability to credibly criticize other countries for violating human rights. They gave nations an (unjustified) excuse for violating the rights of terrorist suspects. And, finally, they served as a recruiting tool for terrorist groups. Abu Ghraib, moreover, was not the only blight on the U.S. human rights reputation with respect to its wars in Afghanistan and Iraq. The detainee abuse was endemic and not, as President George W. Bush claimed when the Abu Ghraib scandal broke, a result of a "small number of American service men and women."[49] U.S. personnel abused detainees at many U.S. detention facilities, including the military detention facility on Bagram Airfield in Afghanistan, the detention camps at Guantanamo Bay, and CIA "black sites" located in countries around the world. Some of the abuses led to deaths, as was the case with two detainees at Bagram in December 2002.[50]

Detainee abuse occurred for multiple reasons.[51] U.S. government agencies failed to provide proper training and resources to detaining authorities; some military commanders were grossly delinquent in their responsibilities; some soldiers acted well beyond what the law permitted. Some of the worst abuses resulted from the Bush administration's decision to cast aside the legal protections that international law afforded detainees in times of war. Administration lawyers—particularly from the Department of Justice's Office of Legal Counsel—claimed that the Geneva Conventions did not protect war on terror detainees and provided an interpretation of "torture" that permitted U.S. personnel to apply interrogation techniques, such as waterboarding, that the United States had previously considered unlawful.[52] Investigating these abuses, the Constitution Project's bipartisan Task Force on Detainee Treatment found that "the nation's most senior officials, through some of their actions and failures to act in the months and years immediately following the September 11 attacks, bear ultimate responsibility for allowing and contributing to the spread of illegal and improper interrogation techniques used by some U.S. personnel on detainees in several theaters."[53] The U.S. military was also heavily criticized for detaining individuals who should never have been detained in the first place. This was largely due to another problem: lack of due process guarantees of detainees in Iraq, Afghanistan, Guantanamo Bay, and the CIA's black sites.

Those in authority, however, were not uniformly in agreement about which legal protections applied and which interrogations techniques could be administered. In 2002, a day after White House Counsel Alberto Gonzales advised the president that the Third Geneva Convention did not apply to al Qaeda or the Taliban, Secretary of Defense Donald Rumsfeld rescinded the order by General Tommy Franks to apply the Geneva Conventions to detainees in the field. Also in 2002, the legal advisors to all four branches of the armed services objected to a series of proposed interrogation techniques, with several of them asserting that the techniques contained activities that could result in service members being prosecuted and requesting more time for review. Nonetheless, Rumsfeld approved a series of those proposed interrogation techniques for general use at Guantanamo Bay, including techniques that allowed sleep deprivation, stress positions, deprivation of food for up to twelve hours, handcuffing, and hooding.[54] Journalists reported that several agents from the Federal Bureau of Investigation working at Guantanamo Bay were also uncomfortable being involved with the military's interrogation techniques.[55] Despite these and other internal disputes, however, policies were put in place that enabled and encouraged torture.

The Bush and Obama administrations also came under considerable criticism for the killing and injuring of civilians in night raids and airstrikes, including unmanned aerial vehicle ("drone") strikes carried out by the CIA and U.S. military. In some cases the casualties resulted from criminal acts by U.S. personnel, in other cases only rules of engagement were violated, and there were cases in which rules were followed but civilians were killed regardless. Some U.S. commanders sought to learn lessons and implemented new regulations to reduce civilian harm.[56] Nonetheless, many Afghans and Iraqis could not comprehend why the United States repeatedly made the same types of mistakes and consequently killed or injured innocent people (Afghans and Iraqis often blamed informants who gave the United States false intelligence to settle personal scores). The United Nations and local and international human rights groups also criticized the United States for transferring its detainees to other governments, which then tortured them.[57]

Finally, many critics pointed to a lack of transparency and accountability. The Obama administration, for example, faced bipartisan criticism for failing to disclose where it conducted drone strikes, what legal framework it applied to those strikes, and what legal criteria it used to determine who could and could not be targeted.[58] U.S. detention operations were likewise cloaked in secrecy: the United States refused to reveal in what countries it operated the CIA's "black sites";[59] only starting in 2010 did the government make earnest efforts to allow nongovernmental human rights organizations to visit its main detention facility in Afghanistan and observe Detainee Review Boards;[60] and lawyers representing Guantanamo Bay detainees were subjected to extremely strict rules of classification that restricted their ability to defend their clients.[61]

With such a high premium placed on secrecy, victims of detainee abuse and other abuses struggled to find legal redress. In many cases the government claimed the "state secrets privilege" to shield itself from accountability, a privilege that the courts often accepted.[62] In other cases, the judiciary was so deferential to the executive's wartime authority that courts claimed they were forbidden from judging the administration's actions.[63] While human rights abuses did result in some criminal prosecutions and administrative reprimands and demotions, many of those involved in the abuses, including high-level decision makers, were not brought to justice. Some lawyers, in response, sought accountability in non-U.S. venues, such as the European Court of Human Rights, or under universal jurisdiction laws in foreign countries.[64]

Blockages to accountability were seen in other ways. In Afghanistan, for example, ISAF had on several occasions made quick public denials of allegations of civilian casualties, only to be proven wrong later by human rights groups, investigative journalists, or internal inquiries. It was also problematic that the U.S. military usually did not publicize criminal and administrative actions against its own personnel, and thus the victims of abuses, their families and communities, and the public at large remained unaware that the military was seeking accountability. In these instances, local populations—left with the false impression that the U.S. military allowed its personnel to operate above the law and without regard to the lives of the people in Afghanistan and Iraq that the U.S. government claimed to be protecting—were angry and resentful.

Over time—either through policy choices, staffing changes, elections, or legal rulings—the Bush and Obama administrations rescinded several of the legal memos that led to detainee abuse, adjusted rules aimed at limiting civilian casualties, and provided greater due process guarantees. In some cases, however, the achievements were inadequate or short-lived. In Afghanistan, for example, the U.S. military's 2010 shift toward greater transparency and improved detainee review procedures underwent significant regressions starting in 2011. Moreover, at the time of this writing many human rights lawyers and activists still regarded the lack of U.S. due process guarantees, transparency, and accountability, as well as ongoing cases of civilian casualties, deeply problematic.

President George W. Bush's emphasis on Saddam Hussein's "torture chambers" and "rape rooms" is illustrative of the problems that arise when a government criticizes its enemy for human rights abuses and then commits human rights abuses itself. Those phrases lost most of their rhetorical value with the American public, the public of U.S.-allied countries, and—perhaps most important—the public of the countries the United States was seeking to garner support from when it became known that the United States itself was torturing detainees and abusing them in other ways. The term "rape rooms" nearly disappeared from Bush's speeches with the publication of the Abu Ghraib photographs, and the president "steered clear of prison references when establishing the savagery of the enemy."[65]

Perhaps more detrimental was the fact that America's human rights abuses during the two wars did not quickly fade from memory. U.S. military personnel, who frequently rotated through their deployments, were therefore not directly responsible for the abuses that preceded them, and were also therefore likely to regard each case of abuse as a single, isolated, and deplorable act. Afghans and Iraqis, in contrast, often saw each abuse as part of an accumulated problem that had amassed over several years.[66] Even the earliest of the human rights abuses by U.S. personnel in the Afghanistan and Iraq Wars remained fresh in the minds of local populations years later. What this meant in practical terms was that one act of abuse was linked to every abuse that came before it, regardless of the perpetrator. That, in turn, increased the local population's distrust and lack of confidence in the U.S. military, and even government. Any good faith effort that the military made toward the people of Afghanistan and Iraq was undermined by U.S. human rights abuses from the past; any claim of a successful U.S. human rights accomplishment was open to criticism and skepticism due to U.S. human rights failures, both past and present. This was one of the main consequences that many soldiers needed to better understand when considering what impact human rights abuses and law of war violations had on their war efforts.

The abuses had a direct operational impact, too. Insurgents used U.S. human rights abuses to build support for their agendas, recruit, and justify their violence. The abuses also undermined command authority and caused psychological trauma for the soldiers who carried out or who were exposed to the abuses.[67] Adding to the detriments in Afghanistan, local populations transposed negative attitudes toward U.S. military forces to all ISAF forces, undermining their ability to execute their missions. In addition, these abuses made it more difficult for some U.S. allies to partner with America's war efforts.[68] The United Kingdom, for example, had at times refused to transfer its detainees in Afghanistan to U.S. military custody because of concerns about detainee abuse and lack of due process. Furthermore, residents of both Afghanistan and Iraq, watching U.S. troops capture and detain large numbers of people only to later release them because they posed no threat, became skeptical of U.S. military capabilities to capture real insurgents. These are but some of the negative consequences that the U.S. human rights abuses in Afghanistan and Iraq had on U.S. war efforts.

The U.S. use of relief operations and rule of law reform efforts as weapons of war, as described above, also raised significant questions. While humanitarian assistance and rule of law are essential to local populations in war stricken areas, given the amount of blood, labor, money, and time that the U.S. military spent on them, it is necessary to ask whether those efforts were useful endeavors. Jamie Williamson concluded, based on a review of the limited research available in 2012, that "there is little, if any, evidence that short-term humanitarian assistance initiatives, when implemented by international forces, have benefited the overall counter-insurgency strategy, especially in Afghanistan."[69] Moreover, international law requires that a military allows humanitarian relief agencies to provide assistance impartially and without adverse discrimination; it also prohibits the military from fighting a war by starving the civilian population and targeting objects indispensable to the civilian population's survival.[70] While international law does not strictly prohibit the military from carrying out relief operations in sync with its COIN approach (in fact, in some situations international law requires the military to provide such assistance), the underlying spirit of humanitarian assistance is for it to be provided on the basis of the population's needs and not on military advantage. In talking about how the military should allow impartial and independent humanitarian agencies to operate, Williamson put it this way: "the beneficiaries of aid and relief are those who are in need and who are suffering because of the conflict, not those who might be strategically important in overcoming insurgents."[71] This principle seems in direct contrast to the military's underlying notion of using relief operations as a war weapon.

But risks remain even when military relief operations distribute assistance impartially and without adverse discrimination. When militaries provide relief assistance, insurgents have come to regard all assistance—both that provided by the military and that provided by independent relief organizations—as part of the war effort. In that scenario, the independent humanitarian relief workers become targets, as do all humanitarian projects, including schools and hospitals. And when U.S. forces killed civilians or U.S. human rights abuses were reported, this association of humanitarian workers with the U.S. military further increased their risk. The fact that military operations were administered out of some PRT sites also made those relief efforts targets for their close links to the war efforts. As a result, many NGOs demanded that the military limit its role in relief operations.[72] Many in the military have considered this approach impractical and overly principled, but humanitarian relief organizations are protective of their independence, which if jeopardized may not only cause them security concerns, but also destroy their access to people living in insurgent-held areas (i.e., the insurgents may refuse the humanitarians' safe passage and attack them) and threaten their reputation and thus efficacy in future conflicts.

Like humanitarian assistance, strong rule of law is essential. But, also like humanitarian assistance, problems result when the military attempts to strengthen the rule of law as a means to defeat insurgents. In Afghanistan the United States was, generally speaking, in a relatively poor position to lead by example with regard to rule of law. This was not only due to its human rights record and a lack of transparency and accountability, but also because in the beginning of the war the United States provided financial and military support to Afghan warlords who were suspected of committing many of the atrocities in the 1990s civil war. Many Afghans hoped that the warlords responsible for those crimes would be brought to justice. Instead, the United States partnered with them and strengthened their position in Afghan politics. When the United States then criticized corrupt Afghan government officials, the inevitable response was that the Americans had helped to put them in power. The United States also provided considerable support to Afghanistan's National Directorate of Security (NDS) and to other security officials that were notorious for abusing detainees. Many Afghans therefore saw U.S. rule of law efforts as being at cross-purposes with other military, intelligence, and political strategies. They thus saw the U.S. rule of law efforts as either disingenuous or low in priority, despite the fact that Afghans had continuously demanded a strong rule of law from their previous governments.

Using rule of law to military ends also influenced the development of Afghanistan's legal system and procedures. It tended to create a system of rules that favored prosecutors, judges, convictions, and police but not judicial review mechanisms and the defense counsels who protect the rights of suspected criminals. The United States also seemed to favor technical projects, such as building courtrooms, providing human rights trainings, and training police, that did not respond to underlying causes of rule of law deficiencies, such as bribery, corruption, and the police being used for criminal enterprises.[73]

Responding to this imbalance, many Afghans regarded the justice system as one-sided and unable to provide the fairness and predictability required in any strong rule of law system; military actions thus worked against the counterinsurgency goals of increasing local support for the government through rule of law. When the United States, and its military in particular, encouraged President Karzai on several occasions to adopt a U.S.-like military internment regime, the United States put itself in the awkward and inconsistent position of pushing for strong rule of law on the one hand, while on the other pushing the Karzai administration to violate Afghan constitutional law and its international human rights obligations.[74]

The U.S. military's efforts to reform the Afghan National Police (ANP) was also at odds with its rule of law commitments. It was in 2009, when U.S. leaders deployed a robust COIN approach, that the United States also ramped up its efforts to turn the ANP into what amounted to an auxiliary security force to the Afghan military for purposes of fighting insurgents.[75] While it is difficult to determine the exact impact of the military-led police reform efforts in Afghanistan, several issues are important to consider: Militaries and law enforcement institutions often have different rules of engagement and standards on the use of force, handling detainees, and evidence collection. As a result, when law enforcement activities become militarized, there can be a rise in the use of lethal force, an increase in the detainee population and detainee abuse, and a thinning out of due process. There is also a risk of limited transparency and accountability. Some of these results are militarily beneficial, at least in the short term. Still, it is worth considering that a more militaristic approach to policing can erode the relationship of trust between the police and local communities that is pivotal to successful and sustainable policing. Using police to fight insurgents can also result, as it did in Afghanistan, in a civilian policing gap, in which there were too few police focused on the problems of common crime and on maintaining peace and order outside the counterinsurgency context.

Conclusion: Looking Forward

The United States has had a varied relationship with human rights, both at home and abroad. The Afghanistan and Iraq Wars demonstrate that the U.S. government identified benefits in using human rights on the battlefield to build public and international support against its enemies. It did this by highlighting its enemies' human rights abuses and its own human rights accomplishments. The military also used relief operations and rule of law reform projects in Afghanistan and Iraq to fight its enemies. This was largely done as part of the COIN doctrine, which the 2006 version of the Army Field Manual on Counterinsurgency defined as "military, paramilitary, political, economic, psychological, and civic actions taken by a government to defeat insurgency."[76]

Yet, difficulties may arise when the U.S. military uses human rights as a weapon of war, including in contexts where U.S. personnel commit human rights abuses. In the Afghanistan and Iraq Wars, these abuses led to the erosion of the military's reputation at the local and international levels, which then prevented the United States from claiming a high moral authority. There were also serious operational consequences, whereby military operations that leaders claimed benefitted the local population evoked suspicion and allies refused to work with the United States. But, as this chapter has shown, even if the United States had not committed human rights abuses, the uses of relief operations and rule of law reform efforts as war weapons create their own complex and difficult issues. Any relief and rule of law reform operations must be able to respond to the questions of whether it is appropriate, necessary, and useful for the military to get involved in these activities and what consequences may arise if the military does get involved.

The premise that military action against suspected terrorists and terrorist groups will long be a focus of the military raises the additional important question—not discussed in this chapter—of whether it is even possible to have counterinsurgency and counterterrorism (CT) operations occurring in the same theater of war. They are two drastically different approaches to warfare. In Afghanistan, for example, Special Operations Forces and Intelligence Community activities often resulting in the death, injury, or detention of civilians have discredited the COIN efforts to build trust and confidence in the local populations. It will be imperative moving forward for military strategists to consider how, if at all, COIN and CT can coexist without one undermining the other.

Admittedly, the concerns raised here are based on wars in which the United States deployed large numbers of troops. That may not be the case in future conflicts. The drawn-out U.S. military interventions in Afghanistan and Iraq have made the United States war weary, and Americans will likely resist sending heavy deployments of soldiers to fight abroad—unless, of course, there is another September 11–type attack. The Department of Defense has used a "light footprint" approach already in Somalia, Yemen, Pakistan, and elsewhere. Thus the questions become, with no, or few, combat troops on the ground abroad, will it be easier for the military to use human rights as a weapon of war? Do light-footprint war efforts reduce the potential for human rights abuses? A light footprint may reduce risks, but it will not eliminate them. This is largely because a light-footprint approach requires considerable cooperation between governments, including abusive ones. U.S. military and other government agencies will therefore want to train and assist foreign security forces, share intelligence, and, at times, conduct joint military operations. In such situations, as has occurred in the past, if the U.S. military provides assistance to foreign security forces with poor human rights records, it will nonetheless draw both local and international criticism. Certain U.S. laws mitigate against this problem by restricting funding going to such abusive forces, but it nonetheless occurs frequently. In other words, even when the United States looks to gain military influence and security abroad while reluctant to deploy substantial fighting forces, a light footprint offers neither a political nor an operational panacea to the issues that this chapter raises.

NOTES

This chapter was written in the author's personal capacity. The author thanks Kate Clark, Ralph Mamiya, Christopher Rogers, Joshua Sussman, and the editors of this book, Beth Bailey and Richard H. Immerman, for their valuable comments and feedback. All errors remain the author's own.

1 United Nations Office of the High Commissioner for Human Rights (hereafter UNOHCHR), "The Core International Human Rights Instruments and Their Monitoring Bodies," http://www.ohchr.org/EN/ProfessionalInterest/Pages/CoreInstruments.aspx.

2 UNOHCHR, "Human Rights Bodies," http://www.ohchr.org/EN/HRBodies/Pages/HumanRightsBodies.aspx.

3 Ibid.

4 M. Glen Johnson, "The Contributions of Eleanor and Franklin Roosevelt to the Development of International Protection for Human Rights," *Human Rights Quarterly* 9, no. 1 (February 1987): 19–48.

5 Ibid.; President Franklin D. Roosevelt, "The 'Four Freedoms'" (annual message to Congress, January 6, 1941), http://www.fdrlibrary.marist.edu/pdfs/ffreadingcopy.pdf.

6 Johnson, "Contributions of Eleanor and Franklin Roosevelt," 24 and 30.

7 A. J. Hobbins, "Eleanor Roosevelt, John Humphrey: and Canadian Opposition to the Universal Declaration of Human Rights: Looking Back on the 50th Anniversary of UNDHR," *International Journal* 53, no. 2 (Spring 1998): 332.

8 United Nations, "United Nations Treaty Collection, Status of the Convention on the Rights of the Child as of August 5, 2014," http://treaties.un.org/Pages/ViewDetails.aspx?src=TREATY&mtdsg_no=IV-11&chapter=4&lang=en; and Human Rights Watch, "US: Senate Misses Opportunity on Disability Convention: Ratification Vote for Treaty Falls Short" (December 4, 2012), http://www.hrw.org/news/2012/12/04/us-senate-misses-opportunity-disability-convention.

9 Beth Van Schaack, "The United States' Position on the Extraterritorial Application of Human Rights Obligations: Now Is the Time for Change," *International Law Studies* 90 (2014), https://www.usnwc.edu/getattachment/a88e97e5-11ec-4dfb-a013-4cfa5f8efe5a/The-United-States--Position-on-the-Extraterritoria.aspx.

10 White House, "National Security Strategy" (May 2010), http://www.whitehouse.gov/sites/default/files/rss_viewer/national_security_strategy.pdf.

11 David P. Forsythe, "American Foreign Policy and Human Rights: Rhetoric and Reality," *Universal Human Rights* 2, no. 3 (July–September 1980): 43–44.

12 David P. Forsythe, "Human Rights and Foreign Policy: In the Next Millennium," *International Journal* 53, no. 1 (Winter 1997–98): 118.

13 President William J. Clinton, "Address to the Nation on Airstrikes Against Serbian Targets in the Federal Republic of Yugoslavia (Serbia and Montenegro)" (March 24, 1999), http://www.presidency.ucsb.edu/ws/?pid=57305.

14 President George W. Bush, "President Asks American Children to Help Afghan Children" (October 12, 2001), http://georgewbush-whitehouse.archives.gov/news/releases/2001/10/20011012-4.html.

15 Laura Bush, "Radio Address by Laura Bush to the Nation" (November 17, 2001), http://georgewbush-whitehouse.archives.gov/news/releases/2001/11/20011117.html. Kate Clark has noted that the Taliban's pulling off women's fingernails for wearing nail polish is an urban myth. Kate Clark, email, January 19, 2014.

16 "Report: Iraq Intelligence 'Dead Wrong': Bush Says Fundamental Changes Needed in Spy Agencies," *CNN*, April 1, 2005, http://www.cnn.com/2005/POLITICS/03/31/intel.report/index.html.

17 U.S. Senate Select Committee on Intelligence, "Report of the Select Committee on Intelligence on Postwar Findings about Iraq's WMD Programs and Links to Terrorism and How They Compare with Prewar Assessments" (109th Congress, 2nd Session, Senate, September 8, 2006), http://www.intelligence.senate.gov/phaseiiaccuracy.pdf.

18 "Bush Declares War," *CNN*, March 19, 2003, http://www.cnn.com/2003/US/03/19/sprj.irq.int.bush.transcript/.

19 President George W. Bush, "President's Radio Address" (March 15, 2003), http://www.gpo.gov/fdsys/pkg/PPP-2003-book1/pdf/PPP-2003-book1-doc-pg266.pdf.

20 President George W. Bush, "Address to the Nation on Iraq" (March 17, 2003), http://www.cnn.com/2003/WORLD/meast/03/17/sprj.irq.bush.transcript/.

21 President George W. Bush, "Address to a Joint Session of Congress and the American People" (September 20, 2001), http://georgewbush-whitehouse.archives.gov/news/releases/2001/09/20010920-8.html.

22 President George W. Bush, "President Building Worldwide Campaign Against Terrorism" (September 19, 2001), http://2001-2009.state.gov/s/ct/rls/rm/2001/5028.htm.

23 Laura Bush, "Radio Address."

24 President George W. Bush, "President Speaks to the United Nations General Assembly" (September 21, 2004), http://georgewbush-whitehouse.archives.gov/news/releases/2004/09/20040921-3.html.

25 President George W. Bush, "Presidential Address to the Nation" (October 7, 2001), http://georgewbush-whitehouse.archives.gov/news/releases/2001/10/20011007-8.html.

26 United Nations, "Humanitarian Appeal for Iraq: Revised Inter-agency Appeal, 1 April–31 December 2003" (June 2003), http://reliefweb.int/appeals/2003/files/irq-03flash2.pdf.

27 Department of the Army, "Counterinsurgency—Field Manual 3-24" (December 15, 2006), 6-1, emphasis added.

28 Ibid., D-6, D-7.

29 The terms "shape-clear-hold-build" and "clear-hold-build-transfer" are also used. Anthony H. Cordesman, "'Shape, Clear, Hold, Build, and Transfer': The Full Metrics of the Afghan War" (Center for Strategic and International Studies, February 18, 2010), https://csis.org/files/publication/100302_afghan_metrics_combined.pdf.

30 Jamie Williamson, "Using Humanitarian Aid to 'Win Hearts and Minds': A Costly Failure?," International Review of the Red Cross 93, no. 884 (December 2011): 1040.

31 Department of the Army, "Tactics in Counterinsurgency—Field Manual 3-24.2" (April 21, 2009), 4–9, http://armypubs.army.mil/doctrine/DR_pubs/dr_a/pdf/fm3_24x2.pdf.

32 Ibid., 5–23.

33 Stephen Carter and Kate Clark, "No Shortcut to Stability: Justice, Politics and Insurgency in Afghanistan" (Chatham House, December 2010), 20, http://www.chathamhouse.org/sites/default/files/public/Research/Asia/1210pr_afghanjustice.pdf.

34 Ibid.

35 Ibid., 4.

36 Paul Fishstein and Andrew Wilder, "Winning Hearts and Minds? Examining the Relationship between Aid and Security in Afghanistan" (Feinstein International Center, January 2012), http://fic.tufts.edu/assets/WinningHearts-Final.pdf.

37 Department of the Army, "Counterinsurgency Operations—Field Manual–Interim 3-07.22" (October 1, 2004), 4-4, https://www.fas.org/irp/doddir/army/fmi3-07-22.pdf.

38 Liana Sun Wyler and Kenneth Katzman, "Afghanistan: U.S. Rule of Law and Justice Sector Assistance" (Congressional Research Service, November 9, 2010), http://www.fas.org/sgp/crs/row/R41484.pdf.

39 General Stanley McChrystal, "Commander's Initial Assessment" (August 30, 2009), http://www.washingtonpost.com/wp-dyn/content/article/2009/09/21/AR2009092100110.html.

40 North Atlantic Treaty Organization, "NATO Rule of Law Field Support Mission (NROLFSM)" (Media Backgrounder), http://www.isaf.nato.int/images/media/PDFs/110930rolbackground.pdf.

41 Chris Rogers, "Afghanistan Post-2014: Closing Bagram," JustSecurity.org, November 14, 2013, http://justsecurity.org/2013/11/14/guest-post-afghanistan-post-2014-closing-bagram/; Kate Clark, "65 'Innocent'/'Dangerous' Detainees Released from Bagram: What Secret Documents Say about Afghan and US Claims," Afghanistan Analysts Network, February 13, 2014, http://www.afghanistan-analysts.org/65-innocent-or-dangerous-detainees-released-from-bagram-secret-documents-and-afghan-and-us-claims.

42 Jack Goldsmith, "Thoughts on 'Lawfare,'" Lawfareblog.com, September 8, 2010, http://www.lawfareblog.com/2010/09/thoughts-on-lawfare/#.UtAmDNLkvpU.

43 Mark Martins, "Building the Rule of Law in Theory?," Lawfareblog.com, November 22, 2010, http://www.lawfareblog.com/2010/11/building-the-rule-of-law-in-theory/.

44 Gregg Zoroya, "Northern Alliance Has Bloody Past, Critics Warn," USA Today, October 12, 2001, http://usatoday30.usatoday.com/news/attack/2001/10/12/northern-alliance-usatcov.htm.

45 Joost R. Hiltermann, "Halabja: America Didn't Seem to Mind Poison Gas," New York Times, January 17, 2003, http://www.nytimes.com/2003/01/17/opinion/17iht-edjoost_ed3_.html.

46 George W. Bush, "Remarks by the President at the 2003 Republican National Committee Presidential Gala" (October 8, 2003), http://georgewbush-whitehouse.archives.gov/news/releases/2003/10/20031008-9.html.

47 Department of Defense, "Article 15-6 Investigation of the 800th Military Police Brigade ('Taguba Report')" (May 27, 2004), http://www.dod.mil/pubs/foi/operation_and_plans/Detainee/taguba/TAGUBA_REPORT_CERTIFICATIONS.pdf. See also Seymour Hersh, "Torture at Abu Ghraib: American Soldiers Brutalized Iraqis. How Far up Does the Responsibility Go?," New Yorker, May 10, 2004.

48 Department of Defense, "Article 15-6 Investigation."

49 President George W. Bush, "The President's Radio Address" (May 8, 2004), http://www.presidency.ucsb.edu/ws/?pid=25150.

50 Constitution Project, "The Report of the Constitution Project's Task Force on Detainee Treatment" (2013), 68–72.

51 Ibid., 109.

52 Ibid., 137, 142–43; Evan Wallach, "Waterboarding Used to Be a Crime," Washington Post, November 4, 2007, http://www.washingtonpost.com/wp-dyn/content/article/2007/11/02/AR2007110201170.html.

53 Constitution Project, "Report of the Constitution Project," 9.

54 Ibid., 136–37, 38–39.

55 Jane Mayer, The Dark Side: The Inside Story of How the War on Terror Turned into a War on American Ideals (New York: Doubleday, 2009), 202–4.

56 Department of the Army, "Civilian Casualty Mitigation—Army Tactics, Techniques, and Procedures 3-37.31" (July 18, 2012), http://armypubs.army.mil/doctrine/DR_pubs/dr_a/pdf/attp3_37x31.pdf.

57 UNAMA/UNOHCHR, "Treatment of Conflict-Related Detainees in Afghan Custody" (October 2011), http://unama.unmissions.org/Portals/UNAMA/Documents/October10_%202011_UNAMA_Detention_Full-Report_ENG.pdf; Afghanistan Independent Human Rights Commission and Open Society Foundations, "Torture, Transfers, and Denial of Due Process: The Treatment of Conflict-Related Detainees in Afghanistan" (March 17, 2012), http://www.aihrc.org.af/media/files/AIHRC%20OSF%20Detentions%20Report%20English%20Final%2017-3-2012.pdf; Open Society Justice Initiative, "Globalizing Torture: CIA Secret Detention and Extraordinary Rendition" (February 2013), http://www.opensocietyfoundations.org/reports/globalizing-torture-cia-secret-detention-and-extraordinary-rendition.

58 See Julie Hirschfeld Davis, Laura Litvan, and Greg Stohr, "Obama Faces Bipartisan Pressure on Drone Big Brother Fear," *Bloomberg News*, March 8, 2013, http://www.bloomberg.com/news/2013-03-08/obama-faces-bipartisan-pressure-on-drone-big-brother-fear.html; Human Rights Watch and nine other institutions, "Joint Letter to President Obama on US Drone Strikes and Targeted Killings" (April 11, 2013), http://www.hrw.org/news/2013/04/11/joint-letter-president-obama-us-drone-strikes-and-targeted-killings.

59 Open Society Justice Initiative, "Globalizing Torture," 12.

60 Jonathan Horowitz, "The New Bagram: Has Anything Changed?," *Huffington Post*, March 18, 2010, http://www.huffingtonpost.com/jonathan-horowitz/the-new-bagram-has-anythi_b_365819.html; Jonathan Horowitz, "New Detention Rules Show Promise and Problems," *Huffington Post*, June 20, 2010, http://www.huffingtonpost.com/jonathan-horowitz/new-detention-rules-show_b_544509.html.

61 Carol Rosenberg, "Guantánamo Defense Attorneys Want to Accuse U.S. of Torture—but Can't," *Miami Herald*, October 22, 2013, http://www.miamiherald.com/2013/10/22/3704653/guantanamo-defense-attorneys-want.html.

62 American Civil Liberties Union, "ACLU Asks Supreme Court to Hear Extraordinary Rendition Case" (press release, December 8, 2010), https://www.aclu.org/national-security/aclu-asks-supreme-court-hear-extraordinary-rendition-case.

63 Charlie Savage, "Suit over Targeted Killings Is Thrown Out," *New York Times*, December 7, 2010, http://www.nytimes.com/2010/12/08/world/middleeast/08killing.html.

64 See, for example, Amrit Singh, "European Court of Human Rights Finds Against CIA Abuse of Khaled el-Masri," *Guardian*, December 13, 2013, http://www.theguardian.com/commentisfree/2012/dec/13/european-court-human-rights-cia-abuse-khaled-elmasri.

65 Eran N. Ben-Porath, "Rhetoric of Atrocities: The Place of Horrific Human Rights Abuses in Presidential Persuasion Efforts," *Presidential Studies Quarterly* 37, no. 2 (June 2007): 195–96.

66 See, for example, Open Society Foundations, "The Trust Deficit: The Impact of Local Perceptions on Policy in Afghanistan" (October 7, 2010), http://www.opensocietyfoundations.org/sites/default/files/perceptions-20101007_0.pdf.

67 Joshua E. S. Phillips, *None of Us Were Like This Before: American Soldiers and Torture* (Verso, 2010).

68 Constitution Project, "Report of the Constitution Project," 278.

69 Williamson, "Using Humanitarian Aid," 1052. See also Fishstein and Wilder, "Winning Hearts and Minds?," 68.

70 For a legal review, see Williamson, "Using Humanitarian Aid," 1048–51; and Jean-Marie Henckaerts and Louise Doswald-Beck, eds., *Customary International Humanitarian Law—Volume I: Rules* (Cambridge: Cambridge University Press and International Committee of the Red Cross, 2005), 186–202.

71 Williamson, "Using Humanitarian Aid," 1049.

72 International Rescue Committee, "Aid Groups Urge NATO to Separate Military and Humanitarian Activities to Protect Civilians in Afghanistan," http://www.rescue.

org/news/aid-groups-urge-nato-separate-military-and-humanitarian-activities-protect-civilians-afghanista-4463; Lara Olson, "Fighting for Humanitarian Space: NGOs in Afghanistan," *Journal of Military and Strategic Studies* 9, no. 1 (Fall 2006): 13.

73 Clark, email.

74 See, for example, Tim Golden, "Foiling U.S. Plan, Prison Expands in Afghanistan," *New York Times*, January 7, 2008, http://www.nytimes.com/2008/01/07/world/asia/07bagram.html?ref=bagramairbaseafghanistan; Open Society Foundations Regional Policy Initiative, "Remaking Bagram: The Creation of an Afghan Internment Regime and the Divide over U.S. Detention Power" (September 6, 2012), http://www.opensocietyfoundations.org/reports/remaking-bagram-creation-afghan-internment-regime-and-divide-over-us-detention-power.

75 Cornelius Friesendorf, "International Intervention and the Use of Force: Military and Police Roles" (Geneva Centre for the Democratic Control of Armed Forces, 2012); and Cornelius Friesendorf and Jörg Krempel, "Militarized versus Civilian Policing: Problems of Reforming the Afghan National Police" (Peace Research Institute Frankfurt, 2011).

76 Department of the Army, "Counterinsurgency," 1–1.

PART III

Waging and the Wages of War

7

The Combatants' Experiences

LISA MUNDEY

America's wars are declared by its elected leaders. They are shaped by those leaders' shifting geopolitical visions, by the uncertain knowledge gleaned and analyzed by the Intelligence Community, by military doctrines considered and adopted, by the long and often complex histories and relationships of nations and regions. But in the end, America's wars are fought by its youth.

More than 2.6 million American service members were deployed in Iraq and Afghanistan. These young men and women had their lives disrupted. Some faced combat; others dealt primarily with unrelenting boredom. More than sixty-eight hundred of these men and women were killed in action in the two wars, with almost ten times that number physically wounded and close to thirty times that number diagnosed with posttraumatic stress disorder, or PTSD.

As the American military was sent to fight in distant places, an entire cohort of American children grew up in a nation at war, entering kindergarten in the months before the attacks of September 11, 2001, and graduating high school in the spring of 2014. But this nation at war bore little resemblance to the United States in previous major wars. World War II had subsumed almost everything to its needs, pulling sixteen million men into uniform and touching almost every aspect of home front lives. The Korean War was more limited, and more politically divisive. Vietnam cost 58,220 American lives, and the controversy that raged over that war tore the nation apart. In contrast, the wars in Iraq and Afghanistan remained, for most Americans, on the periphery. Evidence of war appeared in support for the troops: bumper stickers on SUVs, applause in airports, a much-heralded Super Bowl commercial. But as Army Sergeant Sharon Allen wrote in *Operation Homecoming: Iraq, Afghanistan, and the Home Front, in the Words of U.S. Troops and Their Families*, while "everyone says they are supporting us," most civilians "have no idea about who soldiers really are" or what they go through.[1]

This essay illuminates those soldiers—and the marines, sailors, and airmen who served with them in Iraq and Afghanistan. It begins by briefly describing who did, in fact, serve in the nation's first extended wars fought by an all-volunteer force, and then turns to words drawn from the memoirs, blogs, and emails in which service members have tried to relate their experiences to those of us at home. Some of their descriptions are graphic, and some of their language profane. Both, in my judgment, are essential to capturing the combatants' experiences, to emphasizing—in the midst of discussions of doctrine and national strategy and geopolitics—the human scale and consequences of war. In the end, this is a story about the men and women who serve in an all-volunteer force, many of whom deployed multiple times, and how their experiences are largely disconnected from the American society that sent them to war.

Who Serves

The United States ended conscription in 1973, at the conclusion of ground combat in the Vietnam War. Thus all who fought in Iraq and Afghanistan were volunteers. Some of those who had joined in the pre-9/11, post–Cold War years were surprised by the sudden shift in the conditions of their service. The Army had advertised its National Guard as "One Weekend a Month"; a photograph of an Army jeep in Afghanistan bearing the hand-lettered sign "One Weekend a Month, My Ass" cycled through social media across Iraq, Afghanistan, and the United States in the summer of 2003, as Guard units accounted for up to 41 percent of troops deployed to Iraq in the early years of the war.[2]

Because the United States relied on its volunteer force rather than using the draft to fill the ranks in time of extended war, troops were often deployed more than once. Of the 2.6 million who have served in Iraq or Afghanistan, around 40 percent completed multiple tours; some deployed as many as four or five times. They also served longer periods overseas than anticipated, up to eighteen months at a stretch.[3]

Since the Bush administration had not anticipated a drawn-out insurgency in either Iraq or Afghanistan, the call-ups for the second round of deployments surprised some troops. "I figured that the Army was big enough that one unit would not have to go back again and again before this thing was over," Sergeant Alexander Garcia remarked on his second deployment. Although he claimed not to feel resentment, he also said, "I kind of feel like I did my part. Just as I was readjusting to life back home, just as I was starting to feel normal again, this kind of throws me back into the waves."[4] Though the prospect of repeated deployment prompted some to leave military service, others chose to reenlist even knowing that they were likely going overseas again. Some of these men and women believed in the avowed causes of the wars, while "others were driven by powerful loyalty to units and friends. For some it was simply their job."[5] Between 2004 and 2011, some soldiers had no choice whether to stay or go, as the U.S. military began to apply a "stop loss" policy, which prevented individuals from returning home at the end of an enlistment contract if the person's unit was still deployed. The rationale for the policy was "to promote continuity within deployed units," but not surprisingly, the stop-loss policy did not prove popular with troops or with their families.[6]

Recruiting volunteers became more difficult as casualty rates rose, and the military began offering large bonuses on enlistment. The ongoing wars also changed who volunteered: many fewer African Americans (who made up a disproportionate percentage of Army troops, though not in the combat arms) volunteered during this period. Women's enlistment rates also dropped—although almost three hundred thousand women service personnel deployed to Iraq or Afghanistan.[7] In both countries, service women have "patrolled streets with machine guns, served as gunners on vehicles, disposed of explosives, and driven trucks down bomb-ridden roads. They have proved indispensable in their ability to interact with and search Iraqi and Afghan women for weapons." Specialist Veronica Alfaro states bluntly, "I did everything there. I gunned. I drove. I ran as a truck commander. And underneath it all, I was a medic,"[8] while Staff Sergeant Ranie Ruthig remembers, "We've had grenades thrown at us, shooting at us with AK-47's." She adds, "When someone is shooting at you, you don't say, 'Stop the war, I'm a girl.'"[9]

But the demographics of the volunteer force also created its own challenges. A volunteer force is older than a draft-based military. The average age of military personnel during the Vietnam War was about twenty years old; the average age in today's military is about twenty-eight and a half. Many more service personnel are married than previously was the case—sometimes to other service members; many have children (and almost 7 percent of the military is composed of single parents). This creates special difficulties for repeated and lengthy deployments. In addition, as the U.S. volunteer force relies heavily on the Guard and Reserve, which are locally based and built primarily from a population of adults with jobs, calling up Reserve and Guard units not only leaves states without resources in the case of natural disasters, but sometimes strips towns of people playing key roles: firefighters, police officers, teachers, and the like.[10]

In the wars in Iraq and Afghanistan, the main stress of deployment fell on the Army, which supplied 54 percent of the manpower (more than the Navy, Air Force, and Marines combined) and had the most contact with both local populations and enemy forces. The Navy provided engineers, medical support, and staff to train the Iraqi Army; the Air Force primarily offered air support and military police. The Marine Corps, like the Army, saw significant action in both wars. The tours for Army soldiers also tended to be several months longer than those for personnel from the other branches.[11]

Though we tend to think of combat troops when we think about the military, most of the force is composed of support personnel. As Army Captain Benjamin Tupper explains, "for every fighting soldier there are eight to eleven soldiers who serve in logistical and support roles—medics, truck drivers, mail handlers, fuelers, military police—and rarely have contact with enemy forces."[12] Only 11 to 14 percent of U.S. forces serve in combat roles.[13] Nonetheless, because these wars did not have clear front lines and combat zones, support troops often faced danger and uncertainty, particularly when traveling in convoys.

Combatants' Experiences

As in most wars, the combatants' experiences depended a great deal on *when* and *where*: when in the course of each war, and where they were stationed. In both Afghanistan and Iraq, some servicemen slept in the elements, subsisting on MREs (meals ready to eat), while others rested comfortably in beds and drank lattes, safely ensconced behind well-fortified walls of large American bases. Troops found much more austere conditions at the beginning of each conflict than in later deployments. And much also depended on location— whether they were in desert or mountain passes, at a city or rural fire base, in areas primarily friendly or overwhelmingly hostile. Nonetheless, most of the U.S. combatants shared broader categories of experience.

Among the first challenges for American troops in Afghanistan and Iraq was the environment, which—in different ways—increased the difficulty of daily life and of waging war. Temperatures were often extreme, whether the subzero cold of the Hindu Kush Mountains of Afghanistan or the summertime heat of Iraq, where daytime temperatures generally ranged from 105 to 125 degrees Fahrenheit. One Army lieutenant reported that the 120-plus-degree heat he had faced, sitting in a Humvee in Iraq, made it feel "like my eyeballs were boiling."[14] While Iraq's winter weather was moderate, some still found it oppressive. As Sergeant Roy Batty described it, "for most of the year, Baghdad is solidly tan, but in the winter it is a depressing combination of slate gray and shit brown, glazed over with subfreezing temperatures at night."[15]

The terrain in Afghanistan is particularly harsh. A country about the same size as Texas but with a mountain range running from the northwest to the southwest, much of the terrain is arid, with a few fertile valleys along rivers. In this predominately rural and undeveloped region, the military could not rely on roads. "We had brand-new Humvees before we left to come out here," Army Specialist Johnny Rico notes, "but we burn through them! They are all already almost deadlined. We go up and down straight vertical cliffs."[16] As Army Lieutenant Craig Mullaney put it, "NASA would have difficulty building a rover to maneuver in the Afghan countryside."[17]

Both urban and rural environments were difficult. Especially in rural areas, arid conditions meant that dust and sand were inescapable facts of life. Air Force Staff Sergeant Parker Gyokeres, trying to describe conditions in Iraq, pointed his friends and family to their vacuum cleaners. Now, he wrote, "open the canister, and pour it all over you, your bed, clothing, and your personal effects. Now roll in it until it's in your eyes, nose, ears, hair, and . . . well, you get the picture. . . . And, no, there is no escape, trust me. You just get used to it."[18] Mullaney remembers the clouds of dust kicked up by his Humvee. He swears he "swallowed my own body weight in Afghan dust."[19] Sand was everywhere, damaging electronics as well as vehicles.

Urban areas presented different environmental challenges. In Afghanistan, the larger cities had three- and four-story cement structures, all in a state of disrepair after decades of warfare. Army Specialist Rico described a "teeming, overflowing mess of claustrophobic streets and wayward alleys. The streets are open sewers, and piles of garbage litter the intersection." Locals moved around the city in old Toyota pickup trucks, on motorbikes, or even by donkey. And, to Rico, the stench was ever-present: "the ripe smell of rotten fruit and feces reminds me of the monkey cage at the zoo."[20] Like Afghan cities, Baghdad had its "labyrinth of alleys and streets"; troops also described its powerful and unpleasant smell.[21] Marine Lieutenant Nathaniel Fick observed that "sewage flowed through drainage ditches, and trash piles dotted the roadside."[22]

The living, working, and fighting conditions of the troops were also shaped by U.S. military policies and limitations. At first, conditions for U.S. troops in Iraq and Afghanistan were austere. Fick described his physical condition after several days of campaigning as looking "as if I had come to the meeting straight from my cardboard box beneath an overpass. Days of sweat and grime stiffened my uniform. My fingernails were black, and I could feel my toes squishing in my socks. I slept at night with my head out the sleeping bag because I couldn't bear the stench of my own body."[23] Even in 2005 in Afghanistan, the troops of the 25th Infantry Division did not have the chance to shower for the first month of the deployment. "Most of us had worn the same uniform from our first day," Rico explained, "a uniform so slick with sweat and stink that it'd peel off like a bandage."[24] As no supplies materialized, units from the Florida National Guard, for example, had to ration their water and food in Iraq. Troops in those early months in Iraq also relied mostly on MREs, sometimes eating the exact same version of a meal over and over, month after month.[25]

As the wars lengthened and American bases grew larger, the amenities that were available to the troops increased significantly. Forward Operating Bases (FOBs) became so large that they functioned like mini-cities. Some of the troops stationed at these FOBs rarely left the safety of the protective concertina wire; combat troops began to refer to them as "Fobbits," a term consciously connected with the Hobbit characters from *Lord of the Rings*. (Infantrymen also have a more general term for everyone other than them: POGs—People Other than Grunts.) From the perspective of the frontline combatant, the POGs and the "Fobbits have it easy, what with little to no exposure to the enemy, plus all the creature comforts of the FOB—from massages to pedicures to smoothies to 24-7 coffee shops and deluxe chow halls."[26] At the base in Kandahar, Afghanistan, troops ate at Burger King and drank lattes at the Green Beans Café. Flat-screen televisions were on sale at the post-exchange. There was a gym with a climbing wall, Nautilus machines, and aerobics classes. For a soldier coming out from a rural firebase, a place like Kandahar was "like Disneyland."[27]

Similarly, Army Sergeant Kayla Williams remembers visiting a brigade support area in Mosul, Iraq, which served pizza and ice cream,[28] while Sergeant Batty noted that "the surrealism of eating Alaskan king crab every single day for three months at [FOB] Shield was not exactly what I had in mind when I first envisioned coming to this war-torn city [Baghdad]."[29] It is probably not surprising that troops in the field felt some bitterness toward those who lived in such comfort, particularly as there was no difference in pay and benefits of (in the words of Captain Tupper) "a Fobbit and a frontline trigger-puller" under constant threat from the enemy.[30]

The consequences of initial problems of supply were much greater than troops' discomfort. In March 2003 in Iraq, the military most often used un-armored Humvees to ferry troops around. At first, the troops removed the soft canvas doors because they thought they limited their range of motion. Florida Army National Guard Specialist John Crawford recollects that it was a tight fit getting into a Humvee with full battle gear and weapon, so "it [became] easiest just to ride with one foot out of the vehicle sort of half in, half out."[31] As the areas grew more dangerous, a door-less vehicle made Fick feel "ridiculously exposed."[32] It was not long before American troops reattached the doors and started "duct-taping Kevlar to the side of our trucks," as one soldier recalled.[33] The Army sent armor kits to attach to the Humvees, but struggled to keep up with demand.[34]

With a growing insurgency in Iraq in late 2003 and 2004, but a lack of effective planning from policy makers represented by Secretary of Defense Donald Rumsfeld's widely reported quip "you go to war with the army you have, not the army you might want," supply shortages became critical.[35] The press reported that the Army alone "began the war with an estimated $56 billion equipment shortage."[36] Service members needed body armor, armored vehicles, and even spare parts for the vehicles and equipment they did have. It took almost six months for bulletproof vests to arrive for some units in Iraq.[37] "No supplies came our way," recalls Specialist Crawford, "and soon we began commandeering civilian vehicles, our Humvees all [were] broken." They also had problems with the unit's night-vision equipment and Vietnam-era rifles. Equipment shortages were so severe in some units, particularly among National Guard and Reserve units, that relatives bought their loved ones body armor, global positioning devices, and radios.[38]

Finally, the nature of these wars shaped service members' experiences. In both Iraq and Afghanistan, American forces fought an "unconventional" war, one in which it is impossible to distinguish friend from foe. Iraq and Afghanistan had few areas where one could discern a "front line," and in both countries troops faced un-uniformed fighters who could blend into the civilian population. Without clear front lines, female troops found themselves in the thick of the conflict, despite policies that prohibited them from serving in front-line combat units. In Iraq, American troops manned traffic checkpoints, went out on patrols, and conducted raids while insurgents in civilian clothes increased the frequency of their attacks, melting into crowds or disappearing into traffic in their unmarked cars. Captain John Prior remarks, "How can you tell them apart? The same guy that waves at you can shoot you with an RPG [rocket-propelled grenade]."[39] American troops were well aware that unarmed Iraqis in civilian dress with cell phones could be lookouts or could remotely detonate roadside bombs.[40] In Afghanistan too, the Taliban melted back into the villages after an attack, indistinguishable from the civilian population. As Staff Sergeant Glenn Yeager, too young to have experienced Vietnam, muses, "It's not like wars we've fought in the past, wars when you knew who the enemy was, where they were, and knew how to hit them. Now, you can't tell who's who, where they're hiding—or when you do know where they're hiding, it's a place we're not allowed to hit. It's frustrating to all of us."[41]

Even worse, for many, was the possibility that children posed a threat. Both in Iraq and Afghanistan, American service members remarked on the constant presence of children. Sergeant Batty explains that in Iraq, "the kids are everywhere here, and they always cluster around your trucks begging for water or candy or anything. It's cute at first, but it gets annoying after a while, and it's also a security concern. We've seen UAV [unmanned aerial vehicle or drone] footage of kids burying IEDs [improvised explosive devices] and heard intel[ligence] stories of kids attaching magnetic IEDs to Humvees."[42] On some occasions, children even shot at American troops, so it was always difficult to assess a situation accurately.[43]

At the same time, some American troops found children more reliable than adults. First Sergeant Troy Steward noted that in Afghanistan, "Kids are still the best source of information. They will tell the truth as long as they don't think they will get in trouble for it."[44] Often, American troops could sense the situation in a particular village from the presence and friendliness of the children. If an area was hostile, children would not approach the soldiers. If an attack was immanent, the kids would run away. Nonetheless, all were aware that the Taliban had also used children to plant roadside bombs meant for American troops.[45]

In these unconventional wars, Americans discovered that one of the most persistent dangers—first in Iraq and later in Afghanistan—was not from combat, but from the improvised explosive device, or IED. It was estimated in 2006 that an IED went off somewhere in Iraq on average once every fifteen minutes, and the Pentagon acknowledged that IEDs were "the single most effective weapon against our deployed forces."[46] These devices were so common that the explosions accounted for about half of American combat deaths and injuries in Iraq in 2007.[47] The uncertainty of the IED kept American forces constantly vigilant. Troops were given instructions to avoid trash bags and even packages children wanted to give them. Army Specialist Robert Weber told his mother, "Things are getting worse over here, more dangerous. The roads are bad. You don't run over anything even if it looks like a piece of paper."[48] In Afghanistan, IEDs were often constructed using fertilizer and fuel and containers as commonplace as plastic jugs. These homemade explosives accounted for 60 percent of American and coalition deaths in Afghanistan between 2003 and 2014. One sergeant told a reporter, "They tell us to watch out for stacks of rocks, but there's stacks of rocks everywhere here."[49]

In most cases, the IED required an insurgent to detonate it, which sometimes worked in favor of American troops. For instance, Brian Mockenhaupt had been sent out by his company commander to clear an intersection at night. They parked the trucks and started walking around the road, looking for anything suspicious. Someone spotted a small mound of dirt across the road. Unable to tell if it was a bomb from afar, Mockenhaupt and one of his soldiers moved in to investigate in person. "Closer, and closer still, and we see a piece of cardboard," Mockenhaupt remembers. They had to pull it away to see what was underneath. They found "two cylinders, bigger than coffee cans, nestled in the dirt. Two baby blue wires twisted together, run from each into the ground. That's a bomb," he realized. Mockenhaupt's heart skipped a beat and his stomach fluttered. He scrambled backward, signaling his men to get back. Thankfully for them, the trigger man was not around.[50]

While early IEDs were crude constructions, the insurgents became more sophisticated with their production and cleverer in their hiding places. When armored Humvees started arriving in Iraq in 2004, the insurgents created bombs that could penetrate the new armor. They added booby traps and started planting multiple IEDs that would detonate after rescuers arrived. They hid IEDs "under garbage and tires, behind guardrails, [and] inside craters."[51] As Americans increased the frequency of their roadside patrols, the insurgents even started to plant the devices between sweeps of the patrols, a technique Americans variously called "drop and pop" or "stop and drop."[52]

Direct hits from IEDs often proved fatal, and close misses were jarring. San Francisco Chronicle reporter John Koopman, who was riding along for a routine patrol with an Army unit in Ramadi in 2004, experienced a near miss. The explosion sounded like thunder, and it kicked up a cloud of dust, which blocked the sun. Although the blast was fifteen feet in front of the vehicle, it "punched the Humvee like a fist, pushing to the side like a toy car," Koopman describes. The gunner, Army Sergeant Michael Marchetti, shouted, "Goddamn! Goddamn! I can't fucking hear," shortly followed by "I'm good. I'm good." The driver, Specialist Kevin Neff, pushed his foot to the floor to get the truck out of the kill zone and away from the two-foot crater left by the bomb. The soldiers were lucky. The IED had been remotely controlled, and the bomber did not get the timing right.[53]

In 2007, a new mine-resistant ambush-protected vehicle, or MRAP, arrived in Iraq. It had a V-shaped hull to dissipate the force of the blast to protect troops from IEDs. Marine Staff Sergeant Christopher Spurlock credited the new vehicles for saving his life from an IED in Ramadi in 2008. "We came up to a really bad intersection," he describes. "The next thing you know, I was being flipped upside down into the air." When everyone scrambled out of the MRAP, they saw that the entire transfer case had been destroyed. Even with a mangled vehicle and a crater from the bomb, "Everyone was O.K.," he reported.[54]

With IEDs and mortar attacks, blown-up human remains became all too common in Iraq. In August 2004 Army Captain Daniel Murray told his wife, "I've seen hair and brains picked up onto a dustpan, scraped onto it with a stick and handed to me because no one knew what to do with it." Sometimes he had to identify body parts that had been thrown ninety feet away. "I smelled it," he added, "gas, metal, adrenaline, sweat, tears, torn building materials, fresh meat, unwashed blown up body parts."[55]

Some of the injured, including Iraqis, were ferried to hospitals. On board the USNS *Comfort*, a Navy hospital ship, Commander Edward Jewell recorded in his journal one particularly difficult day: "We got creamed with fresh casualties last light, thirty new patients, both sides, all needing immediate and significant intervention. The injuries are horrifying. Ruptured eyeballs. Children missing limbs. Large burns. Genitals and buttocks blown off. Grotesque fractures. Gunshot wounds to the head. Faces blown apart. Paraplegics from spine injuries." Patients continued to come in, including children who were injured and ill. Jewell jotted in his journal, "we have grown to hate the rumble of helos [helicopters] on the flight deck, since it usually means another load of Iraqi patients."[56]

In these unconventional wars, without a clear sense of who constituted the enemy, troops unintentionally injured and killed innocent civilians. Marine Sergeant Rob Sharra recounts an episode early in the war in Iraq. He and his marines were sitting in their vehicles when an Iraqi woman started to walk slowly toward them. Having been warned to watch out for suicide bombers, Sharra perceived her as a threat and feared she carried explosives. Wanting to protect his men, Sharra "picked my weapon up and aimed in. And the sound of my rounds going out got the guys in the other vehicle to open up, as well. And they opened up on her with, I mean, 15 weapons. I mean, she just got torn to pieces." Tragically, the woman had not been a danger. As she fell, Sharra saw a white flag in her hand. The killing devastated Sharra. He remembered thinking, "What the hell happened?" and as the reality kicked in for him, "I was crying, hysterical. You know, this woman got killed by my actions. I mean, that was something that plagued me."[57] On another occasion right after the invasion into Iraq, marines fired into a car that refused to stop after warning shots were fired. One bullet hit a three-year-old girl, slicing off the top of her head. Although there were a few cases in which service members intentionally targeted civilians, "collateral damage" such as this exacted an emotional toll on the troops. One marine miserably admits, "dog, whatever last shred of humanity I had before I came here, it's gone."[58]

Combat

The pace of combat operations fluctuated throughout the wars in Iraq and Afghanistan, with a lot of action during the initial invasions, followed by periods of quiet and then spikes in violence. Combat in Iraq began in March 2003 with airstrikes, quickly followed by American and British ground forces. As Army Apache helicopters moved across the border, the pilots were ready for action.

"Six, this is White Four. Coming around the tank on the right," announced one pilot.

"Send it Four."

"The good news is, it's an enemy tank, and it's destroyed. The bad news is, it looks like it was destroyed in Desert Storm" in 1991.

We all chuckle.

"Apache Six, this is Blue One. Negative enemy contact on the left here."

"Well, what was it Blue?"

"It looks like it's, uh . . . a herd of camels."

We could hear a collective groan from the entire troop.[59]

Moments of levity, like this one, were punctuated by more intense episodes. As American troops approached the outskirts of Baghdad, Saddam Hussein loyalists, called Fedayeen, attacked Army and Marine Corps forces. As historians describe it, "vans, pickup trucks, and cars carrying men armed with RPGs, demolitions, and automatic weapons appeared from nowhere on suicide missions."[60] Danger seemingly lurked around every corner. Specialist Crawford remembers, "I spent most of my time watching the rooftops and side roads, looking into my rearview mirror to make sure no one was creeping up on my car from behind."[61]

After a short period of quiet, violence in Iraq grew tremendously. In June 2003, American troops faced about five hundred insurgent attacks per month; two years later they faced an average of nearly three thousand. The insurgency had continued after the fall of Saddam Hussein, as minority Sunnis fought against American forces as well as the majority Shi'a and Kurdish populations. The Sunni insurgency largely took place in the "Sunni Triangle," which included the cities of Ramadi and Fallujah. There was also a Shi'a revolt from Baghdad into the south and east.[62]

In Afghanistan, coalition forces defeated the Taliban by December 2001, and the Taliban retreated into the Hindu Kush Mountains between Afghanistan and Pakistan to the east. The pace of operations fell into a fairly predictable routine, with wintertime all but ending combat and fighting resuming with the spring thaws. As Captain Tupper, an embedded trainer with the Afghan National Army describes it, "Throughout the summer, the cat-and-mouse game was as predictable as it was violent. The Taliban came out of their mountain hideouts to conduct operations. We would get intel on where they were and go hunting. It would end in one of two ways: We would either engage them and inflict horrible losses on their soldiers, or they would be able to get back to their mountains and disappear. They would only reappear at a time and place of their choosing to sow IEDs, ambushes, and terror."[63]

In order to make themselves less vulnerable targets, commanders instructed their troops to "make our movements unpredictable, never to take the same route at the same time or on the same day of the week" even though they had to patrol the same areas dozens of times each week.[64] Unpredictability not only kept enemies from using predictable movements to plan attacks, but also kept troops from letting down their guard. One female soldier in Afghanistan explains, "After you go outside the wire so many times, you start to feel comfortable or complacent. That will get you killed, and it almost got us killed. So, no more complacency. Every time I'm out, my mind runs through the hundreds of possible ways we could be hit."[65]

Because there were fewer troops deployed to Afghanistan, and the fighting area in that country was larger and more rural than Iraq, American troops relied heavily on airpower to destroy enemy forces. Air support included Navy and Air Force jets, low-flying A-10 Warthogs, and Apache helicopters.[66] Lieutenant Beau Cleland describes the sounds of aerial bombardment: "There isn't some multisyllabic 'kaboom.' It's just every pot and pan in your kitchen hitting the floor simultaneously and then stopping."[67] When the A-10 Warthogs fire their thirty-millimeter Gatling cannons, Mullaney writes, the cannons "spun so fast that you couldn't make out the sound of individual rounds"; "it sounded like a wood chipper grinding thick logs."[68] On the ground, the noise of battle was deafening. "Think of the loudest war movie sequence you've ever seen," Cleland advises, "and multiply that until it would make your ears bleed. Literally. One of our interpreter's ears were bleeding after this last one—he wasn't wearing ear protection."[69]

From the pilot's seat of the A-10, the firefights below look like "a fireworks show gone insane," according to Air Force Reserve Captain Michael Daftarian. As Daftarian made his first approach over one battlefield, the ground forward air controller gave his assent to have the bombs dropped "danger-close" to American troops. Daftarian mentally repeated the pilot prayer, "Please God, don't let me fuck up." He dropped a bomb, dived down to shoot the Gatling cannon on the hillside, and then came back to drop two more five-hundred-pound bombs. Daftarian felt a lump in his throat when he did not see any fire—enemy or friendly—from the ground below and feared he had just killed fellow Americans. He repeatedly called down to the controller and relaxed only when he heard the voice reply, "Two . . . good hits, we're still hunkering down. . . . We still got shrapnel raining down here, but the hillside is gone!"[70]

While getting into a firefight with an enemy could be terrifying, many also report a sense of exhilaration from the pumping adrenaline and realization that they survived. Specialist Michael O'Mahoney and another soldier were on guard duty in an M113 armored personnel carrier. One day, while on duty, O'Mahoney heard the first round of mortar fire hit about one hundred meters away from their vehicle, with a second whistling overhead and landing closer. "Dude, get your fuckin' hatch closed!" he yelled to his partner. "So there we were, an infantryman and a scout, neither of us having been on a 113 before, pulling, punching, slamming, and smashing these hatches that refuse to come down over us to help aid in our protection," he remembers. They managed to duck into the vehicle moments before the closest round hit, a mere ten meters away. "We laughed with each other as he gave me the requisite 'I love you, man,'" O'Mahoney reports.[71] Marine Corps Lieutenant Brian Humphreys recalls a firefight in Iraq in February 2004, when he and his men had come under enemy fire for about ninety minutes yet miraculously none of his fellow marines had gotten hurt. Humphreys thought to himself, "Did that just happen?" as they clamored back into the trucks. As they sat in a traffic circle, weapons at the ready, and hearts pounding, "another thought enters my mind before I have a chance to shut it out," he remembers: "That was fucking awesome."[72]

At other times, troops feel very much out of control of their fate. Joshua Martin, sitting around in a combat housing unit at FOB Delta in Iraq, was playing his guitar with his friend when the first round of indirect fire hit. "We felt the earth shake from beneath us," he writes. "We looked right at one another. We both knew what was going on but I still got up and walked over to him and tapped him on the shoulder saying 'we are getting mortared,'" he notes. At that point they grabbed their weapons and dashed for the bunker. After the attack, Martin remembers, "the fear really started to set in. I would think to myself that during these attacks one round might get lucky. From then on sleep went right out the window. I was afraid I would never wake up. I just made me angry that my life was out of my hands. No control over whether I lived or died."[73] Other soldiers, shaken by near misses, reacted with anger and frustration: "I can tell you I'll be glad when these days are done for me," stated one soldier, "Fuck this shit."[74]

And in the end, war—unlike an action movie—consists of long stretches of boredom. One soldier, returning from guard duty in rural Afghanistan in 2005, remarked to Specialist Rico, "Oh, I've been on tower three for seven consecutive hours. I watched dirt for seven consecutive hours." After guard duty, the soldier went out on patrol. "We pulled security in a dried-up riv-erbed," he explained. "For like three hours. I saw a camel. Mostly just more dirt."[75]

To combat that boredom, in the downtime between duty shifts American troops watched a lot of pirated DVDs and played videogames sold to them by Iraqis and Afghans. They were so bored they would watch or play almost anything. They also made a lot of videos, many of which have featured on YouTube or social media sites. One of these videos, a remake of Lady Gaga's music video "Telephone" by soldiers stationed in Afghanistan, went viral.[76]

In these recent wars, modern technology has connected the home front with the battlefield in ways never seen before. When U.S. troops deployed overseas for war in the past, contact with the home front was often limited to writing letters. Unique today is that troops in Afghanistan and Iraq have had nearly constant access to home through email, phone calls, Skype, Facebook, and more. In the early stages of the wars, service members had only spotty Internet and phone connections with home. So, like troops in the past, they relied mostly on mail. "Mail becomes a miniature Christmas," explains Captain Lee Kelley.[77] Kayla Williams remembers boxes of mail finally catching up to her unit. She received junk food: potato chips, granola bars, and more. The U.S. military is so expert at logistics that mail soon became a regular service, even for those in more rural areas.[78] At one point in 2004, the Army mandated that soldiers send postcards home because "a lot of soldiers were failing to contact their parents and let them know that they were okay, and these worrywart parents were contacting the chain of command," explained Army Specialist Colby Buzzell.[79] As the American presence in Iraq and Afghanistan lengthened, access to the Internet and to phones became commonplace. One Morale, Welfare, and Recreation tent in Kunduz, Afghanistan, in 2011 sported forty plywood cubicles to keep service members linked with home. While access to Facebook and other social media sites had been restricted at first, policy makers relented in 2010.[80]

Frequent communication with home brought all the joys and the problems of home overseas, which sometimes interfered with troops accomplishing their duties. For instance, a "gunner inside an armored vehicle type[d] furiously on a BlackBerry, so engrossed in text-messaging his girlfriend in the United States that he has forgotten to watch for enemy movement."[81] When casualties are taken, however, Internet and phone connections are cut off until the families can be notified.[82] These blackouts often caused panic among the families back home, for they knew that someone from the unit had been hurt or killed—but nothing more.

Since the beginning of combat operations, 2,356 Americans in Afghanistan and 4,489 in Iraq have died as of this writing.[83] These numbers include troops only, not civilian personnel or contractors; adding these casualties would raise the number of American dead significantly.[84] When a service member dies, the survivors conduct memorial ceremonies. When Lieutenant Mullaney lost a soldier in combat, the patrol came back to the base, still covered in muck and blood, to stand for company roll call. At the sound of the fallen soldier's name, there was a pause and a second call of his name. After another long pause, a soldier answered, "Private O'Neill is no longer with us."[85] To commemorate the fallen soldier, the men displayed his combat boots, rifle, bayonet, dog tags, and, in this case, a wide-brimmed camouflage hat. Later, they had a formal memorial ceremony, where the roll call was read again. Seven soldiers fired a three-volley salute. Taps began to play. Everyone snapped to attention. Tears fell.[86] It was a scene played out thousands of times since the tragic events of 9/11 generated the tragedy of two wars. Thankfully, the majority of men and women who served in Iraq and Afghanistan had enough training, skill, and luck to make it back home.

Although the experiences of the troops varied widely from the initial invasions through the increasing violence of dual insurgencies, the experiences of going into combat, coming under mortar fire, and feeling the concussive blasts from roadside bombs were strikingly similar in Iraq and Afghanistan. These experiences set the women and men who served apart from those who know about the wars only from the safety of home.

NOTES

Many thanks to my research assistants Anne Marie Saman and Janina Wojkowski.

1 Sharon Allen, "Combat Musician, Lost in Translation, and the Circle," in *Operation Homecoming: Iraq, Afghanistan, and the Home Front, in the Words of U.S. Troops and Their Families*, ed. Andrew Carroll (New York: Random House, 2006), 158.

2 Bradley Graham and Josh White, "Army to Use Fewer National Guard Troops in Iraq," *Washington Post*, July 1, 2005.

3 Ron Capps, "Long Deployments for Reserves to Continue?," *Time*, May 24, 2011, http://nation.time.com/2011/05/24/long-deployments-for-reserves-to-continue; Lizette Alvarez and Andrew Lehren, "3,000 Deaths in Iraq, Countless Tears at Home," *New York Times*, January 1, 2007.

4 Monica Davey, "The New Military Life: Heading Back to the War," *New York Times*, December 20, 2004.

5 James Dao, "2,000 Dead: As Iraq Tours Stretch on, a Grim Mark," *New York Times*, October 26, 2005.

6 Monica Davey, "Eight Soldiers Plan to Sue over Army Tours of Duty," *New York Times*, December 6, 2004; Johnny Rico, *Blood Makes the Grass Grow Green: A Year in*

the Desert with Team America (New York: Presidio Press, 2007), 176; Larry Shaughnessy, "Gates Makes Good on Promise to end Controversial 'Stop Loss' Policy," *CNN*, June 15, 2011, http://www.cnn.com/2011/US/06/15/army.stop.loss/.

7 General Accounting Office, *Military Personnel: Reporting Additional Service-member Demographics Could Enhance Congressional Oversight* (Washington, DC: GPO, 2005), 10; Department of Defense (DOD), "2011 Demographics" (updated November 2012), militaryonesource.mil; Greg Myre, "Women in Combat: 5 Key Questions" (National Public Radio, January 24, 2013), http://www.npr.org/blogs/thetwoway/2013/01/24/170161752/women-in-combat-five-key-questions; David Burrelli, "Women in Combat: Issues for Congress" (Congressional Research Service, 2013), summary; DOD, "Report on the Impact of Deployment of Members of the Armed Forces on Their Dependent Children" (October 2010), militaryonesource.mil; DOD, "2012 Demographics," 111–12, militaryonesource.mil..

8 Lizette Alvarez, "G.I. Jane Stealthily Breaks the Combat Barrier," *New York Times*, August 16, 2009.

9 Felicia R. Lee, "Battleground: Female Soldiers in the Line of Fire," *New York Times*, November 5, 2008.

10 DOD, "2011 Demographics."

11 Dave Baiocchi, "Measuring Army Deployments to Iraq and Afghanistan" (RAND, 2013), www.rand.org.

12 Benjamin Tupper, *Greetings from Afghanistan, Send More Ammo: Dispatches from Taliban Country* (New York: Nal Caliber, 2011), 110.

13 Mrinal Suman, "Teeth to Tail Ratio: An Archaic Concept," *Indian Defence Review* 21 (October 2006): 74.

14 Michael S. Mundey, interview, November 2013.

15 Roy Batty, "The Dog," in *Doonesbury.com's the Sandbox: Dispatches from Troops in Iraq and Afghanistan*, ed. David Stanford (Kansas City: Andrews McMeel, 2007), 149.

16 Rico, *Blood Makes the Grass Grow Green*, 148. "Deadlined" means that the vehicles are no longer able to operate.

17 Craig Mullaney, *The Unforgiving Minute: A Soldier's Education* (New York: Penguin, 2009), 226.

18 Parker Gyokeres, "Camp Muckmungus," in Carroll, *Operation Homecoming*, 134.

19 Mullaney, *Unforgiving Minute*, 226.

20 Rico, *Blood Makes the Grass Grow Green*, 134.

21 John Crawford, *The Last True Story I'll Ever Tell: An Accidental Soldier's Account of the War in Iraq* (New York: Berkley, 2005), 21.

22 Nathaniel Fick, *One Bullet Away: The Making of a Marine Officer* (Boston: Houghton Mifflin, 2005), 227.

23 Ibid., 292.

24 Rico, *Blood Makes the Grass Grow Green*, 98.

25 Crawford, *Last True Story*, 19, 23; Neela Banerjee and John Kifner, "Along with Prayers, Families Send Armor," *New York Times*, October 30, 2004.

26 Tupper, *Greetings from Afghanistan*, 110.

27 Mullaney, *Unforgiving Minute*, 339.

28 Kayla Williams, *Love My Rifle More Than You: Young and Female in the U.S. Army* (New York: Norton, 2005), 202.

29 Roy Batty, "The Keep," in Stanford, *Doonesbury.com's the Sandbox*, 250.

30 Tupper, *Greetings from Afghanistan*, 111.

31 Jeffrey Gettleman, "Deaths in Iraq Take a Steady Toll at Home," *New York Times*, November 2, 2003; Williams, *Love My Rifle More Than You*, 240; Crawford, *Last True Story*, 38, 206.

32 Fick, *One Bullet Away*, 225–26.

33 Chris Dixon, "Big Wheels for Iraq's Mean Streets," *New York Times*, February 4, 2008.

34 Ann Scott Tyson, "Thousands of Army Humvees Lack Armor Upgrade," *Washington Post*, February 12, 2007.

35 Eric Schmidt, "Iraq-Bound Troops Confront Rumsfeld over Lack of Armor," *New York Times*, December 9, 2004.

36 Tyson, "Thousands of Army Humvees."

37 George Packer, *The Assassin's Gate: America in Iraq* (New York: Farrar, Straus and Giroux, 2005), 300; Rajiv Chandrasekaran, *Imperial Life in the Emerald City: Inside Iraq's Green Zone* (New York: Knopf, 2006), 28.

38 Crawford, *Last True Story*, 19, 23; Banerjee and Kifner, "Along with Prayers."

39 Packer, *Assassin's Gate*, 328.

40 Evan Wright, *Generation Kill: Devil Dogs, Iceman, Captain America, and the New Face of American War* (New York: Berkeley Caliber, 2004), 102.

41 Glenn Yeager, "A Hard Place to Be," in Stanford, *Doonesbury.com's the Sandbox*, 25.

42 Batty, "Dog," 153.

43 Mullaney, *Unforgiving Minute*, 226.

44 Troy Steward, "Lost Innocence," in Stanford, *Doonesbury.com's the Sandbox*, 262.

45 Michael J. Totten, "Anbar Awakens Part I: The Battle of Ramadi," *Michael J. Totten's Middle East Journal*, September 10, 2007, http://www.michaeltotten.com/archives/001514.html; Mullaney, *Unforgiving Minute*, 225.

46 Allan Millett, Peter Maslowski, and William Feis, *For the Common Defense: A Military History of the United States from 1607 to 2012*, rev. ed. (New York: Free Press, 2012), 668; quote from Rick Atkinson, "The Single Most Effective Weapon Against Our Deployed Forces," *Washington Post*, September 30, 2007.

47 Alvarez and Lehren, "3,000 Deaths in Iraq."

48 Packer, *Assassin's Gate*, 372; quote from Alvarez and Lehren, "3,000 Deaths in Iraq."

49 Millett, Maslowski, and Feis, *For the Common Defense*, 668; Atkinson, "Single Most Effective Weapon"; quote from Carlotta Gall, "Remote-Control Explosions Pose Threat in Afghanistan," *New York Times*, August 22.

50 Brian Mockenhaupt, "The Waiting: To Serve in Iraq Is to Be in a State of Deadly Anticipation," *New York Times*, March 12, 2006.

51 Quote from Alvarez and Lehren, "3,000 Deaths in Iraq"; Tom Vanden Brook, "'94 Military Report Panned Humvee as 'Deathtrap,'" *USA Today*, February 4, 2009.

52 James Barron and Kirk Semple, "2 Soldiers, Friends from Queens, Die on a 'Routine' Patrol in Iraq," *New York Times*, March 5, 2005; Mundey, interview.

53 John Koopman, *McCoy's Marines: Darkside to Baghdad* (St. Paul, MN: Zenith Press, 2004), 287–88.

54 Brook, "'94 Military Report"; Sara Wood, "More Mine Resistant Ambush Protected Vehicles Shipped to Middle East," *American Forces Press Service*, August 17, 2007, http://www.defense.gov/news/newsarticle.aspx?id=47093; quote from Dixon, "Big Wheels for Iraq's Mean Streets."

55 Daniel Murray, "In Due Time," in Carroll, *Operation Homecoming*, 304.

56 Edward Jewell, "Life on the USNS *Comfort*," in Carroll, *Operation Homecoming*, 51–53.

57 Transcript of *The Soldier's Heart*, written, produced, and directed by Raney Aronson, *Frontline*, March 1, 2005, http://www.pbs.org/wgbh/pages/frontline/shows/heart/etc/script.html.

58 Wright, *Generation Kill*, 217–18.

59 Denis Prior, "Distant Thunder," in Carroll, *Operation Homecoming*, 27.

60 Millett, Maslowski, and Feis, *For the Common Defense*, 656, 658.

61 Crawford, *Last True Story*, 173.

62 Millett, Maslowski, and Feis, *For the Common Defense*, 661, 664–65; Dao, "2,000 Dead;" Alvarez and Lehren, "3,000 Deaths."

63 Tupper, *Greetings from Afghanistan*, 170.

64 Mullaney, *Unforgiving Minute*, 231.

65 Army Girl, "Combat," in Stanford, *Doonesbury.com's the Sandbox*, 67.

66 Fick, *One Bullet Away*, 129; Mullaney, *Unforgiving Minute*, 315.

67 Beau Cleland, "Getting Shot At," in Stanford, *Doonesbury.com's the Sandbox*, 211.

68 Mullaney, *Unforgiving Minute*, 290.

69 Cleland, "Getting Shot At," 211.

70 Michael S. Daftarian, "Friendly Fire," in Carroll, *Operation Homecoming*, 18–22.

71 Michael O'Mahoney, "Mortar Mornings," in Sanford, *Doonesbury.com's The Sandbox*, 89–90.

72 Brian Humphreys, "Veterans," in Carroll, *Operation Homecoming*, 306.

73 Joshua Martin, "Each Other Is All You Have," *Real Combat Life*, December 30, 2012, http://www.realcombatlife.com/2012/12/30/each-other-is-all-you-have-by-joshua-martin/.

74 David Finkel, *The Good Soldiers* (New York: Picador, 2009), 66.

75 Rico, *Blood Makes the Grass Grow Green*, 94.

76 Ibid., 189, 225, 271; Mullaney, *Unforgiving Minute*, 355; Mundey, interview; Finkel, *Good Soldiers*, 37; "Telephone Remake," YouTube, April 23, 2010, http://www.youtube.com/watch?v=haHXgFU7qNI.

77 Lee Kelley, "Mail Becomes Paramount," in Stanford, *Doonesbury.com's the Sandbox*, 16.

78 Williams, *Love My Rifle More Than You*, 144; Mullaney, *Unforgiving Minute*, 244.

79 Colby Buzzell, "Stuck in This Sandbox," in Carroll, *Operation Homecoming*, 133.

80 James Dao, "Staying in Touch with Home, for Better or Worse," *New York Times*, February 17, 2011; "US Military OKs Use of Social Media," *CNN*, March 2, 2010, http://www.cnn.com/2010/TECH/02/26/military.social.media/.

81 Dao, "Staying in Touch."

82 Stefan Ralph, "Rest in Peace," in Stanford, *Doonesbury.com's the Sandbox*, 76.

83 "Operation Iraqi Freedom" and "Operation Enduring Freedom/Afghanistan," iCasualties.org.

84 Millett, Maslowski, and Feis, *For the Common Defense*, 676.

85 Mullaney, *Unforgiving Minute*, 292.

86 Ibid., 294, 297.

8

Fighting (against) the Wars in Iraq and Afghanistan

DAVID FARBER

1

The great majority of Americans sacrificed almost nothing during the wars in Afghanistan and Iraq. Because the wars were fought with an all-volunteer force, relatively few families were directly affected. Very few upper-middle-class or wealthy families had close relatives at risk in the theaters of war. The wars did cost the American people a great deal of money: direct costs of some $1.5 trillion and total costs estimated to be more than $4 trillion (or close to $300,000 for every American household).[1] But because of major tax cuts passed and implemented during the presidency of George Bush, those costs were passed along to future generations. Wartime Americans, in essence, paid nothing for the wars fought in their name; indeed, despite ballooning war costs they saw their taxes decline. Still, even as the wars directly affected only a relatively few American families in terms of "blood and treasure," the wars in Iraq and Afghanistan became central issues in the political life of the nation and in how the United States was perceived around the world. While removed from most major direct costs, Americans were moved to act by the wars. Though the wars in Iraq and Afghanistan did not produce the kind of antiwar movement that baby boomers remember from the Vietnam War era, the war in Iraq did mobilize millions of people in the United States and around the world in opposition. In particular, the nearly decade-long war in Iraq changed the trajectory of the Democratic Party by mobilizing new citizen activists at the grassroots and netroots and reduced the credibility of the national Republican Party on national security issues among voters, all of which led directly to the presidency of Barack Obama.

2

People both within the United States and around the world responded differently to the American wars in Afghanistan and Iraq. Outside of the United States, people generally expressed skepticism and even disapproval of the American decision to battle against the Taliban regime in Afghanistan, but outside of nations with large Islamic populations they did so with relatively little intensity. While some people around the world did protest the American effort in Afghanistan, such gatherings lacked mass support and were rarely sustained efforts.

Overwhelmingly people around the world understood the connection between the American war in Afghanistan and the 9/11 terrorist attacks. Those attacks had powerfully affected people, even in nations where strong majorities of the population were highly suspicious of or even hostile toward the American government. In Russia, for example, where anti-Americanism remained a powerful force a decade after the fall of the Soviet Union, people responded viscerally to the collapse of the Twin Towers, which Russians watched live on CNN. Russians poured out of their homes and came by the tens of thousands to the U.S. embassy in Moscow and to the U.S. consulate in Saint Petersburg to lay wreaths, offer prayers, and hold candlelight vigils. President Putin appeared live on television to condemn the attacks and to order that all Russian flags be flown at half-mast in solidarity with the American people. Throughout Europe, both in nations with long-standing ties to the United States such as Great Britain and in post–Cold War nations that had only recently allied with America, such as Poland, similar scenes of heartfelt mourning and solidarity were repeated.

Despite such widespread sympathy, public opinion was by no means universally in support of the American decision to move swiftly to war against the Taliban in Afghanistan. Large majorities of people around the world believed that the United States should pursue a diplomatic solution to the Taliban's support and sheltering of al Qaeda. But people in most of the world understood why Americans felt they must destroy al Qaeda's safe haven in Afghanistan, and relatively few people publicly protested against the American act even as foreign governments responded in complex and differing ways to the U.S. request for support.

People in nations with predominately Islamic populations were an exception to this pattern; they did respond more angrily and more publicly. In Indonesia, home to the world's largest Islamic population, people generally did not think the United States had the right to attack the Taliban. Many feared that an attack on the Islamist government in Afghanistan was part of a larger war against Islam and proved that the United States had no regard for Muslim causalities. Throughout 2002, in the relatively new Indonesian democracy, broad protests against the global war on terror broke out in the streets of Jakarta and other major Indonesian cities. Effigies of President Bush and American flags were commonly burned, often outside of a McDonald's restaurant—widely seen in Indonesia as a symbol of the United States. Even as such protests against the American global war on terror, in general, and against the war in Afghanistan, in particular, did occur in many predominately Islamic nations, including Jordan and Iraq, and across Palestine, relatively few other mass protests against the American war in Afghanistan gained traction.

In general the Afghan War was far more popular with the American people than it was with people around the world. At the advent of the Afghan War in October 2001, Americans overwhelmingly approved of the Bush administration's decision to attack the Taliban; according to a Gallup poll taken just hours after the first bombs fell on Taliban strongholds, some 90 percent of Americans said they approved of the action and only 5 percent registered disapproval.[2] While approval ratings would slowly drop off as the war dragged on for more than a decade, a strong majority, at least according to public opinion polls, held on to the belief that the war was "the right thing" to do, at least until the war's waning days in late 2013.[3] America's war in Iraq would fare differently in the minds of the American people. As a result, the two wars would play quite different roles in American politics.

3

The Iraq War, from beginning to end, was wildly unpopular around the world; people in almost all nations registered strong disapproval in public opinion polls, and millions took to the streets to protest what they perceived to be a unilateral and unjustified American invasion of a sovereign nation. Around the world, people condemned the U.S. government and lambasted President Bush for warmongering. In the months leading up to the March 20, 2003, American military intervention in Iraq, tens of millions of people around the world filled the streets to protest the coming war. The biggest global protests occurred on February 15, 2003, when some thirty million people declared their opposition to the American led invasion. A million or more people demonstrated in Rome, Madrid, and Barcelona; half a million or more came out in London and Berlin, while hundreds of thousands turned out in Melbourne and Paris; similar demonstrations clogged public plazas and streets in Cape Town, Havana, Bangkok, Dhaka, and hundreds of other cities.[4] In terms of sheer numbers of people and countries involved, the protests represented an unprecedented display of global public opinion fervently lined up against American policy. America would go to war in Iraq against the wishes of masses of people around the world.[5] In part due to such passionate public condemnation of the war by the world's citizenry, few governments cooperated directly with the United States in the Iraq War, and many bluntly condemned the action.

People around the world opposed the Bush administration's policy to go to war in Iraq for quite varied reasons. The membership in that opposition was quite varied, as well. Certainly some members of the international community opposed the American government's decision to wage war on Saddam Hussein's Iraq because they had little or no trust in American foreign policy generally. Even people in nations long allied with the United States perceived the war in Iraq through a darkening lens. According to opinion polls taken in 2003, some 75 percent of all European Union citizens believed that the United States was a "poor, or negative force for world peace, for the fight against poverty, and for international protection."[6] The Bush administration's unilateral decision to invade Iraq hardened those perceptions. Writing in 2007, the Italian scholar of international relations Federico Romero concluded, "The war in Iraq has eroded—perhaps even demolished—the main pillars of the transatlantic trust that defined the post–World War II era: the perception that U.S. international attitudes were, on balance, helpful for democracy and prosperity; and the notion that European interests had a place in Washington's deliberations."[7]

Especially in countries with large Islamic populations, many people were suspicious of America's aggressive role in the Middle East; they suspected pro-Israel sentiments and a hunger for Arab oil played powerful roles in the rush to war. Almost all dismissed President Bush's claims that America had to invade Iraq to fight the threat of terrorism and weapons of mass destruction and to bring democracy and human rights to the Iraqi people. Many perceived the Bush administration as an arrogant, militaristic, imperialistic global bully.

Antiwar rhetoric in nations with large Islamic populations was the most heated and, from the perspective of even antiwar Americans, hyperbolic. The vice president of Indonesia and head of that nation's Islamic coalition party, the United Development Part, declared soon after the war had begun, "Who is actually the terrorist, the one who is against human rights? The answer is the U.S. because they attacked Iraq, they are leaders of terrorists, the initiators of war." A newspaper editorial in the widely read *Koran Tempo* echoed those sentiments, dismissing the Bush administration's claims that overthrowing Saddam was just and necessary, stating that in Indonesia, the word "Bush" "symbolizes the new world colonizer and terrorist."[8] In Turkey, a nation that had long-standing ties to the United States, a leading politician dismissed American claims that Iraq represented an imminent danger to the world; he argued that America invaded Iraq to seize its oil and that the Bush administration might have its sights set next on Turkey's massive boracite holdings. In 2004, a novel, *Metal Firtuna* (metal storm), played out that scenario—of an American military attack on Turkey aimed at seizing the national wealth of the Turkish people—for an anxious public. The novel sold over half a million copies, much to the dismay of the American undersecretary of defense and ardent proponent of the Iraq War, Douglas Feith, who visited Turkey and publicly insisted that such anti-Americanism cease. Less than two years after the Bush administration launched the war in Iraq, 82 percent of Turks polled by the BBC stated that it was not terrorists but President Bush who represented the greatest threat to global security. Large majorities of people polled in other predominately Islamic nations expressed similar feelings.[9]

Many Americans, too, held strong opinions against the Iraq War, both before the war commenced in March 2003 and repeatedly during the war's many nadirs. At least among those who carefully followed the news, these antiwar Americans understood that they stood with global opinion and mourned their nation's international disrepute. Such domestic antiwar sentiments were, however, muted during the war's very beginning. And certainly at the moment the Iraq War began, only a small minority of Americans held antiwar sentiments. A large majority had come to accept the necessity of the war.

Just before the war began, President Bush had appeared on national television to explain why Americans must fight Iraq and topple the Saddam Hussein regime despite the lack of certain proof of Iraq's threat to the United States: "Facing clear evidence of peril, we cannot wait for the final proof—the smoking gun—that could come in the form of a mushroom cloud." President Bush also argued that Saddam had forged close relations with terrorists, including al Qaeda, and that "alliances with terrorists could allow the Iraqi regime to attack America without leaving any fingerprints."[10] After a drumbeat of such prowar "messaging" from President Bush and his national security team, the Iraq War was widely accepted and even popular with Americans during its first few months. People rallied around U.S. troops in harm's way and eagerly awaited news of the capture of the Saddam regime's "weapons of mass destruction." Seizing these weapons, Americans had been told, was the major reason for the American war.

Soon after the war began it became painfully clear that Iraq did not possess the claimed weapons of mass destruction, nor did any proof exist of connections between the Saddam regime and the 9/11 terrorists or al Qaeda. A little more than two years after the Iraq War began, a majority of Americans had turned against the war, telling public opinion pollsters that they believed it had been a "mistake." That level of antiwar disapproval peaked shortly before the 2008 presidential election, with over 60 percent of Americans expressing disapproval of "Bush's war."[11]

4

Before the Iraq War had commenced, Americans had joined in the global protests against the Bush administration's planned "preventative war" in Iraq. Demonstrators numbering in the hundreds of thousands marched in San Francisco and New York, and protesters rallied in hundreds of other places. One American activist stated that the protests in the weeks before the Iraq War actually commenced felt in spirit and practice like the antiwar movement that had risen up in the 1960s to protest against the Vietnam War. Many activists predicted that if and when the Bush administration actually went to war, the strength and militancy of public protest and street demonstrations within the United States would increase dramatically, just as had happened during the Vietnam War.[12]

In the United States, however, people opposed to the American war in Iraq did not generally follow the protest template laid out in the sixties. Many of the activists and organizers first involved in the extraordinary street protests and public rallies against the war, especially as the Iraq War dragged on, turned instead to new forms of political organizing. Capitalizing on new communication and information-dissemination media, key antiwar activists used both traditional grassroots and the newly devised "netroots" activism to mobilize a new progressive political base within the Democratic Party. That progressive base, focused and unified in opposition to the Bush administration's war in Iraq—though not solely so focused—would play a fundamental role in winning dark horse candidate Barack Obama's Democratic Party nomination for the presidency and contribute greatly to his victory in the 2008 presidential election. Obama's victory, however, did not, much to the frustration of many of his progressive supporters, lead directly and immediately to an end to the war in Iraq or to other key Bush administration policies in the global war on terror that Obama had pledged to stop.

Antiwar Americans, in the months and then days leading up to the Iraq War, presented a broad array of arguments against President Bush's planned "preventative war." And unlike the early days of the sixties antiwar movement, dissent came from all sections of the political spectrum. In the immediate run-up to the war, a faction of well-known conservatives were more outspoken against the war than were their liberal counterparts.

Several prominent conservative pundits and political operatives decried the war as contrary to American global interests. Pat Buchanan, a renowned conservative writer and media personality who had challenged George H. W. Bush for the Republican presidential nomination in 1988, was the most blunt of these right-wing critics. Labeled a "paleoconservative" in the media for his vitriolic opposition to the "neoconservatives" who influenced President Bush's foreign policy strategy, such as Paul Wolfowitz, Richard Perle, William Kristol, and Douglas Feith, Buchanan echoed the charges made by some of Iraq War's international Islamic critics: invading Iraq was far more in Israel's interest than it was in that of the United States. In the pages of *American Conservative* magazine, Buchanan wrote, "We charge that a cabal of polemicists and public officials seek to ensnare our country in a series of wars that are not in America's interests. We charge them with colluding with Israel to ignite those wars. . . . We charge that they have alienated friends and allies all over the Islamic and Western world through their arrogance, hubris, and bellicosity."[13]

While few other well-known conservatives expressed such heated and pointed critiques, many expressed doubts about the purpose and outcome of the war. In the run-up to the war, House Majority Leader Dick Armey, a staunch conservative and Republican stalwart, urged his president not to attack Iraq: "If we try to act against Saddam Hussein, as obnoxious as he is, without proper provocation, we will not have the support of other nation states who might do so. . . . I don't believe that America will justifiably make an unprovoked attack on another nation," Armey said. "It would not be consistent with what we have been as a nation or what we should be as a nation."[14] Key national security advisors to former President George H. W. Bush voiced similarly worded, blunt warnings against what they perceived to be a rush to war planned by the administration of George W. Bush. The administration's increasingly bellicose statements on the need to rid Iraq of the dictator Saddam Hussein divided the conservative ranks. Only the war itself would close those ranks as conservatives and Republicans, more generally, rallied around the flag and their president.

Liberals and other progressives, both within and outside the political establishment, spoke out in much larger numbers against the war. Few outright supported the move to war, but their ranks, too, were divided. While many progressive activists and nationally known Democratic officeholders condemned a unilateral American war in Iraq, several leading liberal politicians voiced their concerns about the war cautiously and with carefully phrased caveats.

During October 2002 Senate debates over authorization of President Bush's use of military force in Iraq, those divisions within the liberal political establishment were revealed. Senator Edward Kennedy, long past any presidential aspirations but still seen as a leader of liberal Democrats, unsparingly condemned Bush administration fearmongering. He quoted from a declassified CIA report: "Unprovoked by a U.S. military campaign, Iraqi President Saddam Hussein is unlikely to initiate a chemical or biological attack against the United States."[15] He urged that the rush to war be slowed and reappraised. Kennedy was not alone.

Perhaps the most blunt and outspoken opponent of the war was a relatively moderate Democratic senator from West Virginia, the venerable Robert Byrd. Calling on his decades of public service, Byrd insisted that the war was wrong and that Senate approval of such a war was motivated by political fears of appearing weak on terrorism in the days leading up to the 2002 congressional elections: "As sure as the sun rises in the east, we are embarking on a course of action with regard to Iraq that, in its haste, is both blind and improvident. We are rushing into war without fully discussing why, without thoroughly considering the consequences, or without making any attempt to explore what steps we might take to avert conflict." He systematically dismantled President Bush's case for war against Iraq: "No one supports Saddam Hussein. If he were to disappear tomorrow, no one would shed a tear around the world. I would not. My handkerchief would remain dry. . . . But the principle of one government deciding to eliminate another government," he argued, "using force to do so, and taking that action in spite of world disapproval, is a very disquieting thing. I am concerned that it has the effect of destabilizing the world community of nations. I am concerned that it fosters a climate of suspicion and mistrust in U.S. relations with other nations. The United States is not a rogue nation, given to unilateral action in the face of worldwide opprobrium."[16] Byrd spoke for many but did not represent a majority, even among Senate Democrats.

Most leading liberal officeholders did not decry President Bush's insistence on the need for military force. Nor did their actions in the days leading up to the American attack on Iraq demonstrate a clear stand against the "preventative war." The most equivocal of those leading liberals was Massachusetts Senator John Kerry, who was very much laying the groundwork for his 2004 bid for the presidency. Kerry demonstrated an approval of war against Saddam Hussein, if necessary, even as he proclaimed he was no advocate of a rush to war. Many could not follow the rhetorical path he tiptoed along.

In the forty-five-minute soliloquy Senator Kerry gave during the Senate debate over authorizing force in Iraq, he sought middle ground on waging war. He insisted that the Bush administration approach the United Nations with its concerns so as to gain international support for curtailing the Saddam regime. Nonetheless, he argued that the Senate should give President Bush the authority to use military force against Iraq: "As bad as he is, Saddam Hussein, the dictator, is not the cause of war. Saddam Hussein sitting in Baghdad with an arsenal of weapons of mass destruction is a different matter. In the wake of September 11, who among us can say, with any certainty, to anybody, that those weapons might not be used against our troops or against allies in the region?" Furthermore, Kerry argued, "while the administration has failed to provide any direct link between Iraq and the events of September 11, can we afford to ignore the possibility that Saddam Hussein might accidentally, as well as purposely, allow those weapons to slide off to one group or other in a region where weapons are the currency of trade? How do we leave that to chance?"[17]

Kerry urged his colleagues to vote in favor of authorizing the president's use of military force in Iraq. Kerry carried the day: twenty-nine of fifty Democrats, including New York Senator Hillary Clinton, voted to give President Bush the unilateral authority he sought. All but one of the Senate's forty-nine Republicans also sided with the president's plan for war.

Outside of the Capitol, stalwart progressives did speak out directly against the impending war. One of those progressives, the relatively little known governor of Vermont, Howard Dean, used his anti–Iraq War position to stake out a run for the Democratic presidential nomination. Just before the war commenced, he delivered an antiwar speech in Iowa, the state that first selects delegates to the presidential nominating convention: "I do not believe the President should have been given a green light to drive our nation into conflict. . . . To this day the President has not made a case that the war against Iraq, now, is necessary to defend American territory, our citizens, out allies, or our essential interests." Presciently, Dean also argued that President Bush seemed to have no plan to secure peace in Iraq once American troops had overthrown the Saddam regime and that the war in Iraq would far more likely diminish American influence in the Middle East and around the world than increase it. "We must be smart as well as tough," he concluded.[18]

Throughout the weeks leading up to the war, many others, with far less immediate ambition than Dean, also registered their disapproval of Bush's preemptive strike. One of those speakers was a second-term member of the Illinois State Senate. On October 2, 2002, the day that the Iraq War resolution was introduced in both houses of Congress, Barack Obama spoke before around two thousand people gathered at a Chicago antiwar rally. It was one of a great many such rallies held that day in communities around the United States. Neither the Chicago rally nor the then-unheralded Obama had any immediate impact, but both proved highly significant for what they portended about U.S. political activism in the years ahead.

A small faction of the still relatively weak progressive movement in the United States organized the Chicago rally: big-city white political operatives.

Many of these operatives had roots in the sixties New Left; in the seventies they became involved in urban politics, almost always in coalition with insurgent African American Democratic Party–linked individuals. In the case of the 2002 Chicago antiwar protest, the march organizer was a woman named Marilyn Katz, who had been a leader in the sixties New Left flagship organization Students for a Democratic Society and later a campaign organizer and communication specialist for Puerto Rican and African American candidates in Chicago, including the breakthrough African American mayor Harold Washington in 1983. Also involved in the Chicago anti–Iraq War rally was a longtime Chicago liberal activist, philanthropist, and early Obama backer, Bettylu Saltzman. At these women's behest, the relatively unknown Barack Obama condemned an American war in Iraq.

In pitch-perfect form, Obama presented the political vision that would become so useful to progressives in the years ahead. Without equivocation, he blasted Bush's planned war in Iraq: "I know that an invasion of Iraq without a clear rationale and without strong international support will only fan the flames of the Middle East, and encourage the worst, rather than best, impulses of the Arab world, and strengthen the recruitment arm of al-Qaida. I am not opposed to all wars. I'm opposed to dumb wars." Using the refrain "You want a fight, President Bush?" he attacked Bush for seeking exactly the wrong war. Obama instead proposed a war against oil dependency, a war against hopelessness in too many poor, predominately Islamic nations, and, overarchingly, "the battles that we need to fight. The battles against ignorance and intolerance, corruption and greed, poverty and despair."[19] Obama had begun to outline an alternative if vague progressive position to the Bush administration's pro–oil industry, pro-rich, unilateralist, and bellicose approach to the world. He also demonstrated—or in 2002 simply symbolized—the power of urban liberalism. This progressive base had been pushed to the sidelines in the national Democratic Party for more than a decade.

Obama's speech, although not a national story as he was several years away from becoming a national figure, excited many progressives in Chicago and directly contributed to his successful 2004 election as junior U.S. senator from Illinois. Obama's speech gave him a powerful record as an early, principled opponent of the war in Iraq. Progressive activists in the United States, when the time was right, would help elevate this prescient anti–Iraq War spokesman to a figure of presidential stature.

5

The time was not right for antiwar activists and politicians in the weeks and then months right after the Bush administration ordered the attack on Saddam. In the United States, and for that matter in much of the world, street protests, public rallies, and heated criticism against the Bush administration's war in Iraq dropped quickly once the fighting commenced. In the United States at least, that relative quiescence among antiwar activists was driven by two major factors.

First, the American war effort appeared to be a stunning success. On May 1, 2003, just six weeks after American troops marched into Iraq, President Bush landed on the deck of the USS *Abraham Lincoln* in a Lockheed S-3 Viking wearing a military flight suit, posed for pictures, and then gave a victory speech before a red, white, and blue banner proclaiming "Mission Accomplished." He announced, "In the Battle of Iraq, the United States and our allies have prevailed." Praising America's service personnel, he continued, "Because of you, the tyrant has fallen and Iraq is free."[20] The American people, by a large majority, cheered on their president. Public opinion polls taken in the days right after the announcement registered a 70 percent approval rating for President Bush's job performance. Given that less than 47.9 percent of Americans had voted for him back in November 2000, those numbers reveal that a large number of Americans who had not been Bush supporters had rallied around the president's actions and were pleased by the extraordinary performance of the American military and its commander in chief. Local antiwar activist Ron Jacobs recalled that in the immediate aftermath of the victory speech, within the antiwar movement "most of its members and organizers had reluctantly surrendered their determination, acknowledging another victory for the U.S. war machine."[21]

Second, antiwar activists and critics were reluctant to speak out and organize aggressively against the Iraq War in its first few months out of respect for the men and women who were on the ground and in the air actually fighting for the United States. Here was a lesson painfully learned from the antiwar movement that had struggled to end America's involvement in Vietnam during the 1960s and early 1970s. At that time a great majority of antiwar activists had been careful to separate out their criticism of the policy makers who managed the war from the young people who actually fought it (and charges that protesters often spat on returning soldiers or called them baby killers are simply not true—if such events happened they were rare and never part of any organized protest). Nonetheless, antiwar activists almost never spoke positively about America's service personnel in Vietnam, about their bravery or sense of duty. Instead, that generation of antiwar activists urged young men to resist conscription into the armed forces—often suggesting that it was better and even braver to refuse to fight in Vietnam than it was to lawfully serve. Vietnam-era veterans, and many other Americans who lived through that era, felt strongly that antiwar activists had treated veterans shabbily and had dishonored their service. Such feelings had polarized the nation, and memories of that hard time were still felt more than thirty years later.

In a related vein, antiwar Americans were also well aware that an all-volunteer force was fighting the Iraq War. The United States had ended conscription more than thirty years earlier, in the immediate aftermath of the Vietnam War. No one would be drafted to fight in Iraq. Instead, a tiny percentage of the American people, disproportionately drawn from working-class families of the small towns and rural areas of the South and the West, would do all of America's fighting and dying. Out of guilt, out of a sense of gratitude, out of a sense of common decency, very few Americans, even those most fiercely opposed to the war, wanted the men and women who were risking and sometimes sacrificing their lives to feel any less than honored for their service. From all sides of America's debate about the utility and the legitimacy of the Iraq War would come a heartfelt but soon clichéd sentiment: "Thank you for your service."

As a result of America's rapid progress in battle in the early months of 2003 and antiwar proponents' respect for—and tactical concerns about being perceived as disrespecting—the service of the all-volunteer military, outspoken opposition to the ongoing war was slow to mobilize. Most elected officials rallied around the troops and Bush. In May 2003, Kerry, who was already well into his campaign for the 2004 Democratic Party presidential nomination, hit the political notes he thought would be pleasing to a majority of Americans, including Democratic Party primary voters, telling a national television audience, "I would have preferred if we had given diplomacy a greater opportunity, but I think it was the right decision to disarm Saddam Hussein. And when the president made the decision, I supported him, and I support the fact that we did disarm him."[22]

6

Few nationally prominent officeholders stood against this political tide. An exception was Vermont Governor Howard Dean. Throughout 2003 and then into 2004 he continued to oppose the Iraq War, a stand fundamental to his run for the Democratic presidential nomination. Dean was a good, proven politician, but his campaign stood out for the legion of activists he attracted. These activists—a large majority of them attracted to Dean's anti-war stand—helped to mainstream a new style of campaign organizing and voter mobilization: politics at the netroots.

These "Dean-iacs" were part of a broader progressive effort to bring a new generation of activists into politics using blogs and social media sites. The progressive bloggers and their websites and those to which they linked began to form a counterpublic on the Iraq War and the broader Bush-driven global war on terrorism. Like the teach-in and underground newspaper movement of the Vietnam War era, this nascent counterpublic aimed to do more than inform. Just as labor unions had been vital sites for New Deal working-class Democrats, college campuses for the sixties New Left and anti–Vietnam War protests, churches for both black civil rights activists and white New Rightists, so key anti–Iraq War interactive websites became an organizing portal, a mode of political participation for a new breed of progressive activists. In the early twenty-first century, at least for a segment of the population, political consciousness would be formed at the (web)site of information production. While relatively few in number, these netroots activists proved to be key sources for voter mobilization efforts, early campaign donations, and a general sense of political "buzz" that could generate broader media and popular interest in unheralded, outsider political figures. Progressives had been looking for a new source of organization building: the blogosphere would become vital to that effort. The Dean campaign was their first major national attempt to organize electorally at the netroots.

MoveOn.org was one of the very first of these key progressive websites. Sponsored by wealthy and tech-sophisticated Silicon Valley entrepreneurs, it was founded in 1998 to fight conservative Republicans' attempt to impeach President Bill Clinton over the Monica Lewinsky sex scandal. MoveOn.org became an early anti-Bush site that connected people opposed to the Iraq War. The site's backers saw that people drawn to their site, first to sign a petition opposing Clinton's impeachment, hungered to do more. They founded MoveOn PAC, which used social media and a dedicated website to become a major fund-raising source for progressive-oriented Democratic congressional candidates across the United States. MoveOn was a partisan site tightly knotted to the Democratic Party and proved to both Democratic officeholders and fellow progressives that digital media could be used to raise money from people previously unaffiliated with any traditional progressive causes or partisan politics.

Others followed down MoveOn's path. Particularly successful was an upstart site, the Daily Kos, which grew out of founder Markos Moulitsas's desire to find and foster like-minded, previously unaffiliated progressive-oriented individuals. He was also driven by a specific political agenda. He felt particular frustration with progressives' longtime reliance on single-issue organizations that lobbied on behalf of a specific policy such as abortion rights or environmentalism. He wanted to mobilize more broadly on behalf of progressive Democrats. Kos, as he was known, wanted to link progressive activism more directly to the Democratic Party and so move the Democrats in a more pointedly progressive direction and, like many younger progressives, also simply felt locked out of the normal channels of progressive political involvement and advancement. His sense of frustration and desire to participate would be replicated over and over again by many others.[23]

Kos's blog, the Daily Kos, was founded in March 2002 and exploded in March 2003 when Moulitsas began to promote Howard Dean's upstart campaign for the 2004 Democratic presidential nomination. Kos was thrilled by Dean's blunt and unapologetic antiwar rhetoric and appreciated Dean's outspoken opposition to the Bush tax cuts. Kos, who lived in the Bay area, blogged Dean's March 2003 speech before the California Democratic Party: "What I want to know is what in the world so many Democrats are doing supporting the President's unilateral intervention in Iraq? What I want to know is what in the world so many Democrats are doing supporting tax cuts which have bankrupted this country and given us the largest deficit in the history of the United States?"[24] Moulitsas was not alone in promoting the antiwar, nonestablishment Dean candidacy.

Dean immediately attracted the attention and zealous backing of Kos-like, web-savvy young political activists looking for an alternative to Kerry, the center-of-the-road, cautious Democratic Party front-runner. These netroot activists began the first major web-based campaign site that featured bloggers and the ability of individuals to freely interact: Deanforamerica.com. They also glommed onto Meetup.com to facilitate physical meetings across the country of Dean supporters. Some seventy-five thousand Dean supporters attended these meetings in more than six hundred communities.[25] They also furiously raised money online, targeting small donors. The Dean-iac netroot activists succeeded in propagating Governor Dean as a credible antiwar candidate despite his lack of support from traditional Democratic interest groups and donors.

Governor Dean failed to win the 2004 Democratic nomination, unable to overcome the established network of party interest groups and political donors that rallied around Kerry. His candidacy, however, revealed both the power and excitement self-avowed antiwar progressives at the netroots had brought to the campaign process and the utility bloggers had in exciting the passions and involvement of new political actors. United by their opposition to Bush's war in Iraq, a new progressive force had been mobilized. After some twenty-plus years of conservative domination of the grassroots activist landscape, netroots progressives, fired up by their opposition to the Iraq War, had emerged ready to battle the right.[26] Despite their reservations about Senator Kerry's antiwar bona fides, most progressive antiwar activists rallied around Kerry after he secured the nomination.

By the fall of 2004, the war had become a major campaign issue. Immediately before the 2004 election, the American people were still generally supportive of President Bush's battle, but nearly as many believed that the administration had deliberately misled the American people about weapons of mass destruction in Iraq.[27] Americans largely were anxious and confused about the war, even as a small majority hung onto the belief that it had been worth the costs. In the months just prior to the 2004 presidential election, Democratic presidential nominee Kerry had turned very much against the war, saying he would never have supported the effort had he known that the Bush administration had deceived the American people about Iraq's weapons programs. He used the faltering and ever more costly war as a campaign issue against President Bush. Kerry's antiwar position was strengthened by Americans' discomfort with the grave human rights abuses American soldiers had inflicted on Iraqis held at Abu Ghraib prison, revelations widely publicized by a carefully documented report aired April 28, 2004, on *60 Minutes*. But Kerry's new antiwar message was undermined by the cautious, vaguely prowar stance he had declared during the debate over authorizing force in Iraq. The Bush campaign unrelentingly lambasted Kerry as a "flip-flopper," and the colorful phrase stuck, weakening his campaign and harming his attempts to use the war against Bush.[28]

7

After Kerry's narrow defeat to Bush in the 2004 presidential election, the Democratic Party establishment, heavily pressured by its new activist base, turned to Howard Dean for leadership, naming him chairman of the Democratic National Committee. Chairman Dean, his fellow Democrats hoped, would bring his antiwar netroot supporters into the party's activist base. After taking up the chairmanship in early 2005, Dean declared, "This party's strength does not come from consultants down. It comes from the grassroots up."[29] Dean advocated for a simple and straightforward progressive policy base for the Democratic Party: in terms of foreign policy, oppose the war in Iraq and work with—not against—America's international allies on global problems; in domestic policy, stop giving tax breaks to giant oil companies and the wealthiest Americans; and as a major policy goal, create a national health care plan.[30] The new party activists brought into the Democratic Party were not single-issue progressives, but their passionate antiwar sentiments unified them and fueled their commitment to electoral politics.

By no means were all antiwar activists narrowly focused on the Democratic Party and traditional electoral politics.[31] As the Iraq War become ever more deadly and costly, and ever more obviously not a "mission accomplished," antiwar activism spread across the United States. Increasingly, somber antiwar activists simply wanted the war to end. They focused on the terrible human toll it was taking on American service personnel. The most influential of those protests was the vigil held by Cindy Sheehan, whose son Casey, an Army specialist, was killed in action along with seven other young soldiers on April 4, 2004. His death came nearly a year after President Bush's "Mission Accomplished" victory speech aboard the *Lincoln*.

Soon after Casey's death, a grieving Sheehan told a newspaper reporter that she was not sure she understood what her son had died defending in Iraq. By the time of President Bush's inauguration in January 2005, Sheehan had become an antiwar activist, cofounding a small organization dedicated to ending the war: Gold Star Families for Peace. Members had all lost a family member in the war. On August 6, 2005, Sheehan began a vigil outside President Bush's Crawford, Texas, ranch; she told journalists that she simply wanted to meet with the president and would wait in her makeshift camp until she had the opportunity to discuss with him why her son and other parents' children had died in Iraq. Her vigil captured international attention and kept people's focus on the war's devastating effects.[32] MoveOn.org and other antiwar groups organized vigils across the country in support of Sheehan's efforts to make people understand that President Bush had lied to the American people about going to war, that he was lying when he told them the war had been won, and that thousands of American men and women were dying in Iraq because of those lies.

According to polling data, American public opinion began turning against the Iraq War in early 2005, but only in 2006 did that dissatisfaction harden.[33] In the months leading up to the November 2006 congressional elections, the war became a central issue in a way it had not during the 2004 presidential election. Progressive antiwar activists at the netroots threw themselves into electoral politics, championing antiwar Democratic candidates around the country by raising money for them and by promoting and participating in grassroots activities such as registering new voters, canvassing districts to identify sympathetic voters, and working on Election Day to bring those voters to the polls. MoveOn.org alone had amassed an email list of some three million people who could be solicited for campaign funds and district-by-district grassroots activism.

Progressives worked hard and contributed directly to a massive electoral turnaround. Thirty-one new Democrats were elected to the House of Representatives, enough new members to restore a Democratic majority in the House for the first time since 1994. In the House's 435 elections, Democrats gained some 6.5 million more votes than did Republicans. The Senate Democratic caucus also recorded a major pickup, netting seven seats, returning its control to the Democrats. Antiwar progressive activists' turn to electoral politics had been a resounding success.[34]

Still, not everybody opposed to the Iraq War supported this electoral strategy. Just as some on the political left had argued in 2000 that the choice between George Bush and Democratic candidate Al Gore presented little more than a decision between Tweedledee and Tweedledum, so too did some leftist antiwar activists insist that working for any Democratic Party candidate was a fool's errand. Alexander Cockburn, an internationally known "man of the left," argued that "the mainstream anti-war movement . . . is captive to the Democratic Party." The result of this captivity, Cockburn continued, was a relatively passive antiwar movement that accepted the Democratic Party's continuing funding of the Iraq War even as the Democrats claimed their opposition. Cockburn and other militant antiwar activists insisted that the antiwar movement should have been far more militant, taking to the streets and demanding an end to the war in Iraq. Cockburn, a veteran of the Vietnam antiwar movement, understood that confrontational militant demonstrations would almost surely have resulted in little or no change in American policy in Iraq. However, he argued, immediate policy change should not really be the primary goal of a dissident social change movement. He offered a different perspective: "Anti-war movements are often most significant in their afterlife—schooling a new generation in attitudes and tactics of resistance."[35]

By and large, the netroots antiwar progressives rejected Cockburn's old left perspective on the making and meaning of a dissident political culture. The netroots movement, cheered by their electoral success in the November 2006 congressional elections, even as they were frustrated by the Democratic Party's incremental approach to ending the Iraq War in 2007, began looking forward to the 2008 presidential election. They, and many other Americans opposed to "Bush's war," sought a strong antiwar candidate. The mainstream antiwar movement believed they could have a major voice in electing the next U.S. president.

By 2008, many nationally known politicians had come out strongly against the Iraq War. Even some conservative Republicans had lost faith. Senator Richard Lugar, one-time chair of the Foreign Relations Committee and a leading Republican voice on foreign policy and national security, had turned against his president's leadership and called for a staged troop withdrawal. Democrats were even more outspoken, and none of the contenders for the party's presidential nomination supported the Iraq War. However, only one candidate had a spotless record opposing the war. Thanks to his October 2, 2002, speech, Senator Barack Obama could declare an unwavering antiwar stance. His main competitor, New York Senator Hillary Clinton, could not, having voted in favor of giving President Bush the authority to wage war on Iraq.

8

Barack Obama had many things going for him besides his antiwar bona fides. He was a powerful and effective stump speaker; he was untouched, as he often said, by the contentious politics of the sixties; he was obviously highly intelligent and deeply informed on the issues; and he was the first African American elected official to have the talent and the timing to become a serious aspirant to the presidency. For his supporters Obama was, as his campaign slogan stated, "change we can believe in."

After narrowly beating Senator Clinton for the Democratic Party presidential nomination, Obama crossed swords with his Republican opponent, Arizona Senator John McCain, over the war in Iraq. McCain, a Vietnam War veteran who had been held captive by the North Vietnamese for nearly five and a half years, was an ardent war supporter. He vowed that if he were elected president the troops fighting in Iraq would not face the same dishonor he and his brothers in arms had been forced to swallow in Vietnam. He would not withdraw American troops from Iraq until the war was won. During the presidential campaign McCain blasted Obama for losing faith in the war. He insisted during the first 2008 presidential debate, "We are winning in Iraq. And we will come home with victory and with honor." He assured Americans that "we will succeed and our troops will come not in defeat, that we will see a stable ally in the region and a fledgling democracy."[36]

In response to McCain's assertions, Obama expressed a starkly different view: "Six years ago, I stood up and opposed this war at a time when it was politically risky to do so because I said that not only did we not know how much it was going to cost, what our exit strategy might be, how it would affect our relationships around the world, and whether our intelligence was sound, but also because we hadn't finished the job in Afghanistan. . . . Senator McCain and President Bush had a very different judgment." Obama continued, "And I wish I had been wrong for the sake of the country and they had been right, but that's not the case. We've spent over $600 billion so far, soon to be $1 trillion. We have lost over 4,000 lives. We have seen 30,000 wounded, and most importantly, from a strategic national security perspective, al Qaeda is resurgent, stronger now than at any time since 2001." In concluding, Obama drew a clear division between himself and McCain: "So I think the lesson to be drawn is that we should never hesitate to use military force, and I will not, as president, in order to keep the American people safe. But we have to use our military wisely. And we did not use our military wisely in Iraq."[37]

Antiwar activists flocked to the Obama campaign, which drew heavily on the netroots activists to build the most powerful and effective social media campaign electoral politics had ever seen. That campaign extolled Obama's attributes, showcasing his principled stand against the war, his charismatic personality, and his promise to reverse the course of the Bush years. The campaign unendingly tied Senator McCain to President Bush's policies. By the fall of 2008, President Bush, with approval ratings stuck around 30 percent, had become so unpopular that the two-term president made not a single campaign appearance on behalf of McCain, who pledged to maintain Bush's wars. Overwhelmingly, Americans disapproved of Bush's war in Iraq. But by late September Americans were also deeply anxious about the free-falling bank and real estate crisis that was plunging the United States—and much of the world—into a deep economic recession.

To highlight those debacles and showcase Obama's promise to bring fundamental policy changes to the White House, the campaign built on the successes MoveOn.org and other progressive social media to create an unprecedented web presence. The Obama campaign understood the power of the relatively new Facebook, gaining almost two and a half million supporters (the McCain campaign eventually joined in but recorded just more than six hundred thousand). The Obama campaign hosted its own YouTube channel, boasting more than eighteen hundred videos. All told, Obama's online videos were viewed some 889 million times (335 million more views than McCain's videos received). The Obama social media machine also raised an unprecedented amount of campaign funds, more than $750 million, upending the traditionally huge Republican advantage. By greatly expanding the use of social media, the Obama campaign achieved an unprecedented donor base: some three million people donated to the Obama campaign, with about half of those donations coming in amounts of two hundred dollars or less. The netroots mobilization against the Iraq War had become a critical component of Barack Obama's campaign in 2008.[38]

Barack Obama won the election by a whopping 9.5 million votes. The Obama campaign's netroots political machinery contributed to a record number of voters turning out. Some 131.3 million Americans voted, with nearly 70 million supporting Obama. The only major candidate in either party to oppose the Iraq War from its beginnings in late 2002 had become the president of the United States.

Around the world, people celebrated Obama's victory; in many nations his popularity easily surpassed his support in the United States. Global public opinion had lined up in overwhelming numbers against the Bush presidency and his supporter, McCain. Unalterably opposed to America's war on Iraq, people feared America's belligerency and the Bush administration's seeming contempt for world opinion; they wanted a restrained American foreign policy that would once again work as a global partner for peace, stability, and prosperity. In Europe especially people believed Obama shared their views, and in his early days in office his popularity reached extraordinary levels— some 86 percent expressed their confidence in America's new president. The Japanese were similarly enthralled; Obama had an 85 percent confidence rating there. Even in countries not normally sympathetic to any American president, Obama polled well, with 55 percent of Mexicans and 62 percent of Chinese indicating confidence in America's new president. Only in predominately Muslim nations, such as Egypt, Jordan, Lebanon, Pakistan, and Turkey, did large majorities maintain their suspicions of the American government, even as Obama replaced Bush.[39] Bush's wars had deeply harmed America's reputation in many predominately Islamic nations, and it would take more than a change in personnel to heal those wounds.

Stateside, progressives believed that President Obama—their candidate— could and would quickly end the war in Iraq. Many hoped that he would efficiently bring the war in Afghanistan to a close as well. They expected Obama to repudiate the most aggressive of the Bush administration's antiterrorist policies. In particular, progressives believed that Obama would keep his campaign promise to close America's brutal Guantanamo Bay detention camp for suspected terrorists and bring detainees to trial. Overwhelmingly, in the months that followed President Obama's January 2009 inauguration, progressives supported their president and waited for him to act. On many issues they would wait a long time.

President Obama meant to close down the Guantanamo Bay detention camp. Within days of being sworn in he issued an order to close it no later than 2009 and to bring the detainees to trail either in the United States or abroad. The Democratic Party–controlled Congress rebelled and stopped Obama. Members of Congress were reacting to the fears of their constituents, many of whom were still too scared of possible terrorist threats to countenance on American soil civilian trials of men many believed to be in league with al Qaeda. The facility remains open; some prisoners have been held there for well over a decade without any trail to determine their guilt or innocence.

Obama also continued the core policies laid out by the Bush administration on the global war on terror. In most key areas, he actually intensified the fight. While running for president he had blasted the Bush administration for not doing more to bring al Qaeda ringleader Osama bin Laden to justice. Obama pushed his national security team hard to find and kill bin Laden. On May 2, 2011, they did. Similarly, Obama brought the war home to al Qaeda and allied terror groups throughout the Middle East, the Near East, and the Horn of Africa. The Obama administration oversaw a brutal Predator drone war, as well as a series of covert operations that resulted in the deaths of hundreds, if not thousands, of people. The strikes were effective in killing terrorists operating in Afghanistan, Pakistan, Yemen, and other nations, but innocent civilians as well.[40] Progressives were appalled at the Obama administration's willingness to use such a brutal means to pursue terrorist targets. Tom Hayden, who once helped lead the anti–Vietnam War movement and then decades later campaigned for Obama, spoke for many who had opposed Bush's wars: "[Obama] does things that would be unthinkable from a antiwar perspective. . . . I think a lot of people thought he would do a better job for us."[41]

Obama also chose to continue the war in Afghanistan. Here he had promised nothing different. Even during his October 2002 speech in which he had condemned the planned war in Iraq, he had clearly stated that he did support the effort to rid Afghanistan of al Qaeda and the Taliban regime that had supported bin Laden and his fellow violent anti-American jihadists. Only slowly, after first supporting a troop surge, did President Obama begin to wind down the American war in Afghanistan, promising to bring home American troops in 2014.

While President Obama sometimes deeply disappointed factions of the antiwar movement that had helped him to win the presidential nomination and then twice the presidency, he did stay true to his core commitment. He had promised to bring the American war in Iraq to an end. And while it may have taken him longer than some in the antiwar movement would have wished, he succeeded. The last American troops left Iraq, as Obama had said they would, in the last days of 2011. Marilyn Katz, the progressive activist who had arranged for Barack Obama to speak out against the Iraq War in October 2002, gave the president his due: "He was an anchor for building the antiwar movement," she said. "We decided that our vehicle would be in Barack Obama. . . . This is a guy who made his promise and kept his promise."[42]

9

For those who opposed the American wars in Afghanistan and Iraq, the struggle to end the wars had been immensely frustrating. They had watched tens of thousands of people die. Internationally, only a minority of people ever accepted the legitimacy of America's turn to war in Afghanistan and Iraq to seek revenge for the 9/11 attacks and to solve the problem of international terrorism. Americans were far more accepting of the Bush administration's call to arms. While Americans became impatient with the lack of success in the bloody fight in Afghanistan, majorities supported the campaign for nearly a decade, and no major politicians challenged the need to attack al Qaeda and the Taliban. Only in the summer of 2010, as the war seemed to have become yet another quagmire, did public opinion turn against the military struggle, though most expressed only weariness with the war, not a sense of betrayal or a belief that the United States had made a fundamental mistake in sending troops to Afghanistan.[43]

Iraq had always been a different struggle for Americans. While early success had convinced a majority of Americans for a time that the war was just and necessary, millions of Americans joined people around the world in opposing the Bush administration's "preventative war." A vibrant, peaceful antiwar movement struggled from 2002 to find a means to end the war. By 2004, many activists had chosen to align themselves with the progressive wing of the Democratic Party as the best way to fight the Bush administration's fierce commitment to the war. While the antiwar movement's first candidate, Vermont Governor Howard Dean, had not been able to win the party nomination in 2004, his candidacy helped to inspire a "netroots" movement that fast developed into a smart and sophisticated grassroots campaign that energized progressives around the nation. These progressives helped to elect a wave of antiwar congressional candidates in 2006. Soon thereafter these progressives, fueled and united by their antiwar beliefs, pushed Barack Obama to national prominence, then Democratic presidential candidate, and finally two-term president of the United States. While the antiwar movement had only limited success in changing American policy, its reliance on netroots organizing and social media was instrumental in changing democratic practice in the United States and the fortunes of a once obscure local politician named Barack Obama.

NOTES

1 For direct costs, see the running totals collected by the National Priorities Project, http://nationalpriorities.org/cost-of/, and for an article on the total estimated costs,

see Ernesto Londono, "Iraq, Afghan Wars Will Cost $4 trillion to $6 trillion, Harvard Study Says," *Washington Post*, March 28, 2013, http://articles.washingtonpost.com/2013-03-28/world/38097452_1_iraq-price-tag-first-gulf-war-veterans.

2 David W. Moore, "Public Overwhelmingly Backs Bush in Attacks on Afghanistan," Gallup News Service, October 8, 2002, http://www.gallup.com/poll/4966/public-over-whelmingly-backs-bush-attacks-afghanistan.aspx.

3 Jeffrey M. Jones, "In U.S., Half Say U.S. Should Speed Up Afghanistan With-drawal," Gallup Politics, March 15, 2012, http://www.gallup.com/poll/153260/Half-Say-Speed-Afghanistan-Withdrawal.aspx.

4 Angelique Chrisafis, "Millions Worldwide Rally for Peace," *Guardian*, February 16, 2003, http://www.theguardian.com/world/2003/feb/17/politics.uk.

5 For a nuanced look at international opinion during the post-9/11 era, see David Farber, ed., *What They Think of US: International Perceptions of the United States since 9/11* (Princeton: Princeton University Press, 2007).

6 Federico Romero, "The Twilight of American Cultural Hegemony," in Farber, *What They Think of US*, 165.

7 Ibid., 166.

8 Melani Budianta, "Beyond the Stained Glass," in Farber, *What They Think of US*, 31.

9 Nur Bilge Criss, "Turkish Perceptions of the United States," in Farber, *What They Think of US*, 62–68.

10 "Bush: Don't Wait for Mushroom Cloud," CNN.com/Inside Politics, March 8, 2002, http://edition.cnn.com/2002/ALLPOLITICS/10/07/bush.transcript/.

11 Andrew Dugan, "On 10th Anniversary, 53% in U.S. See Iraq War as Mistake," Gallup Politics, March 18, 2013, http://www.gallup.com/poll/161399/10th-anniversary-iraq-war-mistake.aspx.

12 Jeremy Varon, email, September 25, 2013; Varon is a prominent scholar of antiwar activism during the Vietnam War era as well as a veteran activist who organized against the Iraq War and related Bush administration policies.

13 Pat Buchanan, "Whose War?," *American Conservative*, March 23, 2003, http://www.theamericanconservative.com/articles/whose-war/.

14 "Armey: 'Unprovoked War Would Be Illegal,'" *Chicago Tribune*, August 9, 2002, republished on CommonDreams.com, http://www.commondreams.org/headlines.shtml?/headlines02/0809-08.htm.

15 "Authorization of the Use of United States Armed Forces Against Iraq—Continued—(Senate—October 09, 2002)," *Congressional Record*, S10166, https://beta.congress.gov/congressional-record/2002/10/09/senate-section/article/S10164-1.

16 Senator Robert C. Byrd, "Rush to War Ignores U.S. Constitution," October 7, 2002, http://www.swans.com/library/art8/zig078.html.

17 "Authorization of the Use of United States Armed Forces," S10173. Both Kerry quotes appear on this page.

18 Howard Dean, "Defending American Values—Protecting American Interests" (Drake University, February 17, 2003), http://www.crocuta.net/Dean/Transcript_of_Foreign_Policy_Speech_at_Drake-Feb17_2003.htm.

19 "Transcript: Obama's Speech Against the Iraq War" (October 2, 2002), http://www.npr.org/templates/story/story.php?storyId=99591469.

20 Remarks by the President from the USS Abraham Lincoln, "President Bush Announces Major Combat Operations in Iraq Have Ended," http://web.archive.org/web/20041020235150/http://www.whitehouse.gov/news/releases/2003/05/iraq/20030501-15.html.

21 Ron Jacobs, "A Look at the Movement Against the US War in Iraq," Counterpunch, July 12–14, 2013, http://www.counterpunch.org/2013/07/12/a-look-at-the-movement-against-the-us-war-in-iraq/.

22 "Secretary of State John Kerry Says as a Senator He 'Opposed the President's Decision to Go into Iraq,'" PolitiFact.com, http://www.politifact.com/truth-o-meter/statements/2013/sep/13/john-kerry/secretary-state-john-kerry-says-senator-he-opposed/. This article is a great source on Kerry's evolving position on the Iraq War.

23 See Jerome Armstrong and Markos Moulitsas, Crashing the Gate: Netroots, Grassroots, and the Rise of People-Powered Politics (White River Junction, VT: Chelsea Green, 2006). Throughout this article I am much influenced by the analysis of Democratic Party politics and the role of the netroots presented in this book.

24 Quoted in Armstrong and Moulitsas, Crashing the Gate, 138.

25 Michael T. Heaney, Matthew E. Newman, and Dari E. Sylvester, "Campaigning in the Internet Age," in The Electoral Challenge: Theory Meets Practice, ed. C. Craig and David B. Hill (Washington, DC: CQ Press, 2010), 170

26 Dean and his "Dean-iacs," besides opposing Bush on the issue of the Iraq War and tax cuts for the wealthy, also rescued the issue of health care from its burial during the first Clinton administration. Dean insisted that a national health care plan was the single most needed policy in the United States. Health care for all was an interesting choice for the progressive forces; it was not a program aimed at the poor, who after all are covered by Medicaid in the United States; nor was it something labor unions were interested in because they, too, had long before made health care insurance a major part of any contract they negotiated for their members. So national health care was a solution for an essentially unaffiliated, unorganized group for whom no particular progressive faction or organization had focused its attention. National health care was a middle-class, progressive cause in the United States. President Clinton had seen it as such, too, and now, as Dean phrased it, the Democratic wing of the Democratic Party—that is, the progressive wing—was making it their central affirmative domestic issue.

27 Opinion polls taken shortly before the election showed around 51 percent of Americans thought it had not been a mistake to go to war, even as about 47 percent thought the Bush administration had misled them about the need to go to war. "Iraq," Gallup, http://www.gallup.com/poll/1633/iraq.aspx. This is a very useful site that includes a number of historic polls on American public opinion on Iraq and the Iraq War.

28 See, for example, Judy Keen, "Bush: Kerry Repeatedly Flip Flops on Iraq War," USA Today, August 10, 2004, http://usatoday30.usatoday.com/news/politicselections/nation/president/2004-08-10-bush-talks_x.htm.

29 Quoted in Armstrong and Moulitsas, *Crashing the Gate*, 151.

30 In some ways at least, the new progressives operating at the netroots level bare a more than passing resemblance to the American progressives of a century ago. Mostly middle class in orientation and identity, they are less invested in economic redistribution or safeguarding of the poor or even working class than they are in safeguarding the secular and well-educated middle class from the outrages of the corrupt and insatiable wealthy and the religious, moralistic, and antiscience demands of the often but not exclusively lower and middling income social conservatives. The new progressives were a mainly postracial, postfeminist, post–Great Society sort—whose progressivism was driven most of all by the Bush administration's odd mélange of war, evangelical religion, and hyper-capitalism that was given urgency by the Bush administration's muscular use of state power to advance its agenda.

31 For a suggestive analysis of the partisan views of antiwar activists, see Michael T. Heaney and Fabio Rojas, "Partisans, Nonpartisans, and the Antiwar Movement in the United States," *American Politics Research* 35, no. 4 (July 2007): 431–64.

32 See Gold Star Families for Peace, http://www.gsfp.org.

33 "Iraq," Gallup.

34 The war was a major contributor to Democrats' success, but it was not the only issue. President Bush's poor handling of Hurricane Katrina as well as Republican Party corruption scandals played important roles, too.

35 Alexander Cockburn, "Whatever Happened to the Anti-War Movement?," *New Left Review* 46 (July–August 2007), http://newleftreview.org/II/46/alexander-cockburn-whatever-happened-to-the-anti-war-movement.

36 All quotes are taken from the September 26, 2008, presidential debate transcript: http://elections.nytimes.com/2008/president/debates/transcripts/first-presidential-debate.html.

37 Ibid.

38 A useful source on the Obama campaign is Larry Sabato, *The Year of Obama* (New York: Pearson, 2010), especially the essays by Girish J. Gulati, "No Laughing Matter: The Role of the New Media in the 2008 Election," 187–203; and Michael Cornfield, "Game-Changers: New Technology and the 2008 Presidential Election," 205–30. Facts and figures are drawn from these two essays.

39 Historic international polling data are provided in "Global Opinion of Obama Slips, International Policies Faulted" (Pew Research Global Attitudes Project, June 13, 2012), http://www.pewglobal.org/2012/06/13/global-opinion-of-obama-slips-international-policies-faulted/.

40 The drone casualty numbers are classified and therefore hard to calculate. See "Counting Deaths from Drone Strikes" (Human Rights Institute, Columbia Law School, 2015), http://web.law.columbia.edu/human-rights-institute/counterterrorism/drone-strikes/counting-drone-strike-deaths.

41 Zachary A. Goldfarb and Juliet Eilperin, "Syria Situation further Strains Obama's Relationship with the Antiwar Movement," *Washington Post*, September 13, 2013, http://www.washingtonpost.com/politics/syria-situation-further-strains-obamas-relation-

ship-with-the-antiwar-movement/2013/09/13/06c9b0f2-1bb9-11e3-a628-7e6dde8f889d_
story.html.

42 Ibid.

43 Elizabeth Bumiller and Allison Kopicki, "Support in U.S. for Afghan War
Drops Sharply, Poll Finds," March 26, 2012, *New York Times*, http://www.nytimes.
com/2012/03/27/world/asia/support-for-afghan-war-falls-in-us-poll-finds.html.

9

Limited War in the Age of Total Media

SAM LEBOVIC

The wars in Iraq and Afghanistan were fought in an age of media sat-uration. The big three television networks of the postwar era had been supplemented by a plethora of cable channels, including a number devoted to twenty-four-hour news coverage. And the wars were the first fought wholly in the age of the Internet: journalists could update their stories rap-idly; the blogosphere provided a new arena for columnists to opine about the wars and foreign policy; even deployed soldiers could publish blogs about their military experiences. According to basic democratic principles, this range of media channels should have made for a more informed pub-lic: with more media, more information should have been provided to the public; and with access to more information, the public should have been more informed.

And yet, on a variety of fronts, the public was woefully misinformed about the wars in Iraq and Afghanistan. In the lead-up to the invasion of Iraq in March 2003, as many as 68 percent of Americans believed that Iraq had played a role in the attacks of 9/11, with 13 percent believing that "conclusive evidence" of such a relationship had been found.[1] Half of the respondents in a Knight-Ridder poll believed that one or more of the 9/11 hijackers were Iraqi citizens, even though none of them were.[2] Such misunderstandings were not solely a product of the rush to war. Between June and September 2003, after the end of the initial invasion, polls revealed that 60 percent of Americans still believed at least one of three demonstrably false things about the war: that clear evidence had been found that Saddam Hussein had worked closely with al Qaeda, that weapons of mass destruction (WMDs) had been found in Iraq, or that world public opinion had favored the U.S. invasion of Iraq.[3] And as the wars in Iraq and Afghanistan dragged on, Americans would remain ig-norant about the basic facts of combat. In July 2003, only 23 percent of Ameri-cans could correctly estimate whether the presence of European soldiers in the peacekeeping force in Afghanistan numbered in the tens, the hundreds, or the thousands.[4] In March 2008, only 28 percent of U.S. adults were able to approximate the level of American casualties in the Iraq War.[5]

How, in the midst of the information age, did the American public remain so misinformed, uninformed, and confused about the wars in Iraq and Afghanistan? Why did the proliferation of media not produce a more perfect "marketplace of ideas" as we might so easily assume? Broadly speaking, scholars provide two different sorts of explanations for the failure of the media to produce an informed public. Extending the economic metaphor of the "marketplace of ideas," we can call them "supply-side" explanations and "demand-side" explanations. Supply-side explanations focus on the ways in which information is supplied to the public by the government and journalists, while demand-side explanations focus on the ways in which consumers of the media make use of that information.

On the supply side, I argue below, it is important to understand how journalists rely on official sources for their reporting, and how official sources can mislead journalists and the public, as well as limit access to important information. On the demand side, it is important to pay attention to the relationship of the individual consumer to the media, analyzing the ways in which individuals internalize stories from the media and considering the possibility that the proliferation of entertainment media might be distracting public attention from questions of war and peace, or desensitizing citizens to the horrors of war. My aim is to raise questions and sketch problems more than it is to provide a final account of media practice in the wars. But in general, I want to suggest that it is important that we think about the use of media channels in their social, economic, and political contexts. In other words, rather than considering the technological potential of new forms of media in the abstract, it is better to think about how the media are actually used to communicate information, uses that are often shaped by specific historical contexts.

Close to 90 percent of Americans relied on TV as their primary news source during the wars. For that reason, I draw the majority of my examples from that medium. But this analysis should also apply to print and online media, not least because content often circulates from one medium to another. Most Internet users in March 2003, for instance, received their online news from TV network sites, newspaper sites, or government sites.[6] Nonetheless, the emphasis on one medium provides coherence to a subject that risks sprawling.

* * *

The best place to start is on the supply side, where we can see how information gets into the news. What sources do news reports rely on? Overwhelmingly, journalists rely on official sources. In early 2003, the media watchdog organization Fairness and Accuracy In Reporting (FAIR) surveyed news reports on

Iraq for a week on either side of Colin Powell's fateful February 5 presentation at the United Nations, in which he presented the administration's case for war. Of the 393 talking heads and sources who appeared on-camera in stories on the ABC, NBC, CBS, and PBS evening news programs in this period, two-thirds were American, and three-quarters of those were current or former government officials. FAIR found that only one official U.S. source, Massachusetts Democratic Senator Ted Kennedy, could be considered opposed to the war (a judgment made on the generous grounds that he had asked what the length and cost of the invasion would be).[7] A more detailed follow-up study looked at 1,617 on-camera sources on network evening news programs as well as on Fox and CNN in the three weeks after bombing started in Iraq in March 2003. It found that over three-quarters of all news sources were American, that 68 percent of American sources on the news were current or former government officials, and that two-thirds of those official sources were military sources. Academics and representatives from think tanks and nongovernmental organizations, by way of contrast, made up only 4 percent of the sources. In other words, the talking heads whom Americans heard on the news were overwhelmingly American and predominantly spoke in an official capacity. And almost half of all American sources were from the military.[8]

At the most obvious level, these statistics suggest a problem in the way that news organizations presented the debate about the war. Foreign perspectives were drowned out: in October 2003, 81 percent of sources on the media were American, 10 percent were Iraqi, and the rest of the world split the remaining airtime.[9] Moreover, pro- and antiwar positions were not presented equally as two sides to the issue: 64 percent of the guests espoused prowar positions, and only 10 percent espoused antiwar positions.[10] Even a weaker definition of media balance, in which the media represent political positions according to their popularity, was not met, as antiwar positions were substantially underrepresented on the news as compared to their prevalence in the population. Although polls suggested that roughly a quarter of Americans were opposed to the war, and despite the presence of large-scale antiwar protests, only 3 percent of U.S. sources expressed opposition to the war on the news.[11]

Reliance on official sources is not a new phenomenon. Numerous studies have shown that media coverage of wars and foreign policy in the second half of the twentieth century tends to rely on official sources, and that the range of debate in the media therefore tends to reflect the range of debate within official circles. Media scholars call this the "indexing" theory of news coverage—the range of debate in the media is "indexed" to the range of debate between officials. When officials disagree about a policy, the media will present a vibrant debate about the policy. When officials agree about a policy, journalists will find it difficult to present anything but consensus around an issue.[12]

Media coverage of the Vietnam War provides a case study of the indexing theory in history. It is often imagined that hostile media coverage of the Vietnam War undermined the war effort. But in reality, media criticism of the Vietnam War lagged behind public opposition to the war. Beginning in 1965, antiwar protests drew ever-larger crowds, and by the end of that year public approval of President Lyndon Johnson's handling of the war had begun to drop.[13] By mid-1966, according to Gallup polls, America was deeply divided about the Vietnam War. In March of that year 26 percent of the public believed the war was a mistake, but by the end of summer that number had jumped to 36 percent. Despite occasional reversals, opposition would continue to rise in 1967—reaching 47 percent by October.[14]

But until the Tet Offensive at the start of 1968, television editorial commentary ran four to one in favor of the war. After Tet, television opinion became more unfavorable to the war, but this was because the Tet Offensive encouraged greater levels of *official* discontent with the war. Close to half of all antiwar sources cited on the news were public officials, and reflected increasing political tension over the war, such as the disputes aired in Senator William Fulbright's hearings. And much coverage of antiwar protestors remained critical or dismissive. The range of debate in the media thus mapped onto the range of debate among political elites, not the range of debate occurring in the public.[15]

It is easy to understand why the media tend to rely on official sources. To begin with, it is cheaper and easier to speak to officials—they hold regular press briefings, issue statements, and are available and prepared for interviews. This means that officials are often given more prominent platforms in the news than are less powerful political actors. It also means they are identified as important and authoritative voices. Although 80 percent of all news sources are identified by name on the nightly news, 42 percent of antiwar sources were unnamed in the opening weeks of the Iraq War. Whereas official sources often engaged in sit-down interviews on-screen, antiwar voices were largely expressed through brief interviews with anonymous members of the public and one-sentence sound bites.[16]

More foundationally, the modern demands of objectivity in journalism heighten media dependence on official sources. Journalists need to make many decisions in the course of constructing a news story out of the dizzying array of facts, opinions, interpretations, and voices that could be included in their coverage. The task of the objective journalist is to avoid partisanship or bias in making such decisions, and relying on and quoting the statements of experts and public officials provides journalists with an apparently easy way to remove their own political judgments from their decisions about what is newsworthy. According to professional norms, journalists exercise little judgment in quoting official sources: the statements of officials in power are almost always newsworthy simply because government officials are newsmakers. Similarly, it often makes sense to seek the expertise of officials or former officials. In the process, of course, journalists *are* nonetheless making news judgments, and repeating the positions of officials can easily slant the news.[17]

Such slanting can take obvious forms, such as the disproportionate amount of prowar coverage on the nightly news. But it can also take more subtle forms as journalists find themselves unintentionally echoing the attitudes and perspectives of official sources. Although a number of post-9/11 journalists disliked the phrase "the global war on terror," which they found to be amorphous, vague, and highly ideological, they nevertheless found themselves using it in their stories. Sometimes, this was simply because they were quoting an official who used the phrase, and the practices of objectivity required that they present the official's statements without criticism. "I don't classify the war on terror," explained one reporter, "the president uses the phrase, I quote him using the phrase. . . . It's not my responsibility to define it." Indeed, as another reporter pointed out, to refer to the "so-called war on terror" in reports would appear to be a breach of objectivity, an act of editorializing if not a form of sneering partisanship. Moreover, journalists soon came to rely on the phrase "global war on terror" as an easy shorthand that captured a complex range of events, even if this meant naturalizing the assumption that "global war on terror" was an objective description of a global phenomenon, rather than a political label and the product of a series of controversial government policies.[18] Thus the standards of objective journalism helped portray the position of the administration as neutral and objective, while criticism of the administration increasingly appeared biased and subjective.

In the Iraq War, two factors exacerbated this problematic reliance on official sources. First, in the context of war, a number of journalists eschewed their commitments to objectivity and rallied to the flag. Such saber rattling and partisan patriotism are most often associated with the Fox News Channel, and not without reason. Despite its claims to be "fair and balanced," a number of the network's on-air commentators made very clear their political commitments. Brit Hume, for instance, dismissed the requirements of objectivity because "neutrality as a general principle is an appropriate concept for journalists who are covering institutions of some comparable quality. This is a conflict between the US and murdering barbarians."[19]

But such sentiments were not unique to Fox. Shortly after the invasion of Iraq, CBS's Dan Rather told Larry King that "I'm an American. I never tried to kid anybody that I'm some internationalist or something. And when my country is at war, I want my country to win. . . . Now, I can't and don't argue that that is coverage without a prejudice. About that I am prejudiced."[20] Indeed, although much media criticism has focused on the jingoistic excesses of Fox, it would be a mistake to assume that the problems of war coverage were specific to that channel. Fox coverage *was* highly prowar, and viewers of Fox were more likely to hold the mistaken belief that Iraq had WMDs or ties to al Qaeda than viewers of any other channel.[21] But Fox represented an extreme example of a systemic problem. Indeed, Fox wasn't always the worst offender. CBS gave the lowest amount of screen time to antiwar sources in the month after the invasion of Iraq. Only one of its 205 sources, or less than 1 percent, expressed an antiwar stance; 3 percent of sources on Fox expressed antiwar sentiments.[22]

Reliance on official sources in the lead-up to the Iraq War was made particularly problematic by the fact that the administration engaged in a coordinated campaign to build support for the war through the media. The administration of George W. Bush included a number of neoconservatives and muscular nationalists who had long advocated for the need to depose Saddam Hussein. In the aftermath of 9/11, and especially in the wake of the apparently successful war in Afghanistan, the administration reached a decision to prepare public opinion for a war in Iraq. In August 2002, the White House established an Iraq Group in order, as Bush's Press Secretary Scott McClellan later put it, to "campaign to convince Americans that war with Iraq was inevitable and necessary."[23] That campaign kicked off in early September. As White House Chief of Staff Andrew H. Card explained, "From a marketing point of view, you don't introduce new products in August."[24] Administration officials fanned out across the news media, offering interviews that reiterated the key talking points: Iraq had WMDs and was working with al Qaeda. In public speeches, President Bush and other leading officials made the same case.

The basic problem was that the administration based its case for war on a string of falsehoods. A 2008 study by the Center for Public Integrity found that administration officials had made 935 false statements to the public in the lead-up to the war. George Bush made 232 false statements about WMDs alone; Colin Powell made 244 false statements.[25] Given the media's reliance on official sources, and journalists' understandings of objectivity, such statements went largely unchallenged. Rather, they reverberated throughout the media, making the case for war appear far stronger than it in fact was and thereby misleading the public. On one level, then, the media's failure to act as a watchdog can be attributed to its own faults and professional practices. The *New York Times* public editor, for instance, suggested that the paper's coverage had been "credulous" and overly deferential to anonymous sources.[26]

But the ability of the media to challenge the case for war, and for the public to develop an independent opinion about the basic facts of the situation, was also undermined by a deeper problem. The Bush administration was selectively quoting from controversial intelligence reports as it built its case for war, and those intelligence reports were classified and unavailable to the media or the public. This allowed the administration to selectively leak classified information to the news media to bolster its case. When Vice President Dick Cheney appeared on *Meet the Press* on September 9, 2002, for instance, he quoted Judith Miller's *New York Times* story to support his claim that Iraq had acquired aluminum tubes that could be used to build a centrifuge to produce uranium. It was in fact highly questionable whether the tubes were for uranium production, but the *New York Times* story was based on a selective leak that portrayed those tubes as far more damning than they were.[27] By citing the *New York Times* story as if it was authoritative, Cheney was being doubly deceptive: he was both veiling the contested nature of classified intelligence assessments, and acting as if the *Times* story provided an independent verification of his administration's position rather than an echoing of it. For the public to understand that, however, it would have been necessary to have access to the full intelligence reports, or, at the very least, for journalists to discuss the limits of their sources in a more transparent fashion. But in the context of widespread official secrecy, the administration had carte blanche to present its case for war, and the public had little ability to challenge or critically assess the facts of the matter. Information moved from officials to the news media in a selective and strategic fashion. From there it flowed out to shape public attitudes to the war.

This centrally coordinated effort to manage the flow of information through the news continued once the war began. In a Pulitzer Prize–winning investigative report in 2008, *New York Times* journalist David Barstow revealed that the Pentagon closely briefed the former military officials who acted as talking heads on television news programs in order to shape news coverage of the war. These seventy-five talking heads, many of whom worked for military contractors and had an interest in maintaining friendly relations with the military establishment, were meant to act as "message force multipliers" and "surrogates" for official policies and attitudes to the war. When news broke that troops in Iraq were dying because of inadequate body armor, for instance, one Pentagon official wrote to colleagues to say that "I think our analysts—properly armed—can push back in that arena." In all, Barstow concluded, the careful management of talking heads to regulate the news coverage of the war constituted a "symbiotic relationship where the usual dividing lines between government and journalism have been obliterated."[28]

Efforts to manage news about the war also extended to coverage of combat. Because of the widespread myth that the media produced domestic opposition to the Vietnam War, government officials have sought to regulate combat coverage in every subsequent conflict. In the 1983 invasion of Grenada, for instance, the media were barred from combat areas until the conflict was essentially over. This tactic provided the Reagan administration with unprecedented control over information about the intervention, but it also produced a backlash. In the invasion of Panama in 1989 and in the First Gulf War in 1991, the media were therefore organized in pools that could report on the war, but only under close supervision by the Defense Department. Granting the media some access also allowed the Pentagon to more carefully develop its briefings for the press—providing them with information that presented American warfare and military technology in its most flattering light. In what were then state-of-the-art facilities, military representatives briefed media pools on the unprecedented efficiency of smart bombing.

Beginning with the interventions in Bosnia and Kosovo, the Department of Defense began to provide reporters with even greater access to war zones by embedding them within combat units. The same system was employed in Iraq and Afghanistan—some six hundred journalists would be assigned to combat units, deploy with them, and report firsthand on their experiences. For the Defense Department, such a system promised two benefits. First, by placing U.S. and allied journalists on the frontline of combat, the Defense Department tried to minimize the ability of foreign governments to spread misinformation about U.S. conduct during the war. Second, stories from embedded journalists would showcase the U.S. military to the public at home. Critics, though, suggested that placing journalists within army units would make them overly familiar and dependent on those units and reduce the psychological distance journalists needed to report objectively on war. Embedding, it seemed to many, was more a Faustian pact than victory for the media or guarantee that the public would be fully informed about the true nature of combat.[29]

It is tricky to calculate the extent of bias in reports filed by embedded journalists. Academic studies differ in their conclusions—largely because it is difficult to quantify "objectivity" in a news report, and because objectivity varied by journalist, report, and network (one study, for instance, found that

62 percent of reports on Fox News could be considered neutral in tone, compared to 96 percent on ABC and CBS).[30]

But more important than questions of individual bias was the systematic, if subtle, slanting that embedding produced. Most reports filed from embedded journalists were live, and many focused on the first-person experience of the journalist—in one study of embedded journalism in the first six days of the Iraq War, 77 percent of stories featured no sources but the journalist. The stories naturally privileged the point of view of the journalist and the journalist's unit. They focused on the U.S. experience of war, not the experiences of civilians, and certainly not Iraqi perspectives. And as first-person stories from the thick of the action, journalistic stories could not provide big-picture accounts of the war—they were shards of lived experience, not synthetic accounts of strategy.[31]

Combined with the traditional difficulty of reporting on a complex, multifaceted war as well as the new desire for round-the-clock news stories, impressionistic journalistic accounts helped to create a number of errors in reporting on the invasion. By March 27, only eight days after the invasion began, Greg Mitchell, of the newspaper trade journal *Editor and Publisher*, could cite fifteen stories that had been incorrectly reported and had created an impression of easy victory.[32] Three of them were reports that the port city of Umm Qasr had been taken by Coalition forces; the *Guardian* would later observe that Umm Qasr had been reported as being "taken" nine times before it actually was.[33]

On April 9 the impression of an easy victory became solidified when the news aired images from Firdos Square in Baghdad, where a crowd of Iraqis tore down a statue of Saddam in apparent celebration of their liberation. The heavy U.S. military presence in the square, the fact that many foreign journalists were staying nearby, and the relatively small crowd of Iraqis involved would later lead to speculation that the event had been staged or faked. Such suspicions are understandable. The Bush administration had shown itself to be adept at managing the media. And on May 1, when a jet carrying Bush landed on the USS *Abraham Lincoln* and the president declared victory before a "Mission Accomplished" banner, the administration showed that it wasn't averse to producing media spectacles to convince the public that the war was over. (The May 1 event provides a textbook example of what historian Daniel Boorstin called "pseudo-events"—events that were planned for the sole purpose of being reported on, in order to create a self-fulfilling image of reality.[34])

But in Firdos Square, the debate about fakery misses the larger point. It is true that a military psychological operations officer was present in the square, and that he insisted that a conspicuous American flag be replaced by an Iraqi flag to minimize the impression of U.S. occupation. But that simply testifies to the fact that this was a war waged in front of the cameras, and that all participants were constantly aware of the need for image management. And it is true that the crowd was far smaller and less intense than it appeared on television, but that was not necessarily a sign of manipulation. Ever since a study of a political parade in Chicago in the 1950s, media scholars have known that through the use of close-ups, television reports can create a greater emotional impact for viewers at home than the live experience has on spectators in person.[35]

The real story of Firdos Square is how the images were received at home—where the media treated them as proof that the war was going as smoothly as official pundits had predicted. Images of the statue coming down were shown on Fox every 4.4 minutes on April 9 and every 7.5 minutes on CNN, crowding out images of combat that were occurring elsewhere in Baghdad at the same time. Television commentators repeated ad nauseam that this was an historic occasion. (Fox, predictably, was particularly hyperbolic—David Asman declared that his "goosebumps have never been higher than they are right now," and Brit Hume opined that "this transcends anything I've ever seen."[36]) Government officials, watching the images, basked in success. In the wake of Firdos Square, coverage of the war shifted accordingly. The amount of war coverage on the evening news dropped rapidly from the week before Firdos to the week after: by 66 percent on ABC, by 58 percent on NBC, and by 70 percent on Fox News.[37] Of course, the war was not over—there had been only 139 U.S. deaths from combat before Firdos Square. By 2010, 4,400 U.S. soldiers had died in Iraq—the vast majority of them after Bush declared "Mission Accomplished."[38] But impressionistic reporting, combined with an administration that skillfully shaped the sources of information available to the news, helped to create the impression that the war had concluded. As in the coverage of Firdos Square, so in the news coverage of the wars more broadly: without the presence of bad-faith journalism, reporting based on official accounts created false impressions.

* * *

Focusing on the supply side helps explain how the news gets made, but what did the public make of all this? To what extent were the problems on the supply side exacerbated, or even trumped, by problems on the demand side? Scholars' answers to such questions depends in part on how they understand the impact of media messages on audiences. In the early twentieth century, many scholars believed that audiences were completely susceptible to media messages, and that the media worked like a hypodermic needle, directly injecting ideas into people's brains. If one accepts this understanding, no demand-side explanations would be necessary—the problematic messages in the media would completely account for public opinion about the wars.

But a number of studies of American elections conducted in the middle decades of the twentieth century found that media messages had much more limited effects. People, these studies revealed, based their opinions less on the media than on the views of their neighbors, colleagues, and families, and their opinions were remarkably resistant to changes in media messages. Those who embrace this approach see supply-side explanations as much less important in explaining public attitudes to the wars. They would focus more, for example, on preexisting community attitudes than media messages.

As is so often the case when scholars have proposed two radically opposed theories, a middle-of-the-road theory eventually emerged. In the case of media reception, many scholars now believe that media messages have more of an effect on audiences than limited effects theorists believe, but less of an effect than early theorists presumed. In particular, scholars focus on a number of ways in which media messages intersect with preexisting attitudes and beliefs. They argue that information in the media matters, but so do factors on the demand side.

First, media coverage of a story can play an important role in determining how much attention the public pays to a story. A study of the attitudes of voters in the 1968 election found that exposure to media messages did not determine *what* voters thought about an issue, but it did determine *whether* voters thought about that issue. (In other words, extensive coverage of economic issues would not guarantee that voters would think a certain way about the economy, but would guarantee that they would think that economic issues were important for the election.)[39]

In the case of the wars in Iraq and Afghanistan, it seems plausible that the decline in media coverage after the initial invasions helped to remove the wars from public consciousness. Faced with tight news budgets, networks reallocated resources away from the conflicts after the intense opening stages of the war—media attention was diverted from Afghanistan to Iraq in early 2003, and then media attention shifted from relatively low-level constant fighting in foreign lands to "sexier" topics like the 2004 election cycle back home. Fast-breaking stories displaced coverage of incremental combat and occupation. In 2001 there were 1,288 minutes of Afghanistan coverage on network nightly news; by 2005, Afghanistan featured in only 147 minutes of coverage.[40] Similarly, Iraq received 4,100 minutes of coverage on the nightly news broadcasts of the three networks in 2003, but only 1,000 minutes in 2007.[41]

Of course, it is not media messages alone that determine whether members of the public think an issue is important. Studies from the Vietnam era, for instance, show that Americans who had relatives serving in the war paid more attention to the conflict than those who had no personal ties to it.[42] But with an all-volunteer army, most Americans had little direct connection to the wars. The lack of media coverage intersected with this fact to render the wars quite literally out of sight and out of mind for many Americans, contributing to the public's lack of attention to the wars.

Furthermore, it has become clear that media messages more powerfully shape public attitudes when they intersect with preexisting beliefs and attitudes about the world. Complex events are necessarily framed by the media—certain elements of stories are highlighted, certain interpretations are emphasized, and certain narratives are imposed to simplify and make sense out of what could be a bewildering number of details. Such broad media frames can shape how audiences interpret and internalize public events.[43] This process was clearly at work in the wars in Iraq and Afghanistan. The plausibility of false claims that Saddam Hussein was involved in 9/11, or that he was developing WMDs, was heightened by the ongoing presentation of Saddam as a threat, a dictator, and an enemy since the time of the First Gulf War in 1991. The desirability of a war to oust the Taliban was heightened by a surge of media coverage in late 2001 that framed the war as an act of women's liberation. Such messages tapped into long-standing tropes about misogyny in the Arab world, and even older imperialist tropes that Western civilization would liberate women from backwardness.[44] And both wars were framed as part of a "war on terror," a framework that was made plausible by decades of media presentations of Arabs as terrorists.

The point is not that such frames are entirely false—Saddam was a brutal dictator, the Taliban did oppress women, and the 9/11 hijackers were terrorists from the Middle East. But insofar as these facts operated as broader generalizations and moral frameworks, they encouraged simplistic understandings of the wars. To understand why the public was less than fully informed about the wars, it is necessary to explore not simply how the wars were framed in the media, but also why those frames resonated so powerfully with the public. Doing that requires understanding the history that produced broader public attitudes to terrorism and to the culture and politics of the Middle East.

Beyond the way that the public interprets media messages, there are two broader demand-side problems that might help explain why the public perceived the wars in inaccurate ways. The first potential problem is that after decades of war coverage, the public may have become desensitized to the horrors of war. Susan Sontag made a particularly eloquent version of this argument in an essay on photography in the early 1970s. War photographs, Sontag observed, are presumed to create moral outrage among the public, and to shock the public into opposition to war. But, she continued, the public becomes desensitized to such images over time—what was once shocking becomes banal, and ever more horrific images need to be produced to create moral outrage.[45]

It is plausible that after decades of war photography, television footage, and violent war movies, the public has become somewhat numb to the shock of war; perhaps it is easier to ignore the horrors of war than ever before. It is significant, for instance, that the images from Iraq and Afghanistan that produced the most moral outrage were images of shocking, and highly personalized, suffering: the photos of the tortured and humiliated prisoners at Abu Ghraib, or the haunting image of the wedding of Tyler Ziegel, a Marine Sergeant who was severely burned in Iraq.

It is worth remembering, nevertheless, that images of wartime violence have been carefully managed in American history. During World War II, Americans did not see images of dead American soldiers until late in 1943, when *Life* magazine, after consultation with the U.S. government, published a photo of corpses washed up on a beach in Papua New Guinea. Similarly, television footage of Vietnam was far less bloody than most imagine. Although there were some notable exceptions, most reports featured no violence at all—according to one study of 2,300 television news reports, only 76 showed violence.[46]

And little violence was on view in reports on the war in Iraq. A study of 1,820 stories filed by embedded journalists found that while 30 percent showed images of battle, only 4.4 percent showed coalition casualties, only 3.3 percent showed civilian casualties, and only 0.4 percent showed Iraqi casualties.[47] Another study of 5,087 shots of firefights found that only 15 percent showed casualties.[48] In part because of moral concerns about showing violence on television, and in part because of the location of embedded journalists, television viewers saw many bullets fired, but they did not see what those bullets hit. Combined with official information policies designed to downplay casualty numbers—bans on footage of the returning coffins of U.S. war dead, and a decision not to count Iraqi casualties—it seems that the U.S. public was sheltered from many of the worst horrors of the war.[49] Nonetheless, Sontag's argument is worth thinking about, as it is entirely plausible that a broader culture of media violence has helped dull public reactions to the wars even in the absence of particularly violent images of recent wars.

The final problem on the demand side arises from an entirely different perspective. Rather than suggesting that the public was misinformed by media frames, or that there was too much misinformation in the news, it is possible that in the age of media abundance people are simply turning off the news. For some, this seems to be a generational issue—one 2007 study, for instance, found that up to 50 percent of young adults pay little to no attention to the daily news.[50]

But there is also a deeper issue that affects all citizens. Rather than use the proliferation of media channels to focus on news about war and peace, it seems that many people use media channels to avoid the news and to consume other sorts of media: reality TV, dramas, celebrity gossip, sport. In an age of more limited media, people had less ability to regulate how much news they consumed—everyone had access to more or less the same information on more or less the same number of channels (all three networks, for instance, played the evening news at the same time). With the rise of cable and the Internet, however, it is far easier for individuals to manage how much news they consume—news junkies can watch the news twenty-four hours a day; those who are disinterested in the news can avoid it altogether by seeking out other content. Political scientist Markus Prior has explored how these changes have changed public knowledge of political issues. He found that with the shift from limited to abundant media channels there has been a polarization of political knowledge—news junkies now do better on political knowledge tests than individuals in the age of limited media, but most people who prefer entertainment to news now do worse than individuals in the age of limited media. This seems to suggest that many people are becoming less informed about the news because they are paying less attention to the news.[51]

Concern that the public pays too little attention to the news has a long history—journalist Walter Lippmann made much the same case when he wrote one of the first books on the role of the media in modern democracies in 1922. So it warrants emphasizing that such an argument can take two forms (indeed, both were present in Lippmann's work).[52] First, the argument can take an elitist form. One can suggest that the problem is the fault of the public—that they are too stupid, or lazy, or ignorant to read as widely and as critically as they should. Very quickly, such an argument can begin to flirt with undemocratic remedies. But there is also a populist version of the argument. One could suggest that the problem is the fault not of the public, but of broader social and political conditions. The public doesn't read as widely, closely, and critically as they could not because they are incapable of doing so, but because they don't have the opportunity or incentive to do so.

Many factors could contribute to this problem: education levels shape one's ability to make sense of the media, poverty impedes one's ability to afford

cable subscriptions and Internet access, and so forth. To take but one example, people are working long hours to make ends meet during difficult
economic times—this makes it harder to find the time and energy to devote
to careful consideration of public affairs. Similarly, decades of political scandal have heightened public cynicism about public affairs, and alienated large
sections of the public from politics. Why spend precious time and energy to
understand political affairs when politics is conducted by a remote political class, seems unlikely to produce meaningful change, and often descends
into infighting, corruption, and petty ineptitude? Entertainment, at least, can
provide some distraction and solace from the indignities and difficulties of
everyday life. If we want to look for problems on the demand side, in other
words, it is important to think carefully about the social and political context
in which media messages are consumed—about the way that the media and
politics fit into the broader lives of citizens.

* * *

It isn't possible in an essay of this scale to resolve once and for all what created the public opinion that helped lead the United States into the wars in
Iraq and Afghanistan and facilitated the length of U.S. engagement in the
conflicts. It is entirely likely, of course, that problems on both the supply and
demand sides intersected to misinform the public about the wars, and that
some people were misinformed by particular governmental statements, others paid little attention to the news, others believed in particular framings,
and so forth.

Thinking about problems on both the supply and the demand sides, however, reminds us that the proliferation of media channels in the information
age does not straightforwardly produce a more robust marketplace of ideas,
a better informed public, or a more perfect democracy. The wars provide an
opportunity to think historically about how information actually gets into the
media, and how media messages actually influence the public—processes that
depend on relations of power and history. And the wars remind us, as citizen-
consumers of the media, of the need to reflect critically on the information
that we find in the media, and on the ways in which we use the media to make
sense of our world.

NOTES

1 Steven Kull, Clay Ramsay, and Evan Lewis, "Misperceptions, the Media and the
Iraq War," *Political Science Quarterly* 118 (Winter 2003–4): 572.

2 Tom Zeller, "How Americans Link Iraq and Sept 11," *New York Times*, March 2,
2003.

3 Kull, Ramsay, and Lewis, "Misperceptions, the Media and the Iraq War," 575.

4 "Public Supports Expanding Afghanistan UN Peacekeeping Force beyond Kabul" (Program on International Policy Attitudes Media Release, July 8, 2003), http://www.pipa.org/OnlineReports/Afghanistan/Afghanistan_Jul03/Afghanistan_Jul03_pr.pdf.

5 Pew Research Center for the People and the Press, "Political Knowledge Update: Awareness of Iraq War Fatalities Plummets" (March 12, 2008), http://www.people-press.org/2008/03/12/awareness-of-iraq-war-fatalities-plummets/.

6 Susanna Fox, Lee Rainie, and Deborah Fallows, "The Internet and the Iraq War" (Pew Internet and American Life Project, April 1, 2003), http://www.pewinternet.org/Reports/2003/The-Internet-and-the-Iraq-war/Part-1.aspx; Kull, Ramsay, and Lewis, "Misperceptions, the Media and the Iraq War," 581.

7 FAIR, "In Iraq Crisis, Networks Are Megaphones for Official Views," March 18, 2003, http://fair.org/article/in-iraq-crisis-networks-are-megaphones-for-official-views/.

8 Steve Rendall and Tara Broughel, "Amplifying Officials, Squelching Dissent," May 1, 2003, http://fair.org/extra-online-articles/amplifying-officials-squelching-dissent/.

9 John Whiten, "If News from Iraq Is Bad, It's Coming from U.S. Officials," February 1, 2004, http://fair.org/extra-online-articles/if-news-from-iraq-is-bad-its-coming-from-u-s-officials/.

10 Rendall and Broughel, "Amplifying Officials, Squelching Dissent"

11 Ibid.

12 W. Lance Bennett, "Toward a Theory of Press-State Relations in the United States," *Journal of Communication* 40 (June 1990): 103–27; Jonathan Mermin, *Debating War and Peace: Media Coverage of U.S. Intervention in the Post-Vietnam Era* (Princeton: Princeton University Press, 1999).

13 Sheldon Appleton, "The Public, the Polls, and the War," *Vietnam Perspectives* 1 (May 1966): 6–7.

14 Joseph Carroll, "The Iraq-Vietnam Comparison," Gallup Poll, June 15, 2004, http://www.gallup.com/poll/11998/iraqvietnam-comparison.aspx.

15 Daniel C. Hallin, *The "Uncensored War": The Media and Vietnam* (Berkeley: University of California Press, 1989), 201.

16 Rendall and Broughel, "Amplifying Officials, Squelching Dissent."

17 Gaye Tuchman, "Objectivity as Strategic Ritual: An Examination of Newsmen's Notions of Objectivity," *American Journal of Sociology* 77 (January 1972): 660–79.

18 Seth C. Lewis and Stephen D. Reese, "What Is the War on Terror? Framing through the Eyes of Journalists," *Journalism and Mass Communication Quarterly* 86 (Spring 2009): 92, 95.

19 Sean Aday, "The Real War Will Never Get on Television: An Analysis of Casualty Imagery in American Television Coverage of the Iraq War," in *Media and Conflict in the Twenty-First Century*, ed. Philip Seib (New York: Palgrave Macmillan, 2005), 147.

20 Kull, Ramsay, and Lewis, "Misperceptions, the Media and the Iraq War," 593.

21 Ibid., 582, 589.

22 Rendall and Broughel, "Amplifying Officials, Squelching Dissent."

23 Walter Pincus, "Records Could Shed Light on Iraq Group," *Washington Post*, June 9, 2008, http://articles.washingtonpost.com/2008-06-09/politics/36861311_1_nuclear-program-nuclear-weapon-intelligence.

24 Elisabeth Bumiller, "Bush Aides Set Strategy to Sell Policy on Iraq," *New York Times*, September 7, 2002.

25 Charles Lewis and Mark Reading-Smith, "False Pretenses" (Center for Public Integrity, January 23, 2008), http://www.publicintegrity.org/2008/01/23/5641/false-pretenses.

26 Daniel Okrent, "The Public Editor: Weapons of Mass Destruction? Or Mass Distraction," *New York Times*, May 30, 2004.

27 Michael Isikoff and David Corn, *Hubris: The Inside Story of Spin, Scandal, and the Selling of the Iraq War* (New York: Crown, 2006), 34–36.

28 David Barstow, "Behind TV Analysts, Pentagon's Hidden Hand: Courting Ex-Officers Tied to Military Contractors," *New York Times*, April 20, 2008.

29 Michel Haigh, Michael Pfau, Jamie Danesi, et al., "A Comparison of Embedded and Nonembedded Print Coverage of the U.S. Invasion and Occupation of Iraq," *Harvard International Journal of Press/Politics* 11 (Spring 2006): 140–42.

30 Sean Aday, Steven Livingston, and Maeve Hebert, "Embedding the Truth: A Cross-Cultural Analysis of Objectivity and Television Coverage of the Iraq War," *Harvard International Journal of Press/Politics* 10 (Winter 2005): 12.

31 Pew Research Project for Excellence in Journalism, "Embedded Reporters: What Are Americans Getting?" (April 3, 2003), http://www.journalism.org/2003/04/03/embedded-reporters/.

32 Greg Mitchell, "15 Stories They've Already Bungled," *Editor and Publisher*, March 27, 2003, http://www.editorandpublisher.com/PrintArticle/15-Stories-They-ve-Already-Bungled.

33 Annie Lawson, Lisa O'Carroll, Chris Tryhorn, and Jason Deans, "War Watch: Claims and Counterclaims Made during the Media War over Iraq," *Guardian*, April 11, 2003.

34 Daniel J. Boorstin, *The Image: A Guide to Pseudo-Events in America* (1962; repr., New York: Random House, 2012).

35 Peter Maas, "The Toppling: How the Media Inflated a Minor Moment in a Long War," *New Yorker*, January 10, 2011, http://www.newyorker.com/reporting/2011/01/10/110110fa_fact_maass.

36 Sean Aday, John Cluverius, and Steven Livingston, "As Goes the Statue, So Goes the War: The Emergence of the Victory Frame in Television Coverage of the Iraq War," *Journal of Broadcasting and Electronic Media* 49 (September 2005): 321–22.

37 Ibid., 326.

38 Terry H. Anderson, *Bush's Wars* (New York: Oxford University Press, 2011), 236–37.

39 Paul Lazarsfeld, Bernard Berelson, and Hazel Gaudet, *The People's Choice: How the Voter Makes Up His Mind in a Presidential Campaign* (New York: Columbia University Press, 1948); Maxwell E. McCombs and Donald L. Shaw, "The Agenda-Setting

Function of the Mass Media," *Public Opinion Quarterly* 36 (Summer 1972): 176–87; Todd Gitlin, "Media Sociology: The Dominant Paradigm," *Theory and Society* 6 (September 1978): 207–11; David H. Weaver, "What Voters Learn from Media," *Annals of the American Academy of Political and Social Science* 546 (July 1996): 34–47.

40 Sherry Ricchiardi, "The Forgotten War," *American Journalism Review*, August–September 2006, http://www.ajr.org/article.asp?id=4162.

41 Sherry Ricchiardi, "Whatever Happened to Iraq?," *American Journalism Review*, June–July 2008, http://www.ajr.org/article.asp?id=4515.

42 William M. Hammond, "The Press in Vietnam as Agent of Defeat: A Critical Examination," *Reviews in American History* 17 (June 1989): 314.

43 Robert M. Entman, "Framing: Toward Clarification of a Fractured Paradigm," *Journal of Communication* 43 (Autumn 1993): 51.

44 Carol A. Stabile and Deepa Kumar, "Unveiling Imperialism: Media, Gender and the War on Afghanistan," *Media, Culture and Society* 27 (September 2005): 772.

45 Susan Sontag, "In Plato's Cave," in *On Photography* (New York: Farrar, Straus and Giroux, 1973), 3–24.

46 Hammond, "Press in Vietnam," 315.

47 Aday, Livingston, and Hebert, "Embedding the Truth," 13.

48 Aday, "Real War Will Never Get on Television," 148–49.

49 Elisabeth Bumiller, "U.S. Lifts Photo Ban on Military Coffins," *New York Times*, December 7, 2009; Bradley Graham and Dan Morgan, "US Has No Plans to Count Civilian Casualties," *Washington Post*, April 15, 2003.

50 Thomas E. Patterson, "Young People and the News" (Joan Shorenstein Center on the Press, Politics and Public Policy, July 2007), 13–14.

51 Markus Prior, "News v Entertainment: How Increasing Media Choice Widens Gaps in Political Knowledge and Turnout," *American Journal of Political Science* 49 (July 2005): 577–92.

52 Walter Lippmann, *Public Opinion* (New York: Harcourt, Brace, 1922).

10

"Watching War Made Us Immune"

The Popular Culture of the Wars

ANDREW C. MCKEVITT

On January 23, 2007, President George W. Bush delivered his seventh State of the Union address, his sixth since the 9/11 attacks and the resulting military action against al Qaeda and the Taliban in Afghanistan in the fall of 2001, and his fourth since the U.S. invasion of Iraq in March 2003. With so many American lives at stake overseas, the president devoted much of his speech to foreign policy. Iraq, in particular, cast a long shadow over the historical moment—the president mentioned Iraq or the Iraqi people thirty-four times in the speech (up from sixteen the previous year), reflecting the nation's 2006 eruption into full-scale insurgency against occupying U.S. forces and a civil war between the various factions vying for power in post-Saddam Iraq.[1] Americans watched anxiously as 2006 proved to be the war's bloodiest year yet. Drawing on the historical memory of Vietnam, critics increasingly used the word "quagmire" to describe the rapidly deteriorating political and military situation. Less than three months prior, voters expressed their frustration with the war by electing a Democratic majority to Congress, giving the opposition party majorities in both houses.

The day following the State of the Union address, *Talk of the Nation*, a daily politics program on National Public Radio, invited a half dozen shapers of culture and politics to discuss the national Zeitgeist in the aftermath of Bush's speech. Host Neil Conan spoke with author and screenwriter Nora Ephron, country songwriter Merle Haggard, and two prominent scholars. The guests expressed a variety of opinions, most criticizing the president for what they saw as an aggressive foreign policy that had devastated the lives of millions of people in Iraq and throughout the Muslim world.

Then Conan turned to Frank Miller, the author of critically acclaimed graphic novels, some of which had inspired recent popular Hollywood films—*Batman Begins* (2005), *Sin City* (2005), and, most recently, *300* (2006), a high-octane, blood-soaked account of the three hundred Spartan warriors who stood against the amassed armies of Persia in the Battle of Thermopylae. The film adaptation of *300* had proved wildly successful, grossing more than two hundred million dollars in theaters and entering the popular consciousness through imitation and parody.[2] It also proved controversial, with critics charging it with racist and homophobic representations of Persians— here, stand-ins for the West's new enemy, Islamists. Even the president of Iran, Mahmoud Ahmadinejad, accused the filmmakers of "psychological warfare" aimed at "plundering Iran's historic past and insulting this civilization." In director Zack Snyder's interpretation, Persian king Xerxes is both effeminate and grotesque, a monstrous creature who surrounds himself with all the orgiastic pleasures of the senses that the ascetic Spartans, disciplined warriors from childhood, deny themselves. Relying on duty, honor, and courage, the Spartans unquestioningly sacrifice their lives in bloody battle to save their civilization from Xerxes's monstrous, mindless, marauding hordes. This "porno-military curiosity" of a film delivered its message with all the subtlety of a shield smash to the face: Western civilization's values will allow it to triumph over the East.[3]

Miller, his voice raspy and quivering, assessed the "state of the homefront," arguing that "our country and the entire Western World is up against an existential foe that knows exactly what it wants, and we're behaving like a collapsing empire." Echoing the message of *300*, Miller explained, "We're constantly told that all cultures are equal, and every belief system is as good as the next. . . . For some reason, nobody seems to be talking about who we're up against and the sixth-century barbarism that they actually represent." He continued, "I hear people say, 'Why did we attack Iraq?' . . . Well, we're taking on an idea. Nobody questions why after Pearl Harbor we attacked Nazi Germany. It was because we were taking on a form of global fascism. We're doing the same now." "Well," said Conan, "[Nazi Germany] did declare war on us." "Well, so did Iraq," Miller retorted.[4]

Of course, Iraq did not declare war on the United States in 2003. But Miller's conflation of Saddam Hussein's Iraq with an "existential foe," a "sixth-century barbarism" embodied in "global fascism," presents historians with an opportunity to unpack the tangled relationship between popular culture and U.S. military activity around the world in the wake of the September 11 attacks. The very concept of a global war on terror is replete with complications and inaccuracies. But popular culture is not shaped by accurate understandings of military and political strategy, campaigns, and tactics; rather, ideas and understandings about the U.S. role in the world bleed into each other, and in that regard the global hunt for Osama bin Laden and senior al Qaeda leaders, the war to oust the Taliban and crush its insurgency, and the invasion and occupation of Iraq all blended together in the popular imagination.

Indeed, for many influential makers of culture (including Frank Miller) such distinctions did not exist. Therefore, in analyzing the popular culture of this era, historians cannot isolate that surrounding the Iraq War from portrayals of the global war on terror (GWOT) overall.

In conflating the GWOT and the specific wars, Miller—and U.S. popular culture in general—followed the lead of the Bush administration, which cultivated and encouraged messy popular understandings of U.S. military action abroad so as to implicitly connect all post-9/11 military action to that tragic day. None other than Vice President Dick Cheney reinforced this sloppiness by repeatedly and publicly asserting, contrary to CIA assessments, that Saddam Hussein and al Qaeda were linked. As a result, when Miller spoke on the radio in 2007, more than 40 percent of Americans believed that Saddam Hussein had helped to finance, plan, or carry out the 9/11 attacks.[5] Widespread misinformation about and misunderstanding of the GWOT emanated from the highest levels of the U.S. government and filtered into popular culture.

The metaphorical construct of a global war on terror underlay the vast array of films, television programs, music, literature, and video games that both reflected and shaped the ways Americans made sense of their country's military response to the September 11 attacks. A "global" war is grand, epic, and fantastic; a war on "terror" is a war not against a specific group of people or nation but against an idea, a universal human experience. Defining the U.S. global engagement on such terms made it easy for popular culture to move into the realm of fantasy in the broadest sense of the term. While very different popular culture creations, both director Peter Jackson's *The Lord of the Rings* film trilogy (based on J. R. R. Tolkien's novel) and the wildly popular television series *24*—the former set in the fictional universe of Middle Earth and the latter set in a fictional twenty-first-century United States—were epic fantasies: highly stylized, imagined worlds in which stand-ins for the righteous West (innocent but determined hobbits; actor Kiefer Sutherland's courageous and persevering Jack Bauer) do battle against an existential threat. Both the film trilogy and the television series helped Americans simplify a complicated world. Pennsylvania senator and future presidential candidate Rick Santorum, for example, clumsily equated Tolkien's "Eye of Mordor" with al Qaeda's focus on the insurgency in Iraq.[6]

The fantastic notion of an epic global war on terror, then, provides a framework for understanding the role popular culture played in defining the U.S. post-9/11 military response. In general, most popular culture did not confront the GWOT directly. Instead, it interpreted the military and political response to 9/11 through allegory and metaphor. When a film, television series, or video game did try to create a realistic representation of any aspect of the GWOT, the response was—with rare exceptions—indifference, controversy, or scorn. From *300*'s ancient Greece to the reimagined *Star Trek*'s twenty-third century, from the unexplored galaxies of *Battlestar Galactica* to the Gotham of Christopher Nolan's *Batman* trilogy (inspired, too, by a Frank Miller graphic novel), the epic fantasy ruled. Popular culture portrayed the GWOT not unlike how George W. Bush articulated the GWOT—as an apocalyptic, universal struggle between good and evil. The Bush administration's vision of a singular "global war on terror," light on material demands but nearly totalitarian in its ideological imperatives, casting the struggle against al Qaeda, the Taliban, and Saddam Hussein in existential terms, defined the films, television, video games, books, and even music that offered a context in which popular American attitudes evolved in the post-9/11 era. This chapter surveys these texts to demonstrate the varied ways in which popular culture fought on the many fronts of the GWOT.

***

Few examples better illustrate the intersection of epic fantasy and the GWOT than the popularity of superhero film franchises in the post-9/11 era. By one count, U.S. film studios produced nearly twice as many superhero films in the dozen years after the September 11 attacks as they did in the fifty years of the second half of the twentieth century. These post-9/11 films included three of the ten highest grossing films of all time—*The Avengers* (2012), *The Dark Knight* (2008), and *The Dark Knight Rises* (2012).[7] Superhero films met the political and cultural needs of Americans confronting a GWOT by promising viewers satisfying resolutions to apocalyptic, existential challenges.

The apotheosis of superheroism started where the proverbial buck stopped, with the president. In a feminist critique of post-9/11 American culture, journalist Susan Faludi pointed to the ways in which the U.S. news media "seemed eager to turn our guardians of national security into action toys and superheroes." Political commentators like former Reagan speechwriter Peggy Noonan celebrated George W. Bush's muscular response to the attacks, suggesting that at any moment the president could "tear open his shirt and reveal the big 'S' on his chest." The media transformed a range of administration officials from functionary bureaucrats into courageous heroes ready to battle the "evil-doers" (as the president dubbed the nation's enemies). *Vanity Fair* magazine published a spread of photographs of cabinet officials accompanied by superhero nicknames: Dick Cheney as "The Rock"; secretary of the newly created Department of Homeland Security, Tom Ridge, as "The Protector." Faludi argues that Americans responded to September 11 "not by interrogating it but by cocooning ourselves in the celluloid chrysalis of the baby boomer's childhood," that is, in the mythology of 1950s Westerns, with their lone, heroic protagonists riding into town to save vulnerable and desperate women and children.[8]

Administration officials, including the president's closest political advisor, Karl Rove, convened several dozen Hollywood producers just two months after the 9/11 attacks to discuss how filmmakers could contribute to the war effort. Chairman of the Motion Picture Association of America, Jack Valenti, an aide to Lyndon Johnson during the Vietnam War, said he "heartily endorse[d] Hollywood getting involved to help out in any way we can in this war." Rove asked the gathered executives to consider a number of themes that conveyed the GWOT's sense of apocalyptic fantasy, including "the Sept. 11 attack was a global attack requiring a global response" and "the war is a war against evil."[9] The meeting produced no agreement on the kinds of films Hollywood would produce, but the studios' superhero fixation over the following decade—likely driven more by box office receipts than patriotic duty—both reflected the fantastic vision of the GWOT and offered narratives that helped Americans make sense of epic struggles against existential threats.

The best example is Christopher Nolan's tremendously successful *Batman* trilogy—*Batman Begins* (2005), *The Dark Knight* (2008), and *The Dark Knight Rises* (2012)—which combined grossed more than one billion dollars in the United States. Nolan took Miller's vision of a tortured, gritty vigilante and set him in a fictional universe parallel to that of the GWOT. Over the course of three films, the Dark Knight (played in this iteration by Christian Bale) battles against the League of Shadows, a secret international organization intent on "purging" the world of its sins and vices. The extremist—even fundamentalist—philosophy of the league's leader, Ra's al Ghul (Liam Neeson), echoed that of Osama bin Laden, and the radical commitment of his followers alluded to the fanaticism of suicide bombers ready to die for an otherworldly cause. Batman frequently resorts to extralegal means, such as using an advanced tracking system that allows him to monitor all of Gotham City's residents' movements through their cell phones, to save an imperfect but nevertheless tolerant and liberal society. The vigilante fantasy of Nolan's *Batman* trilogy gave Americans the vicarious opportunity to refight the GWOT, except this time without the strictures of a massive government bureaucracy beholden to a constitution and democratically elected lawmakers. Superhero vigilantes provided for the ultimate in revenge fantasies, though they were not without critics. In a 2013 critique in *Salon*, Richard Cooper questioned the morality of superior beings singlehandedly carrying out justice—be it Batman, Superman, or Iron Man. "Superheroes are a bunch of fascists," he concluded.[10]

Audiences have read a variety of other fantasy and science fiction texts in light of the GWOT. Tolkien's *Lord of the Rings*—reinterpreted by Peter Jackson in the most expensive set of films ever produced—has been read as an allegory for international relations since its first publication in the 1950s. Despite Tolkien's insistence that the book "is neither allegorical nor topical," generations of Americans have imposed their own world onto Middle Earth and the hobbit Frodo's quest to destroy an all-powerful ring. It, like other texts, was easily reinterpreted in light of the GWOT. One twenty-first-century scholar, writing about Jackson's *Lord of the Rings*, posits Sauron—the evil "Lord" of the book's title—as Osama bin Laden, the ghostly and terrifying "ringwraiths" as terrorists, and the insular hobbits as Americans. An alternative reading by antiwar activists framed George W. Bush as Sauron, even creating an image that spread online of the president wearing the power-granting ring.[11]

Similarly, one of the most profitable film franchises ever, *Star Wars*, made its own GWOT connections with the 2005 release of the second trilogy's final film, *Revenge of the Sith*. Protagonist Anakin Skywalker, whose transition from heroic Jedi Knight to evil Sith Lord the film chronicles, at one point warns his mentor, "You're either with me, or you're my enemy," an obvious echo of George W. Bush's early GWOT admonition to the world, "You're either with us or against us." *Star Wars* creator George Lucas said that in the second trilogy, Skywalker's personal shift to the "dark side" symbolizes a republic's descent from democracy to imperial dictatorship. He wrote the original story in the 1970s, inspired by Richard Nixon and Vietnam, but found the contemporary allusions to George W. Bush and Iraq worth emphasizing.[12]

Many successful films attempted to narrate the GWOT through allegory and metaphor. Yet a genre of film specifically about the various conflicts of the GWOT also emerged. In general, the more a film tried to adhere closely to real-world events such as the Iraq War—the further it tried to distance itself from the realm of fantasy—the less likely it was to have success at the box office. This trend led *Indy Week* editor David Fellerath to wonder, "Why are the Iraq War movies tanking?" Fellerath drew comparisons to the generation of successful films and filmmakers that emerged in the 1970s from the Vietnam conflict. The Vietnam War was a counterculture war, he argued, and that was reflected in everything from the college students who protested against it to the comportment of the soldiers who fought it and the filmmakers who tried to capture it. The countercultural visionaries of the 1970s—Francis Ford Coppola, Robert Altman, Martin Scorsese, and Michael Cimino, among others—created "fresh, idiosyncratic and personal films," Fellerath wrote. These were nuanced films that dissected their subjects with a scalpel. In contrast, he continued, contemporary filmmakers had applied a "bludgeon of conventional liberal outrage" to the Iraq War.[13]

Fellerath used the occasion of the release of *Redacted*, a film by veteran director Brian De Palma, to illustrate how Hollywood's "conventional liberal outrage" was driving movie audiences away. De Palma ranked among the most talented young filmmakers in the 1970s and had directed his own critically acclaimed Vietnam War film, 1989's *Casualties of War*. His 2007 *Redacted* tells the story of a horrific 2006 incident in al-Mahmudiyah, Iraq. A group of U.S. army soldiers raped and murdered a fourteen-year-old girl, executed her family, and then tried to hide the crime by burning the remains. De Palma chose a documentary-style technique to tell the story, interspersing real footage of events in Iraq with his own dramatic rendering. Missing, according to Fellerath, is "a sense of the surreal and the absurd" that made films about Vietnam, such as Coppola's *Apocalypse Now*, so powerful; he argued that *Redacted* and its ilk are "so deadened by their earnest self-importance that they're dramatically inert."[14]

Perhaps for this reason films about the Iraq War tanked at the box office. *Rendition* (2007) featured A-list actors including Meryl Streep, Reese Witherspoon, and Jake Gyllenhaal, but grossed less than ten million dollars domestically. *Lions for Lambs* (2007), also starring Streep along with superstars Tom Cruise and Robert Redford, made only fifteen million, less than half of its production budget. Angelina Jolie starred in *A Mighty Heart* (2007), which portrayed the story of journalist Daniel Pearl, who was murdered by al Qaeda militants in Pakistan in 2002. The film earned less than ten million at the box office. Despite a star-studded cast that included Tommy Lee Jones and Susan Sarandon, *In the Valley of Elah* (2007) brought in less than seven million in ticket receipts.[15] The winning actor-director combination behind the billion-dollar *Bourne* film franchise—Matt Damon and Paul Greengrass—produced a major flop in 2010's *Green Zone*, a big-budget action-thriller *roman à clef* about the Bush administration's "cooked" WMD intelligence. Hollywood could be forgiven for believing that by 2010, after opposition to the war in Iraq had helped carry a Democrat to the presidency, enough Americans would turn out to see a film highly critical of the way the previous administration misled the country to war. But politics did not translate into ticket sales. The list of critically acclaimed, star-studded, but underperforming films goes on—*The Kingdom* (2007), *Grace Is Gone* (2007)—so much so that the historian must try to explain this obvious pattern of failure in trying to use popular culture's signature medium to confront the GWOT.

In addition to their "earnest self-importance," what else accounts for these films' failure? In 2010, it is clear, audiences preferred films that eschewed reality for fantasy or science fiction: every one of the top ten films of that year fit into one of those two categories. Compare that to the last pre-9/11 year, 2000, in which only two of the top ten highest-grossing films could be classified as either. These data are not isolated; they are part of a broader pattern across the decade. Of the ten highest-grossing films of each year in the decade following 2001 (that is, the top one hundred films from the years 2002–11), 79 percent fall into the category of fantasy or science fiction, loosely defined. Compare that to the decade preceding 2001 (1991–2000), in which only 33 percent of the hundred highest-grossing films could be labeled fantasy or science fiction. The American public, "perhaps sufficiently enervated and confused by reality," as *New York Times* critic A. O. Scott put it, "was not eager to see it recreated on screen."[16]

Of course, as any good social scientist will tell you, statistical correlation is not necessarily causation. Other explanations exist for the dominance of fantasy narratives in the last decade—one could argue, for example, that advances in computer-generated imagery (CGI) technology gave filmmakers new tools for telling fantasy and science fiction stories they always wanted to tell. Historical analogy also proves instructive in explaining the failure of realistic drama. The classic films of the Vietnam War were *all* produced after the war ended in 1973 and the United States retreated from South Vietnam in 1975. The trio of early classics about the war—*Coming Home* (1978), *The Deer Hunter* (1978), and *Apocalypse Now* (1979)—appeared years after the end of the conflict. The only Hollywood film produced during the conflict that told a story set in the contemporary war was John Wayne's *The Green Berets* (1968), which the screen legend both starred in and directed. Wayne, an outspoken anticommunist in a left-leaning industry, made the film to counter the growing antiwar movement. Critics hated it.[17] The other notable Vietnam-era film, *M*A*S*H* (1970), critiqued the U.S. war effort in Southeast Asia by telling a story about the U.S. war effort in Northeast Asia during the Korean War.[18] *M*A*S*H* was a critical and commercial success because it spoke to popular attitudes of the moment through allegory rather than realism.

The films that defined Americans' collective memory of Vietnam all came years after the war's end. Filmmakers really hit their stride in the 1980s, producing classics such as Oliver Stone's *Platoon* (1986) and *Born on the Fourth of July* (1989) and Stanley Kubrick's *Full Metal Jacket* (1987). So while box office numbers demonstrate that audiences in the first post-9/11 decade were not ready for films about the GWOT, "the real definitive treatment of the Iraq war," argues media scholar Robert Thompson, "won't happen until we have a handle on what this Iraq war ultimately meant."[19] By the 1980s Americans had enough distance from the Vietnam War to begin to process it publicly, their struggle to do so highlighted by the debate over Maya Lin's design for the Vietnam Veterans Memorial.[20] Presumably, some years must pass after the 2011 U.S. withdrawal from Iraq before Americans come to grips with the totality of that experience.

The one filmmaker who proved an exception to the trend of commercial and critical failure was Kathryn Bigelow. In 2008's *The Hurt Locker*, which follows a three-man Explosive Ordinance Disposal (EOD) squad in Iraq, and in 2012's *Zero Dark Thirty*, chronicling the hunt for Osama bin Laden, Bigelow found success by making the GWOT visceral for audiences. She won the 2010 Academy Award for Best Director for *The Hurt Locker* while the film won the Best Picture award. The film stars Jeremy Renner as Staff Sergeant William James, a master in the art of defusing the improvised explosive devices (IEDs) that litter the hot, dusty, menacing landscape of Baghdad. Like an artist, "more like a jazz musician or an abstract expressionist painter than like a sober technician," James is single-minded in his focus, exposing himself to risks and fiddling recklessly with lifesaving gear because it stands in the way of him doing what he does best.[21] James gets high from the adrenaline rush; "war is a drug," viewers learn at the film's outset.

Critics praised *The Hurt Locker*'s "crackling verisimilitude" and "hyperbolic realism."[22] But this also made the film a magnet for criticism from Iraq War veterans. Unlike *Green Zone* or *Lions for Lambs*, the film does not moralize about an unnecessary war and the culpable leaders who started it. Instead, screenwriter Mark Boal based the story on his experience as a journalist embedded with an Army EOD unit in 2004. The only perspective the viewer gets is of soldiers, their dialogue minimal but their implied trauma powerful, their attention too occupied with surviving to think about who is to blame for their tenure in Mesopotamia. With realism setting the film's tone, real soldiers found reasons to question Bigelow and Boal's representation of combat. The film, one veteran argued, was "plagued by unforgivable inaccuracies" and thus "more a Hollywood fantasy than the searingly realistic rendition that civilians take it for."[23] Paul Rieckhoff, founder of Iraq and Afghanistan Veterans of America, feared that the depiction of James's reckless cowboy behavior would give Americans false impressions of veterans' experiences in Iraq. "Films, almost more than anything, will be the way Americans understand our war," he said, tellingly. "So we feel that there is a responsibility for filmmakers to portray our war accurately. We see ourselves as watchdogs."[24] Boal, on the other hand, claimed artistic license was necessary to show "just how hellish this war is."

Bigelow's second GWOT film garnered similar acclaim and generated even more controversy. *Zero Dark Thirty* recounts the decade-long effort to capture or kill Osama bin Laden. It follows a fictional CIA agent named Maya (Jessica Chastain), whose single-minded focus on hunting Osama bin Laden comes to define her years with the agency. She spends the film gathering intelligence, fighting for resources from a resistant bureaucracy, and eventually tracking the al Qaeda leader to a compound in Pakistan, where a team of Navy SEALs finally kills the world's most wanted man. Film critics universally lauded *Zero Dark Thirty* for its sophisticated approach to the GWOT. The *New York Times*' Manohla Dargis said it "shows the dark side of that war. It shows the unspeakable and lets us decide if the death of Bin Laden was worth the price we paid."[25]

Bigelow and Boal intended to create a "reported film" as Bigelow called it, one based on years of research. Critics found reasons for skepticism. Questions focused on the scenes in which CIA agents at "black sites"—top-secret facilities outside the United States and thus theoretically outside U.S. law—subjected suspects to "enhanced interrogation techniques," that is, torture, to extract intelligence about future terrorist activities. In order to dramatize years of intelligence gathering, the film cuts corners. For example, the torture and interrogation of Ammar al-Baluchi, who was instrumental in financing the 9/11 attacks, leads directly to his confession of actionable intelligence. Acting CIA Director Michael Morell criticized this simplistic portrayal, saying, "The film creates the strong impression that the enhanced interrogation techniques . . . were the key to finding Bin Laden. . . . That impression is false." A bipartisan group of senators, including John McCain and Dianne Feinstein, called the film "grossly inaccurate," with "the potential to shape American public opinion in a disturbing and misleading manner." The "film's degree of emphasis on torture's significance," wrote journalist Steve Coll, "goes beyond what even the most die-hard defenders of the CIA" would claim. Political provocateur Naomi Wolf went so far as to compare Bigelow's work to that of another pioneering woman director and "great, but profoundly compromised filmmaker": Nazi Germany's Leni Riefenstahl.[26]

✳✳✳

The cultural power of the Bush administration's vision of the GWOT manifested powerfully just ten days before the U.S. invasion of Iraq, when popular music became one of the first metaphorical battlegrounds on which Americans clashed to define the meaning of the inevitable real war. The 2006 documentary *Shut Up & Sing!* chronicles the wartime experiences of the Dixie Chicks, the best-selling all-female act in the history of American popular music. At a London concert in March 2003, lead singer Natalie Maines sparked a firestorm of outrage when she said, "We do not want this war, this violence. And we're ashamed that the President of the United States is from Texas."[27] During the resulting national backlash, conservatives accused the Dixie Chicks of treason and worse; they organized drives to collect and destroy the band's CDs. The same country music stations that made the Dixie Chicks superstars stopped playing their chart-topping songs. Talk-show hosts mixed gendered language with intimations of violence, as when former presidential candidate Pat Buchanan referred to them as the "Dixie Twits," and Fox News's Bill O'Reilly said that the women "should be slapped around." That the Dixie Chicks were not only outspoken but outspoken *women*, speaking out against a war defined by a cowboy president and the invented male superheroes in his administration, determined much of the public response to Maines's comments. Legendary country music acts Willie Nelson and Merle Haggard, for instance, both openly criticized the war but neither experienced any repercussions.[28] Escalating rhetorical rage even led to threats of physical violence; the film documents a threat to murder Maines at a July 2003 concert in Dallas. Compared to Jane Fonda's 1972 visit to North Vietnam, where she called U.S. leaders "war criminals" and posed with an antiaircraft gun, Maines's mildly critical swipe at a divisive president seemed innocuous. Yet Fonda's career rebounded quickly, while the backlash against the band effectively ended their pop-music dominance.

The Dixie Chicks struggled to define their place in the tense politics of the Iraq War's early months. They posed nude on the cover of the May 2003 issue of *Entertainment Weekly*, tattooed in the contradictory labels critics and defenders had applied to them in the preceding weeks—"Dixie Sluts," "Saddam's Angels," "Brave." The infamous image represented the band's ambivalence about their status as free speech warriors, portraying both vulnerability and fearlessness. Maines engaged in a public feud with another country musician, Toby Keith, who earlier in 2002 had cashed in on the September 11 tragedy with a hit song, "Courtesy of the Red, White, and Blue (The Angry American)." Keith's paean to the U.S. military response to 9/11 climaxed in a warning to terrorists: "We'll put a boot in your ass / It's the American way." "It's ignorant," Maines said of the song, "and it makes country music sound ignorant," to which Keith responded with his own concert backdrop image showing Maines cuddling up to deposed Iraqi dictator Saddam Hussein.[29]

Toby Keith offered an insidious sort of low-intensity patriotism that burrowed into the American popular consciousness in the post-9/11 era. Taking its cue from President Bush's summons to "get about the business of America" and "get down to Disney World" in order to help fight the GWOT, post-9/11 popular patriotism substituted a mixture of militarism and consumerism for the calls to sacrifice that previous global wars demanded. Americans conspicuously consumed the GWOT, adorning their automobiles, homes, and bodies with crude slogans of violent revenge. An "Al Qaeda Hunting Club" or "I do not brake for turbans" bumper sticker could nestle next to a yellow ribbon car magnet, indicating that the owners "support the troops." One billboard advertisement summed up this conspicuous patriotism best: "Ask not what your country can do for you. Ask, 'Can I get this shoe in a size seven?'"[30] Toby Keith's patriotism was easy, inexpensive, and everywhere in the conservative parts of the United States that had once made the Dixie Chicks famous.

Having lost much of their support in the country music establishment, the Dixie Chicks never again reached the heights of early 2003. But they continued to write and responded to their critics musically. Their 2006 album included "Not Ready to Make Nice," a song about the band's lack of regret and unwillingness to apologize, a sentiment easier to express as Iraq descended into insurgency and civil war that year. By the time George W. Bush left office in January 2009, with historically low approval ratings, the reaction to Maines's comments seemed like a fever dream. "Watching war made us immune," Maines sang on 2006's "Easy Silence." Americans adopted an "Easy Silence" about the Iraq War, the band suggested, finding it more comfortable to follow the herd and say nothing than to speak out against an unjust invasion and a cheap brand of patriotism. The Bush administration's vision for a globe spanning, potentially endless, epic GWOT, as much a television event as a lived experience, fed the "Easy Silence" and made Americans immune to the real consequences of complex wars.

∗

The first decade of the GWOT coincided with the emergence of television as a serious creative medium. Series like *The Sopranos* (1999–2007), *The Wire* (2002–8), and *Mad Men* (2007–15) demonstrated that the small screen, as well as the big, could tell compelling stories. Here, too, the GWOT served as real-life fodder for fictional storytelling, though as on the big screen television series that tried to adhere to real-world events were overshadowed by fantasies.

The decade's greatest GWOT television fantasy was unquestionably *24*. The show about a counterterrorism unit in Los Angeles began filming months before the September 11 attacks and first aired in November 2001, just in time to inject fantasy-laced adrenaline into the traumatized national psyche. The show's unique structure presented the GWOT with a sense of urgency and panic that neither policy debates nor the dull drone of the twenty-four-hour cable news networks could provide. Each season of *24* began at a specific time (e.g., twelve o'clock a.m.), and every episode in the season charted one of the twenty-four hours that followed in "real time." The show's argument about the contingency of modern antiterrorism convinced at least some viewers that fighting terrorism hinged on high-stakes moments in which heroes must violate the law for a greater good. Even Supreme Court Justice Antonin Scalia defended protagonist Jack Bauer's questionable ethics; when a Canadian judge joked, "Thankfully, security agencies . . . do not subscribe to the mantra, 'What would Jack Bauer do?,'" Scalia, walking around Bauer's use of torture to extract intelligence from a terrorism suspect, retorted, "Jack Bauer saved Los Angeles. . . . He saved hundreds of thousands of lives." "Are you going to convict Jack Bauer?" he asked. "People in the Administration love the series, too," said 24's creator, Joel Surnow. "It's a patriotic show. They *should* love it."[31]

Like *Zero Dark Thirty*, 24 attracted criticism because of its depiction of the use of torture. The show increasingly relied on torture for major plot points, with Bauer frequently turning to extralegal means to accomplish necessary goals that legal strictures prevented. The centrality of torture, wrote Adam Green in the *New York Times*, communicated to viewers that, "regardless of good intentions, those seeking to protect suspects' rights risk abetting terrorist activities, to catastrophic ends." Taking a jab at neoconservative defenders of "enhanced interrogation techniques," Devin Gordon suggested in *Newsweek* that 24 was "either a neocon sex fantasy or the collective id of our nation unleashed."[32] Secretly, critics of torture agreed, some Americans harbored fantasies of a Jack Bauer–like hero emerging to win the GWOT.

As with films, television series that attempted to depict realistically the various conflicts of the GWOT failed commercially. Most notable was *Over There*, produced by television veteran Steven Bochco, whose many successes included *Hill Street Blues* (1981–87) and *NYPD Blue* (1993–2005). Set in Iraq after the U.S. invasion, *Over There* made history in 2005 as the first television series to take place in an ongoing war. (Though series like *Gomer Pyle, U.S.M.C.* and the television adaptation of *M*A*S*H* aired during the Vietnam War and made obvious allusions to that conflict, they did not take place in Vietnam.) The show chronicles the experiences of a U.S. Army unit in its first deployment to Iraq. Striving for realism, *Over There*'s creators engineered intense battlefield scenes replete with graphic depictions of violence. Critics complained that the show's producers worked too hard to depoliticize the war, to present a show "about survival, nothing else," but ultimately they failed "to make palatable TV out of a problematic war."[33] Veterans of the conflict also found fault with the show. Multiple press outlets queried Iraq War veterans on their impressions, and the responses were overwhelmingly negative.[34] At the end of the show's first season, the FX Network cancelled it because of poor ratings. Americans rejected all popular cultural productions that took place "over there"; not a single film, television show, or video game set primarily in Iraq achieved any real success in the decade after the U.S. invasion.

Contrast *Over There* with *Battlestar Galactica* (2004–9), which had a successful run of seventy-five episodes as well as two films on the Sci-Fi Channel. *Battlestar Galactica* is a "space opera," a complex narrative of love and loss and intergalactic warfare occurring at an ambiguous historical moment. Earth has suffered an apocalyptic attack from a humanoid race called the "Cylons." The series tracks the humans who survived the Cylon "holocaust" as they flee their enemies and trek through many galaxies in search of a new home world. Though the time and place were alien to Americans in the twenty-first century, the plot lines rang all too familiar. The series' third season, in particular, borrowed its story line directly from the GWOT. Having found an inhabitable planet, the humans face a Cylon invasion, which results in human defeat and Cylon occupation. A resistance develops and human insurgents turn against humans who collaborate with the Cylons, even resorting to suicide bombers to attack a graduation ceremony for new human police recruits. The season premiered in October 2006, just as the headlines from Iraq portended more violence and chaos; the twelve months that followed proved to be the deadliest for real-life coalition forces. *Battlestar Galactica* succeeded where *Over There* failed, however, because its fantasy setting allowed its creators—winners of a Peabody Award for their efforts—to rewrite the GWOT, drawing on American anxieties about conflicts like Iraq but ultimately providing satisfying resolutions.

***

If the novel was the entertainment medium of the nineteenth century, and film and television the media of the twentieth, then video games are the medium of the twenty-first century. They are also the medium of a generation, the millennials, Americans born roughly between the late 1970s and the early 1990s, united less by chronological bookends and more by the shared experience of coming to political and cultural awareness in the wake of September 11. In the first decade of the twenty-first century millennials directed their purchasing power toward video games, as the industry's annual revenues roughly matched Hollywood's.[35] Surely it was for these reasons that the U.S. military began taking video games seriously after 9/11. For recruitment, training, and public relations purposes, all branches of the armed forces took advantage of video game technology. Thus the intersection of video games and the GWOT provides a rich window on the cultural history of the early twenty-first-century United States and in particular on the popular culture of the millennial generation.[36] As an innovative new medium, video games performed unique cultural work in helping millennials and other make sense of the GWOT.

Video games taught the millennial generation a new visual rhetoric of war. One of the first major revelations from WikiLeaks, the international organization founded by Australian activist Julian Assange with the intention of publishing classified state documents, was an April 2010 video titled "Collateral Murder," which showed an Apache helicopter firing on a group that included two Reuters journalists, both of whom were killed in the attack. Many observers, including Assange, observed that the leaked footage looked like a video game, in particular a scene from the popular *Call of Duty* series in which the player takes on the role of a gunner in an AC-130 gunship attacking enemy ground forces—many of them retreating from the attack.[37] The low resolution of the real-world camera intersected with the high-resolution graphical representation of the game to create two nearly indistinguishable texts. Similarly, in May 2011 the *New York Times* published video footage taken by the helmet camera of a soldier in Afghanistan documenting tense moments in the midst of a Taliban ambush. Even the *New York Times* reporter commented on the similarities to popular first-person shooter video games such as *Call of Duty* or *Battlefield*, and the footage went out across the Internet with a clear subtext: this footage looks like the games young people play.[38]

Video game technology also generated cultural anxieties about the representation of war and its consequences, and in this regard it performed similar work to new mass media technologies in other modern wars—from photography in the Civil War to film in World War II to the impact of television during the Vietnam War. New media technologies have the potential to disrupt clean narratives of heroism to reveal the messiness of combat, bringing home with increasing visceral intensity the consequences of sending young people to die in war. After 9/11, video games became the latest incarnation of the techno-anxiety generated by new forms of communication and documentation.

One striking example was the 2009 controversy over a game called *Six Days in Fallujah*. The game claimed to offer players the chance to step vicariously into the boots of a U.S. Marine in the 2004 Battle of Fallujah, the bloodiest engagement for U.S. forces in the eight-year Iraq War. The developers spent four years and twenty million dollars on production. To ensure accuracy, they worked closely with Marines who had fought in the battle; in fact, it was a group of Marines who first approached the developer about making the game.[39] Despite the enthusiastic participation of combat veterans, *Six Days in Fallujah* attracted intense controversy. One Iraq War veteran, critical of the claims to realism and accuracy, wrote, "A 'realistic' war game is not going to be fun—who wants to play a game where you sit around doing nothing, punctuated by raiding the wrong house and tearing apart the home of an irate Iraqi family, or sitting around on a convoy until your vehicle gets hit by an IED and your character dies, with no clear enemy in sight? Who wants to play that?"[40] The developers maintained that they were, like documentary film-makers, recording a crucial moment in American military history, but critics questioned how a game could rival a documentary film's accuracy if the game did not use real names of participants and if a player could manipulate events and change the outcome. Faced with such objections—and most particularly, protests from family members of those killed in action during this battle—the Japanese publisher, Konami, relented and canceled the game's publication.

Video games have likewise done work on behalf of the U.S. military. In 2008, in a large shopping mall on the outskirts of Philadelphia, the U.S. Army opened an information and recruiting office called the Army Experience Center. Far from the typical unassuming recruiting office in a nondescript strip mall, this twelve-million dollar, fifteen-thousand-square-foot complex aimed to entertain, with more than eighty video-gaming stations, interactive video exhibits, a replica command-and-control center, and Humvee and Blackhawk helicopter combat simulators. In two years of operation, the Army Experience Center welcomed forty thousand guests and signed up more than two hundred recruits. "Basically, it's mission accomplished," an Army spokesman said, explaining why the center closed in July 2010.[41]

While the facility was designed to impress with shiny, expensive hardware, at its heart was a piece of software, a video game called *America's Army*. First produced and published in 2002, it was released to the public as a free download and updated more than a dozen times in the decade that followed. *America's Army* is a remarkable artifact of the early twenty-first-century U.S. wars: it has been, in its various incarnations, a powerful recruiting tool, a malleable training device, a public relations platform, and a lightning rod for controversy, which it generated in the form of regular protests at the Franklin Mills Mall.[42]

Finally, video games shaped the ways soldiers of the millennial generation made sense of combat, providing them with accessible cultural references for articulating their experiences. Describing a particularly harrowing moment during his tour in Iraq, one Marine corporal recalled, "I was thinking one thing when we drove into that ambush: *Grand Theft Auto: Vice City*." Detailing the fear he felt during his first combat experience, one Army sergeant said, "once I pulled the trigger, that was it, I never hesitated. . . . It felt like I was playing 'Ghost Recon' at home."[43] A Marine who served in both Iraq and Afghanistan confessed, "Combat itself was somewhat like a video game for me. Our weapons can shoot over 1000m accurately. I would see a distant flash, sight in, press the triggers, and no more flash. I barely saw anyone from either side injured or killed." He continued to describe how the best-selling game *Call of Duty 4: Modern Warfare* "had a profound effect on me, because it made me stop and think about what happened to those on the receiving end of my weapons. I was not expecting that reaction at all and it wasn't easy to deal with."[44]

Tellingly, the games soldiers played, like those in the *Call of Duty* series, portrayed only GWOT fantasies. Sometimes they smartly complicated players' understandings of violence and war—powerful scenes included the player dying helplessly in a nuclear attack and, elsewhere, aiding in a terrorist attack on a Russian airport—but ultimately the games' narratives of triumph reaffirmed that the GWOT was a war to be fought and won in the realm of fantasy. The cultural history of the GWOT must consider the ways in which video games as both a medium and a series of texts provided GWOT veterans and the millennial generation more generally with a well of cultural references from which to draw in articulating both combat experiences and understandings of a complicated global war.

***

It may seem counterintuitive to conclude a survey of early twenty-first-century popular culture with the most traditional of media, novels. Literary fiction takes time to gestate, though, as authors observe and reflect on the impact of national crises like the GWOT, so only after a number of years did thoughtful literary interpretations appear. After all, Tim O'Brien's *Going After Cacciato*, widely considered the first great Vietnam War novel, arrived in 1978, a half decade after the Paris Peace Accords ended that conflict. If anything, then, Americans were lucky to see the publication of a coterie of powerful novels about the Iraq War in 2012, only a year after combat operations ceased.[45]

Two standout novels—Kevin Powers's *The Yellow Birds* and Ben Fountain's *Billy Lynn's Long Halftime Walk*—demonstrate widely different literary approaches to the Iraq War, but both nevertheless offer hope that popular culture may one day effectively help Americans make sense of the conflict. "The war tried to kill us in the spring," says Private Bartle, the twenty-one-year-old protagonist of *The Yellow Birds*, in the novel's memorable opening. The story that follows is a stark, elegiac tale of a soldier, hardly a grown man himself, struggling with the impossible-to-keep promise he makes to protect an eighteen-year-old recruit. Powers grounded the novel in his personal experience as an Army machine gunner in Iraq. He had found journalistic accounts of the war lacking. "There was lots of information around," he said. "But what people really wanted was to know what it felt like; physically, emotionally and psychologically. So that's why I wrote it."[46] With a poet's sensibility, Powers invokes simultaneously an alien dream world and a nightmarish landscape, all pointing toward a sadness for innocence irrevocably lost. In that regard, Powers adheres to the tradition of war fiction of Ernest Hemingway and Norman Mailer.

Ben Fountain opted to follow another great war fiction tradition, that of Kurt Vonnegut, whose *Slaughterhouse-Five* introduced readers to the irrationality and absurdity of modern war. Fountain narrates the Iraq War not from Baghdad but from Dallas, the quintessential American city, where his titular character attends a football game at Cowboys Stadium as an honored guest. Billy Lynn is the biggest war hero in a squad full of them, a dozen soldiers whose exploits in an ambush an embedded Fox News camera crew happened to catch. Brought to a Thanksgiving-day game to be the stars of a farcically elaborate halftime spectacle, Billy and his squad encounter an array of memorable characters, from the entrepreneurial team owner interested in financing a film about Billy's squad to the Cowboys players offering to go to Iraq to "help y'alls bust some raghead ass"—so long as they return to the States in time for training camp. The shopping-mall patriotism that the Bush administration encouraged is on full display among the assorted constituencies the squad encounters. They all pay lip service to the search for "double y'im dees" in "Eye-rack," to "nina leven," and to "dih-mock-cruh-see." "Billy suspects his fellow Americans secretly know better," writes Fountain, "but something in the land is stuck on teenage drama, on extravagant theatrics of ravaged innocence and soothing mud wallows of self-justifying pity." For everyone except the squad, destined to return to combat in Iraq, the GWOT remains a fantasy to watch. Culminating in a halftime concert featuring the pop group Destiny's Child, starring its soon-to-be megastar Beyoncé Knowles, and replete with a PTSD-inducing fireworks extravaganza, *Billy Lynn's Long Halftime Walk* brilliantly critiqued a decade of the intersection of popular culture and war.

Fountain's sharp satire highlighted the extent to which many Americans used popular culture in the post-9/11 era to create superficial paeans to patriotism while they lost themselves in epic fantasies, rewriting and refighting the GWOT on film and television and with their thumbs. On the other side of the world, however, the U.S. military continued to fight real, complicated wars. At the outset of the GWOT George W. Bush proclaimed that the entire world was "either with us or against us," and his administration subsequently articulated a totalitarian vision of a virtually unlimited global apocalyptic struggle against the "evil doers." Speaking to a journalist, the president's chief political advisor, Karl Rove, reportedly said, "We're an empire now, and when we act, we create our own reality."[47] The administration's global political and military agenda defined the boundaries of popular culture during the GWOT, encouraging fantasy worlds that competed with reality and left many Americans immune to the real consequences of U.S. foreign policy in the post-9/11 era.

NOTES

For valuable comments on an earlier draft of this chapter I wish to thank my colleagues in the Department of History at Louisiana Tech University, especially David M. Anderson. I also want to thank the students in my "America and the World since 9/11" class for helping generate ideas for this piece and Marilyn Young for thoughtful suggestions at the review stage. I am grateful to the organizers and participants at the Afghanistan and Iraq Wars symposium at the Center for the Study of Force and Diplomacy at Temple University for the opportunity to contribute.

1 "President Bush's 2007 State of the Union Address," *Washington Post*, January 23, 2007.

2 "300 (2006)," Internet Movie Database, http://www.imdb.com/title/tt0416449/.

3 Quoted in David Denby, "Men Gone Wild," *New Yorker*, April 2, 2007.

4 "Writers, Artists Describe State of the Union," *NPR*, January 24, 2007.

5 Terry H. Anderson, *Bush's Wars* (New York: Oxford University Press, 2011), 104–5; Brian Bralker, "Poll: What Americans (Don't) Know," *Newsweek*, September 4, 2007.

6 Tim Grieve, "Rick Santorum and the 'Eye of Mordor,'" *Salon*, October 17, 2006.

7 "List of American Superhero Films," Wikipedia, http://en.wikipedia.org/wiki/List_of_American_superhero_films; "All Time Box Office—Domestic Grosses," Box Office Mojo, http://boxofficemojo.com/alltime/domestic.htm.

8 Susan Faludi, *The Terror Dream: Fear and Fantasy in Post-9/11 America* (New York: Metropolitan Books, 2007), 47–48, 4.

9 Quoted in Rick Lyman, "A Nation Challenged: White House Sets Meeting with Film Executives to Discuss War on Terrorism," *New York Times*, November 8, 2001; Dade Hayes and Pamela McClintock, "War Chores for H'W'D," *Variety*, November 12, 2001.

10 Richard Cooper, "Superheroes Are All a Bunch of Fascists," *Salon*, November 30, 2013.

11 Ken Gelder, "Epic Fantasy and Global Terrorism," in *From Hobbits to Hollywood: Essays on Peter Jackson's Lord of the Rings*, ed. Ernest Mathijs and Pomerance Murray (New York: Rodopi, 2006), 101–18.

12 Stuart Croft, *Culture, Crisis, and America's War on Terror* (New York: Cambridge University Press, 2006), 216; Barry Caine, "Behind the Force," *InsideBayArea*, May 17, 2005, http://www.insidebayarea.com/bayarealiving/ci_2739299.

13 David Fellerath, "Why Are the Iraq War Movies Tanking?," *Indy Week*, November 28, 2007.

14 Ibid.

15 All box office returns are searchable at www.boxofficemojo.com.

16 A. O. Scott, "Soldiers on a Live Wire between Peril and Protocol," *New York Times*, June 25, 2009.

17 See, for example, Roger Ebert's review from June 26, 1968, reproduced at "The Green Berets," RogerEbert.com, http://www.rogerebert.com/reviews/the-green-berets-1968.

18 Less memorable films that also addressed some aspect of the war or its impact included *Welcome Home, Soldier Boys* (1971) and *Dead of Night* (1974).

19 Quoted in Soren Andersen, "Iraq War-Themed Films Can't Find an Audience," PopMatters, January 1, 2008, http://www.popmatters.com/article/iraq-war-themed-films-cant-find-an-audience/.

20 On the controversy over Lin's design, see Patrick Hagopian, *The Vietnam War in American Memory: Veterans, Memorials, and the Politics of Healing* (Amherst: University of Massachusetts Press, 2011).

21 Scott, "Soldiers on a Live Wire."

22 Kenneth Turan, "'The Hurt Locker,'" *Los Angeles Times*, June 26, 2009; Scott, "Soldiers on a Live Wire."

23 Christine Davenport, "Some Iraq, Afghanistan War Veterans Criticize Movie 'Hurt Locker' as Inaccurate," *Washington Post*, February 28, 2010.

24 Quoted in Ibid.

25 Manohla Dargis, "By Any Means Necessary," *New York Times*, December 17, 2012

26 Quoted in Steve Coll, "'Disturbing' & 'Misleading,'" *New York Review of Books*, February 7, 2013; Naomi Wolf, "A Letter to Kathryn Bigelow on Zero Dark Thirty's Apology for Torture," *Guardian*, January 4, 2013. Historian Marilyn Young earlier had noted similarities between Bigelow and Riefenstahl in her review of *The Hurt Locker*. See Marilyn B. Young, "*The Hurt Locker* War as a Video Game," *Perspectives on History* 47 (November 2009), http://www.historians.org/publications-and-directories/perspectives-on-history/november-2009/the-hurt-locker-war-as-a-video-game.

27 *Shut Up and Sing*, directed by Barbara Kopple and Cecilia Peck (2006; New York: Weinstein Company, 2007), DVD.

28 "Destroying the Dixie Chicks—Ten Years After," Saving Country Music, http://www.savingcountrymusic.com/destroying-the-dixie-chicks-ten-years-after.

29 "Fresh Dixie Chicks Row Erupts," *BBC News*, June 3, 2003.

30 Geoff Martin and Erin Steuter, *Pop Cultures Goes to War: Enlisting and Resisting Militarism in the War on Terror* (Lanham, MD: Rowman & Littlefield, 2010), 9, 95.

31 Quoted in Colin Freeze, "What Would Jack Bauer Do?," *Globe and Mail* (Toronto), June 16, 2007; quoted in Jane Mayer, "Whatever It Takes," *New Yorker*, February 19, 2007.

32 Adam Green, "Normalizing Torture on '24,'" *New York Times*, May 22, 2005; quoted in Hillary Profita, "Just a TV Show?," *CBS News*, January 17, 2007.

33 John Leonard, "Baghdad Blues," *New York Magazine*, July 2005.

34 David Carr, "Iraq Veterans Question 'Over There,'" *New York Times*, August 24, 2005; M. L. Lyke, "These Soldiers Say 'Over There' Is Bogus," *Seattle Post-Intelligencer*, July 25, 2005.

35 "How Much Do You Know about Video Games?," Entertainment Software Rating Board, http://www.esrb.org/about/video-game-industry-statistics.jsp; "Hollywood Breaks Revenue Record of $9.68 Billion," *USA Today*, December 9, 2009.

36 For a practical guide to approaching video games as historical sources, see Jeremy K. Saucier, "Playing the Past: The Video Game Simulation as Recent American History," in *Doing Recent History*, ed. Claire Potter and Renee Romano (Athens: University of Georgia Press, 2012), 201–24. For a detailed critical reading of video games and contemporary war, see Corey Mead, *War Play: Video Games and the Future of Armed Conflict* (Boston: Houghton Mifflin Harcourt, 2013).

37 "Collateral Murder—Wikileaks—Iraq," YouTube, April 3, 2010, http://www.youtube.com/watch?v=5rXPrfnU3Go; Michael McWhertor, "U.S. Army Accused of 'Video Game'-Like Behavior in Disturbing Iraq War Video," Kotaku, April 5, 2010, http://kotaku.com/5510188/us-army-accused-of-video-game+like-behavior-in-disturbing-leaked-iraq-war-video.

38 "Combat in the First Person: Haruti," *New York Times*, May 25, 2011.

39 "The Battle over the Battle of Fallujah," *Newsweek*, June 5, 2009.

40 Quoted in "Gamer War Vet Fears that Six Days in Fallujah Will Dishonor Those Who Served in Iraq," *Game Politics*, April 8, 2009, http://www.gamepolitics.com/2009/04/08/gamer-war-vet-fears-six-days-fallujah-will-dishonor-those-who-served-iraq.

41 "Video Game-Heavy Army Recruiting Center at Philadelphia Mall Closing at End of July," *Fox News*, June 10, 2010.

42 See "Shut Down the Army Experience Center," http://shutdowntheaec.net/.

43 Quoted in Saucier, "Playing the Past," 201, 214.

44 Quoted in Brian Ashcraft, "Video Games on the Front Lines," Kotaku, February 12, 2011, http://kotaku.com/5757648/video-games-on-the-front-lines.

45 A full survey of recent literature would also include David Abrams, *Fobbit* (New York: Grove Press, 2012); T. Geronimo Johnson, *Hold It 'Til It Hurts* (Minneapolis: Coffee House Press, 2012); Joydeep Roy-Bhattacharya, *The Watch* (London: Hogarth, 2013); Phil Klay, *Redeployment* (New York: Penguin, 2014); and Roy Scranton and Matt Gallagher, eds., *Fire and Forget: Short Stories from the Long War* (Cambridge: Da Capo, 2013). For reviews of recent literature, see Michael Lokesson, "Passive Aggression: Recent War Novels," *Los Angeles Review of Books*, October 1, 2013; and Ryan Bubalo, "Danger Close: The Iraq War in American Fiction," *Los Angeles Review of Books*, December 25, 2013.

46 Quoted in Paul Harris, "Emerging Wave of Iraq Fiction Examines America's Role in 'Bullshit War,'" *Guardian*, January 3, 2013.

47 Quoted in Ron Suskind, "Faith, Certainty and the Presidency of George W. Bush," *New York Times Magazine*, October 17, 2004.

PART IV

Lessons and Legacies

11

Veterans' Readjustment after the Iraq and Afghanistan Wars

DAVID KIERAN

On March 28, 2008, Jimmy Rice landed at Baltimore's Thurgood Marshall
International Airport. A Baltimore County police officer in civilian life, Rice
had been deployed to Iraq as a technical sergeant in the 175th Security Forces
Squadron of the Maryland Air National Guard. Rice was welcomed enthusiastically. Balloons hung from airport walls. His family and members of his
church held colorful posters and small American flags. His wife declared that
the anticipation made her "feel like a high school kid again with the little but-
terflies." His son, meanwhile, predicted a quick return to normalcy, telling a
television reporter "We're just going to go home and eat and we might play
Wii."[1]

The scene was both heartwarming and familiar. During the Iraq and Afghanistan Wars, Americans consciously worked to replace the archetypal—
but primarily apocryphal—image of the spat-upon Vietnam veteran with
scenes of gratitude and celebration, and the notion that returning troops deserved admiration became a powerful current in American public life.[2]

Jimmy Rice's experience would indeed have been unrecognizable to many
of his predecessors. During World War II, deployments lasted for the war's
duration, and sailing home took weeks. During Vietnam, most veterans, the
average age of whom was nineteen and many of whom were draftees, usually served for a single year before quickly returning to their communities
amid an increasingly unpopular war.[3] Rice was significantly older than these
men. He has a wife and children. He was not a draftee but a volunteer, not
a full-time soldier but a reservist. Moreover, March 2008 was also not his
first homecoming but his fourth, and in 2008 there was no guarantee that he
wouldn't be deployed again—by 2012, one-fifth of the military had deployed
multiple times.[4]

Rice's experience thus paralleled that of many of the two million U.S. Iraq
and Afghanistan veterans. This chapter is about the experiences of those veterans. It begins with a historical survey of debates over what services military
veterans required and deserved. It then turns to the homecoming of the two
and a half million veterans of the wars in Iraq and Afghanistan.[5] Most of these

men and women, often with the help of new government benefits, returned to their families and careers with the ease that Rice's son predicted.[6] A significant minority, however, has found the transition more difficult. This chapter explores five of the challenges that many returning veterans faced: living with significant physical and psychological wounds, returning to marriages and families, healing from the trauma of sexual assault, accessing care in rural areas, and finding employment amid an economic crisis.

There have been spectacular failures in veterans' care—the 2007 revelation that veterans at Walter Reed Army Medical Center were living in squalor, or the VA's continuing struggle to address disability claims in a timely fashion—and it has often been the case, as journalist Aaron Glantz puts it, that "the veteran still needs to fight to get [his or her] benefits: and that means tangling with hostile and cumbersome bureaucracy at the Department of Veterans Affairs."[7] Yet it is not only, as Glantz and others have suggested, a problem of government bureaucracy or political malfeasance.[8] Elected officials and the Department of Veterans Affairs have sought to improve services for veterans, but even well-intentioned efforts have fallen short. These shortcomings are, fundamentally, because those responsible did not anticipate the length and brutality of the wars. Thus they did not develop the policies and devote the resources required to meet such unanticipated needs, leaving the VA persistently reacting to, rather than proactively addressing, the challenges faced by veterans of these wars.[9] Many veterans, as a consequence, struggle to secure timely treatment for physical and psychological wounds, to integrate back into their families and communities, and to find civilian employment after years of war.

These struggles, and the undisputed governmental failures that have exacerbated them, raise two significant questions that persist well after the wars' end: What are veterans' needs, and what is the nation's obligation to meet them?

* * *

Debates about what debts the nation owes its veterans began in the Revolution's aftermath, when Continental Army veterans complained that they had not received promised pensions.[10] The Civil War's devastating physical toll, which included nearly fifty thousand amputations, encouraged many Americans to support a substantial pension system and veterans' employment programs.[11] However, by the late nineteenth century, as historian Megan Kate Nelson explains, "a significant level of disagreement existed regarding the amount and scope of these benefits," and Americans increasingly feared non-veterans abusing the benefit system.[12]

After World War I, veterans (aided by newly empowered organizations like the American Legion and the Veterans of Foreign Wars) supported legislation to provide a "bonus" that retroactively increased veterans' wartime salaries, but such legislation was opposed by successive presidential administrations that deemed it fiscally irresponsible.[13] A "bonus" that paid veterans about a dollar per day of service, plus interest, either upon their death or in 1945 eventually passed over Calvin Coolidge's veto.[14] However, after the 1929 crash veterans increasingly demanded immediate payment. Their protests culminated with the self-proclaimed "Bonus Expeditionary Force" occupying Washington, D.C., during the spring and summer of 1932.[15] Public support for the protestors ebbed and flowed. Initially tolerant, politicians and supportive journalists eventually "dismiss[ed the marchers] as desperate men without any real purpose," but after the U.S. Army tear-gassed the veterans and forced them from the city, the protesters gained renewed sympathy.[16] By that fall's election, the Bonus March had been folded into broader discussions of the Hoover administration's response to the Great Depression.[17]

It may thus seem unsurprising that World War II veterans benefitted from generous access to health care and low-interest home and education loans under the newly created G.I. Bill.[18] Yet despite "virtually unanimous support for aid to veterans" during World War II, the bill's passage was not undisputed.[19] Some conservative legislators feared the bill would reinvigorate New Deal social programs and would "subvert freedom and individual initiative"; for some southern legislators, racist discourses about African Americans' laziness and tendency to exploit government largess likely influenced their opposition.[20] Here again, the sense that veterans deserved benefits in exchange for their sacrifices and required sufficient services to ease their return to civilian life collided with claims about the need to reign in government spending, to promote personal responsibility, and to eradicate fraud.

For thousands of veterans, the G.I. Bill facilitated the college education and home loans that enabled access to the burgeoning postwar middle class. Life in those suburban homes, however, was not always idyllic. Many veterans silently suffered with undiagnosed posttraumatic stress disorder, and both alcoholism and rage were common.[21] Images of the troubled veteran, however, are most familiar from Vietnam's aftermath, and it was after that war that questions about the nation's obligations to its veterans took on new urgency. Many veterans returned disillusioned by what they had seen and done, and many turned against the war.[22] Others, however, felt mistreated or ignored.[23] Veterans struggled both against popular representations that portrayed them as deranged sociopaths and with concrete problems of unemployment, substance abuse, and depression.[24] The 1988 National Vietnam

Veterans Readjustment Survey discovered that while most veterans faced no significant issues, posttraumatic stress disorder, substance abuse, divorce, and general unhappiness affected a great many.[25]

Assistance, however, was not quick in coming. As a presidential candidate Ronald Reagan asserted that veterans "deserve our gratitude, our respect, and our continuing concern"; as president, he did not support substantive expansions of veterans' care.[26] Vietnam veterans, like their predecessors, organized and achieved successes that included the American Psychiatric Association's 1980 recognition of posttraumatic stress disorder as a mental disorder, the creation of storefront readjustment counseling centers, and legislation that attributed many health issues to Agent Orange exposure.[27]

Debates about Iraq and Afghanistan veterans' care are thus part of a long history of debate about veterans' needs and the government's role in providing them. These questions have lately reemerged, even as the Iraq and Afghanistan Wars have raised a new set of challenges for veterans.

From the wars' beginnings, policy makers and military leaders anticipated that returning veterans would struggle to readjust, and avoiding the real or perceived mistreatment of Vietnam veterans was a paramount concern. Six days after the United States invaded Iraq, the *New York Times* reported that "the American armed forces, schooled by the experiences of Vietnam and the first gulf war, have grown far more sophisticated in their approach to the psychological pressures of battle."[28] The military asserted that soldiers were not being rushed home from combat zones without time to process what they had seen, with the Army promoting "a new, corporate-style employee assistance program that will offer up to six personal counseling sessions, advice on dealing with stress and tips for families reuniting after months of separation."[29] For most veterans, these programs were sufficient. Most returned to fulfilling personal and professional lives without long-term issues. Many veterans, including those who made the easiest transition, were helped by the post-9/11 G.I. Bill. The development of this legislation illustrates both the lack of preparation for the scale of demand and the tensions between felt obligation to America's war veterans and concerns about government spending and the impact of a such a broad-based program. The post-9/11 G.I. Bill was the product of the realization, five years into the war in Afghanistan and as many veterans were leaving the military, that the existing Montgomery G.I. Bill was not meeting Iraq and Afghanistan veterans' needs. That bill provided "up to $1,100 a month for a maximum of thirty-six months" to service members who had served a three-year enlistment; regulations specified that the benefits be used within ten years of leaving the military.[30] But as Glantz points out, this is "an amount that didn't come close to covering most of a modern college education," and many veterans were left struggling to pay their bills and finish their degrees.[31] Furthermore, the G.I. Bill benefits were not equally available. Reservists and National Guard troops received fewer benefits overall than did other veterans.[32]

Fixing the G.I. Bill proved contentious. Senator Jim Webb (D-VA) introduced a bill in 2007 that would offer veterans "the highest tuition rate of a public university in [a veteran's state], as well as a housing stipend," or to "match whatever assistance [a private] school provided them" in exchange for three years of service.[33] The Bush administration, however, called the legislation too expensive; it also pointed out that generous education benefits might well undercut reenlistment.[34] Members of Congress, however, saw the new G.I. Bill as paying a debt owed to soldiers—Representative Gabrielle Giffords (D-AZ) remarked that "we have a solemn responsibility to our service members, and one way to fulfill that responsibility is to help them prepare for life after they leave the military"—and, perhaps more cynically in a time of war, as an important recruiting tool.[35] Montana senator John Tester (D) called it a step toward "making military service a more practical option."[36]

Bush ultimately accepted an expanded G.I. Bill as part of a larger war-funding bill that did not set a timeline for withdrawal from Iraq. Yet even with an improved G.I. Bill, college-bound veterans have faced challenges. Some of these are inherent in the legislation and the bureaucracy that administers it. In 2013, the Iraq and Afghanistan Veterans of America complained that keying benefits to in-state tuition rates limited veterans' choice of institution.[37] VA backlogs have made it difficult for some veterans to receive their benefits in a timely fashion.[38] More troubling is that many veterans have enrolled in for-profit institutions, which some activists and lawmakers fear are predatory.[39] In a 2009 Senate hearing, Senator Kay Hagan (D-NC) explained that "with the generous post-9/11 benefits package and given their high tuition at many of the for-profit schools, a veteran can easily exhaust the benefits pursuing a degree at a for-profit institution. And to the dismay of the veteran, in many cases their accumulated credits are not recognized, if they attempt to transfer."[40]

Veterans returning to college have had practical concerns as well. Many are substantially older their classmates, find it difficult to adjust to the comparatively relaxed atmosphere of college campuses, or must learn how to accommodate injuries that can inhibit academic success.[41] Colleges have assisted veterans by creating—often because of student veterans' activism—special counseling services, veterans' centers and associations, and, at the University of Iowa, a course: "Life after War: Post-Deployment Issues."[42] Such programs, paired with veterans' own tenacity, have produced remarkable results.[43] By

2013, over a million Iraq and Afghanistan veterans—about 40 percent of the total number that had served—had attended college.[44]

* * *

Veterans who have taken advantage of the post-9/11 G.I. Bill are among the majority of those who served in Iraq and Afghanistan. With sufficient resources and support, most of the veterans of the twenty-first-century U.S. wars have successfully transitioned to civilian life or to positions of greater responsibility within the military and now enjoy successful careers and fulfilling personal lives. This has not, however, been true for all veterans, and a significant minority have struggled to adapt to the new realities that the war has created.

Many service members returned home with serious injuries and lasting disabilities. In over ten years of combat operations, 6,840 American service members were killed and more than 51,809 were injured.[45] This figure may represent only about 2.5 percent of the total number of men and women who have served in Iraq or Afghanistan, but for those individuals the changes wrought by injury have often been significant. Many of these injuries are the results of improvised explosive devices (IEDs), which have been termed the "signature weapons" of these conflicts. A 2007 report from the Joint Forces Staff College found that the military had been unprepared for their widespread use.[46] Because U.S. troops struggled to detect and defuse IEDs or equip vehicles with sufficient armor to protect troops, many veterans are returning with significant injuries.[47] Journalist Ann Jones explains that "more than half the soldiers hit by IEDs lose both legs and often fingers, a hand, or an arm, as well."[48] Over fifteen hundred men and women have lost at least one limb in Iraq or Afghanistan, making amputation one of the most prevalent physical injuries of these wars.[49] More than three dozen service members have lost three or more limbs.[50] These veterans will require lengthy physical and occupational therapy as well as permanent accommodations in the form of prosthetics and accessible homes and vehicles.[51]

IEDs are also a leading cause of traumatic brain injury. TBI, which occurs when the brain violently collides with the skull, has affected 287,911 troops.[52] TBI has radically altered many veterans' ability to work, study, or maintain a relationship. Jonathan Barrs, a North Carolina veteran who suffered TBI after two IED explosions in Iraq, explains that "dealing with TBI is like a living horror film over and over again." He describes missing medical appointments and job interviews, struggling to complete his course work, and frequently snapping at his girlfriend.[53] Psychological injuries are also prevalent; as of December 2012, the VA had screened 256,820 Iraq and Afghanistan veterans "for potential PTSD."[54]

Many veterans are thus returning home with serious injuries. The high incidence of injuries that will require long-term or even lifelong care is in part the result of the high survival rate for injuries in these wars.[55] The relationship between the number killed and number injured is much different than in previous wars.[56] During World War II a quarter of U.S. casualties were fatalities; in Iraq the percentage is half that, and in Afghanistan it is even lower.[57] This is because advances in military equipment and medical care make it possible for service members to survive injuries that would previously have been fatal.[58] This high survival rate has left those who care for veterans, as one official put it in 2010, "unprepared for the complexity of injuries we were seeing because servicemembers would not have survived these types of injuries in previous conflicts," underresourced, overwhelmed, and scrambling to develop effective treatments, and it has left many veterans struggling to recuperate.[59]

Political leaders and even VA officials have widely recognized that the VA was unprepared to treat both physical and psychological disorders. In a 2005 Senate hearing, then-Senator Barack Obama complained that "our preparation for the wars in Iraq and Afghanistan did not adequately consider what these wars would mean for our Department of Veterans Affairs," and noted a VA report's conclusion that "the VA does not have sufficient capacity to meet the needs of new combat veterans."[60] Three years later, a witness before another congressional committee explained that "with the possibility of more than 300,000 new cases of mental health conditions among Iraq and Afghanistan vets, a commensurate increase in treatment capacity is needed. . . . [And] the expansion of trained providers is already several years overdue."[61] And in 2011, an official in the VA's Office of Rehabilitation Services explained that "at the outset of the current conflicts, it is fair to say we were unprepared for the complexity of injuries we were seeing because servicemembers would not have survived these types of injuries in previous conflicts."[62]

This lack of preparation has manifested itself in staff shortages. In 2011 the National Academies declared that "there is a critical shortage of health-care professionals—especially those specializing in mental health—to meet the demands of people returning from theater in Iraq and Afghanistan and their family members. The psychologists, psychiatrists, social workers, and other mental health professionals who do serve the military and veteran communities have large caseloads . . . and this results in underserved patients and high rates of burnout and turnover."[63] VA physicians and social workers routinely have many more clients than their civilian counterparts, which in turn reduces the quality of care that they are able to provide.[64]

These shortages have left many veterans frustrated and unable to receive adequate, timely care. Johnson, for example, complained in a 2010 congressional hearing that he waited nearly two years for a diagnosis, and that in the meantime "I went through all the Army treatment, I went through part of the VA treatment, and it took them 21 months to discern that it was a traumatic brain injury, and that is really scary. Because you can't get the treatment that you need timely enough to benefit you."[65] Three years earlier, Brady Van Engelen, who had been shot in the head in Baghdad in 2004, had told Congress that "there were just too many patients and not enough case managers to oversee the process. . . . The VA is overwhelmed by the numbers of claims filed and patients needing attendance. We did not prepare for this and it is painfully evident. My generation is going to have to pay for this and we will be paying for years and years."[66]

The VA has worked diligently to address these gaps. In a 2008 hearing, the VA reported that it had hired nearly four thousand mental health workers over the past three years and opened sixty-five new Vet Centers.[67] Two years later, VA officials touted greater collaboration with Defense Department providers and new treatment centers for Iraq and Afghanistan veterans, and some veterans groups acknowledged that many veterans were receiving excellent treatment.[68] Questions persist about how effectively the military is screening service members for TBI and how easily veterans can access care, but by 2010 the VA had opened 108 polytrauma care centers, was sponsoring significant research on TBI, had created assisted living programs for veterans, and claimed to be "screening every OEF/OIF veteran who comes to us for care for Traumatic Brain Injury." Medical professionals, veterans, and veterans' family members universally agree that TBI treatment has drastically improved.[69] By 2013, an undersecretary of veterans affairs could boast that the VA had hired thirteen hundred new mental health providers and support staff over the past year, that the VA had embraced new technologies that allowed veterans to access care remotely, and that the number of veterans receiving mental health care in 2012 was three million higher than it had been in 2009.[70]

There have been other successes as well. Prosthetic research represents an area of particularly significant progress. In 2007, the Department of Defense created three specialized Advanced Rehabilitation Centers focused on treating amputees that have been at the forefront of prosthetic development for veterans.[71] As well, universities and medical device companies have created increasingly nimble prosthetics that allow amputees fuller ranges of motion. As a result, many injured veterans are able to engage in strenuous activities including endurance races and, for nearly five dozen veterans, returning to active duty in combat zones.[72] Current research is resulting in even more spectacular advances. A recently developed prosthesis, for example, costs over a hundred thousand dollars and contains "an electronic motor and sensors able to read signals from [an amputee's] brain."[73]

Despite such progress, however, challenges remain. The development of prosthetic arms has not kept pace with those of comparatively simpler prosthetic legs, and lower-limb amputees have readjusted somewhat more easily.[74] Nonetheless, a 2012 VA study found many veterans satisfied with their prosthetics and agreeing that "their 'life is full.'"[75] And while some veterans still complain about accessing VA prosthetic services, a representative of the Paralyzed Veterans of America told Congress in 2010, "Our members are not experiencing a lot of problems getting what they need. . . . The VA's prosthetic services, not unlike the rest of its health care, has become adaptable to changing needs of this generation"; the problems, he suggested, emerged from an overwhelmed system: "You can beat up on the VA for it, but in fairness to the VA, I mean they are seeing demands on their system that they never could have imagined."[76]

The VA's struggles to meet the demands of returning veterans became national news in the spring of 2014. Responding to complaints by veterans and their advocates about the quality of care at VA facilities, the Department of Veterans Affairs' Inspector General's Office launched an investigation that discovered that veterans in Phoenix often waited as long as four months—substantially longer than the two weeks mandated by VA guidelines—to receive an initial medical appointment, and that that delay was being hidden through fraudulent record keeping.[77] The investigation "identified 1,400 veterans waiting to receive a scheduled primary care appointment" at the Phoenix VA.[78] This large waiting list, however, turned out to be the less serious issue, for the investigation also "identified an additional 1,700 veterans who were waiting for a primary care appointment but were not on" the hospital's waiting list, leaving veterans "at risk of being forgotten or lost."[79] Outraged lawmakers decried the department's culture and declared that veterans deserved better care.[80]

The controversy ultimately led to the resignation of VA secretary Eric Shinseki. This leadership change, however, did not solve the problem; the VA's continuing investigation revealed that scheduling problems and long wait times were pervasive at VA medical facilities across the country and that VA schedulers had routinely been encouraged to falsify records. Nonetheless, the *New York Times* reported that the delays resulted from a familiar problem: "the highest impediment to timely care cited was lack of medical staff."[81]

A complex picture thus emerges. The VA deserves some credit for attempting to meet veterans' mental and physical health needs. Nonetheless, veterans still struggle with and are frustrated by an underresourced and overwhelmed system, one that has at times chosen fraudulent behavior instead of the significant institutional change that would be required to meet the growing demand. A 2014 *Washington Post* poll found that "Almost 60 percent [Iraq and Afghanistan veterans] say the VA is doing an 'only fair' or 'poor' job in addressing the problems faced by veterans" and that "nearly 1.5 million of those who served in the wars believe the needs of their fellow vets are not being met by the government."[82] In September 2014, the VA's inspector general acknowledged before a congressional committee that the inability to quickly access care "may have contributed to [veterans'] death[s]."[83] These sentiments suggest that despite the evident progress, additional resources are necessary to meet needs that will endure for decades.

* * *

Veterans' life-changing injuries have also impacted their family members. Many partners have forgone their own careers and education to become caregivers, and many parents have delayed retirement to pay for care or left jobs to care for their adult children. After a 2005 explosion left twenty-year-old Steven Schulz unable to use his left arm or to walk long distances, nearly blind, and with poor impulse control, a reduced attention span, and difficulty speaking, his forty-nine-year-old mother Debbie became his primary caregiver.[84] At a moment when she and her husband "were preparing to become empty nesters," she told Congress, she instead "became Steven's primary caregiver, advocate, life skills coach, chauffeur, secretary, bookkeeper, teacher, drill instructor, medical assistant, physical, occupational, speech therapist and on and on."[85] This new role has required her to leave her teaching position, which she describes as "a financial hardship to our family [that] diminished my retirement benefits."[86] Sean Johnson's mild TBI has also created family problems. He told a congressional panel, "My wife has given me tremendous care and looked out for me, and it is really a strain. A strain on my children, a strain on her work, and she may end up losing her job because she has to be gone all the time to take care of me."[87] Other marriages have sagged under the weight of posttraumatic stress disorder. Journalist David Finkel, for example, describes one veteran and his wife as "a breaking family whose center has become Adam's war wounds" and which simply "gets on with another day of trying to recover, followed by another day after that."[88] Other veterans' spouses tell similar stories. In 2008, Stacy Bannerman, whose husband had served in Iraq as a National Guardsman, lambasted the available VA readjustment programs, claiming that "the VA's mental health professionals preach to the wives about resilience. But they aren't the ones being woken up at three in the morning because their husband has shot the dog, or is holding a gun to your head, or a knife at your throat."[89] For many caregivers, attending to an injured family member also has physical and psychological impacts; caregivers are more likely to suffer from anxiety and depression, to have chronic physical health needs, and to live in poverty.[90]

Even for veterans with minor or no injuries, returning to their families is often challenging. In the all-volunteer force of just under eight hundred thousand service members, about half of the total active-duty force are married, and about 44 percent are parents.[91] For service members, deployments meant setting aside their roles as parents and partners; for spouses and children, they meant increased anxiety and responsibility. The stress was sometimes existential—not knowing where your loved one was or fearing that he or she had been wounded. One veteran's wife explained, "'Waiting is one of the hardest things I've had to do. I wouldn't hear from him for weeks, then I would get into a depression and sit by the phone and wait for it to ring.'"[92] Often, though, practical concerns also created stress. One airman's wife explained, "Stress is a big part of deployments. You are not only a mom and a wife, you have the entire household to take care of. Many of them work, so they are still managing a career. They are taking care of the children, they are taking care of the finance."[93]

Deployed parents have often struggled with guilt over their absence. "'I actually feel like a heel because I feel like I cheated my son out of something,'" an Iraq veteran commented; "'It was like he didn't have a dad. . . . I'm supposed to be a father, and I wasn't for a year.'"[94] For the sixteen thousand single parents who deployed, arranging for child care with family members, some of whom lived across the country, added additional complications.[95] For children, parental deployments often lead to behavioral and academic troubles.[96]

Homecomings are thus freighted with significant expectations and changed relationships. There were the inevitable returns to the daily pressures of managing a household amid changed economic realities.[97] One Marine reservist found that such details now seemed inconsequential: "You think about car payments and bills and arguments in the family and who's going where for the holidays. And you try to compare that with the importance of who's shooting a rifle at you."[98] Another critical issue, though, was how deployments had altered relationships between partners and within families.[99] Returning spouses were often unhappily surprised by changes that had taken place in their absence and by the challenge of negotiating roles with partners who had run households with autonomy.[100] Couples also found that their respective personalities had changed and that they now related to one another differently.[101] Kristin Knealing, whose husband Joshua arrived in Iraq a month after the invasion, found that "'he's definitely not the same person. . . .

He used to laugh and joke a lot, and now he's so much more serious and easier to upset than before. Sometimes I feel like I need to be careful with what I say so he doesn't get mad.'"[102] For his part, Joshua found returning to civilian life a struggle: "'Over there, you can say what you have to say and let your frustrations out, but not here.'"[103]

The *New York Times* catalogued a list of common problems that could quickly escalate to catastrophe: "adultery or sexual addictions; burdened spouses, some of whom are reaching for antidepressants; financial turmoil brought on by rising debts, lost wages and overspending; emotionally bruised children whose grades sometimes plummet; and anxious parents who at times turn on each other."[104] Multiple deployments exacerbated these problems. A 2008 House subcommittee learned that troops deployed multiple times were "more likely to . . . [be] reporting problems of infidelity, and were almost twice as likely in planning . . . for a marital separation and divorce."[105] As Sheila Casey, the wife of the Army's chief of staff, explained in 2009, "with repeated deployments bearing down on them, these young families don't have enough time together to build strong bonds."[106] Here again the reliance on a relatively small force to fight two protracted wars created problems for veterans.

The military endeavored to meet the challenge that deployments posed to marriages—in part out of a desire to retain personnel—by increasing programs such as Strong Bonds, a relationship program run by chaplains. With a mission of "building, strengthening, preserving and restoring Army Families," Strong Bonds hosts more than five thousand events annually that provide returning service members and their partners with opportunities to improve their relationships through weekend retreats that feature icebreaker games, videos from relationship experts, and other activities that the Army promises will allow couples to "practice communication and relationship-building skills, as well as share intimate moments."[107]

These programs, apparently, have been too little, too late. By the end of the decade, both divorces and domestic violence had increased. Whereas in 2003 Fort Stewart's director of community activity and services told senators that her office had "been very focused on the issue of domestic violence, and we have been very successful," a 2008 *New York Times* investigation found "150 cases of fatal domestic violence or child abuse in the United States involving service members and new veterans during the wartime period."[108] Across the armed services, the divorce rate has steadily increased since 2001; among enlisted Army personnel it has risen from 2.3 percent in 2000 to 4 percent in 2011.[109] After thirteen years of war, then, veterans have increasingly found their family lives in turmoil, readjustment hampered by repeated deployments and mental and physical health issues, and the available resources insufficient to the task.

* * *

Many returning veterans face the additional challenge of recuperating from military sexual trauma (MST). Sexual assault affects service members of all genders, but because women have been deployed more frequently during this conflict than previous ones—more than 275,000 women have deployed to Iraq, Afghanistan, or both, compared to fewer than 10,000 who served in Vietnam—more women have been victims of unwanted sexual contact.[110] In 2012, the VA noted that "half of women sent to Iraq or Afghanistan report being sexually harassed," and there were a reported 3,374 sexual assaults against service members in 2012.[111] Like veterans with other mental and physical health issues, MST survivors have often struggled to receive treatment; most have also not received justice. Veterans may be more likely to report sexual harassment after their service ends and when they are seeking psychological care in response to trauma associated with it, but survivors chronically underreport sexual misconduct during their enlistments because they are anxious about their reputations or about being discredited, and because they may have to continue working in close proximity to their attacker.[112] As one witness at a 2010 congressional hearing put it, "some 90 percent of victims . . . never report assaults within the military because its culture is so hostile to them."[113] Those who do report their attacks face obstacles in obtaining treatment. Often, they cannot document that their trauma emerges from a service-connected disability. Such documentation is critical in two ways. First, it allows survivors access to VA care. Perhaps more important, as a representative of the Disabled American Veterans explained, it "represents validation that the event occurred, expresses gratitude for their service to their country, and recognizes the tribulations they endured while serving."[114]

Yet obtaining such documentation can be difficult. One survivor described the process that victims must follow to make a claim, which includes writing a detailed narrative of the event, as "just as traumatic as the original rape or harassment."[115] In cases when the assailant was the same gender as the victim, the strictures of the only recently overturned "Don't Ask, Don't Tell" policy meant that those challenges were multiplied; a service member who reported a same-sex assault risked being discharged for violating the policy.[116] A military culture that one journalist describes as "regard[ing] a woman who reports sexual assault as a traitor, a weakling, a slut, or a liar" has thus created a cycle that exacerbates survivors' trauma.[117]

Even MST survivors who do receive the necessary documentation some-times find it difficult to obtain effective treatment. Survivors report that ther-apists often lack training in sexual abuse counseling or treat survivors' PTSD as illegitimate because it isn't combat-related.[118] Female service members who were assaulted by men have been assigned to coed group therapy sessions.[119] Perhaps worse, many women report being harassed and propositioned by male patients in VA hospitals; twenty-three rapes and sixty-six incidents of inappropriate touching occurred in VA facilities in 2009.[120] Advocates have demanded better facilities in which victims can receive care without fear of reprisals and further victimization, and the Department of Defense has re-sponded by standardizing reporting, increasing confidentiality, and collab-orating with the VA to improve sexual assault treatment. Nonetheless, the *Washington Post* reported in 2014 that "the Pentagon has officially embraced secrecy and anonymity as a means of dealing with the problem."[121] Clearly, more work remains to be done.

* * *

Struggles with mental and physical health issues, family reintegration, and sexual trauma would challenge any veteran, and those challenges are com-pounded when they coexist.[122] They are also complicated by geography. The volunteer force that fought in Iraq and Afghanistan does not represent the nation's demographics. With the move to an all-volunteer force, military recruiters increasingly turned their attention southward and westward, and by 2005 nearly 40 percent of recruits came from the southern United States, while rural states such as Alaska, Montana, Wyoming, and Oklahoma were contributing a disproportionate number of recruits.[123] About 15 percent of the population lives in New England, but only 11 percent of military recruits come from those six states. In contrast, the Southwest is home to 13 percent of the population but contributes 18 percent of military recruits. And while approximately 8 percent of Americans live in rural areas, those regions con-tribute nearly 12 percent of military recruits.[124]

Moreover, more than half a million National Guard and Reserve members supplemented the beleaguered regular forces in Iraq and Afghanistan be-tween 2001 and 2007. By 2007, 13 percent of all National Guard members had deployed more than once.[125] These units face particular challenges, leaving behind civilian lives for a combat deployment that most had not anticipated when they enlisted. Moreover, many Guard and Reserve members often did not mobilize with their "home" units but were called up individually, often because they had been trained to perform jobs that that were in demand in understrength units.

This constellation of factors has left rural veterans, and particularly National Guard and Reserve veterans, facing two unique challenges upon their return. First, these veterans often return to their communities alone, at both a physical and psychological distance from the military; this means, as the Montana National Guard concluded, that they become "isolate[d] . . . from those who can provide mutual support and understanding."[126] This lack of a support system has likely contributed to an increase in PTSD and suicides among returned Guard and Reserve members.[127]

Rural veterans also have greater challenges accessing veterans' services. Rural states tend to have fewer VA facilities, which means that veterans must often travel great distances to receive care. For example, while a Buffalo, New York, veteran could find a Vet Center, two outpatient clinics, and a hospital within seventeen miles of home, a Buffalo, Wyoming, veteran would have to drive thirty-six miles to the Sheridan VA Medical Center.[128] The Disabled American Veterans of Montana annually logs more than 750,000 miles transporting veterans to medical appointments.[129] As the adjutant general of the Montana Guard put it, "One end of Montana is at Washington, DC, and the other end is at Bangor, Maine. You would not convince anyone living in Washington, DC that they would have to drive to Bangor, Maine to get any type of health care."[130] The sheer size of many rural states, the lack of infrastructure, and the relatively small number of resources in those states have made it difficult for veterans to access treatment. While considerable attention has been paid to rural veterans' needs, the climate of fiscal austerity that followed the 2008 economic crisis has not enabled a substantial increase in services for rural veterans.

The economic collapse and its aftermath have also left many veterans looking for work. The federal government and private entities have made significant efforts to hire veterans. By the end of 2011, nearly a third of new federal employees were veterans, thanks largely to the Obama administration's 2010 Veterans Employment Initiative.[131] Obama also announced plans to offer tax breaks to businesses hiring veterans, and the Chamber of Commerce has sought to connect veterans and employers.[132] Nonetheless, the unemployment rate for veterans remained nearly three points higher than the nonveteran rate in December 2011.[133]

Some veterans found that combat skills didn't readily transfer to a civilian work; others found that employers couldn't understand that military training provided transferable skills.[134] More frustratingly, some veterans found that they lacked the formal certification necessary to do the civilian equivalent of their military job. As one frustrated former Navy corpsman, or medic, who had not been hired as a certified nursing assistant because he lacked the requisite paperwork, bitterly complained, "I was more than qualified for the positions that I applied for"; however, because "I did not have . . . that piece of paperwork saying so . . . I am struggling to find a job and utilize the skills that the Navy spent over $1 million and nearly 6 years giving me."[135]

Employment issues have been more pressing for wounded veterans and those in the Guard and Reserves. Jonathan Barrs, the veteran suffering from TBI, found that "I look for jobs, and when the documentation of my Marine Corps career is shown to the interviewer, just the look on their face will say it all . . . I am denied a job just because they see the words 'temporarily disabled.'"[136] For others, particularly those without a college education, there was the question of what employment opportunities were available. As the *New York Times* wrote of one veteran who lost an arm in Iraq, "When it came to the future, he felt only confusion, saying, 'I'd like to live out West, but what kind of job could I do?'"[137] The veteran "had thought about going to college . . . but his limitations always came rushing back. 'I type slow. I write slow. I can't carry heavy things. What am I going to do for work?'"[138]

Reservists and guardsmen have also struggled. As early as 2004, Michael Dickenson, a member of the Wisconsin National Guard, came home from Iraq to find that he had lost his warehouse job because his employer had gone out of business.[139] Others guardsmen had the additional challenge of reclaiming jobs from temporary employees or convincing employers concerned that they might deploy to hire them.[140]

Although the gap between veterans' and nonveterans' unemployment has narrowed, at the end of 2013 Iraq and Afghanistan veterans were still more likely to be unemployed than their civilian counterparts.[141] Here again, early decisions about how the Iraq and Afghanistan Wars would be fought have produced enduring challenges for veterans; the failure to plan for lengthy wars necessitated the deployment of Guard and Reserve troops, and one result is that many of those veterans are marginally employed in the wars' aftermath. For these veterans, service to the nation may not have provided a clear path to economic stability.

* * *

The relatively small number of Americans who served in Iraq and Afghanistan have sacrificed much over a decade of war. Most have returned home to supportive families and satisfying careers, and, statistically, the struggles that this chapter discusses affect a small percentage of veterans. Nonetheless, the thousands of injured veterans, struggling families, sexual assault or harassment victims, and un- or underemployed veterans deserve recognition as a significant legacy of these wars. As the wars conclude, the nation's mixed record in meeting these veterans' needs is cause for concern and demands continued discussion. Many Iraq and Afghanistan veterans will require decades of medical care and financial support, as will their partners and families. In that period, the nation will continue to confront questions of what a society owes its veterans and how that debt should be paid.[142] How Americans answer these questions will in turn determine, in large part, these wars' impact on American culture.

NOTES

1 WBAL-TV11, "Happy Homecoming from Iraq," March 13, 2008, http://www.youtube.com/watch?v=52xCQ6ClYZU.

2 Jerry Lembke, *The Spitting Image: Myth, Memory, and the Legacy of Vietnam* (New York: New York University Press, 1999). For a critique of this supportive culture, see Andrew J. Bacevich, *Breach of Trust: How Americans Failed Their Soldiers and Their Country* (New York: Metropolitan Books, 2013), 1-5.

3 Christian G. Appy, *Working Class War: American Combat Soldiers and Vietnam* (Chapel Hill: University of North Carolina Press, 1993), 27.

4 Anna Mulrine, "Sgt. Robert Bales and Multiple Tours of Duty: How Many Is Too Many?," *Christian Science Monitor*, March 23, 2012.

5 Chris Adams, "Millions Went to War in Iraq, Afghanistan, Leaving Many with Lifelong Scars," McClatchy News Service, March 14, 2003,http://www.mcclatchydc.com/2013/03/14/185880_millions went to war in iraq afghanistan.html?rh–1.

6 David Finkel, *Thank You for Your Service* (New York: Sarah Crichton Books, 2013), 11.

7 Aaron Glantz, *The War Comes Home: Washington's Battle Against America's Veterans* (Berkeley: University of California Press, 2009), 105, 49–53, 111.

8 Dana Priest and Anne Hull, "Soldiers Face Neglect, Frustration at Army's Top Medical Facility," *Washington Post*, February 18, 2007; Steve Vogel, "Veterans Face Another Backlog as a Quarter-Million Appeal Disability Claims," *Washington Post*, September 10, 2013; Glantz, *War Comes Home*, 100–101, 118, 121.

9 Here, I differ from Glantz, who argues that "the sorry state of care for Iraq and Afghanistan war veterans is not an accident. It's on purpose," the result of "its desire to hide the true costs of the war in order to boost public support," and who dismisses the notion that Bush and his allies "believed their own rhetoric about the invasion of Iraq going quickly and easily" and rather "were ignoring wounded veterans by design," though I agree with his sense that the Bush administration erred in predicting a quick and easy war (Glantz, *War Comes Home*, 118–19, 121).

10 Benjamin Cooper, "Debt and Denial: Early America and Its Veterans" (paper, American Studies Association, Washington, DC, November 23, 2013).

11 Megan Kate Nelson, *Ruin Nation: Destruction and the American Civil War* (Athens: University of Georgia Press, 2012), 196, 170, 172, 175; Glenn C. Altschuler and Stuart M. Blumin, *The GI Bill: A New Deal for Veterans* (Oxford: Oxford University Press, 2009), 18–22.

12 Nelson, *Ruin Nation*, 208, 221–24.

13 Stephen R. Ortiz, *Beyond the Bonus March and the GI Bill: How Veteran Politics Shaped the New Deal Era* (New York: New York University Press, 2010), 23–27.

14 Ibid., 27.

15 Ibid., 49; Lucy G. Barber, *Marching on Washington: The Forging of an American Political Tradition* (Berkeley: University of California Press, 2002), 75.

16 Barber, *Marching on Washington*, 94, 97. Ortiz, *Beyond the Bonus March*, 56–57.

17 Ortiz, *Beyond the Bonus March*, 57.

18 Altschuler and Blumin, *GI Bill*, 39; 71.

19 Ibid., 63.

20 Ibid., 63, 66, 69–70.

21 Thomas Childers, *Soldier from the War Returning: The Greatest Generation's Troubled Homecoming from World War II* (Boston: Mariner Books, 2010), 8–9.

22 Gerald Nicosia, *Home to War: A History of the Vietnam Veterans' Movement* (New York: Carroll and Graf, 2001), 15–97.

23 Kristin Ann Hass, *Carried to the Wall: American Memory and the Vietnam Veterans Memorial* (Berkeley: University of California Press, 1996), 88–89.

24 Jeremy Kuzmarov, *The Myth of the Addicted Army: Vietnam and the Modern War on Drugs* (Amherst: University of Massachusetts Press, 2009), 150.

25 Richard A. Kukla et al., *Contractual Report of Findings from the National Vietnam Veterans Readjustment Study* (Research Triangle Park, NC: Research Triangle Institute, 1988), 1, 2, 9, 11, http://www.ptsd.va.gov/professional/articles/article-pdf/nvvrs_vol1.pdf.

26 Ronald Reagan, "Peace: Restoring the Margin of Safety" (address, Veterans of Foreign Wars Convention, August 18, 1980), http://www.reagan.utexas.edu/archives/reference/8.18.80.html.

27 Nicosia, *Home to War*, 198–209, 506–55; Edwin A. Martini, *Agent Orange: History, Science, and the Politics of Uncertainty* (Amherst: University of Massachusetts Press, 2012), 152–71; David Zierler, *The Invention of Ecocide: Agent Orange, Vietnam, and the Scientists Who Changed the Way We Think about the Environment* (Athens: University of Georgia Press, 2011).

28 Erica Goode, "Learning from the Last Time; Treatment and Training Help Reduce Stress of War," *New York Times*, March 25, 2003.

29 Eric Schmitt, "New Army Rules on Ways to Cope With Civilian Life," *New York Times*, May 15, 2003.

30 Glantz, *War Comes Home*, 73

31 Glantz, *War Comes Home*, 73; Amanda Paulson, "Colleges Volunteer Financial Aid for Returning Soldiers," *Christian Science Monitor*, April 17, 2006; Edward Humes, "Time for a New GI Bill," *St. Paul Pioneer Press*, October 29, 2006; House Subcommittee on Economic Opportunity of the Committee on Veterans' Affairs, "Updating the Montgomery GI Bill," 110th Cong., 1st sess. (2006), 8.

32 Humes, "Time for a New GI Bill."

33 Wes Allison, "Lawmakers Urge GI Bill Expansion," *St. Petersburg Times*, April 11, 2008; Glantz, *War Comes Home*, 81. (On legislative debates over the bill, see Glantz, *War Comes Home*, 81–85.)

34 Glantz, *War Comes Home*, 83; "Mr. Bush and the G.I. Bill," *New York Times*, May 26, 2008; Richard Wolf, "G.I. Benefits Stymie Funding Bill; Opponents Say Educational Costs Too Expensive," *USA Today*, May 9, 2008.

35 Representative Giffords of Arizona, "Honoring Our Veterans by Expanding the GI Bill," *Congressional Record*, May 16, 2008, E956; Glantz, *War Comes Home*, 84.

36 Senator Tester of Montana, "GI Bill," *Congressional Record*, June 26, 2008, S6214.

37 "The GI Bill Tuition Fairness Act" (Iraq and Afghanistan Veterans of America, April 13, 2013), http://iava.org/blog/gi-bill-tuition-fairness-act.

38 Colleen O'Connor, "GI Bill Delays Hinder Vets; College-Aid Kinks Slow to Work Out," *Denver Post*, November 1, 2009.

39 "Preying on Veterans," *New York Times*, December 13, 2010.

40 Senate Committee on Health, Education, Labor, and Pensions, "Drowning in Debt: Financial Outcomes of Students at for-Profit Colleges," 112th Cong., 1st sess. (2011), 58.

41 Kevin Freking, "Veterans Are Flocking to Enroll in College as Wars Wind Down," *Huffington Post*, October 17, 2013, http://www.huffingtonpost.com/2013/10/17/veterans-enroll-in-college_n_4117250.html. See also Glantz, *War Comes Home*, 77.

42 Cody Kraatz, "Local Veterans Turning from War to the Classroom," *San Jose Mercury-News*, November 14, 2008.

43 David Wallis, "Coming Home from War to Hit the Books," *New York Times*, March 1, 2012.

44 Freking, "Veterans Are Flocking to Enroll."

45 "Faces of the Fallen," *Washington Post*, March 6, 2015; Hannah Fisher, *A Guide to U.S. Military Casualty Statistics: Operation New Dawn, Operation Iraqi Freedom, and Operation Enduring Freedom* (Washington, DC: Congressional Research Service, 2014).

46 Rick Atkinson, "The Single Most Effective Weapon Against Our Deployed Forces," *Washington Post*, September 30, 2007; Richard F. Ellis et al., "Joint Improvised Explosive Device Defeat Organization (JIEDDO): Tactical Successes Mired in Orga-nizational Chaos; Roadblock in the Counter-IED Fight" (Joint Forces Staff College Joint and Combined Warfighting School—Intermediate Class #07-02, March 13, 2007), www.dtic.mil/cgi-bin/GetTRDoc?AD=ADA473109.

47 Eric Schmitt, "Iraq-Bound Troops Confront Rumsfeld over Lack of Armor," *New York Times*, December 8, 2004.

48 Ann Jones, *They Were Soldiers: How the Wounded Return from America's Wars: The Untold Story* (Chicago: Haymarket Books, 2013), 36–37.

49 David Wood, "U.S. Wounded In Iraq, Afghanistan Includes More Than 1,500 Amputees," *Huffington Post*, November 7, 2012, http://www.huffingtonpost.com/2012/11/07/iraq-afghanistan-amputees_n_2089911.html; Jones, *They Were Soldiers*, 44.

50 Steve Almasy, "The Toll of War Now Includes More Amputees," CNN, October 29, 2012, http://www.cnn.com/2012/05/27/us/amputee-veterans-come-home/.

51 House Committee on Veterans' Affairs, "Hearing on Optimizing Care for Veterans with Prosthetics," 112th Cong., 2nd sess. (2012), 71.

52 Fisher, *Guide to U.S. Military Casualty Statistics*, 4; for background on mild TBI, see Jones, *They Were Soldiers*, 49–52.

53 Senate Committee on Veterans' Affairs, "Oversight Hearing on Traumatic Brain Injury (TBI): Progress in Treating the Signature Wounds of the Current Conflicts," 111th Cong., 1st sess. (2010), 48–49.

54 Epidemiology Program Post-Deployment Health Group, "Report on VA Facility Specific Operation Enduring Freedom (OEF), Operation Iraqi Freedom (OIF), and Operation New Dawn (OND) Veterans Coded with Potential PTSD—Revised" (Washington, DC: Department of Veterans Affairs, 2012), 4.

55 Todd Bowers, "IAVA Testifies before HVAC Subcommittee on Oversight and Investigations," IVAW.org, March 13, 2008, http://iava.org/blog/iava-testifies-hvac-subcommittee-oversight-and-investigations.

56 Glantz, *War Comes Home*, 35.

57 Anthony H. Cordesman, *U.S. Casualties: The Trends in Iraq and Afghanistan* (Washington, DC: Center for Strategic and International Studies, 2008), 3.

58 Glantz, *War Comes Home*, 35; Jones *They Were Soldiers*, 33.

59 Senate Committee on Veterans' Affairs, "Oversight Hearing on Traumatic Brain Injury (TBI)," 6; for one surgeon's description of this, see Jones, *They Were Soldiers*, 42.

60 Senate Committee on Veterans' Affairs, "Is the VA Prepared to Meet the Needs of Our Returning Vets," 109th Cong., 1st sess. (2005), 2, 41.

61 House Committee on Veterans' Affairs, "Implementing the Wounded Warrior Provisions of the National Defense Authorization Act for Fiscal Year 2008," 110th Cong., 2nd sess. (2008), 8.

62 Senate Committee on Veterans' Affairs, "Oversight Hearing on Traumatic Brain Injury (TBI)," 6.

63 Institute of Medicine, *Returning Home from Iraq and Afghanistan: Preliminary Assessment of Readjustment Needs of Veterans, Service Members, and Their Families* (Washington, DC: National Academies Press, 2010), 73; Glantz, *War Comes Home*, 96.

64 House Committee on Veterans' Affairs, "The U.S. Department of Veterans Affairs Fiscal Year 2008 Health Budget," 110th Cong., 1st sess. (2008), 52.

65 House Subcommittee on Oversight and Investigations, Committee on Veterans' Affairs, "Transitioning Heroes: New Era, Same Problems?," 111th Cong., 2nd sess. (2010), 5–6.

66 House Committee on Veterans' Affairs, "The Impact of Operation Iraqi Freedom/ Operation Enduring Freedom on the U.S. Department of Veterans Affairs Claims Process," 110th Cong, 1st sess. (2007), 22.

67 Ibid., 102.

68 House Committee on Veterans' Affairs, "Healing the Physical Injuries of War," 111th Cong., 2nd sess. (2010), 13, 32.

69 Glantz, *War Comes Home*, 41–44; Senate Committee on Veterans' Affairs, "Oversight Hearing on Traumatic Brain Injury (TBI)," 6, 18, 142.

70 Senate Committee on Veterans' Affairs, "VA Mental Health Care: Ensuring Timely Access to High-Quality Care," 113th Cong., 1st sess. (2013), 53.

71 "Extremity Trauma and Amputee Center of Excellence," Health.mil, n.d., http://www.health.mil/About-MHS/Organizational-Overview/Extremity-Trauma-and-Amputation-Center-of-Excellence. Jones is critical of the trumpeting of these advances; see *They Were Soldiers*, 79–84.

72 Cynthia Billhartz Gregorian, "Local War Vet Will Test Prosthetic Leg in Grueling Race," *St. Louis Post-Dispatch*, March 14, 2013; Tim Craig, "Soldier Who Lost Leg in Afghanistan Vowed 'I Will Return.' This Is What It Took to Get Back," *Washington Post*, May 1, 2014.

73 James Dao, "Learning to Accept, and Master, a $110,000 Mechanical Arm," *New York Times*, November 27, 2012.

74 Ibid.; Department of Veterans Affairs, Office of the Inspector General, *Healthcare Inspection: Prosthetic Limb Care in VA Facilities* (Washington, DC: VA Office of the Inspector General, 2012), 47–48, 53.

75 Department of Veterans Affairs, Office of the Inspector General, *Healthcare Inspection*, 68.

76 Ibid., iv, 62–65; House Committee on Veterans' Affairs, "Healing the Physical Injuries of War," 13, 14.

77 Wesley Lowery and Josh Hicks, "'Troubling' Report Sparks New Wave of Calls for VA Chief's Resignation," *Washington Post*, May 28, 2014; Department of Veterans Affairs, Office of the Inspector General, "Interim Report: Review of Patient Wait Times, Scheduling Practices, and Alleged Patient Deaths at the Phoenix Health Care System" (May 28, 2014), 1.

78 Department of Veterans Affairs, Office of the Inspector General, "Interim Report," 1.

79 Ibid., iii.

80 Greg Jaffe and Josh Hicks, "Shinseki Faces Tough Questions on VA Scandal, Vows to 'Accomplish a Mission,'" *Washington Post*, May 15, 2014.

81 Richard A. Oppel, Jr., "Audit Shows Extensive Medical Delays for Tens of Thousands of Veterans," *New York Times*, June 10, 2014.

82 Rajiv Chandrasekaran, "Poll: Majority of Iraq, Afghan War Vets Struggle with Physical and Mental Problems," *Bangor Daily News*, March 30, 2014.

83 Curt Devine and Scott Bronstein, "VA Inspector General Admits Wait Times Contributed to Vets' Deaths," *CNN*, September 18, 2014.

84 House Committee on Veterans' Affairs, "Implementation of Caregiver Assistance: Moving Forward," 112th Cong., 1st sess. (2011), 31; for a similar story, see also Jones, *They Were Soldiers*, 89.

85 House Committee on Veterans' Affairs, "Implementation of Caregiver Assistance," 3.

86 Ibid., 31.

87 House Subcommittee on Oversight and Investigations, Committee on Veterans' Affairs, "Transitioning Heroes," 6.

88 Finkel, *Thank You for Your Service*, 11.

89 House Subcommittee on Health, Committee on Veterans' Affairs, "Mental Health Treatment for Families: Supporting Those Who Support Our Veterans," 110th Cong., 2nd sess. (2008), 7.

90 House Veterans' Affairs Committee, "Implementation of Caregiver Assistance: Are We Getting It Right?," 112th Cong., 1st sess. (2011), 29.

91 Office of the Deputy Undersecretary of Defense (Military Community and Family Policy), "2011 Demographics: Profile of the Military Community" (Arlington, VA: Department of Defense, 2012), 43, 118.

92 Michael Zwelling, "Coming Home; The War in Iraq Has Produced a Class of Veterans Not Seen for Decades: Soldiers Dealing with the Trauma of Prolonged Combat," *Buffalo News*, August 7, 2005.

93 Senate Subcommittee on Personnel, Committee on Armed Forces, "Issues Affecting Families of Soldiers, Sailors, Airmen, and Marines," 108th Cong., 1st sess. (2003), 65.

94 Zwelling, "Coming Home."

95 Donna St. George, "Yearning to Be Whole Again; Sergeant Sees the Light after a Year of Emotional, Family Turmoil," *Washington Post*, November 24, 2006; on these struggles, see Laura Browder, *When Janey Comes Marching Home: Portraits of Women Combat Veterans* (Chapel Hill: University of North Carolina Press, 2009), 101–2, 104.

96 Sandra G. Boodman, "Deployments Disrupt Kids," *Washington Post*, December 16, 2008.

97 Dave Hirschman and Moni Basu, "Georgia's Guard: The 48th: Stress in Iraq, and at Home; Deployment Can Leave Families in a Financial Lurch," *Atlanta Journal-Constitution*, June 9, 2005.

98 Peter Slevin, "When the War Comes Home; For a Marine Reserve Company That Saw Death in Iraq, Returning to Life in Ohio Is an Unexpected Battle," *Washington Post*, October 30, 2006.

99 Glantz, *War Comes Home*, 11.

100 Maureen Oth, "Fort Bragg's Deadly Summer," *Vanity Fair*, December 2002; David Hanners, "After a Rifle Is Set Down, a New Fight Begins," *St. Paul Pioneer Press*, April 25, 2006. This was a common lament of returning POWs (Natasha Zaretsky, *No Direction Home: The American Family and the Fear of National Decline* [Chapel Hill: University of North Carolina Press, 2007], 50–52).

101 Jones, *They Were Soldiers*, 120–23.

102 Zwelling, "Coming Home."

103 Ibid.

104 Lizette Alvarez, "Long Iraq Tours Can Make Home a Trying Front," *New York Times*, February 23, 2007.

105 House Subcommittee on Health, Committee on Veterans' Affairs, "Mental Health Treatment for Families," 63.

106 Senate Committee on Armed Services, "Department of Defense Authorization Appropriations for Fiscal Year 2010," 111th Cong., 1st sess. (2009), 116.

107 "Memorandum of Instruction—Total Army Fiscal Year 2013 Strong Bonds Program Management, Resourcing and Training" (July 26, 2012), http://explorepsa.com/asb/download/SB_MOI_FY_2013.pdf; Birch Carleton, "News: What Is Strong Bonds?" (Army Strong Bonds Program, December 16, 2010), http://www.strongbonds.org; Kaytrina Curtis, "Strong Bonds Builds Better Marriages" (Army Strong Bonds Program, March 21, 2011), http://www.strongbonds.org; "PREP Marriage Enrichment for ARNG Married Couples" (Army Strong Bonds Program, n.d.), https://www.strongbonds.org/.

108 Senate Subcommittee on Personnel, Committee on Armed Services, "Issues Affecting Families of Soldiers," 55; Lizette Alvarez and Deborah Sontag, "When Strains on Military Families Turn Deadly," *New York Times*, February 15, 2008. See also Jones, *They Were Soldiers*, 120–25 and 133–37.

109 Office of the Deputy Undersecretary, "2011 Demographics," 50; Glantz, *War Comes Home*, 16.

110 Asha Anchan, Kelsey Hightower, and Caitlin Cruz, "'Back Home': Female Veterans Often Find Unwelcoming System, Insensitive Treatment," *MinnPost*, August 30, 2013, http://www.minnpost.com/politics-policy/2013/08/back-home-female-veterans-often-find-unwelcoming-system-insensitive-treatmen; Diane Carlson Evans, "Vietnam Women's Memorial Foundation" (2014), http://www.vietnamwomensmemorial.org/vwmf.php. See also Glantz, *War Comes Home*, 20. Within the debate over military sexual trauma, there has been some inconsistency regarding terminology, with the term "unwanted sexual contact" sometimes encompassing behaviors that range from inappropriate comments to rape. The debate on these matters would benefit from additional clarity (this point was first raised by Aaron O'Connell, "Confronting Social Change: Gender, Sexuality, and the U.S. Military" [paper, Organization of American Historians, Atlanta, March 12, 2014]). As well, it is important to distinguish between the reporting practices of veterans and those of active-duty service members, as each operates in a different bureaucracy and has different resources available.

111 Gregg Zoroya, "VA Finds Assaults More Common; Study Shows More Happen in War Zones," *USA Today*, December 27, 2012; Jennifer Steinhauer, "Sexual Assaults in Military Raise Alarm in Capital," *New York Times*, May 8, 2013.

112 Helen Benedict, *The Lonely Soldier: The Private War of Women Serving in Iraq* (Boston: Beacon, 2009), 68–69, 81–82; Glantz, *War Comes Home*, 114; House Committee on Veterans' Affairs, "Healing the Wounds: Evaluating Military Sexual Trauma Issues," 111th Cong., 2nd sess. (2010), 8–9; Jones, *They Were Soldiers*, 130.

113 House Committee on Veterans' Affairs, "Healing the Wounds," 7.

114 Ibid., 7–14.

115 Ibid., 15; see also Glantz, *War Comes Home*, 112–13.

116 House Committee on Veterans' Affairs, "Healing the Wounds," 15.

117 Benedict, *Lonely Soldier*, 81.

118 House Committee on Veterans' Affairs, "Healing the Wounds," 14–15.

119 Ibid., 13.

120 Ibid.; Government Accountability Office, "VA Health Care: Actions Needed to Prevent Sexual Assaults and Other Safety Incidents" (Washington, DC: GPO, 2011), 13.

121 Stephanie McCrummen, "The Choice," *Washington Post*, April 12, 2014.

122 Polytrauma refers to multiple, coexisting combat injuries. See House Committee on Veterans' Affairs, "Healing the Physical Injuries of War," 3.

123 Tim Kane, "Who Are The Recruits? The Demographic Characteristics of U.S. Military Enlistment, 2003–2005" (Heritage Foundation, October 27, 2006), http://www.heritage.org/research/reports/2006/10/who-are-the-recruits-the-demographic-characteristics-of-us-military-enlistment-2003-2005; Beth Bailey, *America's Army: Making the All-Volunteer Force* (Cambridge, MA: Harvard University Press, 2009), 259.

124 Ibid., table 8.

125 Defense Science Board, "Deployment of Members of the National Guard and Reserve in the Global War on Terrorism" (Officer of the Under Secretary of Defense for Acquisition, Technology, and Logistics, 2007), 6, 8, http://www.acq.osd.mil/dsb/reports/ADA478163.pdf.

126 Senate Committee on Veterans' Affairs, "Field Hearing on Addressing the Needs of Veterans in Rural Areas," 110th Cong., 2nd sess. (2007), 52.

127 Kristina Fiore, "PTSD Hits National Guard Soldiers Harder: Study," *ABC News*, June 13, 2010, http://abcnews.go.com/Health/MindMoodNews/ptsd-hits-national-guard-soldiers-harder/story?id=10891094; Greg Jaffe, "Army Sees Suicide Rate Decline Overall, Increase among Guard and Reserve Soldiers," *Washington Post*, January 19, 2011.

128 These statistics are from U.S. Department of Veterans Affairs, "Locations" (n.d.), http://www.va.gov/directory/guide/home.asp.

129 Senate Committee on Veterans' Affairs, "Field Hearing on Addressing the Needs of Veterans in Rural Areas," 4, 7.

130 Ibid., 39.

131 Joe Davidson, "Veterans' Advocates Hail 'Good Numbers' Posted in Early Months of Hiring Initiative," *Washington Post*, September 17, 2010; Steve Vogel, "Veterans Hiring in Past Year Balloons," *Washington Post*, December 14, 2011.

132 Michael A. Fletcher, "Veterans Returning to Jobless Welcome," *Washington Post*, October 17, 2011.

133 Vogel, "Veterans Hiring in Past Year Balloons."

134 Michael A. Fletcher, "After Grim Wars, Some Battle a Grim Job Market," *Washington Post*, December 30, 2010; Fletcher, "Veterans Returning to Jobless Welcome."

135 Senate Committee on Veterans' Affairs, "Veterans' Employment: Improving the Transition From Battlefield to the Workplace," 112th Cong., 1st sess. (2011), 12.

136 Senate Committee on Veterans' Affairs, "Oversight Hearing on Traumatic Brain Injury (TBI)," 49.

137 Sara Corbett, "The Permanent Scars of Iraq," *New York Times*, February 15, 2004.

138 Ibid.

139 Stephanie Armour, "New Veterans Adjust from Battleground to Workplace," *USA Today*, June 18, 2004.

140 Ibid. For a particularly nefarious example of this phenomenon, see Glantz, *War Comes Home*, 25.

141 Jim Garamone, "Veterans Unemployment Rate Dropped in 2013" (Department of Defense, March 20, 2014), http://www.defense.gov/news/newsarticle.aspx?id=121873.

142 Linda Bilmes, "Soldiers Returning from Iraq and Afghanistan: The Long-Term Costs of Providing Veterans Medical Care and Disability Benefits" (paper, Allied Social Sciences Association, Chicago, January, 2007), 3, 16–17, http://www.hks.harvard.edu/fs/lbilmes/paper/Bilmes_vacostwar_010707.pdf.

12

The Lessons and Legacies of the War in Iraq

ROBERT K. BRIGHAM

The Bush administration went to war in Iraq thinking that a uniquely American story would emerge. Steeped in American exceptionalism and clinging to the belief that the United States possessed unlimited power, the Bush White House launched a preemptive strike against Iraq, intending to alter Baghdad's fundamental political outlook by toppling Saddam Hussein and building a lasting democracy in his place. For Bush, democracy itself had a transformative power and its expansion in the Middle East promised to make the United States more secure. The president and his closest advisers believed that the United States needed to promote democracy in the Middle East because it was the lack of representative institutions within these states that drove terrorists to desperate measures. Thus with new democratic institutions, the middle class in Iraq and throughout the region would take ownership of the political process alongside the traditional royal families and authoritarian regimes. Shared power through a more democratic state would transform the Middle East from an unpredictable and potentially dangerous region into a stable and peaceful one. The Bush administration believed in Woodrow Wilson's adage that the United States must make the world safe for democracy. The first piece of the puzzle in the Middle East was Iraq.

Accordingly, the Bush administration invaded Iraq in March 2003. During the first few months of the war, it appeared that the Bush team was correct about the limitlessness of American power. U.S. forces easily drove Saddam Hussein from Baghdad and eventually captured, tried, and executed him. In his place, the United States supported a political process designed to identify representative Kurds, Sunnis, and Shi'ites and bring them together into a government of national reconciliation and concord. Alongside the political program was a robust nation-building effort that focused on preparing key Iraqi industries for privatization and global markets. The Bush administration believed that all good things went together: a quick military victory over Saddam Hussein and his followers, a democracy program, and the privatization of Iraqi industries were the cornerstones of a new Iraq. Supporters of the administration's policies were quick to embrace the American victory, and some even claimed that Bush's grand strategy had deep roots in the nineteenth century, when Thomas Jefferson and John Quincy Adams helped build an empire of liberty.[1] Bush celebrated this belief in fine fashion, declaring "Mission Accomplished" aboard the USS *Abraham Lincoln* in May 2003 when he claimed that the war in Iraq had been won.

But Bush was wrong. To the detriment of America's image and reputation, democracy had not taken root in Iraq; little the United States did there changed Iraqi political outlook and behavior. Despite the sacrifice of over four thousand U.S. servicemen and -women who did everything their country asked of them, the deaths of tens of thousands of Iraqis (many of whom were civilians), and a cost to the U.S. Treasury of hundreds of billions of dollars, Iraq at the time of this writing in 2015 remains at war and undemocratic. The government in Baghdad has done little to create a more just and equitable society. In Iraq today, there are gross human rights violations, the Baghdad government excludes political opponents from national public life and threatens them with jail routinely, the level of corruption in the government and private sector is among the highest in the world, and constitutional provisions protecting minority rights are trampled with impunity. Deadly attacks continue unabated. In May 2014, eight hundred Iraqis were killed, most of them civilians, and 2014 marked the deadliest year in Iraq since 2008. All of this points to the Iraq War's greatest lesson and legacy: there was no political corollary to America's overwhelming military power.

To seasoned foreign policy observers, the Bush administration's faulty predictions about America's transformative power did not come as a surprise. Past U.S. efforts to reshape foreign governments have often met similar fates. Several U.S. presidents have been frustrated by their inability to shape the contours of conflicts and political life in other nation states. McKinley and Roosevelt experienced great difficulties in the Philippines, Wilson was repeatedly frustrated in Mexico, Hoover occupied Nicaragua to no avail, and five successive U.S. presidents failed to influence the government in South Vietnam. The failed nation-building experiment in Iraq had an interesting twist, however. After it became clear in 2004 that earlier declarations of a U.S. military victory were premature, some policy makers in Washington believed that the United States successfully changed its strategy with a "surge" of American military power, leading to the ultimate military victory and the transformation of Iraq. But as this essay shows, although a change in tactics to create "a better war" may have led to operational success on the battlefield, it did little to change the nature of the government in Baghdad. In fact, "the surge" helped create the very conditions that made real, lasting political change so difficult.[2] This phenomenon, and its implications elsewhere around the globe, may well prove to be the war's most enduring legacy.

The factors leading to political failure in Iraq began shortly after President Bush declared a military victory. Bush did not realize at the time that the heaviest fighting was yet to come. The civil war inside of Iraq began to take full shape during the Battle for Fallujah at the end of March 2004, when U.S. Marines found themselves confronting insurgent activity throughout the city. The insurgency quickly spread to other areas of Iraq, including the cities of Ramadi, Mosul, and Najaf, as radicalized Sunnis—some with ties to Saddam Hussein and some who supported al Qaeda—struck at the new Baghdad government and its American allies. Sunni insurgents showed considerable knowledge of antitank operations, and U.S. commanders concluded that they also skillfully demonstrated operational freedom of movement by launching stand-off attacks against U.S. troops. In addition, foreign fighters, some with connections to al Qaeda affiliates operating in Iraq, joined Iraqi Sunnis, creating new problems for the Baghdad government. Further complicating the security picture were scores of local Shi'ite militias who attacked Sunnis (and sometimes even Americans) with regularity. Some of these subnational groups were actually associated with the Baghdad government, including the forces of Mogtada al-Sadr, a radical Shi'ite cleric with a large following who controlled the Mahdi Army. The Baghdad government pledged to keep in check Shi'ite militias and do all that it could to end the sectarian violence in Iraq. Yet for three years the war intensified and the death tolls rose.

The Bush administration faced similar difficulties in its nation-building program. Convinced that rapid privatization was essential to rebuild Iraq, Paul Bremer, director of the Coalition Provisional Authority (CPA), which was responsible for the nation-building program in Iraq, claimed that marketization would "be a wrenching, painful process, but if we don't get their [Iraq's] economy right, no matter how fancy our political transformation, it won't work."[3] The problem was that the CPA had few qualified economists on staff. Instead of experienced technocrats, the CPA often hired people loyal to the Republican Party. "The criterion for sending people over there was that they had to have the right political credentials," explained Frederick Smith, who served as deputy director of the CPA's Washington office. Smith told the story of a young man who had sent his resume to James O'Beirne, the White House liaison at the Pentagon. O'Beirne looked at the resume and proclaimed the young man "an ideal candidate" for a job in Iraq with the CPA because he had worked for the Republican Party in Florida during the presidential election in 2000.[4]

Political patronage produced an economic nightmare in Iraq. But other critics of the CPA have argued that it was not the junior appointments that plagued Iraq's development, but the senior appointees. James Dobbins, a former assistant secretary of state under Presidents Bill Clinton and George W. Bush, wrote in *Foreign Affairs* that "Bremer filled nearly all the senior jobs in Iraq with seasoned professionals and only turned to White House patronage machine when the administration proved unable to staff the more junior posts with career professionals." Still, Dobbins warned, "it is not the junior but the most senior and influential positions that are filled by individuals chosen primarily for their ideological convictions and personal loyalty." Here is where the CPA ran into severe oversight and management problems.[5]

Indeed, for many years following Saddam's ouster, the CPA's initial privatization efforts did little to revive Iraq's economy. Iraqi unemployment was unusually high during the CPA's administration, and its inflation rate was staggering.[6] Several independent reports during Bremer's tenure and through the end of 2006 claimed that average Iraqi citizens were only slightly better off economically under the U.S. occupation than they were under Saddam.[7] In several sectors, the U.S. nation-building effort actually created more problems than it solved. For example, the 2005 per capita income in Iraq was $3,400 per year, just ahead of Cuba's. The 2005 unemployment rate was 25 percent, a figure that would have been significantly higher without jobs in the U.S.-supported armed forces.[8] In 2005, only Zimbabwe had a higher annual inflation rate than Iraq's 40 percent.[9] Bob Herbert of the *New York Times* reported in early 2006 that despite the infusion of sixteen billion in American taxpayer money, "virtually every measure of the performance of Iraq's oil, electricity, water and sewage sectors has fallen below prewar levels."[10] Herbert's sources were U.S. government witnesses who had testified before a U.S. Senate committee hearing.

Compounding Iraq's economic problems was the fact that there was "a virtual youth explosion," making job creation an essential part of nation building. Few of the CPA's policies addressed this issue concretely.[11] Even though the CPA was disbanded in June 2004, replaced by a regularized U.S. embassy in Baghdad, its economic policies still influenced Iraq for many years. Critics of the CPA's handling of the Iraqi economy were plenty, and there is still considerable controversy surrounding the awarding of private contracts to American firms without competitive bidding for the rebuilding of Iraq.

The CPA was plagued by other problems, some of its own making. When Bremer left for Baghdad, he had no agreed-upon plan of action for Iraq, and questions of organizational structure remained unanswered. He would hold the rank of ambassador, but he reported to both the president and the Defense Department. He was the director of the CPA but also the leader of a foreign occupying government. Bremer had a vast mandate from Washington, but limited instructions. There was very little oversight on what he did inside Iraq with Iraqi resources, and, at the same time, too many restrictions on what Bremer could do with U.S. funds.

As is often the case, the civilian ambassador clashed with the military command over security matters. Even though Bremer believed internal security to be his first priority in Iraq, how to accomplish that goal generated intense debate between Bremer and General Ricardo Sanchez, who was commander of the coalition ground forces in Iraq. Sanchez strongly disagreed with Bremer's decision to remove all Ba'athist Party members from the Iraqi national army, believing that this only fueled the insurgency. Bremer believed that Ba'athist who had once supported Saddam Hussein would never support the new Iraqi government. Sanchez disagreed. He also thought Bremer discounted the importance of the violent Shi'ite militias and their ties to the national government. There was even disagreement over how many U.S. troops were needed in Iraq. Bremer concurred with the findings of a report produced by the RAND Corporation, an independent think tank from Santa Monica, California, that had concluded that the United States needed roughly five hundred thousand troops in Iraq in 2003 to fulfill its many obligations. In his memoir, Bremer insists that he raised this issue with the president and with Secretary of Defense Donald Rumsfeld. Neither ever replied.[12] The CPA itself was hopelessly understaffed, leading one Middle East expert and former National Security Council member to conclude that it had "virtually no presence outside of Baghdad," therefore jeopardizing the entire reconstruction effort.[13] General James Conway, who commanded the 1st Marine Expeditionary Force, has suggested that the CPA was unable to meet the Iraqis' expectations for rebuilding their country. Consequently, the Marines stationed west of Baghdad were often forced to "become city managers, chiefs of policy and agricultural experts" because Bremer's local governance teams never arrived.[14]

Despite the CPA's chronic difficulties, there was considerable optimism in Washington when the first U.S. ambassador to post-Saddam Iraq, the veteran foreign service officer John Negroponte, took over for Bremer in June 2004. The administration sent Negroponte to Baghdad to supervise the transition of the CPA into a full-fledged embassy and to coordinate policy with the new interim government of Ayad Allawi, a secular Shi'a who was a member of the Iraqi governing council. Secretary of State Colin Powell suggested that Negroponte had the experience and the wisdom to handle the difficult transition, and that the new interim Allawi government had the full support of the United States. At the time of the transition in June 2004, Powell stated that "complete political transition" in Iraq was just around the corner. The CPA had been a necessary step in the process of Iraq's transition to democracy, Powell concluded, and with the new embassy and Allawi government in place, it was only a matter of time before the partnership between Iraqis and Americans produced the desired results.[15]

Before the Iraqi government could reach its goals, however, security had to improve dramatically. "As recent events have demonstrated," Powell wrote Lauro L. Baja, Jr., president of the UN Security Council in June 2004, "continuing attacks by insurgents, including former regime elements, foreign fighters, and illegal militias challenge all those who are working for a better Iraq."[16] Powell had no idea how prophetic his statement would be. For the next two years, the insurgency grew unabated, matched only by Muqtada al-Sadr's Mahdi Army's (a Shi'ite militia with ties to the government) deadly attacks on Sunnis. American forces were caught inside a civil war that had triangulated rapidly, as foreign elements also joined the battlefield.

"We're not winning the war in Iraq," President Bush told a reporter in late December 2006, but he added, "we're not losing."[17] The president was stumped over what to do next in Iraq to stop the sectarian violence and let the full impact of U.S. nation-building programs be felt by ordinary Iraqis. The November 2006 U.S. elections emphatically showed that the American people no longer supported the president's war and demanded a dramatic change. In the midterm elections Democrats captured the House, the Senate, and a majority of governorships and state legislatures from the Republicans. Bush's approval ratings were at an all-time low, and public opinion polls showed a majority of Americans favored a U.S. withdrawal from Iraq.[18] Yet throughout his political career, Bush had exhibited a penchant for political survival. And sure enough, just when the hour looked darkest, a previously unbending president changed the public's perception of the war in Iraq completely by embracing what is now known as "the surge."

The surge, a substantial increase in the number of combat brigades in Iraq, was promoted by the Bush administration as a dramatic departure from current policy. In fact, General George Casey, who replaced General Sanchez as commander of coalition ground forces in Iraq, had already increased U.S. troop strength in Iraq in August 2006 to "clear insurgent and militia-infested neighborhoods," and most empirical evidence suggests that the violence was actually on the decline in late 2006 before the surge.[19] Still, the president claimed that the surge was a new and bold strategy that promised to rescue victory from the jaws of defeat. The key to the surge was embedding American soldiers with Iraqi civilians to improve security, even if such a move exposed U.S. troops to greater risk. The surge also required a longer-term U.S. commitment to Iraq, because successful nation building inside a counterinsurgency program is measured in decades rather than months or even years.

In a solemn speech to the nation from the White House library on January 10, 2007, President Bush accepted full responsibility for the conduct of the war and admitted that too many mistakes had been made in Iraq. He declared, "The situation in Iraq is unacceptable to the American people, and it is unacceptable to me. Our troops in Iraq have fought bravely. They have done everything we have asked them to do. Where mistakes have been made, the responsibility rests with me." Bush then spoke the words that many had been hoping to hear for so long, "It is clear we need to change our strategy in Iraq." The president outlined the comprehensive review that his administration had conducted and told the nation that he had also "consulted members of Congress from both parties, allies abroad, and distinguished outside experts."[20]

Bush then listed his administration's new priorities in Iraq, and at the top of the list was improved security, especially near Baghdad. The president explained, "eighty percent of Iraq's sectarian violence occurs within 30 miles of the capital. This violence is splitting Baghdad into sectarian enclaves and shaking the confidence of all Iraqis." In the past, U.S. and Iraqi efforts to secure the population had failed, Bush argued, because "there were not enough Iraqi and American troops to secure neighborhoods that had been cleared of terrorists and insurgents, and there were too many restrictions on the troops we did have." To remedy this situation, the Iraqi government was making a renewed commitment to internal security by deploying additional Iraqi brigades across Baghdad's nine districts. But this was not enough. The president argued that for the Iraqis to succeed, they "will need our help." Accordingly, he committed to increasing American force levels to more than twenty thousand additional American troops to Iraq. Bush concluded his explanation of the surge by stating clearly, "Our troops will have a well-defined mission: to help Iraqis clear and secure neighborhoods, to help them protect the local population, and to help ensure that the Iraqi forces left behind are capable of providing the security that Baghdad needs."[21]

One intended benefit of the surge was that it also called on the Iraqi government to increase its commitment to rebuilding the nation through democracy and federalism. The Bush administration had been unable to pressure the Baghdad government to make needed reforms under the old security system, and many thought that an enhanced counterinsurgency program would force the new Iraqi government of Nouri al-Maliki to assume more responsibility. The surge required Baghdad to recast its security operations by focusing on the civilian population. Many in the Bush administration hoped that this change in posture would foster better relations between the Maliki government and the Sunni and Kurdish minorities.

The Maliki government was resistant to change, however, and therefore it did little to alter its policies or tactics. Instead of taking responsibility for the growing discontentment in Iraq, as the Bush administration had hoped, the Maliki government concluded that Iraq's current problems were the result of "the previous regime's policy of minimizing the legitimate roles of government institutions," which "led to their collapse after the collapse of the Head of the Government. All this resulted in significant difficulties and conditions that permitted the growth of corruption and organized crime, especially as the result of the lack of security that followed the collapse of the previous regime. These difficulties came simultaneously with the rise of people's expectations for immediate improvement in all aspects of life."[22] The government claimed it had redoubled its efforts to provide for the public welfare by ending corruption in the nation-building program and at the same time improving relations with Sunnis and Kurds. To achieve these goals, the Iraqi security force (ISF) embraced the enhanced counterinsurgency tactics as well, with its focus on the civilian population. In a national security assessment, the Maliki government pledged to change the course of the war by making dramatic changes to its security operations. It now seems clear that Maliki embraced the surge to continue American support, but not necessarily to achieve the ends to which the United States designed that support. Problems would remain in the ISF throughout the surge. Without major reform in Baghdad, there was little hope of ending the sectarian violence that threatened to tear Iraq apart.

Shortly after the surge began, report after report concluded that security had increased dramatically following the introduction of surge troops and that sectarian violence was down considerably.[23] Toby Dodge, an expert on Iraq, agreed. In a 2007 interview with Foreign Policy, Dodge explained, "General [David] Petraeus had some undoubted successes to sell. There has been a ferocious debate about the metrics and certainly August is an odd month because of the intensity of the heat, so conflict tends to drop off a bit. However, I think violence has undoubtedly dropped off compared to 2006. Iraq, especially Baghdad, was in the midst of a civil war in 2006. In 2007, the surge has stopped or put a pause on that civil war."[24] Many inside the Bush administration believed that the surge showed Iraqis that the United States would see this project through, raising the hopes of even the most skeptical members of the Baghdad government. The additional U.S. troops were all that was needed to increase security in key areas of Iraq such as Anbar province and in and around Baghdad, supporters of the surge claimed, and many wondered why the president had not moved in this direction earlier. According to two popular Iraqi bloggers with a large following in the United States, Mohammed and

Omar Fadhil, the surge resembled the old clear and hold strategy employed in the Vietnam War. People in Iraq, they claimed, had been waiting for the United States to commit the resources needed for the "hold" to materialize. The plan to secure Baghdad, according to the Fadhils, was "becoming stricter and gaining momentum by the day as more troops pour[ed] into the city, allowing for better implementation of the clear-and-hold strategy."[25] Others have suggested that the surge's initial victory was psychological. Enemies of the Baghdad government went into hiding, believing additional U.S. troops made it impossible for their militant groups to operate freely. The number of security tips about insurgent operations increased dramatically following the surge.

Other significant evidence of the surge's success was highlighted by the administration throughout the spring and summer of 2007. Perhaps the most important among these was the "turning" of the Sunnis in Anbar province and areas near Baghdad where sectarian violence was the highest. Beginning in mid-2006 in Ramadi (actually before the surge), the center of government in Anbar province some 110 kilometers from Baghdad, U.S. commanders made the decision to try to employ Sunni insurgents as irregular militias in battles against al Qaeda in Iraq (AQI). The feeling among the U.S. leadership was that AQI had gone too far in its program of violence and, as a result, had alienated many of its former tribal supporters. Organized first as Awakening Councils, then as Local Citizens Councils, eventually these former Sunni insurgents called themselves the Sons of Iraq. The U.S. command "turned" these insurgents away from direct attacks against U.S. troops and toward helping defeat AQI through the payment of large sums of money. Each new recruit was given upward of three hundred dollars per month, a significant sum in rural Iraq, to fight AQI instead of Americans or the Baghdad government.[26] Naturally, it was a great risk to employ and arm those who just weeks before had tried desperately to kill American troops and overthrow the Baghdad government, but many in the U.S. command thought the risk was well worth it given how violent Iraq had become in 2006.

There is theoretical support for such a move inside a broad-based counterinsurgency program. FM 3-24, the Army's new field manual explaining the new counterinsurgency program, moved beyond the "people's war" framework of classic counterinsurgency, where the population naturally sided with the government once the insurgents were removed from the scene, and toward a more sophisticated approach that took the organizational structure of traditional societies into account. Using social scientific thinking, the developers of FM 3-24 recognized the power of local and regional networks of people, understanding correctly that traditional populations were often organized along complex layers of local and regional structures. This was clearly the thinking in Ramadi and the rest of Anbar province when U.S. military leaders went to tribal leaders first to "turn" Sunni insurgents.

Its supporters also thought the surge was responsible for reducing sectarian violence in Iraq because it convinced key Shi'ite leaders, such as Muqtada al-Sadr, that it would be foolish to wage war against the Sunni minority and other Shi'ite factions in the face of increased U.S. troops. In the spring and summer of 2007, various Shi'ite militias attacked each other throughout southern Iraq and in eastern Baghdad. Some were rogue elements of al-Sadr's Mahdi Army, while others were younger militants who had grown too restless to control. In a surprise and risky move, the Baghdad government acted quickly to stop the violence, even using ISF forces against fellow Shi'ites to stem the tide of the fighting. Some ISF troops were fighting against their compatriots inside the various Shi'ite militias. Following this flurry of violence, in August 2007, al-Sadr's forces were involved in a series of attacks against another Shi'ite group, the Badr Corps, in the holy city of Karbala. Sensing an opportunity and a problem with the Karbala street fighting, al-Sadr decided to announce a "freeze" on the Mahdi Army's military activities. He believed that by standing down, he could take full control of the subnational Shi'ite movement with the blessing of the United States and the full support of the Baghdad government.

By standing down, al-Sadr elevated his political position among fellow Shi'ites who wanted revenge against Sunnis for years of brutality, but who also wanted an end to the day-to-day violence propped up by the U.S. counterinsurgency program. By repoliticizing his movement, something even General Petraeus recognized when he called al-Sadr a proud son of Mohammed,[27] al-Sadr moved toward his long-term goal of supreme subnational power. Yet many in the Bush administration drew the wrong lesson. Influential officials, most notably on the National Security staff, saw al-Sadr's freeze as a sign that the surge presented him with too many military problems and that he had thrown his power behind the Baghdad government. Military muscle had produced political change.

From the very beginning of the surge, nevertheless, there were signs that the Baghdad government was not responding well to American calls for reform. Congressional leaders had forced the Bush administration to report regularly on progress in Iraq on a number of social and political fronts in exchange for the surge, and many in Congress grew increasingly worried that the Baghdad government was only paying lip service to the idea of national concord and reconciliation. In September 2007 during hearings in Congress, General Petraeus and U.S. ambassador to Iraq Ryan Crocker claimed that

American troops and their Iraqi counterparts had significantly increased security in key areas of Baghdad and Anbar province and had "dealt numerous
blows to al-Qaeda in Iraq."[28] Petraeus claimed that "the security situation in
Iraq is improving, Iraqi elements are slowly taking on more of the responsibility for protecting their citizens." He concluded, "Coalition and Iraqi security
forces have made progress toward achieving security. As a result, the United
States will be in a position to reduce its forces in Iraq in the months ahead."[29]
Ambassador Crocker concurred. He conceded that it was impossible to give a
timeline for withdrawal, but he expressed his optimism that the new strategy
had produced some needed changes in Iraq already. Crocker believed that
"a secure, stable, democratic Iraq at peace with its neighbors is attainable."[30]

Congressional critics could hardly contain themselves. In an atmosphere
reminiscent of hearings during the Vietnam War, key members of both chambers lined up to criticize Petraeus and Crocker's optimistic reporting on Iraq.
Senator Joseph Biden (D-DE), chairman of the Foreign Relations Committee, began his panel's session suggesting that the surge had been designed
to create the space and time needed in Iraq for a political breakthrough in
Baghdad that simply had not happened. "It's time to turn the corner, in my
view. . . . We should stop the surge and start bringing our troops home."[31]
House member Tom Lantos (D-CA) called on a report issued in late August
by the Government Accountability Office, which had been charged with measuring progress on congressional benchmarks, which claimed that the Baghdad government failed to meet fifteen of the eighteen U.S. targets. According
to the report, "Key legislation has not been passed in Iraq, violence remains
high, and it is unclear whether the Iraqi government will spend $10 billion if
reconstruction funds as promised."[32] Lantos also pointed to a highly skeptical report issued by retired Marine Corps General James L. Jones, who had
been charged by Congress with investigating progress in Iraq. "No amount of
charts and statistics will improve its [the administration's Iraq policy] credibility," Lantos declared in the hearings.[33]

Other members of Congress cited a State Department report claiming
that religious freedom in Iraq had deteriorated sharply during the past year.
Many members of Congress believed that this was most significant because it
tested the Baghdad government's ability and willingness to bring Sunnis and
Kurds into national political life. There were other concerns as well. Some
in Congress suggested that human rights abuses seemed to be on the rise
in Iraq following the surge, not decreasing as the president and others had
predicted. The refugee crisis, long an issue in Iraq, was still a main obstacle
facing the Baghdad government, and for many in Congress it was a key measuring stick of progress in Iraq. Since the surge began, little progress had been

made on bringing Iraq's estimated 2.2 million refugees home or improving the lives of the roughly 1.6 million Iraqis who were internally displaced.[34] Since many of the refugees were Sunnis, congressional leaders simply saw the crisis as further proof that Baghdad had no interest in a government of national reconciliation.

The most heated comments, however, came from Senator Hillary Clinton of New York. Late in the hearings, she cast doubt on all that Petraeus had to say. You "have been made the de facto spokesman for what many of us believe to be a failed policy," she charged. "I think the reports you provide us really require the willing suspension of disbelief." Clinton went on to make the obvious reference to Robert McNamara, Kennedy and Johnson's secretary of defense, who routinely gave progress reports to Congress during the Vietnam War using charts, graphs, and statistics. "Although the charts tell part of the story, I don't think they tell the whole story," she warned. She said the "bottom-up" political reconciliation in Baghdad was at best "anecdotal," and then correctly pointed out that the turning of Sunnis in Anbar province, the most visible sign of surge success, had started well before the surge began. At the end of her remarks, the New York Democrat suggested that there was a lack of clarity in the general's response to earlier questions about American troop levels and political progress in Baghdad, hinting that Petraeus had been purposefully vague. She pressed, "Don't you think the American people deserve a very specific answer about what is expected from our country in the face of the failure of the Iraqi government and its failure to achieve its political agenda?"

General Petraeus looked irritated, but responded calmly. "I don't see quite as big a difference as you do," he said. "I would be very hard pressed at that time to recommend a continuation of our current troop levels" if conditions on the ground were the same in a year as they are now. He added that Senator Clinton's question was "quite a bit hypothetical."[35] There was a tinge of politics in Petraeus's response. He understood that the next president of the United States would most likely come from the Senate Foreign Relations Committee. Most political observers agreed that the Iraq War would be a key issue in the next presidential race and that voters supported an end to the war. The Senate Foreign Relations Committee gave key Democrats a platform to attack those who supported Bush's policies in Iraq.

The congressional hearings and the surge itself highlighted the major problems of a counterinsurgency operation. Because the foreign power is so dependent on the host nation to build bridges to its people and become the providers of public welfare, the foreign power often loses influence over the host government. Clearly the Maliki government understood that the surge was the Bush administration's effort to change the geometry in Iraq by making needed security changes, but to claim political success ultimately Bush needed Maliki to change his ways. The surge had led to operational success on the battlefield, but it did little to change the character of the Baghdad government. It was still illiberal and undemocratic. The major problems facing Iraq stemmed from the lack of institutional strengthening and the failure to embed compliance mechanisms into the Iraqi constitution. These factors gave the Baghdad government the "green light" to isolate its enemies into hardened communities of the disenfranchised. The major problem in contemporary Iraq is that the substantive framework agreements—from the interim constitution to the new constitution to the status of forces agreement—were weak and unenforceable. In short, there was no check on the government's power.

These shortcomings were constantly present in Iraq, and their legacy remains an intractable problem. During the years of the most intense fighting, the government's treatment of refugees highlighted its most significant failures. Refugees have always been a product of war, but the Iraqi refugee crisis is one of the largest forced population movements in the region since 1948.[36] According to Antonio Guterres, the former United Nations High Commissioner for Refugees, no other political issue threatened Baghdad's ability to govern more.[37] From 2006 to 2007, every day an estimated two thousand Iraqis were forced to leave their homes against their will. At the height of sectarian violence, Iraq had 1.6 million internally displaced persons (IDPs).[38] Added to those numbers were the estimated 2.2 million who had left Iraq altogether for sanctuary in Syria, Jordan, and other neighboring countries. Taking on Iraqi refugees put an enormous burden on the host countries and often led to political instability as ideological tensions inside Iraq spilled over its borders. There were also huge social and economic problems for the refugees. According to Human Rights First, an NGO working to secure safe passage for Iraqi refugees to the United States, "most refugees cannot obtain work authorization and many refugees lack legal residence rights."[39]

As international funds for support of Iraqi refugees declined, host countries experienced frustration and fatigue, leading to antirefugee feelings and policies. For example, the leading U.S. ally in the region, Saudi Arabia, constructed a seven-billion-dollar high-tech barrier on its borders to keep unwanted refugees out. Kuwait and Egypt embraced restrictive clauses in their immigration laws to limit Iraqi refugees. While many Iraqi refugees had temporary permission to remain in Jordan and Syria, by 2007 their visas had expired. They lived in constant fear of being returned to Iraq against their will because neither Jordan nor Syria is party to the 1951 Convention Relating to the Status of Refugees. One of the chief principles in this Geneva Convention is that of non-refoulement—a refugee's right to not be returned to a country where he or she is in danger of persecution.

Several disturbing trends illustrated the government's refusal to take national reconciliation seriously notwithstanding the allegedly salutary effects of the surge. One of the more serious was the number of IDPs forced to leave their homes for neighborhoods of like ethnic and religious groups surrounded by protective walls and barriers. Baghdad was once a city of mixed ethnicity and religion. The hardening of Sunni communities to the west of the Tigris in the Dora and Huriya neighborhoods, however, has created a sectarian city. This may have led to a short-term decrease in violence, but these hardened communities might also be the source of future violence. According to Elizabeth Ferris, an expert on refugees and national security, IDPs represent both "a consequence and contributing factor to sectarian polarization."[40]

IDPs are not merely a product of sectarian violence, but rather a key strategy of insurgents and militias seeking to control national and humanitarian geographic space. Johanna Grombach Wagner, adviser to the Director General of the International Committee of the Red Cross, explains that the term "espace humanitaire" was coined by former Médecins Sans Frontières (Doctors Without Borders) President Rony Brauman, who described it in the mid-1990s as "a space of freedom in which we are free to evaluate needs, free to monitor the distribution and use of relief goods, and free to have a dialogue with the people."[41] Under international humanitarian law (as codified by the 1949 Geneva Conventions and their Additional Protocols), the primary responsibility for the survival of the population lies with the authorities, or, in the case of occupation, with the occupying power. If the responsible authorities do not provide the supplies the civilian population needs for survival, they are obliged to permit the free passage of relief consignments. While the United States had cooperated with several different international agencies— the United Nations and the International Red Cross, to name just two—it also insisted as part of its larger counterinsurgency program that Baghdad bear the brunt of the responsibility for the care of IDPs.

But Baghdad's slow response created problems for Bush and then Barack Obama. The Iraqi government delayed incorporating the Guiding Principles on Internal Displacement into any national legislation, nor did it guarantee the basic human rights of IDPs, including freedom of movement and nondiscrimination. There were also vast shortages of food in some neighborhoods, drawing into question the Baghdad government's distribution system.[42] These shortages were so acute in the Sunni areas of Baghdad that many observers concluded that the lack of food was a purposeful policy to weaken the Sunni resistance to the government.[43]

Many U.S. policy makers supported the relocation of Sunnis into hardened communities because such action decreased the violence and created an opportunity for the Baghdad government to illustrate its resolve and commitment to national political reconciliation.[44] By removing international organizations—such as the UN and the Red Cross—as the caretakers of the public welfare and replacing them with the national government, many in Washington believed that relocated Sunnis would be dependent on the government for their very survival and that this dependence would foster political compromise.[45]

It took several years for the Maliki government to understand the political importance of such issues, but eventually in 2009 there were signs of progress. Obama's expert on human rights and national security, Samantha Power, whom the president appointed U.S. ambassador to the UN in 2013, monitored events in Baghdad full-time in order to illustrate how sensitive this issue was to the White House. Obama made it clear that the American people were putting pressure on Maliki to see a dramatic change in Baghdad. It was high time for his government to step up to the demands of national leadership, some administration officials believed, and a U.S. withdrawal would foster that development. Although Obama remained generally positive about the strides Maliki had made in office, others in the administration were still concerned about democracy and human rights inside Iraq.

Despite the Obama administration's initial diplomatic efforts, there remained the perception that Sunnis remained marginalized. The continued disqualification of political candidates, including the candidacy of Saleh al-Mutlaq, a prominent Sunni, in the March 2010 election was a source of great discomfort in Sunni neighborhoods all over Iraq. More disturbing still were reports that the Baghdad government substantially increased death sentences against Sunnis in custody in the run-up to the March 2010 elections. According to Amnesty International, forced confessions led to numerous death sentences in the months prior to the U.S. withdrawal in an effort to intimidate Sunnis.[46] A 2009 United Nations report on human rights abuses in Iraq suggested that violations against Sunnis in prisons and on Iraqi streets were on the rise and that "security in Iraq may not be sustainable unless significant steps are taken to uphold the rule of law and human rights."[47]

Many Sunnis had long complained about their treatment by Maliki's Shi'ite-dominated government. Human rights abuses at a secret prison in the old Muthanna airport in West Baghdad and in Baghdad's al Rusafa detention facility were commonplace. Researchers at Human Rights Watch often told of beatings, whippings, electric shock, and teeth pulling in the government's prisons.[48] Sunnis had seen the March 2010 elections as the moment of their return to national politics, only to find that they had been excluded by the Maliki government once again. Ayad Allawi, a secular Shi'ite and Iraq's former interim prime minister, became the standard bearer in the 2010 election for disposed Sunnis. Born in 1946, Allawi had belonged to the Ba'athist Party before fleeing Iraq in 1976. A longtime critic of Saddam Hussein, he had survived several assassination attempts while living in exile in London. Allawi returned to Iraq in 2003 following the American intervention, a policy he supported wholeheartedly by claiming, "There are no words that can express the debt of gratitude that future generations of Iraqis will owe to Americans."[49]

Although Allawi's Iraqiya bloc (Iraqi National Movement) initially won the national election in March by two seats, it took nearly ten months to sort out a power-sharing arrangement after Maliki challenged the election results. The power-sharing agreement of December 2010 created a shared governance structure that allowed Allawi to name the defense minister, a position important for Sunnis who felt they had been subject to constant harassment by the government's security forces. Maliki refused to approve Allawi's selection, however, and instead appointed himself "as the minister of both interior and defense, claiming that because of the country's tenuous security environment he needed more time to vet the candidates."[50] This left the government in the awkward position of having two prominent leaders and no clear policy agreements.

On the eve of the American withdrawal in December 2011 came another alarming report about the Maliki government. On December 12, 2011, Maliki moved swiftly to consolidate his political power in advance of the U.S. withdrawal by rounding up hundreds of former Ba'athist Party members and evicting Western companies from the Green Zone, the physical center of the government. The Maliki government explained its actions as a deliberate response to a "tip from Libya's government that revealed Col. Muammar el-Qaddafi was working with insurgents to stage a coup."[51] While some arrested did have ties to Saddam's government, most were "laborers, political adversaries of the government, the elderly."[52] One Western analyst believed that Maliki routinely used threats of a coup to attack his political rivals. "Baathism here is a symbol that Maliki uses as his bogyman. It gives them the leeway to go around arresting people. It's about a climate of fear."[53] The Obama White House responded to the raids with conspicuous silence.

The administration's refusal to draw attention to Baghdad's attacks on Sunnis in 2011 intensified the climate of fear inside Iraq as the date for America's withdrawal approached. Many Sunnis believed that rather than creating a national government of goodwill and concord, U.S. intervention had provided enough firepower for the Shi'ites to seize control of the country. Sunnis who had sided with the United States during the surge worried that no one would protect them after the American withdrawal. They feared that all Sunnis would be associated with Saddam's brutal rule, and that Shi'ites and Kurds would seek retribution under the passive eye of the Maliki government.

Some of these fears were realized in the fall of 2011, shortly before the American troop withdrawal. In October Baghdad's security forces arrested over six hundred Sunnis in Salahuddin province, claiming that they were planning a coup. That same month, more than a hundred professors at Tikrit University, in Saddam's hometown, were fired for alleged Ba'athist connections.[54] In the week before the American withdrawal, Baghdad insisted that the former Sunni Awakening Councils disband and decommission their arms. Sheik Ahmed Abu Risha, one of America's staunchest Sunni allies and a leader of one militia estimated at eighty thousand members, suggested that Sunnis would not turn in their weapons. "They want to defend themselves," he reported.[55]

Events in early 2012 did little to stabilize Iraq. Following the American troop withdrawal in December 2011, several radical Sunni groups launched raids against key Shi'a shrines and civilians. On July 23, 2012, AQI, a Sunni-led terrorist group, launched coordinated attacks on over a dozen cities, killing over a hundred innocent people. The attacks, Iraq's deadliest since the U.S. withdrawal, came only days after AQI threatened to resume its offensive against the Baghdad government. The new campaign was called Breaking the Walls, a reference to the walls that surround Sunni communities in their "hardened state." One radical Sunni leader, Abu Bakr al-Baghdadi, claimed that the "majority of Sunnis support al Qaeda and are waiting for its return."[56] To calm Sunni fears, the Maliki government announced in late July 2012 that it would allow some former Sunni officers to return to their posts in the armed services. Following Saddam's overthrow, the CPA dismissed all officers with connections to the Ba'athist Party, causing tremendous turmoil and animosity. Most Sunnis saw the government's gesture as too little and too late. Ayad Allawi described Iraq in the summer of 2012 this way: "Things are not good. Things are bad. The society is split and we don't have a real democracy—we have a mockery."[57]

The U.S. State Department seemed to agree. In its official "2011 Human Rights Report for Iraq," the Bureau of Democracy, Human Rights and Labor reported,

> During the year the following significant human rights problems were reported: arbitrary or unlawful deprivation of life; extremist and terrorist bombings and executions; disappearances; torture and other cruel, inhu-

man, or degrading treatment or punishment; poor conditions in pretrial detention and prison facilities; arbitrary arrest and detention; impunity; denial of fair public trials; delays in resolving property restitution claims; insufficient judicial institutional capacity; arbitrary interference with privacy and home; limits on freedoms of speech, press, and assembly and extremist threats and violence; limits on religious freedom due to extremist threats and violence; restrictions on freedom of movement; large numbers of internally displaced persons (IDPs) and refugees; lack of transparency and significant, widespread corruption at all levels of government; constraints on international organizations and nongovernmental organizations' (NGOs) investigations of alleged violations of human rights; discrimination against and societal abuses of women and ethnic, religious, and racial minorities; human trafficking; societal discrimination and violence against individuals based on sexual orientation; and limited exercise of labor rights.[58]

Furthermore, the State Department concluded that "continuing violence, corruption, and organizational dysfunction undermined the government's ability to protect human rights."[59] Since the American withdrawal, this state of insecurity has become the norm again in Iraq. In 2013, there were several attacks that killed more than a hundred people, and there is no end to the violence in sight.

Political corruption remains a significant problem in Iraq today. In 2012 Iraq scored an 18 on the 100-point Corruption Perception Index scale, placing it "in such company as Haiti (19) and Myanmar (15)."[60] Most Iraqis today believe that provision of basic government services, such as electricity and water, has actually gotten worse due to rampant corruption.[61] According to one former Iraqi cabinet minister, "the Iraqi government is an institutionalized kleptocracy."[62] Others have called Baghdad the "City of Corruption."[63]

Surely this is not the legacy U.S. policy makers intended to bequeath to Iraq when they argued for a preemptive strike against Saddam Hussein. But nation building has always been a perilous task. It is far more difficult to alter a society's political outlook than U.S. policy makers are willing to admit. American military power has become a virtue, but it has political limits. This is certainly the most important lesson we can learn from the Iraq War. The Baghdad government has made significant reforms since Saddam's rule. And it now seems clear that Iraq is no longer a threat to its neighbors, and the replacement of Maliki by Haider al-Abadi as prime minister in summer 2014 is seen by many as an improvement. Still, basic human rights violations occur in Iraq with frequency, and many in the government are complicit. Violence continues unabated, and the Iraqi economy is in a shambles. Billions of U.S. dollars and thousands of lives lost have not changed the fundamental political problems in Iraq.

That Iraq was so impervious to change was and is frustrating to Washington policy makers. Despite America's enormous investment in the war, the occupation, and the withdrawal, Washington has exercised limited influence over their allies in Baghdad. Because counterinsurgency depends so heavily on the host government to deliver the social, economic, and political goods to its people, a foreign power loses initiative and leverage. Baghdad officials knew quite well that the United States was completely dependent on them for success beyond operational tactics, and this decreased America's ability to dictate terms to its allies. When Washington demanded needed reforms, those reforms were slow to materialize or never came at all. This is the nature of counterinsurgency and nation building in the modern world. Now that the Islamic State in Iraq and the Levant (ISIL) threatens to topple the Baghdad government, the need for reform is even more desperate. Will Iraq's allies come to its defense if Baghdad does not form a government of reconciliation and national concord?

Furthermore, the United States lost considerable power, prestige, and influence in the region by promising revolutionary change and then not delivering it. Insurgent movements have been emboldened by America's failures in Iraq, convincing their followers that the United States is impotent. Radicalized Islamic groups, like ISIL, strike at will inside Syria and Iraq, knowing full well that there is little political support in Washington for another military intervention in the region so closely on the heels of the failures of the latest wars. Now that ISIL is on the march against Baghdad, can the Obama administration convince voters and allies that Iraq is again worth saving? And can the United States help save Iraq at acceptable costs and risks? These questions have certainly been made more difficult to answer given America's recent history in the region.

NOTES

1 John Lewis Gaddis, *Surprise, Security, and the American Experience* (Cambridge, MA: Harvard University Press, 2004), 81.

2 For an opposing argument, see Peter R. Mansoor, *Surge: My Journey with General David Petraeus and the Remaking of the Iraq War* (New Haven: Yale University Press, 2013).

3 Rajiv Chandrasekaran, *Imperial Life in the Emerald City: Inside Baghdad's Green Zone* (New York: Knopf, 2006), 68.

4 Ibid., 101.

5 James Dobbins, "Who Lost Iraq?," *Foreign Affairs* 86 (September–October 2007): 67.

6 Central Intelligence Agency, *World Fact Book on Iraq* (Washington, DC: GPO, 2005).

7 Ibid.

8 Ibid.

9 Ibid.

10 Bob Herbert, "The Destroyers," *New York Times*, February 13, 2006.

11 Anthony H. Cordesman, "One Year On: Nation Building in Iraq" (Center for Strategic and International Studies working paper, April 16, 2004), 15.

12 L. Paul Bremer III, *My Year in Iraq* (New York: Thresholds Editions, 2006), 10.

13 Kenneth Pollack, "After Saddam: Assessing the Reconstruction of Iraq," *Foreign Affairs* 83 (January–February 2004), http://www.udel.edu/globalagenda/2004/student/readings/FAAfterSaddam-Pollack.html.

14 Quoted in Michael Gordon and General Bernard Trainor, *Cobra II: The Inside Story of the Invasion and Occupation of Iraq* (New York: Pantheon, 2006), 567.

15 "Letter from the Secretary of State of the United States to Lauro Baja, Jr., President of the Security Council, United Nations, 5 June 2004" (Annex, United Nations Security Council, Resolution 1546, June 8, 2004).

16 Ibid.

17 Peter Baker, "U.S. Not Winning in Iraq, Bush Says for 1st Time," *Washington Post*, December 20, 2006.

18 Gallup poll, http://www.gallup.com/poll/1633/iraq.aspx.

19 "Measuring Stability in Iraq, March 2008 Report to Congress in Accordance with the Department of Defense Appropriations Act of 2008" (Washington, DC: Department of Defense, 2008), 18. For deaths in Iraq, see "Iraq Body Count," http://www.iraqbodycount.org/.

20 White House press secretary, January 10, 2007.

21 Ibid.

22 "Iraq First: The National Security Strategy of Iraq" (Republic of Iraq, Office of the National Security Advisor to the Iraqi Prime Minister, July 22, 2007), http://smallwarsjournal.com/blog/iraqi-national-security-strategy.

23 For the most interesting trending, see "Iraq Body Count," http://www.iraqbodycount.org/database/.

24 Ahmed al-Rubaye, "Seven Questions: Is the Surge Working in Iraq?," *Foreign Policy*, September 26, 2007, http://www.foreignpolicy.com/articles/2007/09/25/seven_questions_is_the_surge_working_in_iraq.

25 Robert Kagan, "The Surge Is Succeeding," *Washington Post*, March 11, 2007.

26 Thomas Ricks, *The Gamble: General David Petraeus and the American Military Adventure in Iraq* (New York: Penguin, 2009), 209.

27 Ibid., 267.

28 "General Petraeus Testifies before Congress on the Status of Iraq," *Congressional Quarterly Wire*, September 10, 2007.

29 Ibid.

30 Ibid.

31 Ricks, *Gamble*, 247.

32 Anne Flaherty and Anne Gearan, "White House Pushes Back on Iraq Report," *Washington Post*, August 30, 2007.

33 See Lantos's comments at http://www.foreignaffairs.house.gov/110/lantos091007.htm.

34 United Nations Commission on Human Rights, "United Nations Refugee Agency–Iraq, Country Operations Profile"; UNHCR Iraq Fact Sheet, "Crisis in Iraq" (September 1, 2008); and OCHA Iraq Office in Amman, "Humanitarian Crisis in Iraq: Facts and Figures" (Representative of the United Nations Assistance Mission in Iraq, November 13, 2007).

35 "General Petraeus Testifies before Congress on the Status of Iraq," *Congressional Quarterly Wire*, September 10, 2007.

36 *Forced Migration Review* (June 2007), http://www.fmreview.org/issues.

37 Ibid.

38 UNHCR, "United Nations Refugee Agency–Iraq"; UNHCR Iraq Fact Sheet, "Crisis in Iraq"; and OCHA Iraq Office in Amman, "Humanitarian Crisis in Iraq."

39 Human Rights First, "Iraqi Refugee Crisis," http://www.humanrightsfirst.org/our-work/refugee-protection/iraqi-refugee-crisis.

40 Elizabeth Ferris, "The Looming Crisis: Displacement and Security in Iraq" (press release, Brookings Institute, August 5, 2008), http://www.brookings.edu/~/media/research/files/papers/2008/8/iraq%20ferris/08_iraq_ferris.pdf.

41 Johanna Grombach Wagner, "An IHL/CRC Perspective on Humanitarian Space," *Humanitarian Exchange Magazine* 32 (December 2005), http://www.odihpn.org/humanitarian-exchange-magazine/issue-32/an-ihl/icrc-perspective-on-humanitarian-space.

42 United Nations Office for the Coordination of Human Affairs, "Acute Shortages in Clash-hit Baghdad Suburbs" (April 10, 2008), http://www.irinnews.org/report/77701/iraq-acute-shortages-in-clash-hit-baghdad-suburbs.

43 United Nations, Humanitarian Coordinator on Behalf of Humanitarian Agencies and Organisations, "Humanitarian Situation Report on Baghdad, Basrah, Wassit and Babylon" (March 30, 2008), http://reliefweb.int/report/iraq/iraq-humanitarian-situation-report-baghdad-basrah-wassit-and-babylon-30-mar-2008.

44 Ken Pollack, "The Battle for Baghdad," *National Interest*, August 25, 2009, http://nationalinterest.org/article/the-battle-for-baghdad-3216.

45 Marc Lynch, "What Does Political Science Literature on Civil Wars Really Say about Iraq?," *Foreign Policy*, September 7, 2009, http://www.foreignpolicy.com/posts/2009/09/07/civil_wars_literature_and_iraq.

46 Amnesty International, "Iraq Must Halt Spiraling Death Sentences," January 18, 2010, https://www.amnesty.org/en/news-and-updates/iraq-must-halt-spiralling-death-sentences-20100118.

47 United Nations, Assistance Mission for Iraq, "Human Rights Report, 1 January–30 June 2009," 4, http://www.ohchr.org/Documents/Countries/IQ/UNAMI_Human_Rights_Report15_January_June_2009_EN.pdf.

48 Samer Muscati, "Iraqis Torturing Iraqis," *New York Times*, May 4, 2010.

49 As quoted in Peter Hahn, *Mission Accomplished? The United States and Iraq since World War I* (New York: Oxford University Press, 2012), 178.

50 Michael Schmidt and Tim Arango, "Bitter Feud between Top Iraqi Leaders Stalls Government," *New York Times*, June 25, 2011.

51 Jack Healy, Tim Arango, and Michael Schmidt, "Premier's Actions in Iraq Raise U.S. Concerns," *New York Times*, December 12, 2011.

52 Ibid.

53 Ibid.

54 Ibid.

55 Andrew Kramer, "U.S. Leaving Iraqi Comrades-in-Arms in Limbo," *New York Times*, December 13, 2011.

56 Associated Press, "Iraq Attacks Kill 110 in Deadliest Day in 2 Years," *USA Today*, July 23, 2012.

57 Ibid.

58 U.S. State Department, Bureau of Democracy, Human Rights and Labor, "Country Report 2011, Iraq," http://www.state.gov/documents/organization/204572.pdf .

59 Ibid.

60 Matt Bradley, "Corruption Continues to Plague Iraq," *Wall Street Journal*, June 21, 2013.

61 Ibid.

62 Patrick Cockburn, "The American Legacy in Iraq," *Nation*, April 8, 2013.

63 Ibid.

13

The Lessons and Legacies of the War in Afghanistan

AARON B. O'CONNELL

"However beautiful the strategy," Winston Churchill once quipped, "you should occasionally look at the results."[1] This is good advice for those seeking to understand the thirteen-year-long war in Afghanistan. Governments undertake wars for specific political purposes, assign their forces tasks accordingly, and, in the end, either accomplish their goals or do not. Thus we must begin by asking these questions: What were the U.S. goals in waging war in Afghanistan? What resources were applied toward those goals? What were the outcomes? And finally, what lessons can one take from this longest war in American history?

Clearly identifying the war's goals is difficult because they changed over time. What began in 2001 as a CIA and Special Forces mission to topple the Taliban and destroy the leadership of the al Qaeda terrorist network evolved quickly into a UN-backed mission to stabilize and rebuild Afghanistan. Once the NATO coalition took command in 2003, the missions further expanded and proliferated. Over the ensuing three years, as U.S. attention shifted increasingly toward Iraq, the United States lacked sufficient resources to make any progress in Afghanistan and the Taliban returned in force. Upon taking office in 2009, President Barack Obama responded to the deterioration by narrowing the war's goals and flooding the country with money and troops. Despite the previous administration's early and accurate concerns about the perils of nation building, the new approach led the Americans to fund almost every government program in Afghanistan. By the final years of the war, the United States was simultaneously fighting the Taliban, recruiting and training the Afghan army and police, advising every government ministry, running the largest literacy program in Afghanistan, and even sponsoring youth orchestras and refurbishing sports stadiums.[2] None of it defeated the Taliban or stabilized the country. By the end of 2014, as the war settled into a stalemate, the Americans handed operations over to the Afghan government and came home, leaving a residual force of ten thousand Americans behind to continue training the Afghans and conduct counterterrorism missions. At that point all the major combatants—the United States, NATO, the Afghan government and the Taliban—claimed victory.

Like so many previous wars in Afghanistan, the first months went surprisingly well.[3] Just days after the September 11 attacks, President George W. Bush issued an ultimatum to Afghanistan's Taliban government, which had hosted Osama bin Laden and his al Qaeda network since 1996.[4] When the Taliban refused the president's demands that they turn over al Qaeda's leadership and dismantle its camps, the president dispatched a small team of CIA personnel and about two thousand Marines, soldiers, and Special Forces personnel who made contact with the remnants of the Taliban's ethnic and political enemies: the Northern Alliance. The Americans' objectives were threefold: topple the Taliban government, destroy al Qaeda's training bases, and capture or kill all terrorists connected to the network.[5]

Two of those three goals were accomplished almost immediately. Supported by American air power, the Northern Alliance retook the country in a few weeks. By the end of the year, the Taliban had fled Kabul, abandoned its camps, and dispersed throughout Afghanistan and Pakistan.[6] Had the United States decided that toppling the Taliban government and ejecting al Qaeda from Afghanistan were the only goals of the war, it could have declared victory before Christmas. (That victory, however, would have likely been short-lived, for without a power-sharing government, international aid, and some kind of security force, the country would have quickly fallen back into civil war.) At this point the United Nations stepped in. Recognizing Afghanistan's instability, and aware that its impact could reach beyond national borders, the UN sent representatives to meet in Bonn, Germany, in December 2001. The resulting Bonn Agreement committed the member states to support a transitional government and facilitate national elections. Accompanying these limited objectives were other, more difficult ones: "promoting national reconciliation, lasting peace, stability and respect for human rights in the country."[7] To do all of this, the UN created a 4,500-man International Security Assistance Force (ISAF), which operated only in Kabul and its immediate environs.[8] American forces—numbering between six and eight thousand throughout 2002—operated independently from ISAF at first, because U.S. leaders neither wanted to lead ISAF nor to place American troops under a foreign commander.[9]

As U.S. forces continued to hunt al Qaeda's remnants in Afghanistan and ISAF prepared the country for elections, the force levels began to rise. In 2003 the UN expanded ISAF's mandate to the whole of the country and the NATO alliance assumed command of all international forces in Afghanistan.[10] (Senior White House officials initially opposed the expansion because they worried that the sort of nation-building mission embraced by the UN would require more troops, create more friction with the Afghans, and eventually encourage an insurgency—predictions that would all eventually prove accurate.)[11] A year later, in 2004, a reasonably fair national election elevated Hamid Karzai to the presidency, accompanied by two vice presidents who represented Afghanistan's other principal political and ethnic factions. By the end of 2004, there were twenty-five thousand troops in Afghanistan, two-thirds of whom were American.[12]

Karzai's election did not signal the end of the Afghanistan mission; in fact, even before Karzai assumed the presidency, the United States and its partners had committed themselves to a host of additional military and nonmilitary tasks: manning Provincial Reconstruction Teams; disarming and reintegrating militias; supporting rule of law; creating a functioning judiciary; and ultimately, doing "everything—including the development of economic alternatives—to reduce and eventually eliminate the threat of drug production and trafficking."[13] In early 2006, the Americans agreed to an even more expansive UN agreement—"The Afghanistan Compact"—that established goals and timelines for security, governance, economic and social development, and counternarcotics. The Compact's fifty-two benchmarks asked for international help for almost every function governments undertake, from managing natural resources to road construction, health and nutrition, higher education, poverty reduction, and private-sector development.[14] By the end of the year, there were forty-three thousand troops in Afghanistan, with the United States accounting for half of the total.[15]

Progress on those goals was spotty at best, and between 2006 and 2008, as Iraq burned and U.S. attention drifted from Afghanistan, the Taliban reinfiltrated from Pakistan and began setting up shadow governments in the southern and eastern regions of Afghanistan. ISAF's numbers grew to sixty-three thousand soldiers, an enormous increase from the original invasion force, but still woefully insufficient to stabilize the country. A separate but complementary insurgency emerged in Pakistan in 2007 and quickly gained strength, threatening Pakistan's stability and worsening its already-bad relations with India. The War in Iraq, which by 2008 required 150,000 American troops, made it impossible for the United States to commit the resources needed to stop Afghanistan's deterioration.[16]

When President Obama took office in January 2009, he inherited a war that was a very different war from the one that began in 2001. The risk of al Qaeda attack coming from Afghanistan had been reduced, but the failure to stabilize the country, coupled with the disaster of Iraq, had inflamed Islamist sentiments worldwide. Afghans' patience with the Westerners had begun to wane and pervasive corruption in the Afghan government was steadily delegitimizing the Karzai regime. Pakistan was in freefall, with over eleven thousand people killed that year alone in 732 major incidents of terrorist violence.[17] The Obama administration was split on how to respond. Some urged the president to shift focus away from the Taliban and to concentrate on targeting al Qaeda, while others warned that a Taliban victory could cause Pakistan to collapse, which might lead to another Indo-Pakistani conflict, this time with nuclear weapons.[18]

President Obama deliberated for a full year before announcing a troop surge that raised force levels in Afghanistan to 142,000 men. He also narrowed the mission and lowered the bar for success. Instead of striving for all fifty-two benchmarks in the Afghanistan Compact, the Obama administration resolved that the United States would work "to disrupt, dismantle, and defeat al Qaeda and to prevent Afghanistan from being a safe haven for international terrorism." This latter goal did not require total victory over the Taliban. Rather, if ISAF could "degrade the Taliban insurgency while building sufficient Afghan capacity to secure and govern their country," the Afghans could win the war on their own.[19] That same year, President Karzai won re-election, but the election was marred by extensive fraud and violence, and American pressure for a runoff election severely strained U.S.-Afghan political relations. Parliamentary elections a year later were similarly problematic and paralyzed the Afghan government for most of 2011.

Despite President Obama's insistence that the new mission was "not fully-resourced counterinsurgency or nation-building," by late 2010, that is exactly what it had become.[20] In keeping with the new counterinsurgency (COIN) tactics that had halted the violence in the Iraq War, the new ISAF Commander, General Stanley McChrystal, insisted that "we will not win simply by killing insurgents." Rather, the coalition needed "to provide a convincing and sustainable sense of justice and well-being to a weary and skeptical populace. We must turn perceptions from fear and uncertainty to trust and confidence." Specific tasks flowed from that mission, which the commander distributed in writing: "Be a positive force in the community; shield them from harm; foster stability. Use local economic initiatives to increase employment and give young men an alternative to the insurgency. . . . Insist government officials serve the people; support those who do. Confront corrupt officials. Protecting the people requires protection from physical harm and abuse of power. With your Afghan counterparts, work to change corrupt behavior that adversely affects the people and the mission."[21]

In July 2010 General David Petraeus took over ISAF's leadership and continued the counterinsurgency efforts McChrystal had begun. Petraeus seemed the perfect officer to salvage the war: besides a glowing army record, he had a Ph.D. from Princeton University and had both developed and implemented the counterinsurgency doctrine that first reversed the tide of violence in Iraq. Unfortunately, what worked for a time in Iraq never took hold in Afghanistan.[22] Violence rose to the highest levels of the war. Over the following four years, ISAF fought the Taliban to a stalemate, handed the war off to the Afghan government, and sent its troops home. At the time of this publication, in 2015, just ten thousand troops remain in Afghanistan to conduct special operations and to train and assist the Afghan National Security Forces. By the end of the year those numbers will decline by half, and by the end of 2016 the last of the troops will come home.[23]

Given how often the goals changed, it seems clear that the United States and its partners lost focus early on and never recovered. Goals and resources were aligned at the outset, but became increasingly mismatched in later years. In the first months of the war, when military forces were pursuing military tasks (toppling the Taliban, hunting al Qaeda, and destroying training camps), the United States had operational momentum and the support of the Afghan people. As the UN and NATO took over, and the United States shifted its focus to Iraq, the missions became more ambitious and decidedly nonmilitary: increasing employment, changing corrupt behavior, turning fear into trust. From 2002 until 2009 the ISAF coalition had neither the right tools for the job nor enough of them. The shift to a counterinsurgency approach (done, it seems, at least partly against the president's wishes) increased the resources dramatically, but also put in the military's hands tasks that more properly belonged to other instruments of national power. By 2010, the U.S. military was attempting exactly what Bush administration leaders had warned against in 2002: using violence and nearly unlimited amounts of money to attempt to transform Afghanistan into a modern, liberal state.[24]

Evaluating Costs

From the goals of war, we now turn to its costs. What resources did the United States invest; what costs did it bear?

The most important costs of war are human. During the thirteen years of American combat operations, 2,352 U.S. military personnel were killed in Afghanistan. Of those killed, 71 percent were soldiers and another 19 percent were Marines; sailors and airmen accounted for the remainder. All but 51 of those killed were men. Of those who died, 85 percent were Caucasian, 8 percent were African American, and other races accounted for the final 7 percent. Three-quarters of the dead were age thirty or below. And, as in all

previous wars, something other than enemy fire caused a significant proportion—22 percent—of the deaths: 366 died from accidents and illnesses and
another 116 from self-inflicted wounds.[25] Another 1,582 private contractors
employed by the U.S. government died in the war as well, bringing the total
American deaths to 3,934.[26] The total number of nonfatal casualties (injuries)
is 20,067, including over 700 amputees.[27]

These numbers are small in comparison to America's previous wars. At the
Battle of Antietam in the American Civil War, more soldiers died in a single
day than throughout the entire Afghan War.[28] The Vietnam War had twenty-
five times as many American deaths and World War II had almost two hundred times in less than one-third the duration. Indeed, of the twelve major
wars in American history, only the Gulf War (383 deaths) and the War of 1812
(2,260 deaths) have been less costly in terms of total American lives lost.

Death, of course, reached beyond the American forces. The Afghan War
was fought by a coalition of fifty separate nations, and non-American ISAF
forces suffered an additional 1,124 deaths.[29] There are no good estimates on
the total number of Taliban killed or wounded in the war. Afghan National
Security Forces (ANSF) casualties have been closely guarded by the Afghan
Ministry of Defense, but the Brookings Institution estimates that 13,729 Afghan soldiers and police have been killed since 2001 and another 16,511 have
been wounded.[30]

Military deaths are only a small part of the total human cost of the war. By
far, Afghan civilians have been the greatest victims of the conflict. Although
a comprehensive accounting of their deaths and injuries is impossible, the
UN has verified at least 17,774 civilian deaths and 29,971 injuries since 2009.
Civilian casualties are harder to gauge before that date, but the best estimates
show that at least another 7,099 were killed and just under 10,000 more were
wounded. (Tallies of injuries occurring before 2007 are possible only by cull-
ing press reports, which are often inaccurate and always incomplete.) Even
with these evidentiary problems, it is likely that Afghans have suffered at least
63,000 casualties between December 2001 and January 2015: roughly 24,000
deaths and another 39,000 injuries.[31] None of these figures include the indirect deaths or injuries of the war—those caused by exposure, starvation,
lack of clean water, and myriad other problems experienced by the 800,000
Afghans who have become internally displaced since 2001.[32]

The details of the war's casualties are important. Scholars estimate that
between 1,000 and 3,400 civilians were killed in the first three months of
fighting, as the Americans used air power to topple the Taliban.[33] From 2002
to 2006, as the Taliban fled and then slowly reinsinuated itself into Afghan
society, violence dropped off dramatically. Two thousand more Afghans died

from the fighting over those five years—roughly one every day.[34] Thereafter, as the United States and NATO increased troops and fighting grew more fierce, the civilian death toll began to rise again: from 1,500 in 2007 to 2,400 in 2009, to a high of 3,699 in 2014. By the UN's estimates, over 70 percent of the civilian casualties have been caused by the Taliban and over half of all civilian deaths (15,210) have occurred since 2010, when the United States began surging forces into the country.[35]

Dollars spent are another cost of the Afghan War, although a full accounting of the financial costs will be impossible for years to come. The 2001 ejection of the Taliban cost approximately $21 billion, and annual costs averaged $18 billion per year from 2002 through 2006. As Afghanistan's security worsened after 2006, the United States responded with significant troop increases. As a result, the costs of the war doubled between 2006 and 2008 and doubled again between 2008 and 2010.[36] U.S. spending peaked in 2011 at $107 billion, representing a staggering average of $293 million per day or more than $12 million per hour.[37] All told, from 2001 to 2014 the United States spent a total of $628 billion to fight the war, and in December 2014 Congress approved another $58 billion for operations in 2015. Therefore, the estimated direct costs of the war are $686 billion over fourteen years.[38] Approximately 92 percent of all war funding went to the Department of Defense; State Department diplomatic operations and foreign aid programs accounted for another 6 percent; and the Department of Veterans Affairs accounted for the final 2 percent.[39] Of the total sum, over 60 percent ($429 billion) was spent in the last five years of the war.[40]

All of these figures understate the true costs of the war, for they include only direct costs. Additional indirect expenses will continue for years after the fighting stops. The United States has already committed to a decade of postcombat assistance for Afghanistan, which will add at least $40 billion to the final bill.[41] If previous wars are any guide, long-term medical expenses for veterans will continue to rise for decades and will peak in forty to fifty years.[42] Already, one-third of returning veterans have been diagnosed with mental health difficulties that range from depression to anxiety to posttraumatic stress disorder, and one of every two veterans has been awarded disability benefits for either a physical or psychological injury incurred during service.[43] In 2013, Linda J. Bilmes, the former chief financial officer of the U.S. Department of Commerce, estimated that the total health care costs for the Iraq and Afghanistan veterans over the next forty years will be $288 billion, of which approximately 40 percent ($115 billion) can reasonably be attributed to Afghanistan.[44]

The choice to fund the war through borrowing rather than by increasing revenues also created additional long-term costs. Between 2001 and 2013, the

United States added $9 trillion to its national debt, of which $2 trillion went to fund the wars Iraq and Afghanistan. This decision added $260 billion in interest payments to the wars' cost. While it is almost impossible to separate spending on Afghanistan from spending on Iraq, the Congressional Research Service estimates that 43 percent of all war spending went to Operation Enduring Freedom; thus, Afghanistan's share of the interest payments adds another $112 billion the war's final cost.[45] Adding together the operational costs, the postwar assistance, the long-term medical costs, and the future debt service leaves us with a daunting total financial cost of the war of approximately $953 billion.

Outcomes and Results

Wars are judged by how they end, not by the resources devoted to them or by the costs the nation bears. Therefore, our final—and most important—step is to assess the war's results. Did the United States and its partners accomplish their shifting and expanding goals? What were the outcomes of the war? Where is Afghanistan now?

First and foremost, the United States succeeded in its initial objectives. The Taliban fled over the border into Pakistan in December 2001 and would not control the formal mechanisms of Afghanistan's government for the remainder of the war. Al Qaeda's bases were destroyed, and at the time of publication, the al Qaeda network had no organized presence in Afghanistan. Navy SEALs killed Osama bin Laden in Pakistan in 2011 in a raid that could not have been conducted without American bases in Afghanistan, and the senior leadership of al Qaeda has been decimated through operations that are similarly dependent on support from Afghan soil. Since 2004, drone strikes on Pakistani soil have killed a total of 119 senior al Qaeda and Taliban commanders, including the group's most experienced planners and fund-raisers.[46] These operations have not destroyed al Qaeda, but it is fair to say the organization is only a shadow of its former self. While the Afghan War may have also helped al Qaeda by attracting both funding and lower-level fighters, the loss of the group's Afghan sanctuary must not be understated. One can attribute the degradation of al Qaeda and the destruction of the organization's leadership at least partly to operations in Afghanistan.

While the United States succeeded in its initial objectives, it failed in almost all of the follow-on ones. Even though the vast majority of Afghans are happy the Taliban is gone, Afghanistan is not safer now than it was in 2002 because the Taliban continues to fight. Moreover, the government is corrupt and ineffectual; the drug problem has exploded; and the Afghan army and police suffer from corruption and high desertion rates. While progress has been made in infrastructure development, health, and education, without long-term international support none of it will be sustainable.

A quick tour of current conditions in Afghanistan makes clear how unsuccessful the follow-on rebuilding and stabilization efforts have been. Security is the sine qua non of a functioning and legitimate state; without it, nothing else is possible. And yet, each year of the war after 2002 saw more troops, more violence, and more civilian deaths.[47] By the U.S. Department of Defense's own assessments, the Taliban in 2013 still had freedom of action throughout much of the country, access to critical resources, and the ability to threaten the Afghan government. In addition to the Taliban, "entrenched criminal networks" contest government control of the highways and rural areas and prey on the civilian population without fear of capture or punishment.[48] In brief, the Afghan people are less safe from arbitrary violence today than when the war began.

They know it too. An Asia Foundation poll of over nine thousand Afghans in 2013 found that roughly three-quarters of Afghans claimed they "would be afraid when encountering international forces" or in traveling from one part to another part of Afghanistan. More than half reported "always, often, or sometimes fearing for their own safety or security or that of their family"—an increase of 11 percentage points since 2012. A similar number reported being afraid to participate in an election.[49] The fact that the Taliban have been responsible for the vast majority of the civilian casualties doesn't seem to resonate. "It doesn't matter which side is right, the Taliban side or the side of the government, the police and army, and the coalition forces," an Afghan man told Human Rights Watch after being wounded in a Taliban attack. "We don't talk about that, we don't judge which one is right. But these are the two groups, and they shouldn't target people like us who are walking on the streets."[50]

One principal reason why security is so poor in Afghanistan is the failures of the Afghan army and police. Even after over fifty-nine billion dollars in U.S. funding, both "continue to suffer from deeply inadequate logistical, sustainment, and other support capabilities and are also deeply pervaded by corruption, nepotism, and ethnic and patronage fissures."[51] Desertion rates in the army hover around 30 percent per year.[52] Reports of abuses by the police remain commonplace, and a 2010 study on corruption in Afghanistan showed that Afghans pay bribes to police more often than to any other government official.[53] Nor do the police seem at all effective in their most basic task of protecting the population: as of 2013, one in five Afghans reported that a member of their family had been a victim of violence or crime.[54] Moreover, keeping the police and army operating at their current levels after 2014 will likely require roughly four billion dollars in international aid—roughly twice as much as the Afghan government can generate on its own in a single year.[55]

Attempts to establish a legitimate government that is responsive to the needs of the Afghan people have encountered similar difficulties. Afghanistan's executive branch remains highly autocratic: the president appoints all of the thirty-two provincial governors and some four hundred district governors, creating ties of loyalty to the state but not necessarily to the people. Government services rarely extend beyond the provincial and district centers.[56] The human capital required to run functioning national and provincial offices is lacking, and qualified applicants remain reluctant to work in government.[57] When taking over the leadership of ISAF in mid-2009, General McChrystal noted that "the weakness of [the government's] institutions, the unpunished abuse of power by corrupt officials and power-brokers, and a widespread sense of political disenfranchisement" had become "as great a challenge to ISAF's success as the insurgent threat."[58] The 2013 end-of-year Department of Defense report to Congress noted that rule of law "continues to be one of [the government's] weakest areas. Pervasive corruption remains a challenge."[59]

In fact, calling corruption a "challenge" radically understates the nature of the problem. Corruption affects almost every Afghan in the country. A 2010 UN survey of over seven thousand Afghans in sixteen hundred villages and cities found that in a single twelve-month period one out of every two Afghan adults paid bribes to government officials to obtain basic public services. In a country with a per capita annual GDP of $425, moreover, the average bribe was $160. All told, Afghans paid out $2.5 billion in bribes in 2010, a sum almost equal to Afghanistan's $2.8 billion drug trade. As a result, "drugs and bribes are the two largest income generators in Afghanistan: together they amount to about half the country's (licit) GDP."[60] Unsurprisingly, fully 59 percent of Afghans felt "public dishonesty" was a greater concern than insecurity or unemployment, and a majority of Afghans believed the problem had worsened over the last five years.[61] In 2009, Transparency International named Afghanistan the second most corrupt country in the world. By 2013, increasing corruption had propelled it into a tie for first place with North Korea and Somalia.[62]

Corruption is not limited to local bribe paying. The sheer quantity of international aid flowing into the country since 2002 has created enormous incentives for graft, and loose customs policies allow massive legal transfers of currency out of the country. By the Afghan Central Bank's own estimate, over four billion in American dollars left Kabul in 2011, mostly on large, shrink-wrapped pallets loaded onto planes by forklifts and destined for Dubai, Switzerland, Malaysia, and Pakistan.[63] In 2010, investigators uncovered a massive defrauding scheme in Kabul Bank, which eventually cost depositors nine hundred million dollars. Several of the bank's largest stakeholders were relatives of the president and the first vice president. As of 2014, only three hundred million of Kabul Bank deposits had been recovered.[64]

American contractors have also found ways to direct reconstruction dollars into their coffers in ways both legal and illegal. The most egregious case of wrongdoing involved the New Jersey–based engineering firm Louis Berger International. The company—which had already been exposed in a scathing 2006 report for its shoddy workmanship in road and school construction—went on to become the largest recipient of USAID dollars from 2007 to 2009, much of which was for a contract to rehabilitate the Kajaki Dam in northern Helmand province.[65] In 2010, investigators uncovered a major cost-inflating scheme that had defrauded American taxpayers of over ten million dollars. Two officials went to prison, and the company paid a fine of seventy million, but the dam project remained plagued by delays and security problems. The United States turned the unfinished project over to an Afghan construction company in 2013. The project is scheduled for completion no sooner than 2017.[66]

Afghanistan's expanding drug problems have also fueled corruption and here, the international community's efforts have been entirely counterproductive. From 2002 to 2013, the United States spent seven billion dollars on programs to eradicate poppy, interdict opium production, and entice farmers to grow legal, but less lucrative, crops.[67] None of it worked. A quick survey of cultivation statistics makes this clear: From 1995 to 2001, thanks to the Taliban's brutal suppression tactics, poppy cultivation declined steadily to just 8,000 hectares. When the Taliban fled, it exploded, rising from 74,000 (2002) to 193,000 (2007) to 209,000 hectares under cultivation (2013). By 2013, half of all of Afghanistan's provinces were growing poppy.[68] This has had effects well beyond the field of health. In 2014, the DoD's inspector general for Afghanistan warned that the "the expanding cultivation and trafficking of drugs" was poisoning Afghanistan's financial sector, undermining the state's legitimacy, "stoking corruption, nourishing criminal networks, and providing significant financial support to the Taliban and other insurgent groups." Afghanistan's drug trade, he concluded, "is one of the most significant factors putting the entire US and international-donor investment in the reconstruction of Afghanistan at risk."[69]

Because of these problems with security, corruption, and drugs, systems for sustainable economic growth have not yet taken root. At first glance, the economic indicators seem promising: since 2001, Afghanistan has enjoyed an annual growth rate of 9 percent, and in 2012 GDP growth jumped to 12 percent. (However, most of that growth has been due to the massive amounts of international aid that will fall off dramatically in the years to come.)[70] The Afghan federal budget is, by any standard, a mess: Currently, the government spends roughly three times as much as it generates in domestic revenues, and fully two-thirds of the federal budget comes from international donors.[71] By 2021, expected revenues will cover only a little more than a third of projected expenditures and, by the Afghan Ministry of Finance's own calculations, the country will require roughly ten billion dollars per year in international support. Afghanistan is not expected to reach financial self-sufficiency before 2025.[72]

Attempts to develop Afghanistan's infrastructure have been partially successful, but many of those improvements are unsustainable. When the United States invaded in 2001, Afghanistan had less than fifty miles of paved roads.[73] Over the ensuing thirteen years, the coalition and assorted nongovernmental organizations graded, improved, or paved another 5,430 kilometers at a cost of over four billion dollars—half of which the United States paid.[74] It was dangerous work and terribly inefficient: as soon as roads were repaired, the Taliban targeted them with improvised explosive devices that could be planted overnight and cost less than twenty dollars to make.[75] Afghan and international contractors responded by paying off local commanders to secure cease-fires, often with U.S. funds that went directly to the Taliban. Because of these security concerns, costs skyrocketed: One sixty-mile stretch of road in Eastern Afghanistan cost almost five million dollars per mile. In 2012, when the coalition handed off the responsibility for road maintenance to the Afghan Government's Ministry of Public Works, road repairs ground to a halt. "Things have gotten so much worse," an Afghan taxi driver told a Washington Post reporter in early 2014. "Now, if we drive too fast, everyone in the car dies."[76]

Despite these grim reports, not all of the news is bad: much progress has been made in the areas of health and sanitation. In 2003, there were fewer than five hundred health facilities in Afghanistan (including hospitals) and only about 8 percent of the population had access to basic health services. In 2011, the Afghan ministry of health reported that more than eighteen hundred clinics were open, with 65 percent of the population having access to basic services.[77] More than half of Afghan households now have access to water from an improved source, compared to just 40 percent in 2003.[78]

Maternal care and infant health have also improved dramatically. Almost half of Afghanistan's women now have their children delivered by a medically trained professional, compared to 26 percent just five years ago.[79] Of women, 68 percent now receive some form of prenatal care from a skilled provider, compared to just 8 percent in 2003.[80] The number of midwives has risen from four hundred in 2003 to more than two thousand in 2010, and during the same period, Save the Children and other NGOs have trained twenty thousand community health workers.[81] As a result, the infant mortality rate in Afghanistan has declined by a third since 2003, and the death rate for children under five has declined by 40 percent.[82] Adult mortality has declined as well: the current life expectancy in Afghanistan is now above sixty, compared to slightly below fifty a decade ago.[83]

Education has seen similar gains. In 2001, there were about one million children in school, only a tiny fraction of whom were girls. Today there are more than eight million children in school, including three million girls.[84] Since the fall of the Taliban regime, four thousand new schools have been built in Afghanistan, and 140,000 teachers have been hired. By early 2013, there were seventeen different universities in Afghanistan—up from two under the Taliban—and seventy-five thousand Afghans were enrolled in university.[85] Like so many gains, however, this progress cannot be sustained without ongoing support from international donors. Afghanistan's universities have an annual operating budget of roughly thirty-five million dollars per year; in 2012, the U.S. Agency for International Development provided over half of those funds.[86]

Given these facts, what conclusions may be drawn about the outcomes of the war? Looking back from this point in 2015, it seems fair to say that the American efforts were at best a wildly inefficient partial success and at worst a failure. Even though U.S. Special Forces and the CIA toppled the Taliban and decapitated the al Qaeda leadership, the coalition failed to secure the people of Afghanistan and contributed to the ongoing destabilization of Pakistan. The Taliban returned and the mission mutated from counterterrorism to nation building to counterinsurgency. The billions in reconstruction dollars made significant—but possibly only temporary—improvements to the health, education, and transportation systems of the country, but none of this was sufficient to generate sufficient support for the Karzai regime. Police and army training did not produce a professional force; in fact, portions of the security forces began preying on the population it was charged with protecting. After thirteen years, the international forces left without a decisive victory.

From Legacies to Lessons

From an accounting of legacies, let us now turn to lessons. What lessons can students of history and politics glean from the war in Afghanistan?

The first critical lesson concerns how states cooperate and compete with each other. The great British statesman Lord Palmerston once reminded his countrymen that states have no eternal allies and no perpetual enemies, only interests that are both eternal and perpetual.[87] The same is true today, and one of the biggest obstacles to success in the Afghan War was the fundamental difference between U.S. and Afghan interests. America's purpose was to destroy al Qaeda and turn the Afghan population against the Taliban so that it could not give safe haven to al Qaeda or other transnational terrorist groups. President Karzai shared these interests in principle; nevertheless, he had larger concerns that shaped his priorities more directly. Landlocked and with hostile regimes on both sides (Persian, Shi'ite Iran to the west and Pakistan—the Taliban's principal supporters—to the east), the new Afghanistan needed military power to strengthen its bargaining position with its neighbors. As one of the poorest, most conflict-ridden countries in the world, it needed massive international aid to rebuild its infrastructure. And, in a multiethnic traditional society where loyalty has always been bought through political patronage, President Karzai needed to keep the country's various warlords and power brokers in his coalition. Pursuing these priorities required one thing: money. Thus, the Karzai regime worked to extract the maximum military and financial resources from the United States for as long as possible. The result was an inflated and corrupt economy, a set of political bargains with predatory warlords, and a bill for the United States than ran in the hundreds of billions of dollars.

The next critical lesson is one that is hammered into military officers from their initial training, but seems lost on some civilian policy makers today: when applying instruments of state power toward national interests, military forces should be used for military missions. When the job was to topple, kill, or destroy, the means and ends aligned well and produced the desired results. When the missions shifted to the more nebulous goals of being a "positive force in the community" and turning "perceptions from fear and uncertainty to trust and confidence," the military was as unsuccessful as an earlier generation had been in trying to win hearts and minds in Vietnam. Afghans saw the Americans for what they were: foreign soldiers with guns who usually brought violence with them, either directly or indirectly. American military officers—oftentimes captains and lieutenants in their early to mid-twenties—found themselves in the difficult position of trying to strike bargains with

Pashtun elders in a culture where age, family ties, and Islamic faith are the foremost determinants of authority and credibility. Afghans found it difficult to trust those who could not claim the sorts of authority and credibility they recognized. The resulting "trust gap" prevented them from actively supporting the government.

The first two lessons are strategic ones—they concern the overall objectives of the war and the types of resources applied toward those goals. A third lesson concerns military tactics—and the tactics of counterinsurgency in particular. "Political power is the central issue in insurgencies and counterinsurgencies," the military's counterinsurgency manual explains. "Each side aims to get the people to accept its governance or authority as legitimate" and "victory is achieved when the populace consents to the government's legitimacy and stops actively and passively supporting the insurgency"[88] This first principle of counterinsurgency—that foreign security forces and advisers, speaking foreign languages and carrying with them both guns and foreign cultures, can somehow increase the legitimacy of a country's government—lacks a foundation in history or logic. Such ideas reflect a failure of imagination that stems from the common human habit of assuming one's own values are universal truths rather than locally constructed norms.

At the far end of this thirteen-year war, it seems clear that redefining Afghans' relationships with their government was always a bridge too far. Afghanistan is not now—and has never been—a liberal state whose rulers draw legitimacy from the consent of the governed. Since Afghanistan became a state in 1747, legitimacy has flowed from three principal sources: the force of arms, Islamic propriety, and overt financial patronage.[89] Sadly, the United States put almost all of its resources into the first of these three paths. By battling the Taliban and training Afghan security forces, the United States tried to give President Karzai a monopoly on the use of force—an impossible task in a country awash in arms wherein almost every adult male ascribes to a culture of honor that demands fighting. Various military and police commanders undermined the effort by targeting rival clans, extracting bribes from ordinary citizens, and, in the end, helped drive the people into the hands of the Taliban.

The second path to legitimacy—being good Muslims and opposing un-Islamic practices—was always impossible for the American "infidels." This explains why as early as 2001 Afghans were asking that ISAF be composed entirely of soldiers from Islamic countries.[90] It is a strange irony that had just a fraction of Americans soldiers converted to Islam and married into the tribes the United States hoped to influence (as the Taliban and al Qaeda did), America might have had lifelong legitimacy in every village with an Afghan-American in it. Though it is admittedly unrealistic as an actual policy, the

1960s slogan "make love not war" might have been the most sustainable way to ensure Afghanistan remained al Qaeda free—and at a fraction of the costs in blood and treasure.

The third path to Afghan legitimacy—creating temporary loyalties through overt, financial exchanges—was also off-limits to the American government because it feared such actions would stoke corruption. Domestic constraints were a major factor, particularly after 2008, as American politicians and reporters railed against the Afghans' misuse of American dollars. An American-led transparency task force helped advance a narrative of being serious on corruption, but did little else. Oversight of the billions flowing into Afghanistan was wholly inadequate. As a result, the Afghans took the money and ran; the U.S. government played the role of the patsy rather than the patron. All of this weakened President Karzai's political bargains with his key stakeholders and convinced him that the United States was plotting against him.

A final—and perhaps most important—lesson concerns the idea of historical lessons themselves. If all the mistakes chronicled here were new ones, one might find it easier to forgive the policy makers who made them. This was not the case. All of the above problems were noted in previous wars, catalogued as mistakes, and shared with the politicians who voted for the wars and ordered their prosecution. It seems that when charting a course for the future, the American government is either unwilling or unable to be mindful of the lessons of the past.

In 1972, as the Vietnam War dragged into its eighth year, the Senate held hearings on the lessons of the war. Presidential adviser Arthur Schlesinger, Jr. offered the most important one: "all the problems in the world are not military problems, and military force is not usually the most effective form of national power."[91] Academics studying Vietnam drew similar conclusions in later years. Failure in Vietnam, two professors from Tufts' Fletcher School opined in 1977, "resulted from trying to substitute military force for effective government. It resulted because of misconceptions about our friends, our enemies, and ourselves."[92] The future commander of the Afghan War understood this lesson well. "Counterinsurgency operations, in particular, require close political-military integration," General Petraeus noted in his 1987 Ph.D. dissertation on the Army after Vietnam. "For while military force may be necessary in a counterinsurgency, it is seldom sufficient."[93] All of this was known by both presidents and their top advisors. And yet, all of them ended up using an almost exclusively military approach to the war.

The challenges of corruption and state weakness were also well known in advance, for both problems had been endemic in the Vietnam War. Before committing to counterinsurgency operations in the future, former Under Secretary of State George Ball testified to Congress in 1985 that we must "be sure that there is a well-defined country to defend, a national will to defend it, and a political structure through which that will is expressed, which means, in turn, a government that is neither corrupt nor oppressive." Ball explained, "We must be certain there is a solid political base strong enough to support the weight of our support, since for us to try to create a base by pushing and pulling and bribing and cajoling native politicians into building an effective government may well be beyond our means."[94] The Department of Defense drew a similar conclusion in 1980: "An agrarian based economy is labor-intensive, relatively inflexible, and is acutely sensitive . . . to the demands of large-scale warfare." Consequently, in future operations in similar countries, the "US presence most likely will contort and eventually cripple such an economy and will force it to become almost totally dependent on massive and sustained US aid."[95]

Applying lessons from one country to another is tricky business, and decision makers may have wisely tried to avoid cramming Afghanistan into a Vietnam-shaped policy template. But the American leadership also had numerous specific examples of how *Afghans* fight wars, and it seemed to have ignored those lessons as well. The British—America's strongest allies in Afghanistan, with whom senior policy makers were in regular consultations— knew well the problems of subduing Pashtun insurgencies in Afghanistan because it had fought three Anglo-Afghan wars against the same tribes that would eventually constitute the Taliban. The specific problems of Afghan xenophobia, perceived insults to Islam, corruption, and the difficulties of controlling warlords were principal reasons for the British failures in those wars.[96] The United States had also watched carefully—and participated in— the ten-year Soviet war in Afghanistan that concluded a decade before the U.S. war began. There too, Afghans mobilized themselves along religious and ethnic lines, relied on sanctuaries in Pakistan, joined the army but then deserted, and, in effect, followed a cost-extracting strategy very similar to the one used by the Taliban in the most recent war.[97] Why did these lessons go unheeded?

Three possibilities seem worthy of research and debate for future historians: First, it is possible that these historical lessons got drowned out by other ones—most notably, the supposed successes of the Iraqi surge in 2007. With the new COIN tactics bearing such obvious and immediate fruit in Iraq, policy makers may have concluded that the long line of counterinsurgency naysayers had been unduly pessimistic (a position that is now in full retreat as Iraq struggles with a new insurgency that is again on the cusp of state failure).

Second, it is possible that all of these historical lessons were considered but dismissed. When policy makers use history, they usually do so badly, either by ignoring relevant lessons or overvaluing inapplicable ones.[98] Finally, it is possible that American decision makers understood all of these lessons, but could not translate them into action. War, like all of politics, is fundamentally an attempt to change how human beings think and act. And as endeavors in fields ranging from romance to finance attest, predicting human behavior has not gotten any more accurate over the years. U.S. policy makers had enormous resources at their disposal for prosecuting the war, but in the end they had to move their views through myriad bureaucracies, international coalitions, and human relationships, none of which were under any one person's direct control.

Asking why the United States missed the lessons of previous wars leads to another question—one in dire need of an answer. How shall the American military and government avoid similar errors in the future given the fact that the ones committed here were already repetitions of earlier mistakes? Not only generals and presidents but also every American has a stake in this question's answer because the military fights in the name of its citizens. Democracy spreads best when it is practiced at home, and that means questioning assumptions, testing propositions, and understanding the past in order to seek better actions in the future. It is never enough to note the lessons of unsuccessful wars; we must all *learn* the lessons and use them to correct false premises and adjust faulty reasoning. Even more important, we must each do our part to make political leaders aware of historical background and context, for such details are very often prerequisites for a successful, sustainable foreign policy. Doing so may be the best legacy of what is now America's longest war.

NOTES

1 Richard Langworth, ed., *Churchill by Himself: The Definitive Collection of Quotations* (New York: Public Affairs Press, 2008), 579.

2 Seth Doane, "Afghan Youth Orchestra Hopes to Bring Peace through Music," *CBS Evening News*, February 12, 2013, http://www.cbsnews.com/news/afghan-youth-orchestra-hopes-to-bring-peace-through-music/; "Taliban's Blood-Soaked Stadium Re-opens as a Peaceful Place," *NBC News*, December 15, 2011, http://worldnews.nbcnews.com/_news/2011/12/15/9468942-talibans-bloodsoaked-stadium-re-opens-as-peaceful-place.

3 On the British and Soviet experiences in Afghanistan, see Thomas Barfield, *Afghanistan: A Cultural and Political History* (Princeton: Princeton University Press, 2010) and Martin Ewans, *Afghanistan: A Short History of Its People and Politics* (New York: Harper, 2002).

4 Lawrence Wright, *The Looming Tower: Al-Qaeda and the Road to 9/11* (New York: Vintage, 2006), 254–68.

5 The war aims are expressed in George W. Bush, "Address to the Nation" (October 7, 2001) and "Address to Joint Session of Congress" (September 20, 2001), www.whitehouse.gov. See also Steve Bowman and Catherine Dale, "War in Afghanistan: Strategy, Military Operations and Issues for Congress" (Congressional Research Service, Report 7-5700, December 3, 2009), www.crs.gov.

6 On the initial invasion, see Gary C. Schroen, *First In: An Insider's Account of How the CIA Spearheaded the War on Terror in Afghanistan* (New York: Presidio Press, 2005).

7 United Nations, "Agreement on Provisional Arrangements in Afghanistan" (Bonn Agreement), 1, www.un.org.

8 On ISAF's origins, see Sean M. Maloney, "The International Security Assistance Force: The Origins of a Stabilization Force," *Canadian Military Journal* 6 (Summer 2003): 6–7.

9 Amy Belasco, "Troop Levels in the Afghanistan and Iraq Wars, 2001–2009" (Congressional Research Service, July 2, 2009), www.crs.gov. For tallies by month, see Hannah Fairfield et al., "Troop Levels in Afghanistan since 2001," *New York Times*, October 1, 2009.

10 UN Security Council Resolution 1386 (2001) established ISAF. Resolution 1510 (2003) expanded the mission. Both are available at www.un.org.

11 On U.S. opposition to ISAF expansion, see Sean M. Maloney, "Afghanistan: From Here to Eternity?," *Parameters* 34 (Spring 2004): 8. See also Maloney, "International Security Assistance Force," 6–7.

12 Ian S. Livingston and Michael O'Hanlon, "Afghanistan Index," figure 1.2, "Other Foreign Troops Deployed to Afghanistan," 5, www.brookings.edu/afghaninstanindex; Fairfield et al., "Troop Levels in Afghanistan since 2001"; Belasco, "Troop Levels," 9.

13 United Nations, "The International Conference on Afghanistan: The Berlin Declaration" (April 1, 2004), 2, http://mfa.gov.af/Content/files/berlindeclaration.pdf.

14 United Nations, "The International Conference on Afghanistan: The Afghanistan Compact" (January 31–February 1, 2006), "Annex I: Benchmarks and Timelines," www.nato.int/isaf/docu/epub/pdf/afghanistan_compact.pdf.

15 Livingston and O'Hanlon, "Afghanistan Index," 5; Fairfield et al., "Troop Levels in Afghanistan since 2001"; Belasco, "Troop Levels," 9.

16 Belasco, "Troop Levels," 9.

17 "Annual Fatalities in Terrorist Violence in Pakistan, 2003–2009," in *Pakistan Assessment: 2010* (South Asian Terrorism Portal), http://www.satp.org/satporgtp/countries/pakistan/assesment2010.htm.

18 On the split within the administration, see Bob Woodward, *Obama's Wars* (New York: Simon & Schuster, 2010). On Pakistan, see Stephen Biddle, "Is It Worth It? The Difficult Case for War in Afghanistan," *American Interest* 4, no. 6 (July–August 2009): 4–11.

19 National Security Adviser, "Memorandum for the Principals: Afghanistan Pakistan Strategy," November 29, 2009, cited in Woodward, *Obama's Wars*, 385–86.

20 Woodward, *Obama's Wars*, 387.

21 General Stanley McChrystal, "ISAF Commander's Counterinsurgency Guidance" (n.d.), http://www.nato.int/isaf/docu/official_texts/counterinsurgency_guidance.pdf.

22 On the differences between Iraq and Afghanistan, see Rick Nelson, Nathan Freier, and Maren Leed, *Iraq versus Afghanistan: A Surge Is Not a Surge Is Not a Surge* (Washington, DC: Center for Strategic and International Studies, 2009).

23 Mark Landler, "U.S. Troops to Leave Afghanistan by End of '16," *New York Times*, May 27, 2014, A1.

24 On nation building, see Deputy Secretary of Defense Paul Wolfowitz and Deputy Secretary of State Richard Armitage, "Testimony as Delivered to the Senate Committee on Foreign Relations: The Situation in Afghanistan" (June 26, 2002). See also, Bob Woodward, *Bush at War* (New York: Simon & Schuster, 2002), 124, 241.

25 Official casualty statistics by war, causes of death, and the demographics of the killed and wounded are available via the Defense Manpower Data Center, https://www.dmdc.osd.mil/dcas/pages/casualties_oef.xhtml.

26 Livingston and O'Hanlon, "Afghanistan Index," 12.

27 All of these occurred under fire; the military has a separate system for accounting for accidental nonlethal injuries. See Defense Manpower Data Center, "Military Casualties, Operation Enduring Freedom—Wounded in Action," https://www.dmdc.osd.mil/dcas/pages/report_oef_wounded.xhtml. For statistics on amputations, see Hannah Fischer, "US Military Casualty Statistics: Operation New Dawn, Operation Iraqi Freedom, and Operation Enduring Freedom" (Congressional Research Service, February 5, 2013), www.crs.gov.

28 For Antietam casualties, see National Park Service, "Casualties of Battle," http://www.nps.gov/anti/historyculture/casualties.htm.

29 For all ISAF deaths by country of origin, see http://icasualties.org/oef.

30 On ANSF deaths, see Livingston and O'Hanlon, "Afghanistan Index" (2015), figure 1.20, "ANA and ANP Personnel Fatalities 2007–2013," 13.

31 For the figures since 2009, see United Nations Assistance Mission Afghanistan (UNAMA), *Afghanistan: Annual Report 2014, Protection of Civilians in Armed Conflict* (Kabul, February 2015), 1; for earlier periods, see Neta C. Crawford, "Civilian Death and Injury in Afghanistan 2001–2011," http://costsofwar.org/sites/default/files/CrawfordAfghanistanCasualties.pdf.

32 The UN estimates that the war has created 805,409 internally displaced persons. See UNAMA, "Afghanistan: Protection of Civilians in Armed Conflict" (2014), 9, http://unama.unmissions.org.

33 See Crawford, "Civilian Death and Injury," 39; Marc W. Herold, "A Dossier on Civilian Victims of United States' Aerial Bombing of Afghanistan: A Comprehensive Accounting," http://cursor.org/stories/casualty_count.htm; Carl Conetta, "Operation Enduring Freedom: Why a Higher Rate of Civilian Bombing Casualties?" (Project for

Defense Alternatives, Briefing Report 13, January 18, 2002), http://www.comw.org/pda/o2010ef.html#appendix1.

34 Crawford, "Civilian Death and Injury," 39.

35 See UNAMA, "Annual Report on the Protection of Civilians in Armed Conflict" (2007–14).

36 Amy Belasco, "The Cost of Iraq, Afghanistan, and Other Global War on Terror Operations" (Congressional Research Service, December 8, 2014), 15; Anthony H. Cordesman, "The US Cost of the Afghan War 2002–2013" (Center for Strategic and International Studies, May 14, 2012), 4.

37 Belasco, "Cost of Iraq" (December 8, 2014), 15.

38 Amy Belasco, "The Cost of Iraq, Afghanistan, and Other Global War on Terror Operations since 9/11" (Congressional Research Service, January 8, 2014), 15. See also Cordesman, "US Cost," 3; Pat Towell and Amy Belasco, "Defense: FY2014 Authorizations and Appropriations" (Congressional Research Service, January 8, 2014), 14.

39 Belasco, "Cost of Iraq" (January 8, 2014), 15.

40 Ibid., 15. See also Cordesman, "US Cost," 3; Kenneth Katzman, "Post-Taliban Governance, Security and US Policy" (Congressional Research Service, January 17, 2014), 56.

41 Sardar Ahmad, "West Will Give Afghanistan $4 Billion per Year: Karzai," *Defense News*, March 22, 2012, www.defensenews.com.

42 Linda J. Bilmes, "The Financial Legacy of Iraq and Afghanistan: How Wartime Spending Decisions Will Constrain Future National Security Budgets" (Harvard Kennedy School Faculty Research Working Paper, March 2013), 5, http://web.hks.harvard.edu/publications.

43 Ibid., 4–7.

44 Ibid., 6. Of the total wounded, 40 percent received their wounds in Afghanistan; 60 percent received their wounds in Iraq.

45 Ibid., 19.

46 Bill Roggio, "Senior Al Qaeda and Taliban Commanders Killed in Air Strikes in Pakistan, 2004—2015," http://www.longwarjournal.org/pakistan-strikes-hvts.php.

47 For troop numbers, see Fairfield et al., "Troop Levels in Afghanistan since 2001." For civilian casualties, see UNAMA, "Report on the Protection of Civilians in Armed Conflict" (2007–14). On the problems of measuring security in Afghanistan, see Gary Owen, "1230 Week: A Look behind the ISAF Metric Curtain," *Sunny in Kabul*, August 6, 2013.

48 Department of Defense, *Report on Progress toward Security and Stability in Afghanistan* (November 2013), 14–15; Government Accountability Office, "Afghanistan: Key Oversight Issues" (GAO 13-218SP, February 2013), 17. See also James R. Clapper, "Worldwide Threat Assessment of the US Intelligence Community" (Statement for the Record for the Senate Select Committee on Intelligence, March 2013), 17.

49 The Asia Foundation, "Afghanistan in 2013: A Survey of Afghan People," 6, http://asiafoundation.org/publications/pdf/1280.

50 Human Rights Watch, "The Human Cost: The Consequences of Insurgent Attacks in Afghanistan" (no. 69, April 2007), http://www.hrw.org/reports/2007/04/15/human-cost.

51 Special Inspector General for Afghanistan Reconstruction (SIGAR), "Quarterly Report to Congress" (January 30, 2014), 4; Vanda Felbab-Brown, "Afghanistan after ISAF: Prospects for Afghan Peace and Security," *Harvard International Review* 35 (Fall 2013): 65.

52 On Afghan army desertion rates, see the Department of Defense's *Report on Progress* for the years 2008–14.

53 UN Office on Drugs and Crime (UNODC), "Corruption in Afghanistan: Bribery as Reported by the Victims" (January 10, 2010), 3–4, www.unodc.org.

54 Asia Foundation, "Afghanistan in 2011: A Survey of the Afghan People," 3.

55 Department of Defense, *Report on Progress* (November 2013), 86–87. The Afghan federal budget for 2013 was $7.04 billion, but two-thirds of that came from international donors. The total value derived from internally generated revenue collection was $2.15 billion.

56 Department of Defense, *Report on Progress* (November 2013), 85–87.

57 Kenneth Katzman, "Politics, Elections, and Government Performance" (Congressional Research Service, November 22, 2013), 32.

58 General Stanley A. McChrystal, "COMISAF's Initial Assessment (Unclassified)" (August 30, 2009), 2–5, 2–10, www.washingtonpost.com.

59 Department of Defense, *Report on Progress* (November 2013), 88.

60 UNODC, "Corruption in Afghanistan," 3–4, www.unodc.org.

61 Ibid., 3–4.

62 Afghanistan, Somalia, and North Korea all tied for last place. See Transparency International's Corruption Perceptions Index for 2009 and 2013, http://cpi.transparency.org/cpi2013/results.

63 Matthieu Aikins, "The Coming Meltdown in Kabul," *Wilson Quarterly* 37 (Spring 2013), http://www.wilsonquarterly.com/in-essence/coming-meltdown in-kabul.

64 Emma Graham-Harrison, "Afghan Elite Ransacked $900 Million from Kabul Bank, Inquiry Finds," *Guardian*, November 28, 2012.

65 David Voreacos, "Berger Group Charged with Fraud in Iraq, Afghanistan," *Bloomberg News*, November 5, 2010; Fariba Nawa, *Afghanistan, Inc.: A CorpWatch Investigative Report*, www.corpwatch.org; International Crisis Group, "Aid and Conflict in Afghanistan" (Crisis Group Asia Report 210, 19, August 4, 2011), www.crisisgroup.org.

66 Shashank Bengali, "US hands troubled Dam to Afghans," *Los Angeles Times*, May 5, 2013.

67 SIGAR, "Quarterly Report to Congress," 10.

68 UNODC, "Afghanistan Opium Survey, 2013, Summary Findings" (November 2013), 5, 17, www.unodc.org.

69 SIGAR, "Quarterly Report to Congress," 10.

70 World Bank, "Afghanistan Economic Update" (April 2013), 3; Katzman, "Post-Taliban Governance, Security and US Policy," 55; Department of Defense, *Report on Progress* (November 2013), 100.

71 Afghanistan's core federal budget for FY2013 was $7.04 billion, and its domestic revenue generation target was $2.15 billion. See Department of Defense, *Report on Progress* (November 2013), 86–87. See also World Bank, "Afghanistan Economic Update," 15; Katzman, "Post-Taliban Governance, Security and US Policy," 58.

72 Department of Defense, *Report on Progress* (November 2013), 87; Katzman, "Post-Taliban Governance, Security and US Policy," 55.

73 Mohammed Abid Amiri, "Road Construction in Post-conflict Afghanistan: A Cure or a Curse?," *International Affairs Review* 2 (Spring 2013): 4.

74 Department of Defense, *Report on Progress* (November 2013), 105.

75 Amiri, "Road Construction in Post-conflict Afghanistan," 9.

76 Ibid., 1–11; Kevin Sieff, "After Billions in US Investment, Afghan Roads Are Falling Apart," *Washington Post*, January 30, 2014.

77 Katzman, "Post-Taliban Governance, Security and US Policy," 69.

78 Afghanistan Public Health Institute, "Afghanistan Mortality Survey 2010," 5; UNICEF, "Moving beyond Two Decades of War: Multiple Indicator Cluster Survey" (2003), 50; UNICEF, "Monitoring the Situation of Women and Children: Afghanistan Multiple Indicator Cluster Survey 2010–2011," xx.

79 Afghanistan Public Health Institute, "Afghanistan Mortality Survey 2010," 9.

80 Ibid., 9.

81 Associated Press, "Afghanistan Life Expectancy Rising as Health Care Improves," *Guardian*, November 30, 2011, 22.

82 UNICEF, "Moving beyond Two Decades of War," 65; UNICEF, "Monitoring the Situation of Women and Children," xix.

83 Associated Press, "Afghanistan Life Expectancy Rising"; Afghanistan Public Health Institute, "Afghanistan Mortality Survey 2010," 12–13.

84 Department of Defense, *Report on Progress* (November 2013), 171.

85 Katzman, "Post-Taliban Governance, Security and US Policy," 69; Department of Defense, *Report on Progress* (November 2013), 108–9.

86 Katzman, "Post-Taliban Governance, Security and US Policy," 60.

87 David Brown, *Palmerston and the Politics of Foreign Policy, 1846–1855* (Manchester: Manchester University Press, 2002), 82–83.

88 Department of Defense, *The US Army and Marine Corps Counterinsurgency Field Manual* (Chicago: University of Chicago Press, 2006), 2, 37, 6.

89 These points are made indirectly in Barfield, *Afghanistan* and Ewans, *Afghanistan*.

90 Maloney, "International Security Assistance Force," 5.

91 U.S. Senate, Committee on Foreign Relations, "Causes, Origins, and Lessons of the Vietnam War, May 9–11, 1972" (Washington, DC: GPO, 1973), 79.

92 W. Scott Thompson and Donaldson D. Frizzell, eds., *The Lessons of Vietnam* (New York: Crane, Russak, 1977), iv.

93 David Howell Petraeus, "The American Military and the Lessons of Vietnam: A Study of Military Influence and the Use of Force in the Post-Vietnam Era" (Ph.D. diss., Princeton University, 1987), 304–5.

94 House of Representatives, Committee on Foreign Affairs, "The Lessons of Vietnam, 99th Cong. 1st Sess., April 29, 1985" (Washington, DC: GPO, 1986), 26.

95 Defense Technical Information Center, *A Study of Strategic Lessons Learned in Vietnam: Omnibus Executive Summary* (Maclean, VA: BDM Corporation, 1980), II-11.

96 Barfield, *Afghanistan*, 110–63; Ewans, *Afghanistan*, 59–70, 86–97, 120–23.

97 Ewans, *Afghanistan*, 189–237.

98 These bad habits are discussed in detail in Ernest R. May, *Lessons of the Past: The Use and Misuse of History in American Foreign Policy* (New York: Oxford University Press, 1973), xi–xii.

TIMELINE

Date	Afghanistan	Iraq
12/24/1979	Soviet Invasion of Afghanistan	
1979		Iranian Revolution
9/22/1980		Iraq invades Iran—Iran-Iraq War/ First Persian Gulf War begins
1980	Babrak Karmal installed as Afghanistan ruler, backed by the Soviet Union; the United States and others supply mujahideen	
1/20/1981	Ronald Reagan inauguration	
12/20/1983		Donald Rumsfeld photographed shaking hands with Saddam
1985	Mujahideen form alliance in Pakistan vs. Soviet troops	
1986	United States supplies mujahideen with Stinger missiles, and Karmal replaced by Najibullah as head of Soviet-backed regime	In November, Iran-Contra came to light
1988	Afghanistan, Soviet Union, United States, and Pakistan sign peace accords	Ceasefire in Iraq-Iran War; Iraq uses chemical weapons against Kurds
1/20/1989	George H. W. Bush inauguration	
1989	Soviet troops depart, civil war continues	
8/2/1990		Iraq invades Kuwait
1/17/1991		Operation Desert Storm
2/28/1991		End of Gulf War (Operation Desert Storm ended officially on 11/30/1995)
4/3/1991		UN Resolution 687 bans Iraq WMDs
4/11/1991		Gulf War ceasefire (UN)

Date	Afghanistan	Iraq
Summer 1991		Iraq destroys WMD equipment
12/25/1991	Soviet Union dissolved	
1992	Najibullah's regime collapses, civil war follows	
1/20/1993	Bill Clinton inauguration	
2/26/1993	World Trade Center bombing	
1994		UNSCOM destroys Iraq's known chemical weapons, neutralize Iraq's nuclear program
June 1995	Clinton labels terrorism a national security issue (rather than a law enforcement matter)	
1996	Taliban seize Kabul	
1996	CIA establishes special unit on OBL	
8/7/1998	U.S. embassy bombings in Kenya and Tanzania	
8/20/1998	Operation Infinite Reach, cruise missile strikes in Sudan and Afghanistan, including suspected bases of OBL	
12/16/1998		U.S. Operation Desert Fox—U.S. air raid on Iraqi military targets; UNSCOM and IAEA pull out of Iraq—ends cooperation between Iraq and inspectors, but it also destroys WMD infrastructure
10/15/1999	UN Security Council links al Qaeda to Taliban; tries to force Afghanistan to hand over OBL for trial	
10/12/2000	Al Qaeda bombs USS *Cole*, killing 17 U.S. sailors	
9/9/2001	Al Qaeda assassinates Ahmad Shah Massoud, commander of the Northern Alliance, ensuring OBL Taliban protection	
9/11/2001	Al Qaeda strikes United States with airliners	
9/20/2001	George W. Bush vows attack on Afghanistan, demanding OBL	

Date	Afghanistan	Iraq
10/7/2001	United States and United Kingdom begin bombing campaign over Afghanistan—Operation Enduring Freedom	
12/7/2001	Taliban forces abandon Kandahar, although the United States doesn't capture Mullah Muhammed Omar or OBL	
12/12/2001	Battle of Tora Bora (through 12/17)	
12/22/2001	Hamid Karzai sworn in	
1/11/2002	20 detainees arrive at Camp X-Ray at Gitmo	
1/18/2002	Bush says Guantanamo (Gitmo) detainees are disqualified from protection under the Geneva Conventions	
1/27/2002	Cheney calls Gitmo detainees the worst of a very bad lot	
1/29/2002		Bush accuses Iraq of being part of an "Axis of Evil" at SOTU address
3/21/2002	Bush administration announces military tribunals system at Gitmo	
March 2002	Operation Anaconda: major large-scale battle in the Shah-i-Kot Valley in Paktia province	
4/25/2002	Construction of Camp Delta at Gitmo completed—410 beds	
7/23/2002		Downing Street Memo meeting—MI6 expressed that Bush wanted to remove Saddam, WMDs or no
9/12/2002		"Grave and Gathering Danger": Bush accuses Iraq of failing to live up to UN obligations regarding WMDs
11/8/2002		UN Sec Council Resolution 1441 gives Iraq a final chance to comply with disarmament commitments; UNMOVIC and IAEA begin inspections again 11/27/2002

Date	Afghanistan	Iraq
12/18/2002	Rumsfeld declares Taliban, al Qaeda "gone" from Afghanistan	
1/9/2003		Report to UN Security Council: inspectors report "no smoking guns"
1/28/2003		In State of the Union, Bush implies Iraq is developing nuclear weapons
2/5/2003		Colin Powell's speech to the UN security council
Early 2003		Global protests against War in Iraq
3/19/2003		Bush launches invasion of Iraq—Operation Iraqi Liberation, later renamed Operation Iraqi Freedom
4/9/2003		Saddam Hussein statue toppled; Baghdad is taken by the United States
4/16/2003		Bush signs $79 bn supplemental spending bill for Iraq
5/1/2003	Rumsfeld says major combat has ended in Afghanistan	"Mission Accomplished"—major combat operations announced ended
5/29/2003		Bush announces that United States found WMDs
8/11/2003	NATO takes control of peace force in Kabul	
8/20/2003		Attack on UN HQ in Baghdad—17 people killed
10/2/2003		David Kay, head of the Iraq Survey Group, tells Congress that United States has yet to find WMD evidence
12/14/2003		Saddam captured
1/4/2004	New constitution approved by delegates in Afghanistan	
1/22/2004		CIA officers in Iraq warn of civil war
4/28/2004		Images of torture at Abu Ghraib revealed
5/11/2004		Video of Nicholas Berg, U.S. contractor, beheaded by militants
6/28/2004		United States transfers sovereignty to Iraq
9/7/2004		Death toll of U.S. soldiers at 1,000

Date	Afghanistan	Iraq
9/16/2004		UN Sec Gen Kofi Annan declares Iraq War illegal
10/7/2004		Duelfer Report: Iraq did not have WMDs
10/9/2004	Karzai elected Afghan president in historic vote	
10/29/2004	Osama bin Laden threatens West in televised message	
11/2/2004	Bush wins reelection	
11/8/2004		U.S. assault on Fallujah—largest military operation since invasion; 11/8/2005: reports that United States dropped white phosphorus
1/12/2005		WMD search declared over
1/30/2005		Iraqis vote to form Transitional National Assembly
3/31/2005		Silberman-Robb pres. commission report on failure to find WMDs
5/1/2005		Downing Street Memo revealed
5/23/2005	Karzai and Bush announce military agreement giving U.S. forces access to Bagram Airfield	
5/30/2005		Dick Cheney says insurgency is in "last throes"
6/28/2005	Operation Red Wings—19 U.S. troops dead	
9/18/2005	Local elections held in Afghanistan	
10/15/2005		Iraqis vote to ratify constitution
10/19/2005		Saddam testifies at Baghdad trial
10/26/2005		U.S. death toll at 2,000
11/15/2005		U.S. Senate votes (79–19) demanding regular reports from WH toward phased pullout of troops from Iraq
11/18/2005		Rep. John Murtha (D-PA) calls for U.S. withdrawal from Iraq
12/15/2005		Iraqis elect Iraqi Assembly
12/30/2005	Detainee Treatment Act of 2005 passed, part of supplemental defense spending bill prohibiting cruel, inhuman, or degrading treatment of prisoners including at Gitmo; establishes CSRTs, requiring use of Army Field Manual for interrogations	

Date	Afghanistan	Iraq
3/19/2006		Bush promises "complete victory" in Iraq
3/19/2006		*Time* reports U.S. Marines killed 15 civilians in Haditha in November 2005
4/12/2006		*WaPo* reports Pentagon concluded in May 2003 that no WMDs had been found
4/13/2006		"Revolting Generals" call for resignation of Rumsfeld
5/20/2006		Jawad al-Maliki, new PM, oversees formation of Iraq's constitutional govt
6/8/2006		Abu Musab al-Zarqawi, leader of al Qaeda in Iraq, killed in U.S. air raid
6/29/2006	*Hamdan v. Rumsfeld* Supreme Court decision holds that Bush administration military commissions violated the Uniform Code of Military Justice and the Geneva Conventions (CA3)	
7/13/2006		Over 140 people killed in Baghdad
July 2006	Bloody resurgence in Afghanistan	3,438 Iraqi civilians died, 1,666 bombs exploded—both records
8/21/2006		Bush says Iraq had nothing to do with 9/11
8/22/2006		Marines begin involuntary troop recalls
10/8/2006		Report—in September 2006, U.S. troop casualties spiked—more than 20,000 to date wounded
10/19/2006		House Veteran Affairs Committee staff report that vets (Iraq and Afghanistan) seeking help for PTSD doubled from 4,500 to 9,000 from 10/05 to 6/06
10/20/2006		Richard Armitage called for withdrawal of troops from Iraq
10/23/2006		Sen. Arlen Specter says there's a civil war in Iraq
10/24/2006		19 percent of Americans believe United States is winning the war in Iraq
11/1/2006		Classified military briefing reports Iraq is "edging toward chaos"
11/5/2006		Saddam sentenced to death
11/8/2006	Rumsfeld resigns as Sec Def—after 2006 congressional midterm elections defeat the GOP	

Date	Afghanistan	Iraq
11/9/2006		Iraq health minister reports 150,000 civilian deaths in Iraq
11/23/2006		144 people die in the war's deadliest attack, in Baghdad
11/24/2006		NBC News starts referring to Iraq as a civil war
12/5/2006		Robert Gates, nominated to Sec Def, says United States is not winning the Iraq War
12/6/2006		Iraq Study Group Report released
12/8/2006		71 percent disapproval of Bush's handling of the war
December 2006		Bush administration pressing for increase in troops to Iraq
December 2006	New Counterinsurgency Field Manual released (Gen. David Petraeus)	
12/30/2006		Saddam executed by hanging
1/3/2007		Death toll of U.S. troops reaches 3,000
1/10/2007		Bush speech announcing surge
January 2007		Nearly 2,000 Iraqi civilian deaths, a new monthly high
2/10/2007		Petraeus takes charge of U.S. forces in Iraq
2/18/2007		WaPo report on terrible conditions at Walter Reed Medical Center
2/21/2007		Tony Blair announces timetable for withdrawal of UK troops
2/27/2007	Bagram Airfield bombing during Cheney's visit	
3/14/2007		Pentagon calls Iraq a civil war
4/9/2007		Iraqi protest against U.S. presence, in Najaf
4/12/2007		Iraqi parliament bombed inside Green Zone
4/19/2007		Sen. Harry Reid declares Iraq "is lost"
5/1/2007		Bush vetoes congressional plan for withdrawal from Iraq
5/10/2007		Petraeus posts open letter rejecting torture
6/11/2007		U.S. forces begin arming Sunni militias

Date	Afghanistan	Iraq
6/16/2007		Coalition death toll hits 4,000
9/16/2007		Blackwater contractors kill 14–17 Iraqi civilians without cause at Nisour Square in Baghdad
11/24/2007		U.S. begins major pullout from Iraq
2/22/2008		Turkey launches ground operation in Iraq against Kurdish rebels
3/23/2008		U.S. death toll at 4,000
4/23/2008		Petraeus promoted to lead Central Command
6/12/2008	Supreme Court rules Gitmo detainees have habeas rights	
7/22/2008	Surge ends	
9/1/2008		United States transfers control of Anbar province to Iraq
9/16/2008		Odierno succeeds Petraeus as Iraq Commander
September 2008	Troop and civilian deaths climb in Afghanistan— deadliest year yet	
11/4/2008	Barack Obama elected president	
1/20/2009	Obama sworn in	
1/22/2009	Obama orders Gitmo closed within a year	
2/17/2009	Obama announces he will send 17,000 more troops to Afghanistan	
3/9/2009		Obama announces 12,000 troops to leave the country by September
3/27/2009	Obama announces new Afghanistan strategy— commits 4,000 additional troops	
4/7/2009		Obama visits Iraq for the first time
4/30/2009		Britain ends combat ops in Iraq
5/11/2009	Gen. Stanley McChrystal named new U.S. commander in Afghanistan	
6/30/2009		U.S. combat troops depart Iraq's cities, however 130,000 U.S. troops remain in the country
12/1/2009	Obama orders troop surge of 30,000 additional troops	

Date	Afghanistan	Iraq
February 2010	NATO-led offensive in Helmand	
3/4/2010		Election in Iraq
6/23/2010	Petraeus replaces McChrystal as Afghanistan war commander	
8/31/2010		Obama declares end to combat mission in Iraq; Operational name changes to Operation New Dawn
9/18/2010	Afghanistan elections	
10/22/2010		WikiLeaks releases trove of documents
5/1/2011	Obama announces OBL's death	
6/22/2011	Obama orders troop reductions of 10,000 by the end of the year, with the other 20,000 surge troops schedule to leave by summer 2012	
12/15/2011		U.S. troops declare an end to operations—more than one million service members served, 4,400 died, and it cost more than $1 trillion
3/6/2013		Special Inspector-General for Reconstruction in Iraq Report shows $10 billion was wasted
6/14/2014	Elections in Afghanistan	
9/8/2014		Selection of Haider al-Abadi as Iraq's new prime minister
9/10/14		Obama announces U.S. airstrikes on Iraq and Syria
9/21/2014	Ashraf Ghani declared president of Afghanistan	

Sources: http://thinkprogress.org/report/iraq-timeline/#; http://www.nytimes.com/interactive/2010/08/31/world/middleeast/20100831-Iraq-Timeline.html#/#time111_3273; http://www.nytimes.com/interactive/2011/06/22/world/asia/afghanistan-war-timeline.html?ref=asia; http://www.washingtonpost.com/wp-srv/world/daily/graphics/guantanomotime_050104.htm; http://jurist.org/timelines/2012/01/guantanamo-bay-timeline.php; http://thinkprogress.org/bin-laden-timeline/; http://www.nytimes.com/2012/05/28/world/at-west-point-asking-if-a-war-doctrine-was-worth-it.html?pagewanted=all&_r=0; http://www.nytimes.com/2006/04/13/washington/13cnd-military.html; http://www.cfr.org/afghanistan/us-war-afghanistan/p20018; http://www.bbc.com/news/world-south-asia-12024253; http://www.npr.org/templates/story/story.php?storyId=4996218.

GLOSSARY

ABU GHRAIB PRISON Iraq prison; site of 2003–4 human rights abuses by the U.S. Army and CIA

AFGHANISTAN COMPACT UN agreement regulating international aid for Afghanistan, 2006

ALEC STATION Special unit created by the CIA to track Osama bin Laden in 1996

AL JAZEERA Arab satellite television news channel

AL QAEDA International terrorist network composed of militant Islamists founded by Osama bin Laden

ANBAR PROVINCE Largest governorate of Iraq, populated by Sunni Muslims

ANP Afghan National Police

ANSF Afghan National Security Forces; the law enforcement and military forces of Afghanistan

AQI Al Qaeda in Iraq

ARAB SPRING Series of revolutionary protests and uprisings across the Middle East in 2011

AVF All-volunteer force, U.S. military recruited without conscription since 1973

BA'ATH PARTY Arab Socialist Renaissance Party; a Pan Arab nationalist and socialist political party

BAGRAM AIRFIELD Largest U.S. military base in Afghanistan

BONN AGREEMENT International agreement to re-create the state of Afghanistan, 2001

BUSH DOCTRINE Foreign policy principles pursued by the George W. Bush administration, including unilateralism, preemptive strikes

CADRE A core group of trained personnel able to assume control, especially in promoting the interests of a revolutionary party

CENTCOM U.S. Central Command, covering North Africa, the Middle East, and Central Asia

CHECHENS Ethnic group speaking Chechen and practicing Islam, most living in Russia

CIA Central Intelligence Agency

CJIATF-435 Combined Joint Interagency Task Force on Detentions Operations, Afghanistan

CJTF-7 Combined Joint Task Force 7, U.S. Army V Corps, Iraq

COIN Counterinsurgency; a comprehensive attempt, involving both civilian and military efforts, to stem insurgencies by focusing on their fundamental causes.

COLD WAR The political, military, economic, and ideological rivalry between the United States and the Soviet Union, and their respective allies, 1947–91

CONTAINMENT U.S strategy to limit the military, political, and ideological influence of the Soviet Union during the Cold War

CPA Coalition Provisional Authority; transitional government of Iraq, 2003–4

CTC Counterterrorism Center at the CIA (U.S.)

DCI Director of central intelligence (U.S.)

DFIP Detention Facility in Parwan, Afghanistan

DIA Defense Intelligence Agency (U.S.)

EMBEDDING Deploying journalists with an assigned U.S. military combat unit

EOD Explosive Ordinance Disposal

FALLUJAH Iraqi city, site of the 2004 battle between U.S. forces and Iraqi insurgents

FEDAYEEN Member of an Arab guerrilla group

FM 3-24/MCWP 3.33-5 Field Manual 3-24/Marine Corps Warfighting Publication 3.33-5, Counterinsurgency Doctrine, 2006, U.S. military

FOB Forward Operating Base; U.S. military

FOREIGN INTELLIGENCE SURVEILLANCE ACT Federal law regulating procedures for physical and electronic surveillance within the United States, 1978

GDP Gross domestic product

GENEVA CONVENTIONS A set of international treaties on the conduct of war that govern the treatment of civilians, prisoners of war, and members of the military no longer able to fight

G.I. BILL Servicemen's Readjustment Act, 1944; post-9/11 G.I. Bill, Veterans Educational Assistance Act of 2008 (U.S.)

GRAND STRATEGY Plans, policies, and programs deployed by a state to balance ends and means in the pursuit of objectives on a broad national level

GUANTANAMO BAY U.S. military base in Cuba; often referred to as Gitmo, site of imprisonment of detainees captured in the global war on terror

GULF WAR War waged by a U.S.-led coalition against Iraq in response to Iraq's invasion of Kuwait, 1991

GWOT Global war on terror

HALABJA Kurdish city in Iraq, site of 1988 Iraqi chemical gas attack

HAZARA Ethnic group speaking Persian and practicing Islam, most living in central Afghanistan

HEGEMON State or organization holding controlling influence over surrounding actors

HEZBOLLAH Shi'ite Islamist militant group and political party in Lebanon

HUMANITARIAN INTERVENTION Military action with the principal goal of ending human rights violations

HUMINT Human intelligence

IAEA International Atomic Energy Agency

IC U.S. Intelligence Community

IDP Internally displaced person; refugee who remains within his or her country

IED Improvised explosive device

IMINT Imagery intelligence

INC—IRAQI NATIONAL CONGRESS Iraqi opposition group against Saddam Hussein

INDEXING THEORY Media theory; news content reflects the range of debate among policy makers

INSURGENCY Rebellion or uprising to seize control of a government by non-state actors

IRAN HOSTAGE CRISIS Diplomatic crisis between the United States and Iran, 1979–81

IRAN-IRAQ WAR Armed conflict between Iraq and Iran, 1980–88

IRAQ LIBERATION ACT U.S. congressional statement of policy, supporting regime change in Iraq, 1998

IRTPA Intelligence Reform and Terrorism Prevention Act, 2004 (U.S.)

ISAF International Security Assistance Force; NATO-led UN security mission in Afghanistan

ISF Iraqi security forces; the law enforcement and military forces of Iraq

ISI Directorate of Inter-Services Intelligence; Pakistan's largest intelligence service

ISIL Islamic State of Iraq and the Levant that seeks to establish a worldwide caliphate; an offshoot of al Qaeda in Iraq and Syria that renamed itself the Islamic State in 2014; this acronym is commonly used by U.S. government officials

ISIS Islamic State of Iraq and Syria; acronym commonly used by U.S. press; see also ISIL

ISLAMABAD Capital of Pakistan

JAWBREAKER Northern Afghanistan Liaison Team, first CIA team to enter Afghanistan in preparation for Operation Enduring Freedom, 2001

JIHAD A holy war waged on behalf of Islam as a religious duty

KARBALA GAP Key approach to Baghdad from the south

KREMLIN Historic fortified complex in Moscow; term is often used to refer to the government of Russia or the Soviet Union

KULTURKAMPF A conflict between cultures or value systems, especially between civil government and religious authorities over control of education and church

KURDS Ethnic group speaking Kurdish, inhabits parts of Turkey, Iran, Iraq, and Syria

MADRASA Religious Muslim school, college, or university, often part of a mosque

MAHDI ARMY Iraqi Shi'ite militia created by Muqtada al-Sadr

MNF-I Multi-National Force Iraq

MoveOn.org Progressive netroots organizing website

MRAP Mine-resistant ambush-protected vehicle

MRE Meal ready to eat (U.S. military)

MST Military sexual trauma

MUJAHEDEEN Islamic faith-based warriors who fought against the Soviet Union in the Afghan War, 1979–89; also appears as MUJAHIDEEN

MULTILATERALISM More than two nations or parties working in concert on an issue in foreign relations

MUSLIM Practitioner of Islam as a religious faith

NATIONAL ENERGY POLICY DEVELOPMENT GROUP Task force to create the Bush administration's energy policy, 2001

NATIONAL INTELLIGENCE BOARD Senior Intelligence Community officials, approve National Intelligence Estimates (U.S.)

NATIONAL SECURITY ADVISOR Assistant to the U.S. president for national security affairs

NATO North Atlantic Treaty Organization; collective security agreement between states in the North Atlantic area

NDS Afghanistan National Directorate of Security

NETROOTS ACTIVISM Political activism organized through online media

NGO Nongovernmental organization

NIC National Intelligence Council; U.S. interagency body for creating reports to reflect the Intelligence Community's composite positions

NIE National Intelligence Estimate; U.S. federal government document reflecting authoritative position of the Intelligence Community

9/11 September 11, 2001; the aerial attacks on the World Trade Center and the Pentagon by al Qaeda

Nixon Doctrine Foreign policy doctrine of the Richard M. Nixon presidential administration; U.S. interests can be served by relying on local allied powers to police their regions

Nonproliferation The prevention of an increase or spread in weapons of mass destruction

Northern Alliance Afghan military front that opposed the Taliban in the Afghan Civil War, 1996–2001

NSA National Security Agency (U.S.)

NSC National Security Council; forum for the U.S. president to consider matters of national security and foreign policy with his senior advisors and cabinet members

OPEC Organization of Petroleum Exporting Countries

Operation Anaconda U.S. code name for the ISAF military campaign against the Taliban and al Qaeda, 2002

Operation Cobra II George W. Bush administration code name for the planning to depose Saddam Hussein

Operation Desert Fox U.S. code name for the 1998 punitive bombing of Iraq for lack of cooperation with international sanctions by U.S. and British military

Operation Desert Shield U.S. code name for the U.S. military buildup to protect Saudi Arabia, 1990

Operation Desert Storm U.S. code name for the Gulf War, 1991

Operation Enduring Freedom—Afghanistan U.S. code name for the military operation in Afghanistan, 2001-

Operation Iraqi Freedom U.S. code name for the military operation in Iraq, 2003–10

Operation New Dawn U.S. code name for the military operation in Iraq, 2010–11

ORHA Office of Reconstruction and Humanitarian Affairs (U.S.)

Pashtun Ethnic group speaking Pashto, inhabit Afghanistan and northern Pakistan

PCTEG Policy Counter Terrorism Evaluation Group (U.S.)

PDPA People's Democratic Party of Afghanistan (socialist)

Persian Gulf Extension of the Indian Ocean, through the Strait of Hormuz

Phase III U.S. military planning for combat operations to remove Saddam Hussein

Phase IV U.S. military planning for the stabilization and reconstruction of Iraq

PKK Kurdistan Worker's Party, Kurd separatist military organization fighting the Turkish state

Predator drone Unmanned aerial vehicle in use by the U.S. Air Force since 1995

Preemptive war Military action taken by a country against a perceived imminent threat

PTSD Posttraumatic stress disorder

RAMADI Capital of Anbar province in Iraq, part of Sunni Triangle

REPUBLICAN GUARD Elite branch of the Iraqi military, 1969–2003

RIO PACT Inter-American Treaty of Reciprocal Assistance; collective security agreement between the United States and the nations of Latin America

ROLFF-A Rule of Law Field Force--Afghanistan

RPG Rocket-propelled grenade

SALAFISM Fundamentalist conservative Sunni Muslim ideology; considers other Muslims infidels

SCUD Soviet-designed short-range tactical ballistic missile

SHARIA Islamic law code that guides all areas of Muslim life

SHI'ITE MUSLIMS Second largest branch of Islam, ca. 10–15 percent of Muslim population

SHOCK AND AWE U.S. military doctrine; demonstrating massive superiority to destroy an opponent's will

SIGINT Signals intelligence

SOCOM U.S. Special Operations Command

SOF Special Operations Forces; U.S. military units specializing in unconventional missions

STOP-LOSS POLICY Involuntary extension of a deployed U.S. military member's active duty

SUNNI MUSLIMS Largest branch of Islam, ca. 85 percent of Muslim population

SUNNI TRIANGLE Iraqi region densely populated by Sunni Muslims

SURGE Increased deployment of U.S. military forces in Iraq, 2007–8, and Afghanistan, 2010

TAJIKS Ethnic group speaking Tajik and practicing Islam, inhabitants of Tajikistan

TALIBAN Afghan Islamic fundamentalist political movement with branches in Afghanistan and Pakistan

TALIBAN REGIME Islamic Emirate of Afghanistan, ruled by Taliban, 1996–2001

TBI Traumatic brain injury

TOKYO CONFERENCE Conference to allocate funding responsibility for rebuilding Afghanistan among ISAF nations, 2002

TORA BORA Cave complex in the mountains of Afghanistan, site of 2001 battle between United States and its allied Afghans, and the Taliban and al Qaeda

TSA Transportation Security Administration (U.S.)

UAE United Arab Emirates

UAV Unmanned aerial vehicle, drone

UDHR Universal Declaration of Human Rights, 1948 (UN)

UIGHURS Ethnic group speaking Uighur and practicing Islam, most living in north-western China

UN United Nations

UNMOVIC United Nations Monitoring, Verification and Inspection Commission

UNSCOM United Nations Special Commission on Disarmament

USAF U.S. Air Force

USCENTCOM U.S. Central Command, covering North Africa, the Middle East, and Central Asia

USMC U.S. Marine Corps

USSOCOM U.S. Special Operations Command

UZBEKS Ethnic group speaking Uzbek and practicing Islam, inhabitants of Uzbekistan

VA Veterans Administration (U.S.)

VOICE OF AMERICA Official U.S. radio institution created during the Cold War to broadcast overseas

WAHABISM Austere form of Islam that insists on a literal interpretation of the Koran

WATERBOARDING Extreme interrogation method that simulates drowning; often identified as torture

WAZIRISTAN Mountainous region covering northern Pakistan and eastern Afghanistan

WHIG White House Iraq Group; task force created to market the U.S. invasion of Iraq

WMD Weapon of mass destruction

NOTABLE PERSONS

ABIZAID, JOHN Commander in chief, U.S. Central Command, 2003–2007

AL-ABADI, HAIDER Prime minister of Iraq, 2014–

ALBRIGHT, MADELEINE U.S. secretary of state, 1997–2001

ALLAWI, AYAD Interim prime minister of Iraq, 2004–5; president of the Governing Council of Iraq, 2003

AL-MALIKI, NOURI Prime minister of Iraq, 2006–14; Iraqi minister of the interior, 2010–14; Iraqi minister of defense, 2010–11

AL-SADR, MUQTADA Iraqi Shi'ite Islamic political leader

AL-ZARQAWI, ABU MUSAB Militant Islamist, leader of AQI, 2004–6

AL ZAWAHIRI, AYMAN Leader of al Qaeda, 2011–; high-ranking member, 1998–2011

ATATÜRK, MUSTAFA KEMAL Founder and president of Turkey, 1928–38

BAKER, JAMES U.S. secretary of state, 1989–92

BARSTOW, DAVID U.S. journalist

BIDEN, JOSEPH Vice president of the U.S., 2009–; U.S. senator (D-DE), 1973–2009

BIGELOW, KATHRYN U.S. film director, screenwriter, and producer

BIN LADEN, OSAMA Leader of al Qaeda until death in 2011

BLACK, COFER Coordinator for counterterrorism, head of the Office of Counterterrorism, U.S. State Department, 2002–4; director of the Counterterrorism Center, CIA, 1999–2002

BLAIR, TONY Prime minister of the United Kingdom, 1997–2007

BLIX, HANS Executive chairman of the United Nations Monitoring, Verification and Inspection Commission, 2000–2003

BREMER, LEWIS PAUL Administrator of the CPA, 2003–4

BRENNAN, JOHN Director of the CIA, 2013–; U.S. homeland security advisor, 2009–13

BUCHANAN, PATRICK U.S. conservative author, politician, and political commentator

BUSH, GEORGE H. W. President of the United States, 1989–93; vice president of the United States, 1981–89

BUSH, GEORGE W. President of the United States, 2001–9

CARD, ANDREW White House chief of staff, 2001–6

CARTER, JIMMY President of the United States, 1977–81

CASEY, GEORGE Commander of MNF-I, 2004–7

CHALABI, AHMED President of the Governing Council of Iraq, 2003; head of the INC

CHENEY, RICHARD Vice president of the United States, 2001–9; U.S. secretary of defense, 1989–93

CLARKE, RICHARD National Security Council Special Advisor ("terrorism czar"), 2001–3; national coordinator for security, infrastructure protection, and counterterrorism, 1998–2001

CLINTON, BILL President of the United States, 1993–2001

CLINTON, HILLARY U.S. secretary of state, 2009–13; U.S. senator (D-NY), 2001–9; U.S. First Lady, 1993–2001

CROCKER, RYAN U.S. ambassador to Afghanistan, 2011–12; U.S. ambassador to Iraq, 2007–9

DEAN, HOWARD Candidate for Democratic presidential nomination, 2004; chairman of the Democratic National Committee, 2005–9; governor of Vermont, 1991–2003

DEARLOVE, SIR RICHARD Head of the British Secret Intelligence Service/MI6, 1999–2004

DEUTCH, JOHN Director of central intelligence, 1995–96

DOSTUM, ABDUL RASHID Afghan warlord and Uzbek tribal leader

EIKENBERRY, KARL U.S. ambassador to Afghanistan, 2009–11

ELBARADEI, MOHAMED Director general of the International Atomic Energy Agency, 1997–2009

FEITH, DOUGLAS U.S. undersecretary of defense for policy, 2001–5

FRANKS, TOMMY Commander in chief, U.S. Central Command, 2000–2003

GARNER, JAY Director of ORHA, 2003

GATES, ROBERT U.S. secretary of defense, 2006–11; director of central intelligence, 1991–93

GHANI AHMADZAI, ASHRAF President of Afghanistan, 2014–

GONZALES, ALBERTO U.S. attorney general, 2005–7; White House counsel, 2001–5

GORBACHEV, MIKHAIL Leader of the Soviet Union, 1985–91

HAASS, RICHARD Director of policy planning for the U.S. Department of State, 2001–3

HAQQANI, JALALUDDIN Mujahedeen, Taliban leader

HAQQANI, SIRAJUDDIN Taliban leader

HAYDEN, MICHAEL Director of central intelligence, 2006–9; principal deputy director of national intelligence, 2005–6; director of the National Security Agency, 1999–2005

HEKMATYAR, GULBUDDIN Mujahedeen; prime minister of Afghanistan, 1993–94, 1996

HUSSEIN AL-TIKRITI, SADDAM President of Iraq, 1979–2003

JACKSON, PETER New Zealand film director, screenwriter, and producer

KARZAI, HAMID President of Afghanistan, 2002–14

KEITH, TOBY U.S. singer-songwriter

KERRY, JOHN U.S. secretary of state, 2013–; U.S. senator (D-MA), 1985–2003

KHAN, MOHAMMED DAOUD President of Afghanistan, 1973–78

KHOMEINI, RUHOLLAH Supreme Leader of Iran, 1979–89; high-ranking Shi'ite cleric (Ayatollah)

LIBBY, I. LEWIS "SCOOTER" Chief of staff to the vice president, 2001–5; assistant to the vice president for national security affairs, 2001–5

MAINES, NATALIE U.S. singer-songwriter, vocalist for the Dixie Chicks

MARTINS, MARK Judge advocate leader of ROLFF-A, 2010–11

MATTIS, JAMES Commander in chief, U.S. Central Command, 2010–13; commander, U.S. Joint Forces Command, 2007–10

McCAIN, JOHN U.S. senator (R-AZ), 1987–

McCHRYSTAL, STANLEY Commander of ISAF, 2009–10

McCLELLAN, SCOTT White House press secretary, 2003–6

MILLER, FRANK U.S. comic book writer and artist

MOULITSAS, MARKOS Progressive activist, publisher of the Daily Kos blog

NEGROPONTE, JOHN U.S. director of national intelligence, 2005–7; U.S. ambassador to Iraq, 2004–5

NIXON, RICHARD M. President of the United States, 1969–74

NOLAN, CHRISTOPHER British film director, screenwriter, and producer

NOOR, ATTA MOHAMMED Afghan Tajik politician and warlord

OBAMA, BARACK H. President of the United States, 2009–

OMAR, MOHAMMED Leader of the Afghan Taliban

O'NEILL, PAUL U.S. secretary of the treasury, 2001–2

PAHLAVI, MOHAMMAD REZA Shah of Iran, 1941–79

PETRAEUS, DAVID Director of the CIA, 2011–12; commander of ISAF, 2010–11; commander in chief, U.S. Central Command, 2008–10; commander of MNF-I, 2007–8

POWELL, COLIN U.S. secretary of state, 2001–6; U.S. chairman of the Joint Chiefs of Staff, 1989–93; U.S. national security advisor, 1987–89

POWER, SAMANTHA U.S. ambassador to the UN, 2013–; senior director of the NSC Office of Multilateral Affairs and Human Rights, 2009–13

PUTIN, VLADIMIR President of Russia, 2000–2008, 2012–; prime minister of Russia, 1999–2000, 2008–12

REAGAN, RONALD President of the United States, 1981–89

RICE, CONDOLEEZZA U.S. national security advisor, 2001–5; U.S. secretary of state, 2005–9

ROVE, KARL White House deputy chief of staff, 2005–7; senior advisor to the president, 2001–7

RUMSFELD, DONALD U.S. secretary of defense, 1975–77, 2001–6

SANCHEZ, RICARDO Commander of the Coalition Ground Forces, Iraq, 2003–4

SCHEUER, MICHAEL Head of Alec Station, 1996–99

SCHWARZKOPF, H. NORMAN Commander in chief, U.S. Central Command, 1988–91

SHARIF, NAWAZ Prime minister of Pakistan, 2013–

SHEEHAN, CINDY U.S. antiwar activist

SHERZAI, GUL AGHA Afghan Pashtun politician and warlord

SHINSEKI, ERIC U.S. secretary of veterans affairs, 2009–14; U.S. Army chief of staff, 1999–2003

STALIN, JOSEPH Leader of the Soviet Union, 1922–53

STRAW, JACK British secretary of state for foreign and commonwealth affairs, 2001–6

TENET, GEORGE Director of central intelligence, 1996–2004

WHITE, THOMAS U.S. secretary of the army, 2001–3

WOLFOWITZ, PAUL U.S. deputy secretary of defense, 2001–5

WOODWARD, ROBERT U.S. investigative journalist, 1970–

WOOLSEY, R. JAMES Director of central intelligence, 1993–95

ZIA UL-HAQ, MUHAMMAD President of Pakistan, 1977–88

Beth Bailey is Foundation Professor at the University of Kansas, where she teaches in the Department of History and is Director of the Military and Society Center. Her current research focuses on military institutions and American society; her most recent book is *America's Army: Making the All-Volunteer Force*. The recipient of numerous prizes and fellowships for her scholarship, she has won two Distinguished Writing Awards from the Army Historical Foundation.

Richard H. Immerman, Edward J. Buthusiem Family Distinguished Faculty Fellow in History and Marvin Wachman Director of Temple University's Center for the Study of Force and Diplomacy, is a historian of U.S. foreign relations. His most recent books are *Empire for Liberty: A History of U.S. Imperialism from Benjamin Franklin to Paul Wolfowitz* and *The Hidden Hand: A Brief History of the CIA*. Currently the Francis W. De Serio Chair of Strategic and Theater Intelligence at the U.S. Army War College, from 2007 to 2009 he served as an Assistant Deputy Director of National Intelligence.

Terry H. Anderson is Professor of History at Texas A&M University. A Vietnam veteran, he has taught in Malaysia and Japan. He has received Fulbright awards to China and Indonesia and was the Mary Ball Washington Professor of American History at University College, Dublin. He is the author of numerous articles on the 1960s and the Vietnam War, co-author of *A Flying Tiger's Diary*, and author of *The Sixties; United States, Great Britain, and the Cold War, 1944–1947; The Movement and the Sixties;* and *The Pursuit of Fairness: A History of Affirmative Action*. His latest book is *Bush's Wars*.

Stephen Biddle is Professor of Political Science and International Affairs at George Washington University. His *Military Power: Explaining Victory and Defeat in Modern Battle* won four prizes, including the Harvard University Huntington Prize and the Council on Foreign Relations Arthur Ross Award Silver Medal. In addition to many other publications, he has presented testimony before congressional committees on the wars in Iraq and Afghanistan, force planning, net assessment, and European arms control. He has also served on General David Petraeus's Joint Strategic Assessment Team in Baghdad in 2007, on General Stanley McChrystal's Initial Strategic Assessment Team in Kabul in 2009, and as a Senior Advisor to General Petraeus's Central Command Assessment Team in Washington in 2008–9.

Robert K. Brigham, Shirley Ecker Boskey Professor of History and International Relations, has taught at Vassar College since 1994. He is the author or co-author of multiple books, including *Argument without End: In Search of Answers to the Vietnam Tragedy*, written with former Secretary of Defense Robert S. McNamara and James G. Blight of Brown University; *Guerilla Diplomacy: The NLF's Foreign Relations and the Vietnam War*; *ARVN: Life and Death in the South Vietnamese Army*; *Is Iraq Another Vietnam?*; and *America and Iraq since 1990*.

Conrad C. Crane, Director of the U.S. Army Military History Institute at Carlisle Barracks, Pennsylvania, holds a B.S. from the U.S. Military Academy and an M.A. and Ph.D. from Stanford University. He joined the Strategic Studies Institute in September 2000 after twenty-six years of military service that concluded with nine years as Professor of History at the U.S. Military Academy. He has written or edited books on the Civil War, World War I, World War II, and Korea, and has published articles on military issues in such journals as the *Journal of Strategic Studies*, the *Journal of Military History*, the *Historian*, and *Aerospace Historian*.

David Farber is Roy A. Roberts Distinguished Professor in the Department of History, University of Kansas. He is author or editor of fourteen books, including *The Age of Great Dreams: America in the 1960s*; *What They Think of US: International Perceptions of the United States since 9/11*; and *Taken Hostage: America's First Encounter with Radical Islam*.

Peter D. Feaver is Professor of Political Science and Public Policy at Duke University, where he directs the Triangle Institute for Security Studies and the Duke Program in American Grand Strategy. From June 2005 to July 2007 he served as Special Advisor for Strategic Planning and Institutional Reform on the National Security Council Staff at the White House, where his responsibilities included the national security strategy, regional strategy reviews, and other political-military issues. In 1993–94, he served as Director for Defense Policy and Arms Control on the National Security Council, where his responsibilities included the national security strategy review, counterproliferation policy, regional nuclear arms control, and other defense policy issues. Among his publications are *Armed Servants: Agency, Oversight, and Civil-Military Relations; Guarding the Guardians: Civilian Control of Nuclear Weapons in the United States;* and *Choosing Your Battles: American Civil-Military Relations and the Use of Force.*

Jonathan Horowitz is Legal Officer for the Open Justice Initiative, where he focuses on human rights, counterterrorism, and the laws of war. Prior to joining the Justice Initiative, he worked at the U.S. embassy in Kabul, where he advised the embassy on its detention policy. He has documented human rights abuses in Sudan, Afghanistan, and Kenya; served as an investigator for habeas lawyers representing Afghans detained at Guantanamo Bay; and is the author of several reports that document human rights abuses in the context of armed conflict and counterterrorism.

David Kieran is Assistant Professor at Washington and Jefferson College. His first book, *Forever Vietnam: How a Divisive War Changed American Public Memory,* was published in 2014. He is also the editor of *"The War of My Generation": 9/11 and the War on Terror in American Youth Culture* (2015). Currently, he is writing *Embattled Minds: The Cultural Politics of Mental Health during the Iraq and Afghanistan Wars,* which will be published by New York University Press.

Sam Lebovic is Assistant Professor of History at George Mason University. He received his Ph.D. from the University of Chicago and spent 2012–13 as a Fellow at the Center for Cultural Analysis, Rutgers University. He won the Paul Murphy Award from the American Society for Legal History for his current book project, *Beyond the First Amendment: The Problem of Press Freedom in the American Century,* which is forthcoming.

Andrew C. McKevitt is Assistant Professor of History at Louisiana Tech University. His research focuses on U.S. cultural relations with other nations in the post–World War II era. He is the winner of the 2011 Stuart L. Bernath Scholarly Article Prize, awarded by the Society for Historians of American Foreign Relations, for his "'You Are Not Alone': Anime and the Globalizing of America." He is completing a book manuscript on the ways that U.S. consumption of goods from Japan during the 1970s and 1980s shaped understandings of what we now call globalization.

Lisa Mundey is Associate Professor of History at the University of St. Thomas in Houston. From March 2002 to May 2005 she served as a Historian for the

U.S. Army Center of Military History (CMH), where she wrote on the U.S. Army's experience in Afghanistan. She is the author of *American Militarism and Anti-Militarism in Popular Media, 1945–1970* and served on the editorial advisory board for the *Encyclopedia of Middle East Wars: A Social, Political, and Military History.*

Aaron B. O'Connell is Associate Professor of History at the U.S. Naval Academy and a Lieutenant Colonel in the U.S. Marine Corps Reserve who has served as a Special Advisor to General David Petraeus in Afghanistan and a Special Assistant to General Martin Dempsey in the Pentagon. He received his Ph.D. in 2009, and his dissertation won the Yale University History Department's Distinguished Dissertation Prize in American History. That dissertation was published as *Underdogs: The Making of the Modern Marine Corps.*

Michael A. Reynolds is Associate Professor of Near Eastern Studies at Princeton University. His research interests include Ottoman history, Russian and Soviet history, comparative empire, international relations, and the Caucasus. Among his publications is *Shattering Empires: The Clash and Collapse of the Ottoman and Russian Empires, 1908–1918.*

INDEX

Abizaid, John, 132, 134–35

Abu Ghraib prison scandal, 133, 157–58, 161, 208, 232

Afghanistan: al Qaeda and, 3, 6, 8, 45, 60, 81, 104–6, 142, 150, 195, 309, 315; Bonn Agreement, 309; Bush on, 151–52; civil war in, 27, 152; current conditions in, 316–22; drones used in, 59, 83, 91–93; drug trade in, 310, 315, 317–18; during the Cold War, 24–26; human rights abuses in, 150–52, 157–65; intelligence community (IC) and, 77–78, 80, 83–84, 90–91; lessons from war in, 9, 13–14, 143, 156, 308, 321–25; media coverage of war in, 220–21, 227, 230, 232; mujahedeen in, 27, 81; nation building in, 8, 128, 308, 316; NATO coalition takes command in, 112–13, 138, 141, 308–9, 312; Obama and, 14, 138, 140, 211, 213–14, 311; Pakistan and, 27–28, 91, 112, 114; public opinion on war in, 214–15, 220–21, 234; relief operations in, 152–53, 164; rule of law in, 154–57, 162–63; September 11 and, 21–22, 126–27, 150, 195; Soviet invasion of, 9, 23, 26–27, 47, 78; surge in, 90, 141–42, 154, 214, 311, 324; Taliban in, 3, 8, 28, 59–60, 64, 72, 90–91, 112–14, 139, 154, 157, 181, 185; U.S. interest in, 24; U.S. goals and objectives in, 45, 47–48, 312; U.S. war in, 1, 3–5, 7, 10–12, 14–15, 21, 45, 54–55, 57–60, 63–64, 90, 93–94, 103, 107–13, 115–17, 127–28, 150, 175, 195–96, 238, 308–9, 311–12, 314–15; Vietnam compared to, 323–24. *See also* Global war on terror

Afghanistan Compact, 310–11

Afghan National Police (ANP), 164

Afghan National Security Forces (ANSF), 115, 142, 312–13

Albright, Madeleine, 52n60, 125

'Alec' Station, 81

Al Jazeera, 42

Allawi, Ayad, 290–91, 301–02

All-Volunteer Force, 12, 176, 194, 205, 271, 274

al-Maliki, Nouri, 15, 135, 138, 292–93, 297–98, 300–03

Al Qaeda: about, 28; in Afghanistan, 57, 81, 92–93, 150, 157, 323; Bin Laden, Osama, 28, 42, 45, 54, 81, 104, 142, 247; alleged link to Saddam, 45, 68, 70–71, 84, 106, 151, 198, 220, 225, 240, 288; detainees linked to, 61, 159, 214; eclipsed by ISIL, 15, 121n18; intelligence on, 63, 78, 81–82, 91; in Iraq, 22, 88–89, 105, 133, 135, 137–38, 240, 294, 296, 302; major attacks on U.S. targets, 42, 81–82; Pakistan and, 6, 8, 57, 60, 84, 92–93, 105, 109, 128, 244; September 11 attacks and, 2–3, 5, 45, 105, 150; U.S. baffled by, 23; war against, 6, 8, 11, 54, 57–60, 83–84, 90–92, 104–5, 107, 109–11, 117, 119, 122n20, 123n40, 127–28, 142, 147, 150–51, 195, 212, 214–15, 238–39, 241, 249, 308–12, 315, 320–21. *See also* Bin Laden, Osama; Global war on terror

al-Sadr, Muqtada, 134, 138, 288, 291, 295

al-Zarqawi, Abu Musab, 135

al-Zawahiri, Ayman, 28, 42, 60, 84

Anbar Province, 134, 137, 293–97

297–98, 300–302; NIC report on, 88–89; NIE on, 85–87, 90; Powell and, 65, 70–71, 87–88, 122, 290–91; reconstruction and nation building, 8, 130–31, 286–90, 293, 295–96, 303–4; refugee crisis in, 296–300, 303; relief operations in, 152–53; sectarian division and violence in, 7, 135, 291–92, 295–96, 299, 301–2, 304; Soviet invasion of, 9; UN sanctions on, 38, 42; and WMDs, 36–37, 45–46, 69–72, 79, 85, 88–90, 129. *See also* Hussein al-Takriti, Saddam; Iraq War; Global war on terror

Iraq Liberation Act, 43

Iraq War: Abu Ghraib prison scandal, 133, 157–58, 161, 208, 232; Bush on, 291–92; Bush Doctrine and, 64; casualties and costs of, 21, 105, 107–8, 116, 119, 184, 189, 229, 287, 314–15; civilians killed by U.S. forces, 159; Congressional hearings on, 296–97; counterinsurgency, 8, 11, 93, 108, 135–36, 140–41, 143, 152, 164, 294, 304, 311–12, 324; drone campaign, 92; embedding and, 227–28, 232, 291; goals and objectives in, 23, 130–31, 286; insurgency, 89, 181, 185, 288, 294–95, 324; IEDs in, 182–83; Iran and, 22, 138; lack of coordination between civilian and military actions, 133; lessons and legacy of, 9, 13–14, 143, 156, 204, 212, 287, 298, 303–04; media support for, 224–25; Obama on, 90, 203, 211–12, 214; Operation Iraqi Freedom, 6, 10, 88, 131; opposition to, 22, 133, 136–37, 196–203, 206–10, 213–15, 222, 248, 296–97; as preemptive war, 7, 9, 21–22, 62, 69, 199, 286, 303; public and world opinion on, 12, 106, 194, 196, 198, 204, 209, 220, 225, 230, 234; "surge" (2007), 8, 11, 89–90, 137, 287, 291–94, 296–99, 302, 324; U.S. abuses and torture in, 158–62, 165; U.S. military efforts in, 11–12, 131–32, 184–85; war resolution

in U.S. Congress, 69; Vietnam War compared to, 7, 12, 238, 243

Iraqi National Congress (INC), 72

Iraqi Security Forces (ISF), 11, 134–35, 296

ISIL (Islamic State of Iraq and the Levant), 15, 48, 121n18, 304

ISIS (Islamic State of Iraq and Syria). *See* ISIL

Jackson, Peter, 240, 243

Jawbreaker, 57–59, 83

Jihad, 6, 25–28, 42, 78, 214

Journalists, 12, 15, 65, 83, 94, 124, 137, 159–60, 209, 220–21, 223–28, 232, 241, 244, 246–47, 250, 252, 262–63, 266, 270, 273, 289

Karbala, 131, 295

Karzai, Hamid, 11, 15, 59, 90, 94, 109, 112–13, 116, 128–29, 141, 154–55, 164, 310–11, 320–23

Keith, Toby, 248–49

Kennedy, Edward (Ted), 200–201, 222

Kerry, John, 94, 201–2, 205, 207–8

Khan, Ismail, 58

Khan, Mohammed Daoud, 25

Khan, Mohammed Fahim, 58–59

Khomeini, Ruhollah, 29–30

Kurdistan Worker's Party (PKK), 40

Kurds, 35, 39–40, 134, 286, 293, 296, 302

Libby, I. Lewis "Scooter," 66

Madrasa, 28

Mahdi Army, 288, 291, 295

Martins, Mark, 155–56

Mattis, James, 135

McCain, John, 211–13, 247

McChrystal, Stanley, 93, 141–42, 154, 311, 317

McClellan, Scott, 65–66

Miller, Frank, 238–42

Moulitsas, Markos, 206–7